Contents

Acknowledgments

This book had its serious beginnings as the result of a Guggenheim Foundation Fellowship in 1972–73. I deeply appreciated the foundation's support then, and I hope that the results fulfill its early confidence in my project. Case Western Reserve has also been supportive, offering me sabbaticals on two different occasions. Likewise, on two occasions I worked for long periods in the Senate House Library of the University of London. The staff there was unfailingly courteous and helpful, generously offering me study space and the full resources of the library.

Two scholars acting in editorial capacities provided me with timely encouragement. Lilian Furst, a guest editor for *Studies in the Literary Imagination*, accepted my essay on Byron's *Don Juan*, and Phyllis Roth, in a similar role for G. K. Hall, offered my comments on Nabokov's *The Gift* a place in her highly selective volume of critical essays on Nabokov. Since I am scarcely a specialist on either writer, these acceptances and the cordial remarks associated with them (Lilian subsequently became a colleague of mine at Case Western Reserve for a year) gave me hope that I had gone beyond the platitudes of the neophyte. Most significant for me, however, has been the criticism of Michael Seidel, a reader for the University of Georgia Press, who went far beyond the call of duty in his exhaustive, supportive, yet sharply critical report. Both the report itself and later personal communication with him helped me to give shape and focus to what had threatened to become a version of Joyce's "chaosmos." I want also to thank my editor Trudie Calvert for trying to save me from stylistic errors and my typist Joyce Martin for her patient attempts to decipher my manuscript. When Joyce fled to the Sunbelt, I relentlessly pursued her through the mails.

For permission to use materials previously published in a somewhat different form I am grateful to the following: the University of Toronto Press for "Mark Twain and Victorian Nostalgia," in *Patterns of Commitment in American Literature*, ed. Marston LaFrance (1967) and for "The Mock-Heroics of Desire: Some Stoic Personae in the Work of William Carlos Williams," in *The Stoic Strain in American Literature*, ed. Duane MacMillan (1979); *Studies in the Literary Imagination* for "Mock-Heroics and Mock-Heroic Narrative: Byron's *Don Juan* in the Context of Cervantes" (Spring 1976); *Genre* for "Wallace Stevens's 'Comedian' and the Quest for Genre" (Fall 1984); G. K. Hall for *"The Gift*: Nabokov's Portrait of the Artist," in *Critical Essays on Vladimir Nabokov*, ed. Phyllis Roth (1984).

The author and publisher gratefully acknowledge the following publishers for permission to reprint lines of poetry in this work.

Alfred A. Knopf, Inc., for poetry by Wallace Stevens from *The Collected Poems of Wallace Stevens*, copyright 1923, 1931, 1935, 1936, 1937, 1942, 1943, 1944, 1945, 1946, 1947, 1948, 1949, 1950, 1951, 1952, 1954 by Wallace Stevens; and *Opus Posthumous*, copyright 1957 by Elsie Stevens and Holly Stevens.

New Directions Publishing Corporation, for poetry by William Carlos Williams from *Paterson*, copyright 1946, 1951 by William Carlos Williams; *Collected Earlier Poems*, copyright 1938 by New Directions Publishing Corporation; *Pictures from Brueghel*, copyright 1962 by William Carlos Williams; and *Collected Later Poems*, copyright 1948, 1950 by William Carlos Williams.

I

The Mock-Heroic Mode

Introduction

Above all he is a gallant gentleman, a man of infinite courage, a
hero in the truest sense of the word. (This important point should
be kept in mind.)

> VLADIMIR NABOKOV
> *Lectures on Don Quixote*

Desperate story telling, one caps another to reproduce a rambling
mock-heroic tale.

> JAMES JOYCE
> *Scribbledehobble, the Ur-workbook for Finnegans Wake*

Cervantes's Drummond Light

I take my cue from Vladimir Nabokov—not, in this case, Nabokov the artist,
who plays the major role in a later chapter of this book, but rather Nabokov
the lecturer at Harvard preparing to teach *Don Quixote* to his students. After
describing assignments and requirements, his first remark to them apparently was a reminder that "*Don Quixote* is, among other things, our training
ground for learning methods of approach to Dickens, Flaubert, et cetera."[1]
Many others, of course, have noted the extraordinary significance of the book
as a "training ground" for writers and critics alike. Using a far more striking
metaphor, Herman Melville described Cervantes's protagonist as a brilliant
beacon: "The original character, essentially such, is like a revolving Drummond light raying away from itself all around it—everything is lit by it, everything starts up to it . . . so that, in certain minds, there follows upon the
adequate conception of such a character, an effect, in its way, akin to that
which in Genesis attends upon the beginning of things."[2] He might have said
as much about the book as a whole. Certainly it was "the beginning of things"
as far as this study is concerned. More to the point, *Don Quixote* provided
crucial illumination for the writers whose work I am concerned with exploring, writers of the nineteenth century and since who felt themselves to be
living beyond or "post" any cultural period in which conventional heroic
narrative could still be credibly written and yet who still remained committed
in some fashion to the values generated by such narrative. Under the pres-
sure of their own necessities, they explicitly identified Cervantes as spiritual
and aesthetic father and, in turn, exploited the complex aesthetic instrument
he had brought into being—an instrument I call the mock-heroic mode.

From Stendhal to Saul Bellow, these writers of mock-heroic narrative on the Cervantine model have been directly and explicitly concerned with the full and complex relation of heroic experience to their own immediate environment. To this issue they respond with ambivalent attitudes and contradictory judgments, their ironic sense modulating at every point whatever emotional and intellectual commitments they may make. In the most general way we can describe the mode as symmetrically tragicomic, expressing at the same time much of the irreconcilability of tragic idealism and much of the sense of absurdity that comes from strong social awareness of the ridiculousness involved in the pursuit of abstractions. Mock-heroic writers are thus squarely torn between affirming the normative reality of experience (comedy) and responding sympathetically to the spiritual ardency of life lived according to absolute values (tragedy)—or, in Albert Cook's vague but suggestive terms, torn between the probable and the wonderful.[3] Mock-heroic is the product of literary sensibilities at once saturated in the mystique of a particular heroic vision (as Cervantes was saturated in the classical epic and medieval chivalry) and totally aware of the distance of this vision from the practical possibilities of their own time and place or perhaps from any temporal dimension.

Writers of mock-heroic tend to be those whose lives have straddled major cultural "breaks," themselves divided like their culture into a youth of high emotional and ideological commitments and a maturity of skepticism, dislocation, and the failure of hope—writers in their own fashion "displaced persons" or "exiles" like their protagonists. Although most lives undoubtedly reflect this pattern in one way or another, it is here intensified by dramatic cultural change such as Byron describes in *Don Juan*:

> Talk not of seventy years as age; in seven
>   I have seen more changes, down from monarchs to
> The humblest individuals under Heaven,
>   Than might suffice a moderate century through.
> I knew that nought was lasting, but now even
>   Change grows too changeable, without being new:
> Nought's permanent among the human race,
>   Except the Whigs *not* getting into place.[4]

At the very least, writers of mock-heroic are among those who have been heavily subjected during the course of their (usually early) experience to a compelling version of the heroic life and who then, by temperament or situation or both, must spend a significant part of their literary careers coming to terms with it in an explicit and self-conscious way. The alternative to such a complete and sophisticated confrontation (assuming one remains committed to epic experience) can be seen in the work of Robert Louis Stevenson: chil-

dren's stories of successful adventure and escape, followed by the later romances capturing (as Robert Kiely puts it) the "mood of the Victorian romantic novelist, enchanted, haunted, all but obsessed, by the persistent image of
epic adventure which, except in brief moments of exceptional vision, appears
to him worn and barren."[5]

Cervantes's own life fits the pattern of dislocation I have described, and for
him, too, *Don Quixote* represents a beginning of things. Even if we acknowledge that in many important ways his novel reflects a rich cultural tradition
and even if we grant that versions of mock-heroic go back at least as far as
Greek literature, Cervantes, nevertheless, does begin anew insofar as he establishes this mode as the *sole remaining context* of heroic experience rather
than as a mere dimension of the clearly dominant environment of the authentic hero and works out the formal implications of such a change. Whereas, let
us say, Falstaff and his antics in *Henry IV, Part I* coexist (up to a carefully fixed
point) within the larger world of kings and princes, Don Quixote has usurped
the role of central hero. In tracing the long history of the fool figure, Walter
Kaiser makes essentially this same point. On one hand, he points out that the
sophisticated use of the fool in narrative goes back to the Middle Ages and
before and certainly flourished in the Renaissance. On the other, he argues
that the fool's change of role in Cervantes's work is revolutionary: "Formerly,
to the optimistic, idealistic view of man which the quattrocento world had
accepted, the fool had opposed a skeptical, realistic view. But it would seem
that the fool's view has come to be accepted by the world, which now finds its
spokesman in the fool Sancho Panza; and Don Quixote is a fool because he is
the only man left who holds his idealism." With the ubiquity of fools, the
irony goes from localized to labyrinthine; "irony [now] does more than affect
the meaning: the irony becomes the meaning."[6] For my purposes at least and
those of the writers with whom I am dealing, the mock-heroic mode finds its
most significant articulation in the complex formal implications of this labyrinth.

Before moving on to a detailed discussion of the general properties of the
mock-heroic mode as given new and enduring shape by Cervantes, however,
one possible source of confusion must be dealt with: the almost exclusive
association of the term "mock-heroic" with satire since the eighteenth century. Either it is defined as a rhetorical method of generating what D. C.
Muecke calls "corrective irony" or, if considered in modal terms, it is identified with eighteenth-century mock-epic, which tended (in the name of satire
or realism) to reduce the full moral resonance and ironic balance of the Cervantine model.[7] Although Cervantes apparently began his book as a simple
"invective against books of chivalry," for the second expedition (Chapter 7)
Sancho Panza is introduced, by Chapter 9 the story has been handed over to

the Arab historian Cide Hamete Benengeli, and from then on, Cervantes, like his knight, is off and running into a wilderness of ambiguities.[8] Even *Tristram Shandy*, the great anomaly of the eighteenth century and obviously relevant if I were writing a full narrative history, is reductive in its own way, concerned less with heroism, less even with the insistent fact (for good or bad) of a present reality than with the central subjective drama of knowing. In Robert Alter's words, it is a "self-conscious novel" whose central purpose is to test "the ontological status of the fiction"—only one of the more complex purposes of Cervantine mock-heroic.[9]

If a concept has troublesome or limited connotations, it might seem better to abandon it entirely. We could, for instance, speak of the "quixotic" mode to describe precisely the literary model stemming from Cervantes's major work and leave mock-heroic in the hands of the students of satire. Mock-heroic is a precise and useful term even at the most basic descriptive level, however, both in the fundamental duality that it sets up and in the connotative and denotative possibilities of its separate components. The hyphen links mockery with passionate spiritual commitments, serious imitation (as we speak of a "mock-up" or "mock-turtle" soup) with acknowledged awareness of the flimsiness and inevitable vulgarity of all imitations, a sense of the "real" or possible with an equal sense of the "ideal" or imaginatively conceivable. The hyphen, I have said, links mock and heroic, though my own word "link" begs the question of relationship. For the moment let me merely note that "link" does not imply either simple integration or simple opposition ("versus") but rather a duality that cannot be reduced and thus somehow, in some fashion, must finally be taken as a whole. Marthe Robert would undoubtedly substitute the word "and" for the hyphen. In her comment on the inclusiveness of what she calls "quixotism," she points out the crucial difference between quixotism and satire: "Whatever literary elements it employs—parody or pastoral, caricature or pastiche—the thrust of the satiric method is to mutilate its model while avoiding any serious confrontation with it. The idea that a declaration suffices to extinguish the influence of the past is precisely one of the serious delusions that quixotism attempts to destroy—not with derision, but with piety *and* irony, respect *and* humor, admiration *and* criticism, compassion *and* rigor, replacing the categorical *either/or* of satire with a distressing *and* carried to the limits of the absurd."[10]

The term remains useful, moreover, as an indication of fundamental subject matter: mock-heroic is invariably about the nature, value, possibility, and desirability of heroic endeavor as variously defined by different authors and by the different historical periods in which the individual mock-heroic works have been written. As Harry Levin has often pointed out, most mock-heroic works—from *The Red and the Black* (the career of Napoleon) to *Herzog* (Moses as prophet and "mountain-climber")—are based loosely or closely on specific literary or historical models of heroic experience.[11] In *Don Quixote* some episodes are based specifically on *The Amadis of Gaul*, and the book as a whole reflects the entire tradition of heroic experience in the classical epic and medieval chivalry. As the Knight sharply reminds Sancho Panza on one occasion: "Get it into your five senses that all my actions, past, present, and future, are very well based in reason and conform in every way to the rules of chivalry. For I know these rules better than any knights who have ever professed them in the world" (*DQ*, 201). Having dismissed any substantial relationship to satire, Robert concludes that the mock-heroic mode seems "much closer to ordinary imitation."[12] Or, rather, in some of its elements it is closer to parody, assuming again a concept of parody that extends beyond its conventional satiric and reflexive functions. I am concerned in this book with the mechanics of ironic affirmation, with parody as a device for continuity and preservation.

In every case, the imitated model involves a version of the heroic life. *Don Quixote*, quite simply, is about knight errantry. Questions involving value and possibility arise only when the relevance of an issue is seriously in doubt. The world of the Cervantine mock-hero is unamenable, sometimes positively hostile to his aspirations, not hostile as in tragedy, where fate must inevitably and finally thwart the endlessly aspiring will, but hostile or indifferent to the very idea of the heroic, providing no real medium for its complete and authentic expression.

The "sole subject" of *Don Quixote*, we are emphatically reminded in the final paragraph, "has been to arouse men's contempt for all fabulous and absurd stories of knight errantry, whose credit this tale of my genuine Don Quixote has already shaken, and which will, without a doubt soon tumble to the ground" (*DQ*, 940). This bald statement by no means describes the final meaning of the book nor is it necessarily a direct statement of authorial intention (since the putative speaker is Cide Hamete). Nevertheless, it surely records what we might call the ground theme of the book, the assumption against which all claims to heroic experience in the novel must be tested— namely, that knight errantry is untrue to the facts of empirical reality (fabulous), unworthy of serious consideration (absurd), and anachronistic and irrelevant to present conditions. Although Don Quixote remains more "genuine" than his fraudulent imitators (a group that extends significantly beyond the obvious example of Avellaneda's false protagonist), he has no status beyond that of a "genuine" human being, plain Alonzo Quixada or Quesada, who lives and dies in a remote Spanish village.

Regardless of its final complex attitude toward heroic experience, *Don Quixote* everywhere affirms the considerable factuality of Cide Hamete's allegation. In Chapter 1 I shall call attention to specific qualities of structure, style, and theme that mercilessly emphasize the banal reality of the world in which Don Quixote must attempt to realize his aspirations. The physical environment of the novel is explicitly naturalistic (all wonders are explained) and blatantly mundane. Although there are many genuine problems of perspectivism in the book, the reader is never in doubt about the identity of objects such as windmills and barbers' basins. The social world, moreover, from peasant to aristocrat, bears no serious resemblance to the society idealized in the chivalric romances. Even at the Duke's castle tournaments have to be literally "staged" for Don Quixote.[13] The Knight himself is well aware of his anachronism, though only very gradually and incompletely aware of its implications for him. "I was born in this iron age of ours to revive the age of gold," he tells Sancho confidently early in the book (DQ, 149). Much later, having encountered "enchantments" very different from anything covered in the old books but still determined "to resuscitate the long-forgotten profession of knight-errantry," he puts the problem of relating past to present in more complex and suggestive terms: "Perhaps chivalry and magic in our own day must follow a different course from that pursued by the men of old." We need, he suggests, "fresh kinds of enchantment" (DQ, 418). Cervantes more than his protagonist will go beyond the literal meaning of this statement to explore its larger possibilities. Nevertheless, the Knight has defined the problem: how to maintain heroic values in an "age of iron." Or can they be maintained and in what fashion? Or even should they be, given the cost of preservation, which in Don Quixote's case is nothing less than madness?

Radical disjunction between the heroic pretensions of the protagonist and the actual banality of his world is basic to all mock-heroic literature. As Ronald Paulson has noted, "Romance itself escaped being ridiculous only because its world was synchronized with the ideal code of manners it represented." For satiric purposes in the eighteenth century and earlier, the pretender was often simply an especially vulgar manifestation of his age (both measured by the satirist against some truly heroic norm). Occasionally, even in the eighteenth century, the pretensions of the knight errant represented positive values, and he was satirically useful as "the ruined exemplar of an earlier and better age."[14] But the fully developed Cervantine form of mock-heroic has a more complicated view of the relation of the pretender to his "real" world, and the primary concern of the form, as Robert suggests, is no longer with moral correction. The protagonist takes on authentic anachronism insofar as his aspirations represent genuine, all-important values that are difficult if not impossible to locate in the present because of his own inadequacies and the intractability or meanness of the present world. In trying, nevertheless, together with his creator, to realize them through what I will call (borrowing a phrase from James Joyce) "desperate story-telling," he may be as absurd as the vulgar pretender, but, because he affirms heroic values, he can never be subject to simple satiric dismissal.[15] Nabokov, significantly, emphasizes this point. In an early lecture to his Harvard students, he rehearsed Don Quixote's noble qualities and urged them above all to keep in mind that the Knight "is a gallant gentleman, a man of infinite courage, a hero in the truest sense of the word."[16] The overwhelming material reality of the society in which the mock-heroic protagonist finds himself, however, cannot be ignored or wished away or somehow "reformed"; it exists as dense and heavy as the phrase "age of iron" suggests. Disjunction is extreme; the impulse to heroic experience remains; but a medium adequate for its present attainment is missing, however often and vividly such a medium may be nostalgically invoked. The protagonist is denied a fulfillment in deeds that is worthy of his central impulse and the higher values that grow out of that impulse.

The mock-heroic mode, in short, is both self-consciously aware of fictions and grounded in an affirmation of gritty reality. Both his banal environment and his world of fictions mock the quixotic protagonist, however noble his values. At the same time, the central concern of mock-heroic is not with ontology per se but with the nature and survivability of these noble values in a transforming context. *Don Quixote* establishes a way of maintaining the spirit and values of heroic experience at a time when they are no longer literally possible. Fictionality remains in the service, not of itself, but of the author's prior humanistic commitment. Involving a fundamental and comprehensive response to loss, Cervantine mock-heroic establishes an "enabling" context that makes possible the transformation of nostalgia and despair into renewed engagement with the heroic values of the past. This, in any case, constitutes the premise I will attempt to demonstrate in the chapters that follow.

A Note on Mode

My concept of mode, like that of mock-heroic, also involves an extension of terms and thus perhaps deserves a word or two of explanation. I go beyond its usual descriptive reference to mood and attitudes, however important these may be as part of a more substantial cluster of formal properties united by "family resemblance." Rather, following the lead of Alistair Fowler, I refer to the entire cluster as a mode, distinguishing, in turn, between the often piecemeal and fragmentary nature of modal clustering and the more elaborate and complete structures of genre and subgenre (what Fowler alternatively calls "kind"). As he explains, "Modal terms never imply a complete external form. Modes have always an incomplete repertoire, a selection only of the corresponding kind's features, and one from which overall external form is absent."[17] Anne Mellor's suggestive definition—mode as "the interaction of ethos and literary techniques"—emphasizes less its certain though incomplete historical relation to kind and more its overwhelming semantic authority within whatever genre vehicle supplies primary form or structure. She quotes Paul Alpers's formulation that "mode is the literary manifestation of the writer's and the ideal reader's assumptions about the world."[18]

Defined in this way, the concept of mode has at least two major advantages. It allows for the discussion within a complex critical context (extending beyond superficial thematic identifications) of works of poetry and prose that in other dimensions have wide and obvious formal differences. At the same time, it invites us to exploit that other dimension of mode—its tendency to linger on as an entity after the more complete kind has disappeared, an "echo" or "shadow" or "double" (those images so dear to the mock-heroic sensibility) of kind. Exploring the "anatomy" of science fiction, Mark Rose has noted how mode, "an abstraction from the genre," survives its genre and leads "to the appearance of new generic forms." He speaks of the "soul" of a genre and its "transmigration," a process which, in the context of the more radical poetics of mock-heroic, I prefer to describe as "transformational," emphasizing by the latter term both change and a certain continuity.[19] I have already mentioned that even parody, in the context of the mock-heroic mode, functions primarily as a device for the transformation of the genre of its target text.[20]

I conceive of a literary genre as instrumental, an aid to interpretation, as Rose puts it, "not a pigeonhole but a context for writing and reading . . . a tradition, a developing complex of themes, attitudes, and formal strategies that, taken together, constitute a general set of expectations."[21] Beyond establishing additional criteria in further discussion of *Don Quixote*, I will pursue the transformations of the mock-heroic mode in several important and representative later works toward a definition finally contextual, tentative, and incremental. I hope that these works will spring into sharper critical focus from the perspective of an appropriate "set of expectations," and I assume also that they will constitute a continuing exploration of the wider implications and fundamental nature of these expectations. The crux of it all remains what these expectations continue to reveal: namely, that the writers I am dealing with (and some neglected; George Meredith and Joseph Conrad jump to mind) have had a far more positive, sustained, and complete encounter with heroic experience than has been generally acknowledged and reveal the tenacious survival of such experience in the very context of environments most hostile to its possibility.

The Mode of *Don Quixote*

> He resolved to outstrip that vanity which awaits all the woes of
> mankind; he undertook a task that was complex in the extreme and
> futile from the outset.
>
> JORGE LUIS BORGES
> "Pierre Menard, Author of *Don Quixote*"

Adventure

At the heart of the impulse to heroic experience is simply the impulse to
adventure. The structure of *Don Quixote* makes clear that the book is not
solely concerned with the ethical and spiritual values (however possible or
impossible) commonly associated with heroic experience, values that, at their
most exalted, lead the Knight to be identified sometimes with the warrior
saints and, indeed, even with Christ. On a more primary level, *Don Quixote* is
concerned with the nature and possibility of adventure. Leon Gottfried has
commented on the "Odysseyan form" of the novel—a tripartite structure
divided into sections he calls "home," "road," and "home." According to
Gottfried, "'home' represents family, social ties, friendship, and finally both
mental health and spiritual salvation. At the same time, however, 'home' in
Don Quixote also represents ignoble poverty (in contrast to the sacred poverty
of the knight errant), envy, misunderstanding, and constriction of opportunity. By way of contrast, the 'road,' though a place of endless material defeats, represents boundless hope and opportunity for heroism, idealism, and
pure devotion."[1]

This larger structure, in turn, is echoed in the episodic nature of the action
and the typical scenario of individual episodes. Alexander Welsh has noted
that "Cervantes referred to the adventures of Don Quixote as *salidas*," which
Welsh (following Henry Fielding) calls "sallies" and glosses suggestively as "a
military operation that is at once defensive and offensive, and usually of uncertain success."[2] Nothing really "happens" in the novel in the sense of a

single action leading to a causally predictable end—in the sense, let us say, that Aeneas' destiny leads him inexorably through significant adventures to the founding of Rome. The disjunctive nature of mock-heroic makes such coherent activity impossible; the protagonist is too much out of synchronization with his environment. His theoretical aims have no practical relationship to the society in which he lives, and thus any possibility of material fulfillment is virtually ruled out. "Instead of progressing," Marthe Robert has observed, the novel "marks time like its crazy hero."[3] What remains, nevertheless, given the protagonist's continued "mad" commitment to life "on the road," is the fact of adventure itself. As one chapter head in *Don Quixote* puts it: "Of adventures that poured on Don Quixote so thick and fast that they trod upon each other's heels" (*DQ*, 837). However commonplace Don Quixote's world may be, it is still one in which adventures of a sort can happen, for it is a world open-ended, indeterminate, responsive in its own way to the human need for change, excitement, and freedom. Cervantes writes that after the Knight had left the castle of the Duke and Duchess and when he "found himself in open country . . . he felt himself in his element, with his spirits reviving for the fresh pursuit of his scheme of chivalries. And, turning to Sancho, he said: 'Liberty, Sancho, is one of the most precious gifts Heaven has bestowed upon man'" (*DQ*, 837). Later on I shall stress that indeterminism, like every other aspect of Cervantes's vision, is not without its ambiguities; it works as rigorously against the abstract schemes of the protagonist as it does against all other fixed structures. Nevertheless, the Knight is basically correct in believing that he lives in a world in which liberty in some form is still operative. Even his more radical dictum that "everything is possible" (*DQ*, 637) is not without an element of truth in the novel. In any case, the central rhythm of the action is a continually renewed movement toward the experience of adventure.

The image of adventures "pouring on" Don Quixote might suggest that he simply responds passively to adventures that befall him. Actually, he usually initiates them willy-nilly from whatever materials are at hand. Life provides a vehicle, but the imagination is the generating source of the adventure. The scenario of most episodes involves an encounter and a transformation; the self, through its capacity for belief and imaginative experience, transforms the encountered object and, so to speak, passes through it into a realm of wonder and adventure. Such an act of transformation is fundamental to the mode: from "is" to "ought"; from common sense to imaginative nonsense; from a "lower" empirical reality to a "higher" world of fairy tale.[4] In the earlier scenes of *Don Quixote*, when Cervantes is more concerned with emphasizing the absurdity of the process, the transformations, however amusing, are thin, superficial, and fairly mechanical: windmills into giants, barbers' basins into helmets, whores into romantic princesses. Later on, as the transformations become more complex and are shared by other characters, we become aware that they are all versions of the central, crucial, endlessly reiterated experience of the novel, which affirms the existence of adventure, defines its nature, and ultimately reveals both its spiritual potential and its material limitations.

In defending books of chivalry and adventure against the strictures of the canon, Don Quixote himself suggests that the prototypal experience of this kind of work involves an act of transformation. Specifically and at some length he describes the following episode as typical:

> For, tell me, could there be anything more delightful than to see displayed here and now before our eyes, as we might say, a great lake of pitch, boiling hot, and swimming and writhing about in it a great number of serpents, snakes and lizards, and many other sorts of savage and frightful creatures; and then to hear issuing from the middle of that lake a most dismal voice crying: "You, Knight, whoever you may be, that gaze on this dreadful lake, if you would reach the treasure hidden beneath these black waters, show the valour of your dauntless heart and plunge into the middle of its dark, burning liquor; for if you do not do so, you will not be worthy to see the mighty marvels hidden within the seven castles of the seven witches who dwell beneath this gloomy water." No sooner has the knight heard this dreadful voice than he abandons all thought for himself, and without reflecting on the peril to which he is exposing himself, or even easing himself of the weight of his ponderous armour, he commends himself to God and his lady, dives into the middle of the boiling lake; and then unexpectedly, and when he least knows where he is going, he finds himself amidst flowery meadows, incomparably finer even than the Elysian fields. There the sky seems to him more transparent and the sun to shine with a new brightness.

The passage goes on to tell of verdant groves, crystalline streams, castles of gold and diamonds, lovely maidens, delicious banquets, and finally the princess under a spell waiting to be rescued (*DQ*, 440–42). The heroic test, the act of spiritual ardency, has brought the hero from the world of fact to the realm of wonder, from the age of iron to that of gold, from life in time to stasis.

For the canon, however, such a passage is mere nonsense, "deliberate lies" (*DQ*, 443); it is patently untrue to literal reality. At the same time, he has no belief in a romantic dimension, in what Nabokov describes as "dreams mingling with reality . . . dreams fertilizing reality."[5] Significantly, in defending the experience described, Don Quixote puts less stress on its empirical truth than on its affective qualities, that is, on the human values generated by reading such stories and by attempts at imitation. The vision described is "delightful," he says; these stories "drive away the melancholy, and improve your temper if it happens to be bad" (*DQ*, 442). He goes on to more serious moral claims: "I can say of myself that since I became a knight errant I have been valiant, courteous, liberal, well-bred, generous, polite, bold, gentle and patient, and an endurer of toils, imprisonments and enchantments" (*DQ*, 442).

In the most famous of his transformations, the Knight apparently attempts to imitate literally the experience of the boiling lake. He descends into the Cave of Montesinos, "journeying through that obscure nether region on no assured or charted road" (*DQ*, 615), falls asleep on a ledge, and then (so he says) wakes up to find himself in an enchanted world of heroes. Sancho ridicules the experience at the time, Don Quixote himself later questions whether what happened was "true" or a dream, and the unsympathetic Cide Hamete claims that the Knight finally retracted his story on his deathbed and "confessed that he had invented it, since it seemed to him to fit in with the adventures he had read in his histories" (*DQ*, 624). Nevertheless, regardless of what precisely took place, he has had an adventure in some genuine sense of the word. Awakening as if from a deep sleep after his companions draw him up from the Cave, Don Quixote tells them that they have robbed him "of the sweetest existence and most delightful vision any human being ever enjoyed or beheld" (*DQ*, 614). But again the claims of adventure do not seem to be merely sensuous and aesthetic, though these loom large. More obscurely but no less surely, the process of adventure can generate a quality of love and loyalty that "home" life does not possess. After his waking, Don Quixote, Sancho, and a young scholar acting as guide to the Cave sit down on the grass and bring out food; "and all three in love and good fellowship ate their lunch and their supper in one" (*DQ*, 614). It is this kind of love that Sancho discovers on his travels and that increasingly (much more than hope of material gain) keeps him, against all dictates of reason and pragmatic reality, with his mad companion.

The fact remains that in the Cave of Montesinos episode as in all others, Don Quixote has had a mock rather than a real adventure; he has had a comic imitation of adventure. He is no Roland or Amadis, the Arcadian world has no substantial existence beyond some form of subjective fantasy, and, of course, in the Cave of Montesinos episode, no useful message is brought back from his imitative Journey to the Underworld. My own rather solemn account of the episode scarcely suggests Sancho's antiphonal mockery or the absurd details that emerge even from the Knight's serious version or parodic echoes that are sounded elsewhere in the novel.[6] From an adult point of view, Don Quixote is a grown-up child "playing" at adventures, as the nineteenth-century practice of relegating mock-heroic adventure almost exclusively to young people will make clear. Indeed, the association of the protagonist's experiences with childhood is ubiquitous to the mode from beginning to end.[7] His experiences are distinguished from the sophisticated and deliberate "games" of the Duke and Duchess only by the personal qualities of naiveté, moral purity, and spiritual ardency that motivate their creation.

But if his adventures are largely the creation of his own imagination, the qualities of self-generation, spontaneity, and spiritual enlargement nevertheless remain basic to whatever positive human significance they may have. In mock-heroic narrative, adventure constitutes the only positive response to the inevitable "imprisonment" in a banal present time that simultaneously robs adventure of any final significance. After the Duke and Duchess have taken over the manufacture of adventure late in the novel, Don Quixote and Sancho eventually become aware that they have lost their own adventure-making power and thus whatever freedom is possible to them. Recognized in Part Two as literary "characters" and increasingly treated as such, they more and more become simply puppets on someone else's stage. This growing involvement in other people's games is concomitant with the eventual decline of the Knight and the final return home of the pair. From all such predetermined "cages" Don Quixote, if he is to remain true to his own spirit, must escape to new encounters on the road. As Sancho, who essentially shares his master's commitments, explains to his wife: " 'There's nothing so pleasant in the world for an honest man as to be squire to a knight errant, that seeks adventure. It's true that most of them one finds don't turn out as much to one's liking as a man could wish. . . . But, for all that, it's a nice thing to be looking out for incidents, crossing mountains, searching woods, climbing rocks, visiting castles, and lodging in inns at your pleasure, with the devil a farthing to pay' " (*DQ*, 457).

Exile and Madness

"I'll tell you some wonders," promises a traveler Don Quixote meets on the road, and the Knight immediately changes his plans so that he can meet the man again (*DQ*, 626). His destiny is to be a pursuer of wonders in a world in which the dimension of wonder has ceased to exist in any substantial fashion. Anachronism is basic to his sense of dislocation; indeed, the crude fact of his anachronism is his most striking and obvious characteristic as he appears in scene after scene using the armor, gestures, and rhetoric of an earlier day. His flights from home are flights into what Robert tellingly calls "anachronistic space." And she adds that "he is essentially a displaced person, condemned to wander ceaselessly on the fringe of perceptible reality," someone who "live[s] his life backwards."[8] Such displacement is always characteristic of the mock-heroic protagonist. Bellow literally makes Mr. Sammler a displaced per-

son and describes Herzog metaphorically in similar terms; Nabokov's principal figures are all, in one way or another, versions of his own exiled self;
Leopold Bloom, another Jew in exile, dreams of Palestine and a righteous
Messiah; Wallace Stevens thinks of himself as "a most inappropriate man / In
a most unpropitious place." His Crispin's first act is to emigrate. And so
forth—I could continue the list to include all the mock-heroes dealt with in
this book.

Another of Don Quixote's later avatars is Rip Van Winkle, who wakes up
to find himself psychically dislocated from the present "time" of his environment, with dress and attitudes carried over from the past. Both are essentially
"reactionary" figures, maintaining and pursuing values already lost. As Coleridge pointed out, Don Quixote's madness may "perhaps be defined as the
circling in a stream which should be progressive and adaptive."[9] He is, in
fact, militantly hostile to the idea of adaptation. "I am only at pains to convince the world of its error in not reviving that most happy age in which the
order of chivalry flourished," he tells the barber in an impassioned speech
defending his alleged madness (DQ, 477); and he goes on characteristically to
attack the effeteness and depravity of the present. Until his death approaches,
he attempts to ignore clock time; when Sancho tells him he was down in the
Cave of Montesinos "a little more than an hour," he replies that by *his* reckoning, he "must have stayed three days in those remote and secret regions"
(DQ, 620). Symbolically and almost literally a mummy ("so lean and withered
that he seemed to be nothing but mummy-flesh" [DQ, 471]), he is driven as
much by nostalgia as by hope, his speech to the barber less a program of
action than an expression of alienation and, in effect, a rationalization of his
extreme need to create a world of wonders. Very early in their adventures
together, Sancho dubs him the "Knight of the Sad Countenance," a phrase
accurately reflecting the sense of loss, falling away, and diminishment that
impels his nostalgic spirit to find in acts of desire and imagination what it
cannot find in life.

From this point of view, Don Quixote's "circling" madness is simply an
index of his need and will to find a heroic dimension in life, an environment
commensurate with his aesthetic, emotional, and spiritual longings. His
madness is paranoiac; the universe *must be* organized around his needs. His
"enchanters" are, to be sure, rationalizing devices, versions of the general
human capacity for reconciling the world of "seeming" with the world of
"being," but Don Quixote raises them to the status of primary powers in an
egocentric universe.[10] He answers the Duchess's doubts concerning details in
the story of Dulcinea by reminding her "that all or most of the things which
happen to me are out of the ordinary course of things which befall other

knights errant, whether they be directed by the inscrutable will of the fates or by the malice of some envious enchanter" (*DQ*, 681–82).

This entire scene, in which the Duke and Duchess "egg-on" the Knight in order to draw him out, is significant in suggesting the degree to which will to belief is the central facet of his character. It is late in the novel, and both Don Quixote and (I suspect) his creator seem increasingly aware of what he is affirming. By this time the literal reality of his vision scarcely concerns him. He as much as acknowledges the Duchess's charge that Dulcinea is a "fantastic mistress" engendered and born in his mind when he admits to her: "God knows whether Dulcinea exists on earth or no, whether she is fantastic or not fantastic. These are not matters whose verification can be carried out in full" (*DQ*, 680). Mocker though she is, the Duchess nevertheless understands precisely what Don Quixote is trying to tell her and assures him that henceforth she "shall believe, and make my whole household believe—and my lord the Duke too, if it is necessary—that there is a Dulcinea in El Toboso, and that she lives today, and is beautiful, nobly born and deserving that such a knight as Don Quixote should serve her" (*DQ*, 681).

Paranoia so defined in mock-heroic involves the willful, obsessive, impassioned attempt of the protagonist to create an environment commensurate with his heroic aspirations. Don Quixote is a Faust in a world without Mephistopheles. When reminded early in the novel by a laborer from his own village that he is "really" Master Quixada, the Knight responds: "I know who I am . . . and I know, too, that I am capable of being not only the characters I have named, but all the Twelve Peers of France and all the Nine Worthies as well" (*DQ*, 54). He refuses to acknowledge here the reality of his name as the limiting boundary of his experience, and this response is characteristic of his "mad" refusal throughout to recognize any distinction between the possible (that which is governed by the laws of probability) and the desirable (that subject only to the imagination). His universe is a seamless web in which he wanders indiscriminately, at one moment denying the authority of his senses (turning the real into fiction), at another—for example, the puppet show—intervening in the patently fictive as if it were literally real. Episodes such as those of the whipped boy or the galley slaves make clear that he is concerned neither with the complexity of causality nor the pragmatism of results but rather with the pure "act" of knight errantry—the self in a demonstration or performance of its heroic potential, the self as "actor." Insofar as his adventures have no serious contexts in life, it is entirely appropriate that they are finally subsumed in the play world of the Duke and Duchess. Yet from Don Quixote's point of view, they must be judged as *attempts* to live ideally in a world in which ideality is impossible, attempts that can be justified to some

extent by the moral, spiritual, and aesthetic qualities that underlie their incep-
tion or inform their performance. Even in the extreme madness of his alienation from reality, this is as far as the Knight can go toward recreating the
romantic landscape of a heroic age. Instead of authentic heroic experience,
the mock-hero is reduced to a potentially endless series of heroic gestures in
the imaginary world he has dreamed into being. As the Russian dramatist
and critic N. N. Evreinoff once observed, Don Quixote creates a "theater for
himself" against the aggressive realities of life, a place where the fairy tale
most dear to the self is willed into existence.[11]

It is all a game, of course. Mock-heroic literature is filled with the games of
the protagonist—desperate games, joyful games, children's games, adult
games. Jorge Luis Borges's protagonist, Pierre Menard, creates for himself the
"solitary game" of reconstructing *Don Quixote* in the twentieth century, a task
difficult in itself and made "impossible from the start" by the addition of
"artificial obstacles." For Borges, such dedication to "useless" and "futile"
tasks is the essence of the quixotic stance and the crux of its human significance: the exercise of pure intelligence as a direct, indeed, proportionate response to the material or rational unreality of the situation.[12] Werner Herzog,
in a recent mock-heroic film called *Fitzcarraldo,* describes his protagonist aptly
at one point as a "conquistador of the useless," a phrase whose full ironic
possibilities resonate throughout the experience of the mode.

Don Quixote himself seems to be increasingly aware that he is involved in
a game, sustained, if at all, by mutual agreement to arbitrary rules and measured by the qualities of amusement, exhilaration, and delight that are the
rewards of play. His own gamesmanship becomes more deliberate and self-
conscious. After listening to Sancho's bizarre and vivid account of touching
the sky while riding the magic horse Clavileño, his initial response is to cast
doubts, but later he goes up to his squire and whispers: "Sancho, if you want
me to believe what you saw in the sky, I wish you to accept my account of
what I saw in the Cave of Montesinos. I say no more" (*DQ,* 735). There *is* no
more to say; the two grown-up boys must finally conspire together, like the
Duke and Duchess, to keep the game going. Late in the novel, when, literally,
the "game is up" with chivalry, Don Quixote contemplates turning to pastoral, another significant play world that has appeared from time to time in
the book. In this new context, transformations from reality to wonder will
again be possible. As he tells Sancho: "I will call myself the shepherd Quix-
otiz and you the shepherd Panzino, and we will wander through the mountains, woods, and meadows, singing here, lamenting there, drinking of the
liquid crystals of the springs" (*DQ,* 902). But the detritus of reality works
ultimately against the best of gamesmen; weariness and death prohibit Don
Quixote from ever appearing in his final pageant.

Regardless of final failure, however, strong elements in the novel support the Knight's attempts to live life as a heroic game and collectively suggest Cervantes's sympathetic understanding of the significance of these attempts. In the first place, as critics have often noted, most of the characters in the book live by one fiction or another—live, that is, on illusions about reality which they insist on viewing as the truth. Sancho's famous remark in defense of his belief that Don Quixote will make him governor of an island emphasizes this point: "If I'm set on isles, other people are set on worse. Everyman's the son of his own deeds; and since I'm a man, I can become pope, let alone governor of an isle" (*DQ*, 423). This is a version of Don Quixote's Faustian brag, but, because he is saner, put by Sancho in a more secure illusionist context. Personal responsibility and freedom are affirmed here even as they continue to be affirmed by the Knight up to the bitter end of his career, but such freedom is defined, in effect, as the right to foster and pursue one's illusions.

Moreover, Cervantes "makes his characters live in a world favorable to illusion."[13] Leo Spitzer some time ago noted that "we have to do not only with the opposition between prosaic reality and fantastic dreams; reality itself can be both prosaic and fantastic."[14] Spitzer is specifically referring to the interpolated stories: characters tell elaborate stories, usually involving themselves; other characters from these stories appear eventually on the actual scene of the novel. The line between "fiction" and "life" is deliberately blurred; recent critical emphasis on metafictions has only made us more aware of this dimension of the novel. In addition, Don Quixote becomes self-consciously a literary character in the second part of the book. Ten years have lapsed between the two parts, his earlier adventures have been chronicled and published, and he is encouraged at this late date to act the fabulous figure of legend—to continue "composing," with substantial help, the story of his life. But such storytelling is only one of the elaborate devices of pageant, disguise, "jokes," and authorial manipulation through which Cervantes explores the nature and meaning of fiction and suggests the degree to which our experience is simply the sum of our imagination.

Finally, as I have previously suggested, to the degree to which personal events *are* simply pageant, game, or story, they can be judged by the quality of performance involved. By this criterion Don Quixote is the supreme player. Like all mock-heroes, he is at least an authentic hero of what Cervantes calls the "wild imagination" (*DQ*, 392). In another of his characteristic responses to the recurring question of the reality of Dulcinea, the Knight says to Sancho: "I imagine all I say to be true, neither more nor less, and in my imagination I draw her as I would have her be" (*DQ*, 210). His role and significance are increasingly associated with art and the artist, and as an artist he has no peers. Increasingly in the novel those who encounter Don Quixote are torn between scorn and dismay at his folly and (more frequently) delight and pleasure in the entertainment he provides. He is "the most amusing of all madmen" (*DQ*, 892). The Bachelor, in fact, is attacked by Don Antonio at the end of the novel for having forced Don Quixote to give up knight errantry: "Don't you see, sir, that no benefit to be derived from Don Quixote's recovery could outweigh the pleasure afforded by his extravagances?" (*DQ*, 892). Unlike most of those who enjoy him, however, and also unlike most of the other storytellers in the book, the Knight's imagination is both moral and aesthetic, an expression of the dream of classical and Renaissance humanism that beauty and truth are profoundly one. His great role or performance includes a fundamental dimension of value. As Howard Mancing puts it, "The difference between Don Quijote and Alonzo Quijano is the difference between the verbs *ser* ('to be,' 'to exist') and *valer* ('to be worthwhile'): Alonzo Quijano *es* ('exists'); Don Quijote *vale* ('leads a worthwhile life'). The only meaningful thing that Alonzo Quijano even did was to become Don Quijote."[15] It is this quality of humane "worth" expressed through imagination, passionate commitment, and moral vision that shapes most of his adventures and distinguishes them in part from the more vulgar and superficial gamesmanship of the couple whom Nabokov aptly calls "the idiotic Duke and his feral Duchess"—the "practical jokers" of the book, endlessly playing their "tricks."[16]

But only in part. Toward the end of the book Cide Hamete, in disgust, links together all the fools in their folly. According to Cervantes's report of his sentiments concerning the final elaborate joke of the Duke and Duchess, "he considers that the mockers were as mad as their victims, and the Duke and Duchess within a hair's breadth of appearing fools themselves for taking such pains to play tricks on a pair of fools" (*DQ*, 916). In addition to his ludicrous misreadings of reality, Don Quixote has other dimensions of absurdity, even of his own form of vulgarity. As a mock-hero he is not only fool but pretender, indeed, imposter, Northrop Frye's *alazon* figure, Joyce's "forger." A decayed hidalgo from backwater Spain, whose best friends are a peasant, a priest, and a barber, with none of the accoutrements—wealth, power, and physical prowess—of the traditional heroic role, Don Quixote is inexorably and fundamentally a part of the banal world he is trying to "rescue." His knowledge of the forms of heroic experience is gleaned largely from his reading of popular romance—secondhand knowledge, much of it as shoddy as its source. Not an authentic hero at all, his only recourse is to try to model himself on heroes; he imitates the rules of chivalry with the literalness and punctilious zeal of the actor, the copyist, or the parvenu and with the same inevitable divorce from actual circumstances. As he explains to Sancho in a characteristic scene on the Sierra Morena, "when any painter wishes to win fame in his art, he endeavours to copy the pictures of the most excellent painters he knows; and this same rule obtains for all professions" (*DQ*, 202). The Knight declares, therefore, his intention to "imitate Amadis, and to act here the desperate, raving, furious lover" (*DQ*, 203). He dismisses Sancho's insistence that there be a "reason" for the histrionics and tells him not to "waste time advising me to give up so rare, so happy, and so unprecedented an imitation" (*DQ*, 203). Futility, absurdity, even fatuity constitute the dimension of mockery in the protagonist's gratuitous act.

All Don Quixote's actions are imitations, and, in a world without heroic dimension, could be nothing else. At best they capture some of the spirit of the original, at worst they are crude caricature. The disjunction I have described previously in relation to the mock-hero's adventures extends to his personal situation: an inexorable gap exists between his impulse to heroism and the commonplace materials of his life and world. The mock-hero, like Don Quixote himself, is a figure at once extraordinary and absurd, potentially tragic in his aspirations yet comic in the limited vehicles available for their expression. The narrator says at one point that Don Quixote's adventures "must be honoured either with wonder or with laughter" (*DQ*, 748). I suspect we respond with both at once.

Parody

We could just as well say of Don Quixote's personal responses and adventures that they are insistently parodic, whether we think of them as parodying matter from the chivalric romances or, more generally, parodying the various ritual postures and actions of heroic myth. The novel in general tends toward parody, and for this reason, Cervantes has been justly celebrated by many critics as the father of the genre. In *The Nature of Narrative*, for example, Robert Scholes and Robert Kellogg describe his work as an attempt to "reconcile powerful empirical [realistic] and fictional [ideal] impulses" and point out that "the novel is not the opposite of romance, as is usually maintained, but a product of the reunion of the empirical and fictional elements in narrative literature." Leo Spitzer's description of the "hybrid genre" of the novel— "born of poetry and of something else, of an extrapoetic factor, of a tendency to encroach upon life, along with an inborn striving toward pure art, a nostalgic yearning back to epic beauty"—remains a useful and suggestive way of beginning any general discussion of the form. At the same time, it clearly directs us toward the more systematic and categorical ambivalence of mock-heroic, that "hybrid" which is a type of what Gary Morson calls "threshold literature"—literature of complex and contradictory generic encoding, literature that reminds us of generic boundaries by their ostentatious transgression.[17]

In this context, the mock-heroic mode is explicitly parodic, if by parody we mean (again I am following Morson) a "double-voiced" utterance "designed to be interpreted as the expression of two speakers." As Morson explains: "The audience of a double-voiced word is therefore meant to hear both a version of the original utterance as the embodiment of its speaker's point of view (or 'semantic position') *and* the second speaker's evaluation of that utterance from a different point of view."[18] With parody, an act of imitation releases this concurrent expression of conflicting voices. In mock-heroic narrative, both protagonist and author are highly self-conscious and deliberate imitators. Both (whether they are more fully dramatized as two or combined as the antiphonal voices of one persona) are centrally concerned with heroism, and both are involved in testing, each in his own way, the possibility of heroic conventions in a real world. Whereas the protagonist is committed to straight imitation, the author, by contrast, is committed only to an imitative form that lays bare the pretensions of the more literal copyist and his model in the context of this same "real" world in which they must somehow function. But these pretensions are laid bare (and here the ambivalence becomes acute) so as to transform the expression of heroic impulse and thus ensure its survival in some form. Instead of the either/or of satire, Cervantine parody involves a complex dialectic between heroic and mundane voices, which searchingly acknowledges and explores the claims of both. The conflicting points of view come together in the aesthetic equilibrium of the style, but they are without formal resolution other than the affirmation of whatever humane values may be revealed in the expression of heroic desire as an end in itself. Paterson's legend on his old ashtray—*La Vertue est tout dans l'effort*—constitutes the only explicit theme of the mode.

The Cave of Montesinos episode can again be taken as a case in point. As my comments may have already suggested, it is a subtle examination of the human significance of the heroic myth of the Underworld Journey, and the results are far from moral condemnation or cynical dismissal—a conclusion to this extent shared by both author and protagonist. At the same time, it ridicules not only the special foolishness of the Knight in literally confusing myth with reality and himself with Durandarte and Montesinos, but the absurd aspects of the myth itself, our creation of elaborate "other worlds" filled with people exactly like ourselves, for example, and especially our search for explanations, directions, and "messages." The episode in every way mocks all simple and final explanations; it limits the claims of all visionary excursions whether literal or imaginary, whether dream, art, or alleged fact. That we never know what "really" happened to Don Quixote on the most literal level and are given alternate explanations is symbolic of the larger significance of this particular episode and, at the same time, a clue to the operation of parody in the entire novel. It works against all absolutes, beginning with human experience conceived in heroic or ideal terms and fictional conventions based on these terms but spreading out to cover every ideal value, fixed type, or single point of view. To this extent, Cervantine parody is reductive and destructive. Don Quixote as the most naive and passionate believer in the book is also the greatest fool. Such parody, however, in denying absolute claims, paradoxically preserves the forms and many of the feelings and values on which such claims are based. To this extent it is a salvage operation far more than a demolition, allowing us to invoke, inspect, and even make substantial emotional and rational commitments to ideals whose absolute dimension may have disappeared and whose practical coefficient may be nonexistent. In mock-heroic, parody is the central stylistic device for suggesting the disjunction of value and fact that I have already noted; but it is a medium in which, nevertheless, the claims of both survive, interact, and make themselves felt in new and vivid comic form.

Parody of action in *Don Quixote* is reinforced by rhetorical parody, which serves ceaselessly to remind us of the potential absurdity of every "type" of character or fixed point of view. The Knight's lyrical and moralistic outbursts are only the most obvious manifestations of a strong and complex tendency in the book. Sancho Panza, for example, who serves, in part, as an earthly and pragmatic foil to the follies of Don Quixote, sometimes becomes, through his own credulous actions and infatuated speech, a parodic echo of the Knight's performance. As the priest observes: "The pair of them seem to be cast in one mould" (*DQ*, 482). But even Sancho's earthiness is parodied; his folk knowledge has congealed into aphorisms, which he piles together indiscriminately for a paragraph at a time. "What a string of nonsense, Sancho! What have all these proverbs to do with the matter we were discussing," Don Quixote asks him on one occasion and goes on to assure him that all *his* actions, in contrast, "are very well based on reason and conform in every way to the rules of chivalry" (*DQ*, 201). Nor is Sancho's rhetoric of direct action invulnerable to irony. After he has agreed to take a florid letter composed by the Knight to the village girl he imagines to be Dulcinea, Sancho promises a reply: "Otherwise let the lady Dulcinea look out. For if she doesn't reply as she should, I take my solemn oath that I'll kick and punch a kind answer out of her guts . . . I'm pretty good at that. She doesn't know me. If she did, I swear she would treat me with proper respect." Again it is Don Quixote, who sees the point, and his rejoinder has general implications: "Really, Sancho . . . as far as I can see, you are no saner than I am" (*DQ*, 213). Speech in Cervantes's novel is less a matter of communication than a revelation of the particular "insanity" of the speaker. Parody of this kind renders every voice suspect, from such "normal" figures as the Gentleman in Green to, finally, the author himself, speaking in his own person or through his narrator—significantly, an untrustworthy "Arab" historian with his own ax to grind. Parody operates by creating an incongruity between form and substance; actions, descriptions, and speeches are rendered ludicrous by their inappropriateness to and distance from the needs and expectations of the particular situation invoked. Sometimes substance seems to fail the high expectations of the form. Introduced to Durandarte in the Cave of Montesinos as his possible savior, Don Quixote hears the enchanted knight respond to Montesinos: "If that should not be, cousin, I say: patience and shuffle the cards" (DQ, 618). Other actions and utterances in this scene are equally incongruous to the solemn expectations of the myth. More often in parody it is inflated, mechanical, or congealed form that is inappropriate or irrelevant to the substantial question at hand. This form of parody characterizes the various rhetorical voices I have previously discussed, and it is equally apparent in the endless dissonance between heroic gesture and material event that marks the Knight's activities.

Parody, in short, is central to the entire theatrical world of mock-heroic. It "decodes" heroic values and their expressive conventions (or any others, for that matter), revealing, in the process, their "archaeology" as local manifestations of time and place; it "recodes" them simultaneously as vital game or performance in the larger context of the opaque, banal, time-ridden world that stands revealed.[19] Language reveals now, in one way or another, only the endless imitations of the characters and the poised ambivalence of the author. As Leo Spitzer long ago observed about words in Cervantes's novel, they "are no longer, as they had been in the Middle Ages, depositories of truths nor, as they had been in the Renaissance, an expansion of life: they are, like the books in which they are contained, sources of hesitation, error, deception—'dreams.' "[20]

But not all the words function in such a fashion. Many in the bluntest terms express simply the cruelty, vulgarity, and endless harsh contingency of commonplace life. As Nabokov emphasized to his students, scene after scene involves "a chaos of pain, inflicted or received."[21] I have already noted this dimension of realism in the novel; we need now to examine further its implications.

Anticlimax

The bathos inherent in the operation of parody is only part of a larger principle of anticlimax in Don Quixote. Episode after episode involves a juxtaposition of expectation with actuality so sharp and so immediate as to suggest on the structural level something akin to the superimposition characteristic of the verbal and narrative parody already described. Every assumption, gesture, and action meets (often instantly) its ironic qualification. Examples are everywhere in the complex dialectic of the two protagonists: the following exchange, for instance, after Sancho has returned from a visit to the peasant girl alleged to be Dulcinea and when the Knight is querying him for details, none of which turn out to be congruent with his hopes:

> "One thing you cannot deny me, Sancho. When you stood close to her, did you not smell a spicy odour, an aromatic fragrance, something unutterably sweet to which I cannot give a name? I mean an essence or aroma, as if you were in some rare glover's shop?"
>
> "All that I can say," answered Sancho, "is that I got a sniff of something rather mannish. It must have been because she was running with sweat from the hard work." [*DQ*, 269]

The hopes of Don Quixote are systematically denied by the crude facts of life. The stylistic juxtaposition in the passage above is a direct reflection of its content and, beyond that, of its essential significance as a representative episode.

Chance occurrence is equally important to the action of the novel and likewise serves to interrupt, often brutally and dramatically, any planned pattern of behavior. Again, a single illustration must serve. As Don Quixote and Sancho enter Barcelona in triumph late in the novel,

> the Evil One, who is master of all mischief, and the boys, who are wickeder than the Evil One—or two mischievous, insolent lads at least mingled with the crowd, and one of them lifting Dapple's tail and the other Rocinante's, fastened a bunch of furze to each. The poor animals felt these strange spurs, and by swishing their tails aggravated their pain to such an extent that with a thousand capers they threw their riders to the ground. Insulted and furious, Don Quixote ran to rid his old horse's tail of its plumage, and Sancho did the same for Dapple. Don Quixote's escort had a mind to punish the boys' insolence, but that was impossible, for they had worked themselves in among the thousands who were following. So Don Quixote and Sancho remounted and, amidst the same acclamations and music, reached their guide's house. [*DQ*, 867]

On this occasion, two performances are ruined by such malignant intrusion, obviously that of Don Quixote (not to mention poor Sancho) responding with appropriate dignity and noble acquiescence to the offer of heroic passage into the city, but equally the performance of the escort, who, in search of entertainment, is putting on an elaborate charade to encourage the Knight's fantasies. For nobody do things work out as planned. The mockers are themselves mocked along with the more obvious fools, and the mocking device at the plot level, here as elsewhere in the novel, is the casual, banal, unexpected happening that forever deprives desire of its appropriate consummation.

Heroic plans are reduced in execution to wild and sometimes brutal farce, but, as Sancho wisely observes, "that's where the truth of the story comes in." He is responding to the Bachelor's suggestion, based on his knowledge of traditional epic, that the Knight's history would have been better "if the authors had left out a few of the countless beatings which Don Quixote received in various encounters" (DQ, 488–89). Sancho, in effect, is aware that in Cervantes's own world it is the unexpected but inevitable pratfall that defines the very nature of reality. The narrator, in his witty reference above to "the Evil One" in the guise of mischievous boys, virtually establishes banal chance as a metaphysical principle; everywhere in the book phrases like "as Fate would have it," "fatal destiny," and "the Devil ordained" are used to introduce often disastrous surprises.[22] What might be expected in the life of someone whose conception of empirical reality is as distorted as that of Don Quixote is, in fact, the common experience of all in the novel. This is the point Thomas Cecial (another pragmatically wise "squire") makes to the Bachelor after the latter, by the merest fluke, has been defeated by the Knight in a jousting contest elaborately designed for the opposite result: namely, that Don Quixote will be beaten and forced by vow to return home. According to Cecial, " 'It's easy enough to plan and set about an enterprise, but it's very often difficult to come well out of it. Don Quixote's mad, and we're sane. Yet he gets off sound and smiling, while your worship comes out bruised and sorrowful. So let's consider now which is the madder, the man who's mad because he can't help it, or the man who's mad by choice?' " (DQ, 561). Cecial seems to suggest that our experience of reality almost always renders ludicrous whatever abstract formulations (whether rational and self-conscious or naive) we might have made of it beforehand. Anticlimax thus functions like parody in the novel to suggest the universal madness of man striving to impose formal order on a world so completely indeterminate as to escape his impositions or so opaque as to ignore them. His "rage for order" is matched only by its practical impossibility.

The anticlimax of individual scenes in Don Quixote is repeated in the outcome of larger episodes and, eventually, in the denouement. The shepherd boy who has been saved from one beating by the Knight, only to be doubly beaten later by his now even more irate master, draws the moral of the entire plot when he reminds Don Quixote pointedly that "the end of the business was very much the opposite of what you suppose" (DQ, 274). In traditional heroic narrative, the protagonist is a shaper and visionary planner working, against whatever interruptions and reversals of fortune, toward the achievement of great ends. Even the tragic overreacher whose ends are finally denied to him profoundly rends and twists the social fabric before his inevitable death. Don Quixote, however, returns home after a series of inconclusive and absurd adventures, and homecoming itself is not a comic consummation (as in, let us say, *The Odyssey*) but simply an act of retirement, a movement toward temporary refuge from exhaustion and failure. Nor can we really describe his death as a tragic extension of character. His final plan to create a pastoral world is thwarted, as usual, by chance occurrence; according to the narrator, "his disposition and end came when he least expected it" (*DQ*, 934). Death is merely the surprise common to all, the surprise to end all surprises, different in magnitude rather than kind from the other anticlimaxes in the novel.

Ambivalence

What attitude, finally, are we to take toward Don Quixote and his adventures? One important characteristic of the mock-heroic mode is that this question is incorporated by a variety of methods directly into the fabric of the narrative. In *Don Quixote* the other characters are as troubled as the reader by the problem of an adequate response to the Knight. As if to reinforce further this identity of concern, Cervantes in Part Two literally makes some of the characters "readers" of the first part published ten years earlier or the false second part written by Avellaneda; they become "critics" of Don Quixote the man but by implication also of the book in its role as transformation of heroic chronicle. A few dismiss his experience as foolish nonsense, a waste of everyone's time. Most, however, respond with an astonishment that is a direct reflection of their bafflement and contradictory feelings.

The adventure with the two lodgers at an inn late in the novel is typical of episodes that reveal these mixed feelings. The lodgers have been reading the false second part of the book; Don Quixote hears them talking, realizes the details are all wrong, and intervenes to set them straight regarding his "true" exploits. The narrator describes their response as follows: "Great was the pleasure the two gentlemen received from hearing Don Quixote relate his extraordinary adventures, and they were alike surprised at his extravagancies and at his elegant manner of recounting them. One moment they thought him a man of sense, and the next he slipped into craziness; nor could they decide what degree to assign him between wisdom and folly" (*DQ*, 852). One aspect of this response is clear enough: their sheer pleasure from Don Quixote's performance. This aesthetic judgment is paralleled by their eventual rejection of the vulgar imitation by Avellaneda that they have been unwittingly reading, "a wretched account, barren of invention, poor in style, and miserably poorest in descriptions, though rich in absurdities" (*DQ*, 853). But on the question of a fixed and precise moral and intellectual evaluation of the Knight they remain puzzled until the end. After Don Quixote and his squire have gone out of the room, the two men are left "amazed at the spectacle of mingled wisdom and folly they had witnessed" (*DQ*, 854). All that they can finally attest is that "these were the authentic Don Quixote and Sancho" (*DQ*, 854). Even Sancho at this point views the Knight and himself as characters in a chronicle and delights in the characterization, which for him has taken on the quality of positive myth: "my master valiant, wise and a true lover, and myself, simple, droll, and no guzzler nor a drunkard" (*DQ*, 853). Sancho justly celebrates the glory of the roles; the complex ironies of role-playing, however, are beyond him, on this occasion at least, though not beyond the other, more detached viewers.

Nor, obviously, are these ironies beyond Cervantes, who detaches himself deliberately from his own novel so that its full ironic potential will be the more powerfully felt and the more complete. He is unequivocal only in his distaste for "narrowness of soul," which for him means a fundamental lack of moral range, imagination, sympathy, understanding, and good humor.[23] His act of withdrawal from the role of primary narrator is another important way in which Cervantes dramatizes the problem of attitude in his book and, in particular, moves away from any possible narrowness of his own. The creation of Cide Hamete opened up many new possibilities, not the least of which was the opportunity for Cervantes to emphasize that he was writing a radically new form of "historical" epic, one that is more reflective of actual life, more inclusive, more "mixed," than earlier prototypes of the genre. Cervantes has in mind the classical distinction between poetry and history; as the Bachelor explains, "It is one thing to write as a poet, and another as a historian. The poet can relate and sing things, not as they were but as they should have been, without in any way affecting the truth of the matter" (*DQ*, 488). It is this last premise which Cervantes calls into question through the figure of Cide Hamete Benengeli, "that most meticulous investigator of every detail of this true history" (*DQ*, 789). As I have already noted, Sancho also challenges the Bachelor's statement: for him at least, "the truth of the story" lies precisely in those details (often awkward, painful, and embarrassing) of the hero's adventures which are usually omitted. In this sense his function in the novel is similar to that of Cide Hamete: both are witness to important elements missing from the heroic chronicle as traditionally written.

Yet to have given the story completely to Cide Hamete would have been simply to turn it into an early exercise in literary naturalism—narrowness in another form. This is not, to be sure, what happens because Cervantes carefully takes back with one hand what he has given away with the other. Cide Hamete is a historian, but an Arab historian ("men of that nation being ready liars" [*DQ*, 78]). He is introduced as narrator presumably to emphasize the realistic level of the novel, but it is done so elaborately and self-consciously that our sense of fictional artifice is strongly heightened. The narrative role is split, and this split merely threatens the total narrative voice as a single, reliable point of view. For Cervantes it was an act comparable to doubling the protagonists (not to mention all the other doubling and parallelism in the book) in the opportunities it offered for the complex and confused interplay of attitude and opinion. Sometimes for long intervals Cide Hamete will seem to disappear, but seldom can we risk the assumption that the sentiments expressed on any particular occasion are necessarily those of Cervantes.

When Cide Hamete does speak to us most directly and plainly, he is probably least reliable: his moralizing at the very end, for example; or his "certainty" that Don Quixote on his deathbed retracted the Cave of Montesinos story as pure invention; or his melancholy sense of life as unstable, cyclical, and speeding to its end without hope of renewal except in eternity. By unreliable I do not mean that these views are completely wrong, only that they are simplistic opinions in a dramatic context rather than objective statements of theme. Cide Hamete's concept of the cycle of life, for example, would seem to have the widest interpretive possibilities; it is relevant to the chapter in which it is found and can also be related more widely to the rhythm and total structure of the novel. Nevertheless, Cervantes immediately intervenes to qualify with his own point of view the tone if not the substance of the Arab's position: "So says Cide Hamete, the Mohammedan philosopher; for many, by the light of nature and without the illumination of the faith, have come to understand the brevity and instability of our present existence and the everlastingness of the eternal life to come" (*DQ*, 811). This Christian emendation hints at a possible change of emphasis away from any dark pagan fatalism.

Cervantes then further qualifies the Arab's statement by imputing to it more rhetoric than substance: "In this place [the first paragraph of a chapter dealing with Sancho] . . . our author alludes only to the swiftness with which Sancho's government ended" (*DQ*, 811). What follows in the chapter is a scene of wild and brutal farce in which Sancho is beaten and terrorized by the Duke's lackeys, who pretend that his island is being invaded. It is all another joke, and when it is over, Sancho is glad enough to leave the "governorship" for his old freedom. Yet he has been a good governor, and even the tricksters have come to love him and regret his departure. There is some element of human loss in his going. But the fact remains that Cide Hamete's solemn invocation of the wheel of fortune (an appropriate theme for chivalric chronicle) has been relentlessly qualified—though by no means qualified out of existence—first by Cervantes's own antiphonal voice, then by its context in the comic action of the chapter. Among the many parodies of the book it takes its appropriate place as a complex parody of editorial intervention. It reminds us of a traditional attitude toward the material in question but, equally important, of the present inadequacy of this attitude as a single point of view.

Celebration is another familiar editorial role, and this, too, is parodied in the novel. When, for example, Don Quixote confronts the lion "with marvelous bravery and a bold heart" (*DQ*, 575), Cervantes is moved to quote directly Cide Hamete's apostrophe: "O brave and incomparably courageous Don Quixote de la Mancha! True mirror to all the valiant knights of the world! Thou new and second Don Manuel de Leon—honour and glory of Spanish knights!" (*DQ*, 575). Such praise ("hyperbole upon hyperbole," as Cide Hamete himself describes it) goes on for an entire paragraph. Don Quixote, we must remember, has insisted that a captive lion be let out of his cage so that the Knight may tear him to pieces. But the lion is saner than the human being: he "took no notice of this childish bravado," and "turned his back and showed Don Quixote his hindquarters. Then he lay down again in his cage with great calmness and composure" (*DQ*, 576). Here, as usual, rhetorical parody, in this case of the narrator, is accompanied by anticlimax at the level of action. Nor does Cervantes spare himself from irony. In his role as naive and enthusiastic collector of material about Don Quixote he is even less critical than Cide Hamete. Indeed, he criticizes the Arab for reticence; "when he could and should have let himself go in praise of so worthy a knight he seems deliberately to have passed on in silence" (*DQ*, 78).

Don Quixote, in short, is grounded on fundamental ironies that defy resolution and toward which no simple and unqualified attitude is possible. The disjunction between heroic myth and actuality, value and fact, desire and realization, imaginative or rationally abstract designs and objective reality is radical and insoluble. The novel encourages sympathy neither with narrow views nor with the search for some kind of "golden mean."[24] Instead, Cervantes rests the meaning of his novel squarely on the tension between interactive but irreconcilable dualities. For the critic of *Don Quixote* and other works in a similar mode the problem is always to avoid collapsing this tension in favor of one of its components. Anne Mellor makes the same point in discussing romantic irony, a later and neighboring mode with which mock-heroic shares a good deal during the nineteenth and twentieth centuries. Such irony, she notes (following Schlegel), "reveal[s] the presence of an authorial consciousness that is simultaneously affirming and mocking its own creation. . . . The work of art should create the same impression as that created by the *buffo* or harlequin figure in commedia dell'arte plays, a dramatic character who both controls the plot and mocks the play." In turn, the critic of ironist books, as D. C. Muecke has warned us, must not take sides or rather, "must take both sides and neither side."[25] In *Don Quixote* the irony is more inclusive than exclusive, at once an act of celebration and preservation and a process of limitation and qualification. In particular, *Don Quixote* and similar narratives preserve something of the flavor of the epic in the very denial of its larger pretensions. The spirit of adventure, the sense of man's capacity for love, belief, and imagination, the sheer delight and refreshment derived from good stories ("they drive away the melancholy," says Don Quixote [*DQ*, 442])—all these qualities emerge still recognizable and vital from the ironic crucible, still vital, indeed, *because of* the crucible, emergent only in its reconstructive context.

But most important, the irony preserves the continuing possibility of human freedom as a viable illusion. Cervantes is the supreme entertainer in a world of entertainments, "the arch magician," as Nabokov calls him in a variant of the *buffo* image.[26] Unlike the other entertainers in his novel, he is aware of the capacity even of this role to become static, mechanical, and life-denying—to create in its own time the sterile pageant world of the Duke and Duchess. The most significant escape of Don Quixote and Sancho is from a hypothetical creator who might have imposed on them his own abstract formulations. In Cervantes's hands they remain like himself, indeterminate figures in an indeterminate world. At the very center of his parodic method lies what Schlegel calls, in a telling phrase, "continuous self-parody"; and through such self-parody Cervantes both celebrates and liberates himself from the peculiar madness of the artist: belief in the order of his own creation.[27] Curiously enough, it is this very freedom from order in novel and novelist that allows *Don Quixote* to operate like Melville's Drummond light, bringing into form and substance whatever is touched by its illumination. Among the most important issues illuminated has been the literary survival of the heroic spirit by way of the mode that Cervantes marked out so brilliantly.

II

Nineteenth-Century Romanticism and the Mock-Heroic Mode

Stendhal's Absurdities

> The discovery of this book [Don Quixote] . . . was perhaps the
> greatest moment of my life.
>
> STENDHAL
> *The Life of Henry Brulard*

For Stendhal, Byron, and many others of the earlier nineteenth-century literary generation the compelling images of heroism were twofold: the political
and martial myth of Napoleon transforming Europe under the banner of liberalism; and the spiritual myth of romanticism, with its promise of the godlike possibilities open to passionate and imaginative selfhood. To be more
precise, these were the energizing myths of their youth; by their maturity (in
fact, as a definition of their maturity), hopes based on the literal realization in
life of these myths had collapsed in the general welter of European reaction
after Waterloo. "I fell when Napoleon did," writes Stendhal simply and
bluntly in his autobiography.[1] The trauma of collapse was fundamental to the
individuals involved and far-reaching in its consequences for the literary
world. The sense of historical anticlimax, the inevitable disillusionment, the
necessity, willy-nilly, of adaptation to a new "bourgeois" world given over to
moral cant and materialism all produced in many of the writers of this period
(only to be repeated, of course, in the wake of the historical catastrophes of
the twentieth century) an irrevocable "split" in their lives. Such a split, in
turn, fractured the potential coherence of personality into selves at once related and sharply different, a fracturing that in their work is often dramatized by
a complex and unresolved dialectic between voices of youth and voices of
maturity or "middle age." This dialectic generates on occasion the particular
mock-heroic of the period, returning writers, in the process, to Cervantes and
the mode already established.

We must now turn to an examination of their work, glancing first directly
at autobiography. Raymond Giraud has noted that "there was in the nineteenth century a veritable flood of confessions of self-division and ambivalence." He quotes Gérard de Nerval's statement—"Je sens deux hommes

en moi"—as suggesting the motivating need behind these confessions.[2] A work such as Stendhal's *Life of Henry Brulard* allows us to study the encounter between these "two men" in its most direct and explicit form and at the same time demonstrates the emergence of mock-heroic from the dynamics of this encounter as it unfolds within the context of Stendhal's sensibility.

Growing up Quixote: The Life of Henry Brulard

Stendhal was well aware of the autobiographical impulse of his time. "What consoles me a little for my impertinence in writing so many *I's* and *me's*," he writes in *The Life of Henry Brulard*, "is that I imagine many quite ordinary people in this nineteenth century are doing likewise. So that about 1880 there will be a flood of memoirs, and I, with my *I's* and *me's*, will only be like everybody else" (*HB*, 140). His autobiography is almost literally a "memoir," an extended record of memory in the act of remembering—fragmentary, disorganized, improvisational, committed only to honesty and the truth. This commitment is far more radical and all-pervasive than that which we take for granted in any serious writer. It is not just the effective means toward a literary end but the end itself—the organizing principle, the final meaning, the core of the aesthetic vision. Stendhal's primary commitment is to the truth of feelings, his own as an "ordinary" man of fifty and especially those of the very young Henry Brulard. He disclaims the necessity for factual autobiography: "I make no claim to veracity except in so far as *my feelings* are concerned; I have always had a poor memory for facts" (*HB*, 86–87). He reiterates essentially the same point later in the book: "I must insist again that I don't profess to describe things in themselves but only their effect on myself" (*HB*, 111). Everywhere Stendhal affirms the central importance and intrinsic validity of feelings, never more central, of course, than in childhood. "I was all feeling," he writes of himself in 1799, "and this excess of feeling has left me with only a few very clear pictures, but no explanation of the hows and whys" (*HB*, 274).

Stendhal is, however, equally committed to the truth about feelings, again dealing with himself at fifty as well as the youthful self that he remembers. This kind of truth involves some of the "explanations" he alludes to in the passage above, but, more important, it involves a perspective on the feelings themselves, a sense of their objective significance that parallels his attempt to record their subjective truth. One result of this total commitment to truth is complex duality of point of view in the autobiography: the mature narrator records honestly and sympathetically the feelings of his youthful self in their dramatic context and measures them pragmatically; the same narrator records with great honesty his present feelings and the processes of his memory and engages in ironic dialogue even with the mature self in the very act of recording.

Something of this duality, to be sure, is part of the normal expectation of most autobiography or autobiographical fiction: a dual time sense (the past of actual events, the present in which they are remembered, reconstructed, and analyzed) and, in effect, a dual protagonist, the youthful (or younger) doer or actor of events and the older narrator recollecting them from a distant, more objective, more mature point of view. At the same time, most autobiography gives the last word to the wisdom of the older figure or at least to the authority of a shaped and "developing" self as selected and ordered by maturity. But Stendhal's *Life of Brulard* carefully avoids structure and formal organization, and his only "wisdom" is a present awareness of the ironic dimension of experience at all ages. Yet even this insight (however carefully presented in the context of dialectic rather than as moral imperative) may finally have tipped the scales too much in favor of "reason" over feeling and destroyed the possibility, from Stendhal's point of view, of autobiography as the vehicle for dealing with certain experiences. Stendhal breaks off the narrative at the most ecstatic moment of his youth, his arrival in Milan to join the Napoleonic forces, because he seems to sense that he may not be able to prevent the original experience from being spoiled in passing through the later narrative process. The last line reads simply: "Tender feelings are spoilt by being set down in detail" (*HB*, 347). The spoilage, he implies earlier, is caused by his confinement to rational forms of expression and by his mature sense of absurdity, which is directly proportional to the strength of the emotions he is recording and reexperiencing as he records ("nothing can cure my folly" [*HB*, 347]). He realizes his own present inadequacy: "I declare I can't go on, the tale is too great for the teller. I realize that I am ridiculous, or rather, unbelievable" (*HB*, 346). The creative and finely balanced tension between passion and irony in the older man cannot encompass (or perhaps is a threat to) his one episode of authentic heroism. Nevertheless, before this final silence, "youth" and "maturity" in the *Life of Brulard* tend to be symbolic notations for fixed but complementary attitudes. Maturity to some extent subsumes the attitude of youth, but it does not supersede that attitude in the sense of destroying or resolving the duality. As Victor Brombert has noted, at the heart of Stendhal's ambiguities and his dialectic is his tendency on all occasions to "view himself as both object and subject."[3]

Stendhal's ironic sense may be viewed psychologically as a protective shield for his feelings (he speaks at one point of how he has learned to "hide" his feelings under irony [*HB*, 279]) or philosophically as the multiplication of simultaneous and often contradictory perspectives, but, in any case, it is the mature man's strategy for survival with integrity in the fallen world of post-Napoleonic Europe. His version of the fall, as my remarks may have already suggested, is concerned with historical diminution, specifically, with man's loss of the heroic dimension as an authentic and viable component of experience. It is the biblical story, interpreted simply as Adam's arbitrary removal from a romantic landscape malleable to his most sublime dreams to a banal reality that leaves him only with poignant but absurd pretensions to the heroic virtues of love and honor.

Not that Stendhal sees his early youth as Edenic. The Golden Age is over, and the imbalances, alienation, and "dreary drama" (*HB*, 51) characteristic of Henry's life prefigure the direction in which history is inexorably moving and which will receive final ratification with the defeat of Napoleon. Even as a very young man, Henry is already the uncertain pretender, caught between the unrealistic but compelling emotional and imaginative demands of his aristocratic Aunt Elisabeth's *espagnolisme* (not to mention the faded echoes of the Enlightenment in his grandfather) and the mean values and narrow views of his bourgeois father, most of his other relatives, and the bulk of Grenoble's provincial society. Already for Henry the heroic myth is a nostalgic dream of the far past. One day, for example, he asks his aunt whether there is a place where orange trees grow in the open ground. She answers by telling him warmly about his great-grandfather, born at Avignon. Stendhal's comment on the episode is significant: "I realize today that I had unwittingly reminded her of the object of her endless longing. She told me that we had originally come from a land even more beautiful than Provence (we, that's to say the Gagnons), that her grandfather's grandfather, in consequence of some disastrous circumstance, had taken refuge in Avignon in the train of some Pope; that there he had been obliged to change his name somewhat and to hide, and had then earned his living as a surgeon" (*HB*, 58). This means, Stendhal points out, that one of his forebears was Italian and affirms the notion of his Italian origin. In his life as well as his fiction, Italy becomes the heroic Eden of his imagination, "a land of delight" (*HB*, 58), a paradise passionately but all too briefly regained during the Italian campaign.

Except perhaps for the Napoleonic interlude, however, young Henry is a mock-heroic, not a heroic figure—Gagnon-Beyle, not simply Gagnon, or rather, an attenuated Gagnon forced to live in a world of Beyle.[4] To become a hero in a mundane environment involves the willed imitation of ancient models; it is an act of the imagination, and the result, if successful, contains more of art than of life. For Henry such imitation is symbolized in the story of the plaster medallions. A friend of his grandfather brings to his house plaster medallions of Roman emperors and empresses and the great men of France, which he has mounted in gilt frames. Stendhal writes: "I never tired of studying the features of those *famous men* whose lives I wanted to imitate and whose writings I longed to read" (*HB*, 149). He tries to make his own plaster models (in this case, an imitation of an imitation) and is characteristically unsuccessful; the plaster does not jell. As Stendhal observes wryly: "Although I never succeeded in making a frame filled with medallions as Father Ducros did, I was always preparing to win glory that way by making a great quantity of sulphur molds." (*HB*, 152). Later on, the boy tries to find living role models. On one occasion he takes money given him by his aunt to be tutored in mathematics by a young "dyed-in-the-wool Jacobin": "To see a man made on the model of the Greeks and Romans, and then wish to die rather than not be like him, took but an instant" (*HB*, 262–63). And, of course, Henry, like so many other youthful protagonists in nineteenth-century literature, tries to find an adequate shape for his heroic dreams in literary models.

As I have previously indicated, the compelling force behind Henry's heroic impulse is the *espagnolisme* of his Aunt Elisabeth, which, however sustained by genuine nobility of character, is itself secondhand, abstract, and unworldly, and even, in its own way, bookish. (According to Stendhal, she complimented anything she admired excessively by saying: "It's as fine as the Cid" [*HB*, 95]). Hers is the heroism of noble feelings, and, in this at least, she is Henry's principal model. As Stendhal describes his youth: "The Spanish feelings imparted to me by my Aunt Elisabeth kept me up in the clouds; I thought of nothing but honour and heroism. I had not the least cunning, not the slightest skill at manoeuvring, not the least trace of smooth-tongued (or jesuitical) hypocrisy" (*HB*, 155). The worldly results of this categorical idealism are pointed out explicitly by Stendhal in another passage: "My Aunt Elisabeth had a Spanish soul. Her character was the quintessence of honour. She completely transmitted to me this way of feeling, whence arose a ridiculous series of follies committed through over-scrupulousness and nobility of soul" (*HB*, 95). Without for a moment disavowing *espagnolisme* (indeed, here and elsewhere he confesses its possession at the time of writing the autobiography), the mature Stendhal can view it from the additional perspective of its worldly efficacy. This is not, let me again stress, the same as assuming a worldly point of view. Stendhal writes elsewhere: "This *espagnolisme*, which I got from my Aunt Elisabeth, makes me even now, at my age, appear an inexperienced child, a madman *increasingly incapable of any serious business* in the eyes of that authentic *bourgeois*, my cousin Colomb (whose exact words these are)" (*HB*, 157). In the eyes of the world, *espagnolisme* is childish or "mad"; Stendhal grants the point but not the pejorative implication. His protagonists in the *Life of Brulard* and the novels are defiantly young, but for him they are absurd rather than simply mad—absurdity in this case being an index of his total awareness, in both tragic and comic terms, of the radical disjunction between noble feelings, heroic daydreams of the self based on those feelings, and the mundane reality in which fantasies must try to find relation and fulfillment.[5]

The pattern of Henry's experience, as we might suspect, is characterized by persistent disappointment and anticlimax. The reality of school, for example, he finds "far inferior to the wild visions of . . . his imagination," his companions not "gay delightful noble companions" but "very selfish little scamps." Stendhal realizes the moral of this early episode: "I have had the same sort of disappointment in more or less everything throughout my life" (*HB,* 170). A later childhood duel finds the same pattern at work. On the way to a dueling ground Henry and his opponent are surrounded by a procession of urchins, "ridiculous and very awkward for us." Once there, for some reason that escapes his later memory, the pistols are not fired and peace is declared, although without reconciliation. The next day he feels "horribly remorseful at having let the affair be settled. It offended all my Spanish daydreams; how could I dare admire the *Cid* after not fighting? How could I think about *Ariosto's* heroes? How could I admire and criticize the great figures of Roman history, about whose doughty deeds I read so often in the work of the unctuous Rollin?" (*HB,* 234–36).

His move to Paris, which was supposed to represent escape from the banalities of Grenoble, completes his education in the psychology of disappointment. In a small rented room (albeit in a house once owned by Condorcet, one of his heroes), Henry asks himself the same question raised by the protagonists of the novels: "Is Paris no more than this?" And Stendhal adds: "This meant: the thing I've longed for so much, as a supreme good, the thing to which I've sacrificed my life for the past three years, bores me" (*HB,* 296). As a young man he remains gauche ("I who thought myself a combination of Saint Preux and Valmont"), and the Parisian drawing room to which he is introduced has nothing in common with his romantic dreams: "The amiability for which I longed was the pure joy of Shakespeare's comedies, the amiability that reigns at the court of the exiled Duke in the forest of Arden." Stendhal's comment is characteristic: "This pure, this light and airy amiability at the court of a bored, dissolute old prefect, who was also, I believe devout!!! Nothing could be more absurd, but my unhappiness, although based on *absurdity,* was none the less very real" (*HB,* 292–94).

One suspects that Stendhal avoided the Italian campaign for fear that the putative climax of the book would turn into anticlimax during the process of composition by an older sensibility. There are already hints of the ridiculous in his picture of Henry on the way to Italy—on horseback, for example (he has never ridden a horse), or in his first encounter with the troops: "Instead of the feelings of heroic friendship which I attributed to them as a result of day-dreaming for six years about heroes, based on the characters of Ferragus and Rinaldo, I caught a glimpse of embittered and ill-natured egoists who often swore angrily at us when they saw that we were on horseback while they were on foot. They nearly tried to steal our horses from us" (HB, 332). After his first exposure to cannon fire, the Paris question recurs to him: "That evening, when I thought about it, I could not get over my astonishment. *"What, was that really all?"* I said to myself. All my life I have been liable to this rather foolish astonishment and to this exclamation; I think it is due to imagination. I have made this discovery, as well as many others, in 1836, while writing this" (HB, 337).

By the end of the book, Henry reminds us of Fabrizio on the road to Waterloo. Human experience, as Stendhal has come to view it in the light of his own life and the history of his times, inevitably leads to anticlimax. On one hand, the heroic vision of the protagonist is solipsistic, based purely on noble feelings and fictions of the imagination; on the other, the objective world is crushingly real but without redemptive value—so banal and corrupt that "success" (or climax) in worldly terms would be far more morally damaging than disappointment and failure. Such worldly success informs the matter and structure of traditional autobiography, and Stendhal burlesqued it in some specimen title pages he wrote for his book. One example must serve: "To Messieurs the Police. There is nothing political in this novel. It is about an enthusiast in every sphere who, gradually disillusioned and enlightened, ends by devoting himself to the *culte des hôtels*" (HB, 348). Stendhal's work and mock-heroic in general, as this note makes clear, deals with disappointment, not with disillusionment. Rather, the dialectic of illusions with the world is unremitting, the claims of both absolute, the resolution forever inconclusive. There are, to be sure, important moments in Stendhal's writing in which his protagonists are allowed brief escape into pure daydream, but, in general, the alternative of romantic apocalypse is as foreign to his sensibility as that of finding values in life as it is.

At first glance, the role of the mature narrator in the *Life of Brulard* might seem to represent a position less vulnerable to irony (and thus more resolved) than the adolescent posturings of Henry. He is, after all, the historian dedicated to the truth, at least the truth of feelings, his discursive style designed to recapture the concrete reality of the past with a minimum of distortion, yet at the same time to reveal, as an act of discovery, the "shape and cause of past events" (HB, 100). Without question his method does reveal the shape and substance of Henry's "follies." But though the distinction between maturity and youth is being sharpened in some ways, it is collapsed in others. I have already mentioned that at fifty Stendhal insists on his continued youthfulness: "I AM STILL IN 1835 THE MAN OF 1794," he writes in capital letters at one point (*HB*, 127). This statement has implications that go beyond its obvious reference to his continued naïveté, impulsiveness, and commitment to passionate feelings. Equally important is his awareness that the final absurdity in his autobiography is his role as composer. His method, so empirical from one point of view, from another is merely a version of stream-of-consciousness, an ego game, the rambling proliferation of trivia, vital to selfhood perhaps but irrelevant beyond the subject. In the *Life of Brulard* the autobiographer is mocked from time to time by a still more objective voice. For example, after a description and analysis of a childhood infatuation with an actress: "I have certainly been getting a great deal of pleasure out of writing for the past hour, trying to describe with real accuracy my feelings in the time of Mlle Kubly; but who the deuce will have the courage to wade through it, to read this excessive pile of *I's* and *Me's? I even find it stinking myself. That's the weakness of this sort of writing in which, moreover, I cannot season the insipidity with any sauce of charlatanism" (*HB*, 187). On another occasion, he interrupts Henry's narrative to include an anecdote from the battle of Wagram and then suddenly adds: "But good heavens! who's going to read all this? What high-falutin nonsense! Shall I ever get back to my story? Does the reader know now whether he's got to 1800, to a crazy boy's first steps in the world, or to the wise reflections of a man of fifty?" (*HB*, 339). Sometimes even Stendhal's footnotes operate in comic antiphony to the material in the main text.[6]

For Stendhal's generation, time is the great betrayer of noble impulses, the ultimate anticlimax. Here again, as Stendhal is too well aware, the feelings of the autobiographer at the moment of composition are not exempt. At one point he angrily condemns the later infamy of some of Napoleon's generals (betrayers in old age of "the noble deeds that made them famous in 1793") but then appeals ironically to the future: "Forgive this long parenthesis, O reader of 1880! Everything I'm talking about will be forgotten by that time. The generous indignation that makes my heart throb and stops me from writing will seem ridiculous" (*HB*, 109). "Maturity," the autobiographer's stance, in other words, has meaning, if at all, only as a relative measure of perceiving time; from a still longer temporal perspective it remains "youthful"—quixotic in its immediate passions, quixotic in its ego involvement, quixotic, finally, in its absurd and futile dedication to the "truth" of selfhood. "One can't see oneself," Stendhal candidly admits after describing a judgment made on him by Montesquieu from the stable dimension of another world ("if there is another world" [*HB*, 110]). Thus in both the roles of author and persona Stendhal becomes the mock-hero of his own mock-heroic autobiography. He is the romantic who cannot romanticize, who cannot simply authenticate his feelings through the medium of a conventional heroic rhetoric. Of the "trifles" of the heart, he says that it "would take a great painter's gift to paint them well" and that he loathes "almost equally descriptions in the manner of Walter Scott and the bombast of Rousseau" (*HB,* 242). Nevertheless, from early childhood he cherished *Don Quixote,* "the only book that did not inspire me with mistrust." His discovery of *Don Quixote* was literally and symbolically an act of imaginative liberation—"perhaps the greatest moment of my life," as Stendhal puts it categorically. He happened upon it by accident (all the rest of his books "had been recommended by tyrants"), and from it began to get a "few forecasts" about the human condition, which were the beginning of intimations later followed up relentlessly in his own work (*HB,* 68–69, 182). *The Life of Brulard* acknowledges and at the same time strongly reflects the influence of Cervantes.

The Absurd Adventures of Julien and Fabrizio

The problem of the protagonists in Stendhal's novels is more or less the problem of his own life brought into higher dramatic focus, namely, the need to live heroically—or to find some equivalent of traditional heroism—in a world without heroic dimension. Authentic heroism was out of the question, heroism such as is described by Mathilde de la Mole when defining heroic love: "a force capable of changing life altogether."[7] This kind of heroism no longer existed. Fabrizio cannot find it at Waterloo; Julien mourns its loss. While he is in the seminary, there is a conscription call from which he is exempt: "This incident moved him deeply. Well then, there goes the moment at which, if I'd lived twenty years ago, a life of heroic action would have begun for me!" (*RB,* 159). Heroism was something of the past, immediate or far distant, historical or legendary: with Napoleon in Italy, at the court of Catherine de Medici or Henri III or Louis XIII, certainly in the pages of Tasso and Ariosto. In Stendhal's novels the present world is a cheap imitation of previous ages. This is not simply an underlying theme of his work but a principle worked out from scene to scene in meticulous detail. In the most general sense, all the characters in his novels are vulgar actors on a provincial stage, with the court at Parma, modeling itself ludicrously on Versailles, a universal symbol of life in post-Napoleonic times.

If all present experience is parodic, the question then becomes the quality of the parody—the style of the performance and the nature and depth of the feelings that inform it. In this game the youthful figures will score highest because of their ardency, their idealism, and their naive and literal commitment to the books of history and fiction in which simple heroics abound. Julien and Fabrizio are prototypes of endless quixotic "boy" heroes of the century, culminating perhaps in Dostoyevsky's Prince Myshkin, boy playing

Christ, and Conrad's Lord Jim, the boy returned to Eden to rule there as Adam redeemed. Stendhal's young men are characteristically orphans, in truth if not in fact, the truth reminding us constantly of the shadowy authentic fathers with whom they are obsessed, of their lack, at the same time, of clear and viable role models, and, finally, of their instinct to repudiate their vulgar "real" fathers. When Julien receives a commission and large sum of money from M. de la Mole late in the novel, his response reflects his fundamental psychological and spiritual concern throughout the book: "He saw himself recognized." In other words, his "true" identity has finally been confirmed. From this beginning he goes on to build even greater fantasies: "Is it actually possible, he asked himself, that I might be the natural son of some aristocrat exiled among our mountains by the terrible Napoleon? At every instant this idea appeared less improbable to him. . . . My hate for my father would be a proof . . . I would no longer be a monster!" (RB, 360). The search for paternal legitimacy is synonymous with the search for an authentic role. Lurking in the imagination or actual background of Stendhal's boys is a heroic father, but they are, for all intents and purposes, Telemachus without Odysseus, or at least Telemachus for whom Odysseus remains only a vague memory or will-o'-the-wisp—an insight Joyce later exploited in his explicit use of the great heroic myth. Fabrizio at Waterloo almost (by chance) encounters the Lieutenant Robert who may have sired him during the Italian campaign. They do not meet, however, and would not have recognized each other if they had; the episode is simply one of Fabrizio's many anticlimaxes during the day.[8]

It is Julien, however, the carpenter's son, reading his collection of bulletins from the Grande Armée and the *Mémorial de Sainte-Hélène* and dreaming of glory when he should be working, who is more obviously the parvenu and whose adventures are more explicitly a self-conscious imitation of the heroic life. Very early in the novel, when asked by a friend to join him in business as a wool merchant, Julien is faced with the choice that informs his actions throughout the book. As Stendhal carefully phrases it: "Like Hercules, he found himself faced with a choice, not between vice and virtue, but between comfortable mediocrity and the heroic dreams of youth" (RB, 59). This statement is rich in implications. In the first place, Julien's options involve only two alternatives, each one deeply qualified: mediocrity (that is, bourgeois life) and heroic *dreams*—not, it should be noted, the possibility of authentic heroism. At the same time, Stendhal suggests that the problem goes beyond the usual ethical questions; for Julien as for Stendhal himself the ethical virtues lay (hopelessly corrupted) in the hands of the middle classes, whose purely materialistic drives were masked by moralistic cant. Rather, for Stendhal and his protagonist there remain the heroic virtues (traditional and romantic) of pride and honor, prowess, passion, and imagination. Julien is presumably operating within the context of a "higher" morality.

Stendhal's reference to vice and virtue, however, linked with his allusion to Hercules (these heroic allusions are endless; in the same episode the two boys are described as preparing supper together "like Homeric heroes"), includes an ironic dimension that reinforces the ironies implied in the given alternatives. Julien's experience is already an attenuation of the heroic life, his alternatives already a poor parody of the great spiritual choices confronted by the authentic hero. It is one thing to dismiss mere middle-class or even certain truly Christian values, but how much moral substance of any kind is involved in the options that face Julien? That he does not choose mediocrity is undoubtedly a sign of his superiority. He is left in pursuit of a chimera, however, and, in addition, the self-conscious tactics of pursuit (the energies and attention devoted to playing the hero) go far toward destroying whatever substance might be realized in the immediate experience. By the end of the novel he wearily abandons these histrionics; in Stendhal's words, Julien in prison was "tired of heroics" (RB, 378).

It is not simply that Stendhal's protagonists are directly thwarted by their environment in their attempts to realize their dreams. This is true enough as far as it goes; the world is sometimes actively hostile, usually opaque to spiritual aspirations, and almost always and inevitably anticlimactic, even at its more dramatic moments. After Julien has completed his conquest of Mme de Rênal, for example, he returns to his room and utters the cry familiar to us from the Life of Brulard: "Good Lord! being happy, being in love, is that all it is?" (RB, 69).[9] But is external reality in any direct and intermediate sense to blame at least on this occasion for the failure of experience? Mme de Rênal is, after all, the incarnation of beauty, naturalness, and passion. Stendhal, in fact, focuses his analysis on the mock-heroic implications of romanticism. Julien's imagination is one important claim to his superiority, yet this same imagination is alienating and abstractive (and thus comically absurd) in two different ways, one relating to Julien's dreaming, the other to his role-playing. Imagination alienates by operating best in the medium of memory and desire (time past and time future). Fulfillment in the present moment, says Stendhal, leaves the dreaming soul astonished and discontented: "Such a soul is accustomed to yearning, no longer has anything to yearn after, and has no memories as yet" (RB, 69). At the same time, the imagination alienates by making one self-conscious—not merely always aware of oneself as an object but always trying aesthetically to shape that object. Julien's anticlimax in love includes the seduction scene, where he puts on a ridiculous performance and succeeds only in spite of himself. Stendhal's analysis of Julien's role-playing on this occasion is significant:

In the moments of supreme delight, victim of his own strange pride, he insisted on playing the role of a man accustomed to triumph over women: he made incredible efforts to spoil the effect of all his own charm. Instead of paying attention to the transports of delight he aroused and to the remorse that sharpened them, he focused his attention entirely on the idea of *duty*. He feared that he would be victim of a fearful disgrace and of perpetual ridicule if he departed from the ideal of behavior he had set for himself. In a word, what made Julien a superior being was precisely the quality that prevented him from seizing a pleasure that lay directly in his path. [*RB*, 69]

Stendhal's protagonists have nothing but imagination to depend on, and it marks their superiority. At the same time, however, the very dynamics of imagination serves to heighten the absurdity of their experience, since the imagination tends to stage a theatrical performance and perfect a subjective role at the expense of an adequate response to external reality. As Stendhal observes with regard to Fabrizio's lack of judgment in critical situations: "The presence of danger gives genius to the sensible man: it raises him, so to speak, above himself; in the man of imagination, it inspires dramatic fancies, bold, it is true, but often absurd."[10] On another occasion he describes Fabrizio as someone who "delighted in savoring the sensations produced by the romantic circumstances with which his imagination was always ready to supply him. He was far from employing his time in patiently observing the real characteristics of things in order to discover their causes" (*CP*, 134). The final sentence here is a splendid definition of the mature realist. Stendhal's own vision, in effect, embraces both points of view. For Stendhal (as opposed to romantic orthodoxy) the paradox of the imagination—and the source in this case of unresolvable mock-heroic tension—is that it increases the gap between self and object, thus enhancing the potential for irony generated by the gap, while remaining the mark of a genuinely superior person.[11]

Nevertheless, as I have already suggested, the environment looms large overall. Included in Stendhal's ambivalent view of romantic attitudes is his full awareness of their cultural context as an expedient for spiritual survival in what Gustave Flaubert terms an age of *muflisme*—"boorishness," in Harry Levin's translation.[12] Far more than outright rejection of these attitudes, some combination of ironic awareness with a degree of continued subjective identification informs much of the literary realism of the nineteenth century and finds its sharpest aesthetic expression in the mock-heroic mode. Literary realism reminds us endlessly and brutally of the contingencies of the material world and, in so doing, shows us the imagination isolated, precarious, and at bay. The pressures on the imagination are increased by cultural poverty and the lack of outlets for authentic adventure. Julien, superior as a human being but without a significant given cultural identity, can devote his energies only to the creation of a "fictional" self based on abstract and distant literary and historical models. Like Don Quixote before him, he is almost as much an artist as his creator, an artist by inclination perhaps but also forced to be an artist by circumstances.

Most mock-heroic narratives are, in effect, portraits of the artist as a (perpetually) young man in which the protagonist not only has aesthetic leanings but, just as important, must use his talents largely for the self-conscious creation of a role based largely on imaginary materials. What he creates, however, is "art" more than life, and these two remain in radical disjunction. Stendhal explicitly labels Julien a nascent artist on at least one occasion (see *RB*, 154–55). Julien and Stendhal are both imitative artists as was Cervantes, who stresses the point in his continual mock-serious efforts to relate his work to classical theories of imitation. I am referring again, of course, to parody: Julien is the naive, Stendhal, the highly sophisticated parodist.

In *Red and Black* Mathilde is also a naive parodist, though at first glance her aristocratic origins would seem to provide a more substantial background for heroics and make self-conscious imitation less necessary. In fact, she is an even more mannered and inauthentic figure than Julien, crippled by the "aridity" and "dry prudence" (as Stendhal terms it, *RB*, 359, 376) of Parisian society and by the subtle disinheritance of a family exiled by revolution, then returning to make their way in the corrupt and reactionary world of the restored Bourbons. Bored, restless, with a "lofty" soul (*RB*, 376) and "chivalric temper" (*RB*, 251), she seeks to play "a role and a great role" (*RB*, 286) and casts about through literature and history for suitable models. When she thinks she is falling in love with Julien, for example, her reaction is typical: "She reviewed in her mind all the descriptions of passion she had read in *Manon Lescaut*, the *Nouvelle Heloise*, the *Letters of a Portuguese Nun*, and so on, and so forth. The only thing in question, naturally, was a grand passion; frivolous love was unworthy of a girl of her age and station. She gave the name of love only to that heroic sentiment that existed in France during the days of Henri III and Bassompierre. . . . What a shame that I don't have a real court, like that of Catherine de Medici or Louis XIII; I feel I could rise to the height of daring and nobility" (*RB*, 251). The role she most wants to play, however, is that of Marguerite of Navarre embracing the severed head of her ancestor Boniface de la Mole, and the opportunity finally comes in a cave where the remains of Julien have been taken after his beheading. Ironically for the dead Julien, he remains at least an important "prop" in a last grotesque performance, even though during the final days of his life he had attempted to renounce heroic playacting. It is also thanks to Mathilde that the cave, an ambiguous symbol of Julien's authentic aspirations as well as his vulgar ambition, undergoes an apotheosis of its own: "By Mathilde's orders, this savage grotto was adorned with marbles sculptured at great expense in Italy" (*RB*, 408).

The bulk of the book involves an arduous confrontation between the two in which love is described persistently in metaphors of politics and war and becomes, in effect, a sustained parody of heroic activity on the part of both characters and novelist.[13] The characters think continually of "performances," "triumph," "carrying the day," literary and historical parallels, "political strategy," "the rules" and live almost entirely locked in a world of personal fantasy. Their games are not communal, scarcely shared at all. At one point Stendhal speaks of Julien significantly as "stirred by his own story like a playwright by his play" (*RB*, 272), after he has created in his imagination a lurid scenario (based, naturally, on appropriate models) involving the vengeance to be wreaked on him by M. de la Mole. In Stendhal there are compelling reasons for this "theatre of the self," but it remains, nevertheless, solipsistic, "mad," objectively ridiculous, and, I suspect, closer to the more obvious prison imagery in his books than critics have hitherto noted.

Stendhal is the sophisticated parodist bringing a dimension of lucidity, maturity, and mockery to the ardency and imagination he so admires in his youthful protagonists. As I have already noted, his use of heroic metaphor, whether simple allusions or in complex patterns such as that dealing with love, is pervasive. His plot, following the inclinations of the protagonists to imitate, is constantly alert to shape the present into an attenuated form of the past. Even the names of his characters echo history and literature. In an editorial note describing their background, Robert Adams points out that "Stendhal, in the *Rouge* as in the *Chartreuse*, was writing about two collapsed and almost identified eras; one way to bring them together was to use names familiar from the earlier period in contexts supplied by the later one" (*RB*, 418). Such a "collapse"—the heart and soul of parody—is naively sought after by the protagonists and triumphantly (but ironically) achieved on every level of the fiction by their creator. Coupled with the parodic style in the generation of ambivalence are the persistent intrusions of the mature editorial voice, the older man in dialogue with the young, both voices together offering us multiple intellectual and emotional responses to the existential situation as it unfolds.[14] In Stendhal's novels the juxtaposition of tragedy and comedy is complete at every level; they are versions of his beloved *opera buffa*. Straight tragedy ("deliberately setting out to arouse emotion") he detested: "It is only *after a comic passage* that my feelings can be deeply moved" (*HB*, 307).

The *Charterhouse* begins in much the same fashion as *Red and Black*, and for a while it seems we will find the same parody of heroic action found in the earlier book. There are, to be sure, a few opening pages of straight heroics with an authentic hero. Lieutenant Robert, the presumed father, is, however, quickly pushed aside in favor of the naive and inexperienced son, and the plot moves on rapidly to Waterloo, Stendhal's most well-known set piece of mock-heroic narrative. Fabrizio's experiences on the battlefield are the supreme example in Stendhal's work of the ardent child trying to play hero on the model of Tasso and Ariosto in an environment that renders his efforts ineffectual and ludicrous. During the entire episode there is almost total disjunction between self and object, conception and empirical reality. Fabrizio has trouble establishing the most basic facts: "Is this a real battle?" he asks another soldier at one point (CP, 38). But for the later Stendhal Waterloo represents the final opportunity even for epic playacting, the last faint echo of adventure. After the Waterloo scenes in the novel, role modeling on historical and literary originals is largely consigned to the completely vulgar parvenu Court of Parma, the mock-heroic in this case taking on a distinctly eighteenth-century satiric and reductionist flavor. With regard to Fabrizio and the other sympathetic characters, Stendhal turns his attention to alternate mock-heroic performances, in particular three which we might label, in turn, mature and self-conscious social games, spontaneous actions, and stasis or pure daydream. All of these new options, like the imitations of Julien, Mathilde, and the very young Fabrizio, are corruptions of authentic heroic activity, yet all, at the same time, are heroic gestures of escape from the particular death-in-life of nineteenth-century boredom—attempts to redeem the self, however temporarily, provisionally, absurdly, from the universal banality of adult experience.

Fabrizio's responses after Waterloo, which I have identified above, are not so much modeled on prototypes from history and literature as they are keyed to the three dominant personalities in his immediate present who influence his life and shape his experience: Count Mosca, the Duchess of Sanseverina, and Clelia. The ultimate appeal of models remains: "I always compare myself with a perfect model which can't exist," is the way Fabrizio puts it in a moment of insight (CP, 147). But the specific answers to the post-Waterloo question—"What will I be?"—are given to him directly or indirectly by his friends.

Mosca is the most explicit "teacher" and parental figure of the three, sharing with the narrator the role of a mature spokesman in dialogue with Fabrizio, conscious of the age gap between them, sympathetic yet critical, a reluctant Sancho Panza to the young man's instinctive quixotism. At the same time, he has adapted his own conduct in the post-Napoleonic world from straight heroics to the creation of an elegant social and political game with which he hopes to ensure his survival (literal and spiritual), his entertainment, and his prosperity.

This game is a significant adult variation of childhood's naive theater of heroes. In "playing" courtier, Mosca, in effect, becomes the self-conscious parodist; with wit and imagination (trying to preserve, not collapse, the distinction between self and model), he attempts to turn the sterilities of provincial court life and reactionary politics into an intellectual exercise which he can dominate through qualities of will, spirit, and imagination. As he explains the direction his life has taken: " 'In Spain . . . under General Saint-Cyr, I braved bullets to earn a decoration and a little glory; now I dress up like a character in a comedy to earn an impressive establishment and a few thousand lire. As soon as I entered this kind of chess game, the arrogance of my superiors offended me and I became determined to occupy one of the highest positions' " (*CP*, 81). In another important passage, the Duchess uses the game metaphor in describing the Court of Parma to her sister-in-law: " 'A court is ridiculous . . . but it's amusing. It's an interesting game, but one whose rules must be accepted. Who ever thought of complaining about the ridiculousness of the rules of whist? And yet, once you're used to the rules, it's pleasant to defeat your opponent with a grand slam' " (*CP*, 88).

Mosca's attempt at such gamesmanship, however, is almost as absurd and ineffectual as the more obvious forms of quixotism that he condemns as impractical in telling Fabrizio (with reference to the imaginative Napoleon's mistaken surrender to the "prudent 'John Bull' ") that "in all ages the base Sancho Panzas of this world have won out over the sublime Don Quixotes in the long run" (*CP*, 151). Mosca (not to mention Fabrizio or the Duchess) cannot sustain the game he has chosen: either at crucial moments he becomes all too literally a courtier and loses sight of ends and values completely or, alternately, his passions make it impossible for him to follow the dictates of his worldly wisdom and technical skill and he reverts to "childish" behavior. Even when he does sustain the game, however, it is largely without significant ends beyond the existential act of playing—a way of demonstrating personal superiority and giving experience some order and proportion but at the expense of the same ironic gap between art and life that I have noted before in mock-heroic narrative. Although apparently absorbed in reality, the heroic spirit, in Mosca's case, continues to operate artistically, ridiculous (as the Duchess implicitly acknowledges) except within the narrow context of the fantasy game it has willed into being from the banalities of the environment.

Mosca's game, indeed, is essentially similar to the more profound "childish game" (*CP*, 292) played by Fabrizio and Clelia late in the novel and from the beginning immanent in the very nature of Clelia.[15] In his analysis of the responses of the Duchess of Sanseverina and Clelia—and Fabrizio's own mirroring of these responses—Stendhal returns again, as with his treatment of the imagination, to ironic versions of the heroic myth of romanticism. The

Duchess is the figure of powerful and spontaneous passion, Clelia the passive daydreamer. Stendhal links them together and at the same time draws a sharp contrast: "The duchess was vivacious, sparkling with mischievous wit, attaching herself passionately, if we may express it thus, to every subject which the flow of conversation brought before her mind's eye. To an equal degree, Clelia showed herself calm and slow to become aroused, whether out of contempt for what was around her, or out of nostalgia for some absent fancy" (*CP*, 228). Contempt and nostalgia are the stock responses of Stendhal's noble souls to the reality of life around them, in effect, the premises from which they all begin their "mad" search for alternatives. Clelia's peculiar madness, familiar to the romantic and Victorian sensibility, involves extreme autistic withdrawal from the temporal world into the stasis of womblike and confined subjectivity—Stendhal's "youthful" image in this case ironically mirroring the pathology of infantilism. Living in the isolated tower of the prison governor's residence, Clelia "enjoyed the kind of freedom to be found in a convent; it was nearly the same happiness she had once expected to attain by becoming a nun" (*CP*, 229). Fabrizio, thrown in the same prison, becomes an initiate to her dreamlike, almost otherworldly state. The echoes of fairy tale are delicate and complex here: the princess kisses her rescuer to sleep, but both, in turn, are wakened to a deeper emotional and spiritual life. And within the restrictions of this fairy-tale game Fabrizio and Clelia achieve genuine heroic stature. The empirical world becomes a place of "terrible exile" from this state of blissful happiness (*CP*, 303). Julien, incidentally, in *Red and Black* finds a similar bliss when "freed" into memory and daydream by his own incarceration.

But from a mature point of view (Stendhal's double vision does not waver for a moment) the fairy tale, however compelling, remains a childish game, just as the tower, freighted though it is with the positive associations of a long metaphorical tradition, remains a grim prison with strong echoes of the Spielberg. Stendhal's tower-prison image is his supreme expression of the ambiguity of mock-heroic games. Fabrizio and Clelia find heroic passion within the walls of the prison (the rules of the game), yet their relationship is at the same time artificial, theatrical (Stendhal making parodic use of melodrama), absurd, and, finally, in its own way, another form of the death-in-life they had sought to escape.

The absurdity is increasingly apparent when the couple reestablishes in the outside world the equivalent of the earlier prison experience. Clelia now binds their relationship in casuistic religious vows; her lover can visit her only at night in the dark. Judd Hubert has explained the significance of this "strange game of hide-and-seek": "It serves at the very least as a means to complicate the relationship and prevent their love from becoming commonplace. Moreover, it shrouds their love in mystery—an absurd and child-ish mystery—and maintains between Clelia and Fabrice a permanent barrier. Finally, this love . . . must somehow remain faithful to its precarious and fabulous origins."[16] In the end their game moves from comic absurdity to something explicitly life-denying as the rules become increasingly tortuous and divorced from human ends. The final crisis is precipitated by an impulse of the heart that the game has come to exclude. Fabrizio develops a perfectly natural desire to see his son every day and live with him; because of the rules, however, arrangements to this end require another elaborate charade: the child must pretend to get sick, pretend to die, and, under pretense of burial, be secreted away to another home. In fact, little Sandrino actually dies from the effects of his artificial confinement, and Clelia follows him soon after, with Fabrizio retiring to the Charterhouse of Parma. The last echoes of the prison imagery are all negative.

In the figure of Clelia and her response to life Stendhal explores the same ambiguities of innocence that would be the peculiar (though by no means exclusive) concern of American writers later in the century. Certainly it repre-sents the determination to exist on a level beyond what Stendhal calls "the sordid pecuniary interests and cold, colorless, commonplace thoughts that fill our lives" (CP, 339). Innocence is heroic in its intentions—that is, in the will to affirm value—and it creates a heroic fantasy world in which banality is absent or magically transformed into the stuff of adventure. Innocence, however, is predicated on an escape from time; it attempts to establish a stasis based either on nostalgic fixation with the past or subjective daydream in the pre-sent. It must necessarily be hostile to growth, change, movement, or adapta-tion, all of which, in a postlapsarian world, are inherent qualities of life. Inev-itably, because stasis cannot be sustained in a real world, the ultimate escape of innocence must be to death.

Finally, there is in Stendhal's work another kind of mock-heroic moment also free from the banal temporality of calculated ends and, at least in its initial manifestation, free even of the need for elaborate games. Georges Poulet has defined it as "a moment of passion which is at the same time, without transition and without any possible differentiation, a moment of ac-tion." Sixteenth-century Italy is the historical source of his mode of passionate and spontaneous action, with the Duchess of Sanseverina its chief exemplar in Fabrizio's immediate circle and an important model from his extreme youth. (He is described in a moment of passion as reverting "to instinct, or, to speak more accurately, to his earliest childhood memories" [CP, 66]). It is a quality akin to the *espagnolisme* Stendhal associated with his aunt, and he has, of course, the most intense identification with it. Passionate feeling, indeed, for Stendhal is the essence of selfhood. As Poulet explains: "The passionate

being does not feel and live under the control of a power which is independent of him. He really *is* his emotion. . . . In whatever direction it carries him,
whether toward crime or amorous ecstasy, the energy in him is never anything but the ardent manifestation of his own self."[17] The ethics of selfhood
(Stendhal's only ethics) are the pride and honor which so totally preoccupy
his characters and relate them, even beyond romanticism, to the figures of
classical epic.

But here as elsewhere in his work Stendhal remains committed to his
sense of historical diminution and his concomitant unwillingness to accept
fully compensatory romantic doctrines of affect. Unlike his protagonists, a
part of him is the mature and objective figure committed to "observing the
real characteristics of things." He observes specifically about the Duchess and
Fabrizio that, insofar as they personify haughty passion, they are essentially
anachronisms from a period when such behavior was consonant with the
entire fabric of society and thus presumably meaningful and efficacious.

In the context of nineteenth-century Europe, these moments of passion
emerge as simply another form of heroic parody. In dealing with them, Stendhal alternates his authorial interventions between ironic apologies to those
whom he assumes are his prudent and philistine Parisian readers ("Fabrizio
had an Italian heart, and I ask that he be excused for it" [*CP*, 132]) and equivalent irony directed at the "madness," "whims," and "childishness" of his
principals, whose erratic impulses give the plot its peculiar jerkiness of
rhythm and lack of firm logic and direction. The subjectively admirable is at
the same time objectively absurd and "pointless." The mature (as well as
childish) Count Mosca can view himself with amusement. During the liberal
revolt, for example, in "a moment of fiery enthusiasm," he bravely defends
the statue of his dead prince against an angry mob to save the widow and her
son from insult: "During that moment I would have given my life for the
prince without hesitation." The Duchess, who has just poisoned the older
prince in bitter anger, nevertheless praises Mosca's action effusively as the act
of an honorable man. Later (objectively) the episode seems ridiculous to him:
"I admit now that it would have been a very stupid way to end. Today the
prince [the new ruler], kind young man though he is, would give a hundred
scudi to have me die of an illness" (*CP*, 354).

Stendhal no more reconciles these different points of view than he adjudi-
cates the double-edged irony of his authorial interventions accompanying the
various "enthusiasms" of Fabrizio: journeying to Waterloo in a burst of romantic rhetoric (Stendhal all through the novel playing off this rhetoric
against a dry narrative tone); visiting Father Blanès, "his true father" (*CP*, 136)
and early instructor in the spiritual mystique of the tower, but at the terrible
risk of Austrian arrest and the Spielberg; or, from pride and vanity more than

passion, pursuing the actress Fausta around Italy, again at great risk to himself and great damage to his best interests. The pursuit of Fausta reveals another irony of the doctrine of passions as practiced in the nineteenth century, an irony which *Red and Black* develops more than *Charterhouse*. An epigraph in the earlier book notes that "to sacrifice oneself to one's passions, well, maybe; but to passions one does not feel! Oh, the sad nineteenth century" (*RB*, 336).

The final anticlimax in *Charterhouse*, paralleling that of the opening chapters, is based on an impulse similar to that which drove Fabrizio to Waterloo and Father Blanès. As I have already noted, the artificial, tenuous, but working balance between fantasy and reality arranged by Clelia and Fabrizio is broken by Fabrizio's sudden desire to see more of his son. Stendhal notes that "it would be difficult to imagine a life more honored, more honorable, and more useful than that which Fabrizio had made for himself before everything was upset by that unfortunate impulse of his heart" (*CP*, 427). "Everything was upset": Stendhal's phrase suggests the degree to which the end of *Charterhouse* serves to give final emphasis to its basic rhythm.

By linking impulse with children's games in a final catastrophe, the ending of the novel suggests also the way Stendhal's treatment of impulse shades off beyond comic absurdity—foolishness—into darker ambiguities. This darker tone is particularly sounded in Stendhal's characteristically dialectical treatment of the concept of vengeance. It is an inevitable by-product of the "Italian" attitude toward life. As the narrator explains: "I am rather inclined to think that the unmoral happiness which Italians derive from vengeance is due to the strength of their imagination; people of other countries do not, properly speaking, forgive: they forget" (*CP*, 319). His comment is made in the context of the Duchess's bitter vengeance on the prince and the people of Parma: the prince poisoned and Parma flooded when she orders opened the reservoir of the Sanseverina palace. She acts consistently, Stendhal stresses elsewhere (see *CP*, 381), from passion, not from morality. Yet she does not escape the penalty of moral guilt: the vengeance was an act "which was not only horrible from the standpoint of morality, but was also fatal to her peace of mind for the rest of her life" (*CP*, 331). Fabrizio in the end feels "he had a great deal to atone for" (*CP*, 430) and moves on to the Charterhouse, a far more sober version of his monastic dream. Julien in *Red and Black* spontaneously avenges himself on Mme de Rênal after learning of her libelous letter to M. de la Mole, then weeps for joy ("his tears sprang from a generous feeling" [*RB*, 367]) and repents when he learns she has not been killed by his bullet. But the ironies here continue to multiply; this murderous act, taken at the expense of the one really genuine and passionate relationship in his life, liberates him, as a prisoner, from ambition and heroic imitations into his own subjective world of nostalgia, memory, and daydream. I have already commented on the ambiguities, in turn, of this freedom. The passionate act in Stendhal would seem to be the ultimate manifestation of existential freedom, yet the Duchess at one point is described as "a slave to the sensations of the moment" (CP, 236), and her melodramatic plottings more and more become a mad game of their own, just as she herself increasingly resembles the genuinely mad poet Ferrante Palla, who, from the beginning, has been her double in caricature (and also, obviously, a parody of the alienated romantic poet).

"My God, give me mediocrity!" reads an ironic epigraph to one of Stendhal's chapters in Red and Black (RB, 359). It is an amusing mockery of his own obsession with the ambiguities of heroism in an unheroic world. His work assumes a disjunction between heroic feelings and values and a world governed on utilitarian principles. This sense of the heroic spirit as "conditioned" suggests Stephen Spender's view of the fate of imagination in the nineteenth century: "The unconditioned centre is where the imagination has power to influence people to transform the outward forms of things. . . . The centre is conditioned when imagination is banished into an individual solitude, shut off from any knowledge of reality outside man's own nature, and from power over the way in which men shape their lives."[18]

Stendhal's work, in short, like Byron's Don Juan, which we must now examine, brings to expression the mock-heroic potential of romanticism. Except during stray moments, his protagonists are refused even the full luxury of solipsism and forced willy-nilly to authenticate their heroic instincts in the context of an iron age whose claims to reality can no longer be ignored or denied. They make fools of themselves, of course, and could not well do otherwise, given a creator so sympathetic to their pretensions yet so determined, like Cervantes before him, to describe the full, hard, empirical truth of the world in which they all must live.

"Half-Serious Rhyme": Byron's
Don Juan

I should be very willing to redress
    Men's wrongs, and rather check than punish crimes,
Had not Cervantes, in that too true tale
Of Quixote, shown how all such efforts fail.

BYRON
Don Juan

Stendhal's mock-heroic protagonists might be seen as "entangled" in their social milieu, the image used by Karl Kroeber to describe the direction taken by Byron's narrative art in *Beppo* and finally in *Don Juan*. According to Kroeber, "Byron does to earlier tales of heroic adventure what Pulci, Boiardo, and Ariosto had done to the traditional stories of Roland, whose heroic prowess, instead of being allowed to operate freely in the grandly simplified world of popular saga, they entangled in the sophisticated intricacies of a highly articulated and complex civilization."[1] This concept of an entangled hero is central to the form of Byron's puzzling masterpiece and basic to any approach to its meaning and its significance to the history of narrative. With *Don Juan* the problem of genre is particularly crucial for an accurate understanding of the poem and, in spite of all the excellent criticism of Byron in recent years, it remains the most controversial and least satisfactorily dealt with.[2]

One immediate source of confusion is that there are satiric elements in the poem (not to mention Byron's well-known predilection for Pope and Fielding) that obviously link it to eighteenth-century mock-heroic. On clear moral, social, and political issues there is no question about the satire. As Byron himself explains:

But Politics, and Policy, and Piety
    Are topics which I sometimes introduce.
Not only for the sake of their variety,
    But as subservient to a moral use;

Because my business is to *dress* society,
  And stuff with *sage* that very verdant goose.   [15.93]

Wellington and Suwarrow, for example, are debased and monstrous figures
when measured against earlier heroes such as Cincinnatus, Leonidus, and
Washington, who fought only for good causes. Byron takes a generally moral
view of war; unlike Stendhal, he has little sympathy with martial "glory"
(that is, pride and honor as expressions of heroic will and energy). As a result, his satiric attack, on occasion, extends into the past to encompass the
bloodier aspects of Homeric epic. The Ismail episode draws together Homer
and the present in a bitter epic parody whose meaning does not lie in any
revealed disequilibrium between ideal model and reality but rather in the
moral horror of both. Juan's own involvement at Ismail is viewed with an
irony different in tone from the indulgence with which he is usually treated.
To be sure, even in this firmly satirical context, the parody is more complex
than it might seem. The episode affirms the continuity of high human courage, and, in the figure of the Khan and his sons, presents us with a modern
version of Priam and his family fighting for home and country. Nevertheless,
these and similar passages on individual men and manners are essentially
satirical attacks on corruptions of more or less simple and fundamental moral
norms. On the brutality of war, the callousness of most military leaders, and
the betrayal of freedom involved in reactionary politics Byron has few doubts
and strong feelings.

The more general thrust of the poem, however, is toward the ambivalence
and dialectical balance of Cervantine mock-heroic and away from the firm set
of values and the *saeva indignatio* of the satirist. In its subordination of satire to
other, very different attitudes, *Don Juan* reflects the change that took place in
mock-heroic between the eighteenth and nineteenth centuries and demonstrates also on occasion a self-conscious awareness of the reasons for this
change. The poem serves as a microhistory of the mode. In the first place,
Byron shares much of Stendhal's sense of the crushing banality of contemporary society, mediocrity so extreme and so uniform as to make most "correction" meaningless and futile:

. . . there is naught to cull
Of Folly's fruit; for though your fools abound,
  They're barren, and not worth the pains to pull.
Society is now one polished horde,
Formed of two mighty tribes, the *Bores* and *Bored*.   [13.95]

Variously expressed, this is one of the great literary clichés of the post-
Napoleonic world, signaling a major change in the stance of the writer to-

ward society and toward his material: "from being farmers, we turn gleaners, gleaning / The scanty but right-well threshed ears of Truth" (13.96). The writer, in other words, shifts from his eighteenth-century didactic role of "cultivator" of society to a more tentative, detached, and alienated stance. His readers, Byron continues, "may be Boaz," but he himself can play only the role of "modest Ruth" (13.96).

But the banality of society recorded in *Don Juan* is only part of the larger emptiness of time and history. A reason more fundamental than social sterility and inertia for the reduction of satire in the poem is a failure of belief in ends or goals—in life as having permanence or redemptive possibility beyond the mere continuity of flux. Byron's satiric role is itself mocked by his pervasive sense of cosmic absurdity. Even more than Stendhal, he can view himself (not just his youthful protagonist) from the temporal dimension of the future, and this elongated view is the chief generative source of irony. As Don Juan rolls on toward Russia, for example, at the beginning of the ninth canto, Byron breaks the narrative to affirm his belief in freedom of thought and hatred of despotism. His rhetoric expands further as he turns his attention to the "sweet child" rescued by Don Juan and riding beside him in the coach:

> Oh Ye! or we! or he! or she! reflect,
>   That *one* life save, especially if young
> Or pretty, is a thing to recollect
>   Far sweeter than the greenest laurels sprung
> From the manure of human clay. . . .   [9.34]

As the first line suggests (not to mention the quibble on "young or pretty"), this moralizing attitude threatens to break into parody. Nevertheless, the rhetoric soars for a stanza and a half more before collapsing in disastrous comic anticlimax:

> Oh ye great authors!—*à propos des bottes,*—
>   I have forgotten what I meant to say
> As sometimes have been greater sages' lots. . . .   [9.36]

In any case, says Byron, it "would have been but thrown away," and he goes on to imagine his message rediscovered

> With other relics of "a former World,"
> When this World shall be *former,* underground,
>   Thrown topsy-turvey, twisted, crisped, and curled,
> Baked, fried, or burnt, turned inside-out, or drowned,
>   Like all the worlds before, which have been hurled

> First out of, and then back again to chaos—
> The superstratum which will overlay us.   [9.37]

A final horrifying fantasy of George IV's being dug up leads Byron to define cosmic time and history as a diminishing cycle:

> Even worlds miscarry, when too oft they pup,
>   And every new creation hath decreased
> In size, from overworking the material—
> Men are but maggots of some huge Earth's burial.   [9.39]

Byron shares Stendhal's sense of historical diminution, but his total perspective is wider, his imagination far less rooted in a nostalgia that can be localized to a particular time or place.

Byron, in short, realized in *Don Juan* that the narrative role of the satirist or moralist is a form of heroic endeavor (literary knight-errantry, so to speak) subject to the same strong, ironic qualification as other forms of heroism. Obviously his own fundamental role encompasses satire within a more comprehensive framework. In a continuing effort to define and defend his intentions he turns on more than one occasion to Cervantes.

The crucial passage is at the beginning of Canto Thirteen. Here Byron speaks of himself not even as "modest Ruth" but as "a mere spectator" (13.7). He still sneers sometimes "because I cannot well do less," but Cervantes has taught him that all efforts to redress wrongs are bound to fail, that all heroism is "mad" in the face of life's opacity (13.7–9). *Don Quixote*, Byron then notes significantly, is a "real epic" (he has been attempting at intervals throughout his own work to describe its relation to traditional epic), and he draws the "great moral" of the book:

> Redressing injury, revenging wrong,
>   To aid the damsel and destroy the caitiff;
> Opposing singly the united strong,
>   From foreign yoke to free the helpless nature—
> Alas! must noblest views, like an old song,
>   Be for mere Fancy's sport a theme creative;
> A jest, a riddle, Fame through thick and thin sought!
> And Socrates himself but Wisdom's Quixote?   [13.10]

The tone as well as the substance of this section is important both to *Don Juan* and to a general understanding of Cervantine mock-heroic. Byron recognizes (or rather, he passionately *feels*) the difference between the satiric or the cynical sneer and the enormous ambivalence of Cervantine mockery, torn between strong sympathy for and identification with the spirit and values of heroic adventure and comic awareness of its ludicrousness as much as its futility. The Knight's adventures, he says, not only fail; they "form a sorry sight." Cervantes's tale is the more sad "because it makes us smile" (13.9). The sense of incongruity expressed here between illusions and the quotidian is too strong even for tragic pretensions (unlike much of Byron's earlier work, which often provides an adequate tragic landscape), let alone the fulfillment of romance; yet these same illusions are not misguided aberrations from some substantial norm, but most of the more elevated human values. The "norm" itself, for Byron at least (Byron, like Stendhal, widening the gap that Cervantes had opened between value and reality), is banality on the social level and cosmic emptiness. Both together constitute Byron's particular lunar landscape, the "waste and icy clime," which is his conception of the essential human environment (8.2). In the same passage on Cervantes Byron also implies that, willy-nilly, the final and perhaps only possible metamorphosis of heroism is into games of the imagination where its now incompatible attributes can exist in a form forever unresolvable. This presumably will be the process of his own poem—in its way a song, a jest, a riddle. Depending on one's point of view, then (the duality extends even this far), the new epic will be either self-destructive (it "smiled away" the Spanish romantic spirit, says Byron, a "perdition," though not done in the spirit of satire) or preservative and transformational to the degree that the heroic spirit continues to exist within the illusional context—immersed, so to speak, in the solution, half acid, half formaldehyde, of irony. It is just such an immersion that Don Juan undergoes within the narrative frame of the poem.

What is missing from the stanzas on Cervantes is any precise indication as to the nature of Byron's own quixotic hero. The actual roles mentioned (redressing, revenging, opposing, freeing, and so on) are those of Don Quixote and, as I have already indicated, to some extent at least the occasional roles of the mature Byron (satirist, lone rebel, political revolutionary, and so on). None of these activities leads us directly to Don Juan. But another passage (4.1–6), this time relating his work to the "half-serious rhyme" of the mock-epic writer Pulci, is more useful in establishing the real locus of heroic values in the poem and the mock-heroic metamorphosis they will undergo. The context of this passage is crucial; it introduces the final canto of Juan and Haidée in love, frames it, in effect, since the canto ends with Haidée dead, Juan in slavery, and the narrator reiterating somberly his theme of change: "I've stood upon Achilles' tomb, / And heard Troy doubted; Time will doubt of Rome" (4.101). He begins on the same note: Time is the great leveler; it works against heroic pride, "which leads the mind to soar too far, / Till our own weakness shows us what we are" (4.1). The sense of time is a dimension of maturity; we ignore or deny it while "Youth's hot wishes in our red veins revel" (4.2). Byron then divides his own life (and, as so often happens in the poem, the *ottava rima* stanza) into two selves, two points of view: boy and man, then and now, hero and mocker:

> As boy, I thought myself a clever fellow,
>   And wished that others held the same opinion;
> They took it up when my days grew more mellow,
>   And other minds acknowledged my dominion:
> Now my sere Fancy "falls into the yellow
>   Leaf," and Imagination droops her pinion,
> And the sad truth which hovers o'er my desk
> Turns what was once romantic to burlesque.
>
> And if I laugh at any mortal thing
>   'Tis that I may not weep; and if I weep
> 'Tis that our nature cannot always bring
>   Itself to apathy. . . .   [4.3–4]

Byron goes on to defend his strange and complex point of view and the art form that has resulted from it by arguing from precedent:

> This way of writing will appear exotic;
>   Pulci was sire of the half-serious rhyme,
>   Who sang when Chivalry was more quixotic,
>   And revelled in the fancies of the time,
>   True Knights, chaste Dames, huge Giants, Kings despotic;
>   But all these, save the last, being obsolete,
>   I chose a modern subject as more meet.   [4.6]

After this introduction, Byron turns to a final treatment of Juan and Haidée's momentary Eden, alternating passages of lyric description with further commentary on the tragedy of time.

Obviously for Byron the "modern subject" equivalent to earlier quixotism is the experience and attitude of youth, the chivalric moment in the personal past of every human being when he has lived as if time ("the real world") did not exist. Spontaneous feeling annuls time and transforms real into ideal; or at least, from a mature point of view, it has the effect of so doing. As Byron comments after describing in Juan and Haidée the language and gestures of passion:

> All these were theirs, for they were children still,
>   And children still they should have ever been;
> They were not made in the real world to fill
>   A busy character in a dull scene,

> But like two beings born from out a rill,
>> A nymph and her beloved, all unseen
> To pass their lives in fountains and on flowers,
> And never know the weight of human hours.   [4.15]

This island idyll—absolute passion in stasis—is at the very center of Byron's vision of heroic youth. At the same time it invokes the image of innocent children so compelling to the entire nineteenth-century mind. In Byron's version, children are, above all, temporal innocents, free (so they think or feel) from the "weight of human hours." "They found no fault with Time," writes Byron in another stanza (4.12); this quality of naive belief and commitment is the primary mark of their distance from the narrator and the measure of their quixotism. The island, as critics have often pointed out, is ringed around with savage seas and ruled by a pirate, himself the cruel victim of history. These frames, like the primary narrative frame, do not deny the idyllic experience but rather add another and complicating perspective to that so splendidly manifested by the youthful protagonists.

Passion for Byron is the great heroic gesture. For him not martial exploits but the possibility of love is the compelling dream of youthful imagination. He observed about himself that his "earliest dreams (as most boy dreams are) were martial, but a little later they were all for love and retirement."[3] His protagonist, of course, is a parody of the lover as hero, his name an echo of one of the "great myths of humanistic naturalism"—the myth, we might say, of sensual apotheosis.[4] Byron specifically describes the senses as

> Those movements, those improvements in our bodies
>> Which make all bodies anxious to get out
> Of their own sand pits, to mix with a goddess,
>> For such all women are at first no doubt.
> How beautiful that moment! and how odd is
>> That fever which precedes the languid rout
> Of our sensations! What a curious way
> The whole thing is of clothing souls in clay.   [9.75]

Again the *ottava rima* falls off in characteristic anticlimax after more or less celebrating (the irony is never completely absent) the "moment" of transformation through the senses in which reality seems to take on the stuff of ideality. It only "seems to" because the sand pits are still there, the goddess is "no doubt" a woman, the narrative dimension of mockery always present like Sancho beside Quixote. The passionate experience is authentic within a larger context of inauthenticity, not absolute, but at its best an "improvement" of the real though far short of genuine transcendence. In Byron's *Don*

Juan as in Stendhal's novels the heroic is nothing more or less than a point of view, an expression of the nobler energies of the self making an "enlargement of existence" (2.173) at certain times (most often during youth) and moods. Nevertheless, as the idyll of Juan and Haidée suggests, transformations can be complete within the inexorable limits of reality. The consummation of his young protagonists is a searching one. They were, Byron writes,

> By their own feelings hallowed and united,
>   Their priest was Solitude, and they were wed:
> And they were happy—for to their young eyes
>   Each was an angel, and earth Paradise. [2.204]

Far from merely debunking heroism or offering us a simple record of disillusionment, Byron's mock-heroic functions as much to locate the heroic as a "real" (possible but also credible, actual) dimension of life—in some way make it viable by making it fully human, although at the cost of making it absurd. In this sense more than in his satiric impulses, Byron's work looks back to eighteenth-century attempts such as Pope's *Rape of the Lock* to salvage epic for a mundane age by giving it a firmly "human" dimension. His epic parody, especially in the Greek island episode, is extraordinarily subtle, invoking and interlocking three potential levels of experience: the ideal (abstract or literary) model, meaningful as a nexus of human aspirations but perhaps undesirable in its marmoreal remoteness from life and in any case unattainable;[5] the ideal-real created by the conjunction of beauty and passion and, inconstant though it is, an increment to reality ("This sort of adoration of the real / Is but a heightening of the *beau ideal*" [2.211]); and, finally, the banal-real, or time-ridden level of social, historical, and cosmic absurdity.

Haidée's discovery and nursing of the shipwrecked Juan, for example (2.129–173), suggests in Byron's treatment all manner of heroic associations, from its obvious parallels with Odysseus and Nausicaa and Dante's Ulysses, to more remote mythological echoes of nymphs in sea caves, to the generic image of mother and child ("like an infant Juan sweetly slept"), and even in one stanza to more specific Christian reference as Haidée hovers over Juan:[6]

> And thus like an Angel o'er the dying
>   Who die in righteousness, she leaned; and there
> All tranquilly the shipwrecked boy was lying,
>   As o'er him lay the calm and stirless air:
> But Zoe the meantime some eggs was frying,
>   Since, after all, no doubt the youthful pair
> Must breakfast—and betimes, lest they should lack it,
>   She drew out her provision from the basket. [2.144]

The stanza once more breaks in half rhetorically, and this time Zoe, the hand-maiden, joins the narrator in playing Sancho to the couple's Quixote. The mockery here is complex: obviously, the ideal dimension is broken and we are brought back to a real world, but the real is by no means completely unattractive. Indeed, it adds a dimension of vitality and coarse material life to the dangerously deathlike atmosphere invoked by the rhetoric of static ideality. At the same time, Zoe's actions are banal, and the dangerous implications of banality are hinted at by Byron in the next stanza: ". . . being less in love, she yawned a little, / And felt her veins chilled by the neighboring sea." Each level of experience invoked by the epic parody qualifies but does not destroy the others. They exist at once, spatially—a full expression of Juan and Hai-dée's world from a multiple, ambiguous perspective. Byron's dry and casual "no doubt" opens up a world palpable enough but totally in doubt: "So little do we know what we're about in / This World, I doubt if doubt itself be doubting" (9.17). He clearly sees his authorial role as that of someone who presents, not resolves, perspectives; the narrative and rhetorical devices in the poem, in turn, work to enhance rather than limit these perspectives. Byron makes clear his position in a gloss of Hamlet's famous duality:

> "To be, or not to be?"—Ere I decide,
> I should be glad to know that which *is being*.
> 'Tis true we speculate both far and wide,
> And deem, because we *see*, we are *all-seeing*:
> For my part, I'll enlist on neither side,
> Until I see both sides for once agreeing.   [9.16]

Hamlet is in doubt about the afterlife, but for Byron the real cause of dialectic is the ambiguity of being itself, an ambiguity that stems from both the integrity and the relativity of individual perspectives.

It is just such integrity that Byron, on the whole, respects in Juan. Although his boy protagonist is not allowed to operate in what Kroeber calls "the grandly simplified world of popular saga," he is, nevertheless, given opportunity for adventure and a substantial measure of freedom throughout the poem. His world, as Alvin Kernan has pointed out, has its own appropriate comic rhythm.[7] Movement, activity, escape, and recovery are basic to Juan's romantic and youthful point of view—his particular version of Stendhal's *espagnolisme*. Like Conrad's Lord Jim, he is offered the widest opportunity for self-expression within the general context of a work that encompasses other perspectives toward the same heroics. Even toward the end of the poem in the firmer social context (and denser banality) of English society, Juan is still engaged in adventure, his final escapade, of course, being a splendid set piece of mock-Gothic.

Because Byron is interested in expressing the particular youthful being of Juan rather than any process of growth toward maturity, he does not involve him, except as casual participant or unwilling victim (the significant exception is Ismail, which I shall discuss later), with those temporal institutions which must inevitably educate, corrupt, or otherwise modify the basic drives and dreams of youth. Our first view of Juan is his escape from the moral and social restrictions of his immediate background—escape from parents to the lonely but more fulfilling role of orphan (that is, the independent child free from a limiting and intrusive adult context). The poem is not a *Bildungsroman*. Juan is representative of a time of life; it is the narrator whose experience has given him the sense of time so central to his own point of view.

What little "development" is apparent in Juan seems to be (with an unfinished poem one can only speculate) toward the full manifestations of his youthful potential or perhaps simply toward renewed expression of this potential in another shape, less purely spontaneous, more formalized. In concrete terms, he moves in the poem from Haidée to Aurora, the different but complementary shapes of sensual apotheosis:

> . . . each was radiant in her proper sphere:
>   The island girl, bred up by the lone sea,
> More warm, as lovely, and not less sincere,
>   Was nature's all: Aurora could not be,
> Nor would be thus:—the difference in them
> Was such as lies between a flower and gem.   [15.58]

Where Haidée invokes a mythological world of sea nymph and goddess, Aurora is the innocent orphan child of history, ambiguously suggesting to the narrator both the compelling power and hopelessness of Edenic dreams. Her expression, he notes, was

> All Youth—but with an aspect beyond Time;
> Radiant and grave—as pitying Man's decline;
>   Mournful—but mournful of another's crime,
> She looked as if she sat by Eden's door,
> And grieved for those who could return no more.   [15.45]

Aurora is equally a historical anachronism; her denial of time extends to her present role as last survivor of a noble Catholic family: "She held their old faith and feelings fast" (15.46). Her proud alienation from English society is complete: "She gazed upon a world she scarcely knew, / As seeking not to know it" (15.47). It is to Aurora that Juan, himself now the incarnate form of beauty and grace, will apparently turn for further expression of the ideal-real moments of youth. Byron describes her influence on him late in the poem and then defines these moments:

> . . . certainly, Aurora had renewed
>   In him some feelings he had lately lost,
> Or hardened; feelings which, perhaps ideal,
>   Are so divine, that I must deem them real:—
>
> The love of higher things and better days;
>   The unbounded hope, and heavenly ignorance
> Of what is called the World, and the World's ways;
>   The moments when we gather from a glance
> More joy than from all future pride or praise. . . .   [16.107–8]

Characteristically, the narrator's perspective moves rapidly, virtually simultaneously, from almost complete identification with Juan and Aurora to melancholy and mature realism—"Alas! her [Cytherea's] star must fade like that of Dian: / Ray fades on ray, as years on years depart" (16.109)—to bathos:

> And full of sentiments, sublime as billows
>   Heaving between this World and Worlds beyond,
> Don Juan, when the midnight hour of pillows
>   Arrived, retired to his. . . .   [16.110]

Mock-heroic is built on layer upon layer of parody. Here the child's game of love, a parody of Eden, is itself parodied (together perhaps with the narrator's own high rhetoric) in the final absurdity of sentimental billows "heaving" between dimensions of reality, those "billows" inexorably linked with "pillows."

Such ironic qualification, however, involves simply a rapid multiplication of perspectives; it never threatens the integrity of Juan's point of view. Only when he becomes naively but deeply involved in the institutionalized horror of Ismail (a passion for glory in this case) does Byron switch in his treatment of Juan from the ambivalent irony of mock-heroic to the reductive irony of satire. Even on this occasion seriously reductive criticism is deflected, first by Juan's action in saving the orphan child and, more important, by Byron's curious introduction of the figure of Daniel Boone. With Juan's heroic image momentarily blurred by his involvement in war, Byron apparently felt impelled to redress the delicate balance between ideal and real with another version of the pastoral dream so basic to the heroic dimension of the poem. Boone is the apotheosis of the pastoral hero, the "child of nature" (8.63), the child-man (while Juan is being "manly"), who has avoided the taint of time and history (and thus maturity) by perpetual escape from civilization: "The free-born forest found and kept them free, / And fresh as is a torrent or a tree" (8.65). With absolute freedom comes eternal newness; the narrator in the same stanza describes Boone and his followers as "a sylvan tribe of children of the chase, / Whose young, unawakened world was ever new." But in the end the narrator characteristically undercuts his emotional and imaginative commitment to the heroic model he has set up and returns to an angry, realistic, carefully detailed account of the battle of Ismail: "So much for Nature:—by way of variety, / Now back to thy great joys, Civilization" (8.68).

The Byronic narrator, it must be emphasized, is as much a mock-hero as is his youthful protagonist, with the distinction, however, that he is self-conscious rather than naive. He is aware that he has not avoided time; the experience of change, variety, and incompletions has brought with it the ironic sense, in this case, a crucial awareness of the distinction between *seeing* and *all-seeing*. It is not so much that he is disillusioned as that he has an ironic attitude toward all illusions, including his own. Illusions are such precisely because they are temporary, partial, and limited ways of seeing, but they are unavoidable because all-seeing is impossible. They are probably even desirable because they motivate our most passionate moments. As Johnson, a mature surrogate of the narrator, explains to Juan while both are awaiting sale by the Turks into slavery: "Time strips our illusions of their hue" (5.21). We shed them, he says, year by year as a snake sheds its skin. Yet Johnson is forced to recognize the ambiguous logic of his metaphor. He concedes that we always get another skin "bright and fresh, / Or fresher, brighter" (5.22) after the old has been cast off. Their present situation seems to Johnson merely a symbol of the lives of most men, who are slaves "To their own whims and passions" (5.25). He in turn prides himself on the knowledge he has gained and the possession of the "right point of view" (5.23), but his pretensions in this scene are mocked by the insistently pragmatic comments of Juan, who under the circumstances naturally yearns for knowledge to be in some way substantial, functional, and operative. Johnson's knowledge has little substance beyond a sense of time and cycle and certainly "leads to" nothing, not even disillusionment (he has married again and again, like the snake shedding skin). In Byron's poem as in all narrative in the mock-heroic mode, illusions and ironic awareness coexist without the resolution that "disillusionment" (loss of illusions) would seem to imply. The pursuit of wisdom is one of the quixotic games of adulthood, the claim of knowledge one of its absurdities. As the narrator observes about himself:

> . . . I love Wisdom more than she loves me;
> My tendency is to philosophize

On most things, from a tyrant to a tree;
But still the spouseless virgin *Knowledge* flies.
What are we? and whence came we? what shall be
Our *ultimate* existence? What's our present?
Are questions answerless, and yet incessant.   [6.63]

The narrator has a strong sense of what might be called the "in-between"—of suspension at the center of unresolved contraries. Life itself he describes as "between two worlds," hovering

. . . like a star,
'Twixt Night and Morn, upon the horizon's verge.
How little do we know that which we are!
How less what we may be!   [15.99]

He is himself middle-aged,

. . . when we hover between fool and sage,
And don't know justly what we would be at—
A period something like a printed page,
Black letter upon foolscap. . . .   [13.1]

His point of view, in other words, is squarely between identification with the passionate and illusional world of youth and the objective, self-conscious realism of old age, "hovering over" both but completely committed to neither. He yearns to play observer, while Juan "takes an active share" (see 11.69–70), and to some extent this does describe their difference. This distinction, however, is far from complete because "hovering," in fact, involves not lack of commitment but ambivalent or multiple commitments. Time and again we have noted the complex range of attitudes expressed by the narrator (often, through parody, expressed at once) toward Juan's adventures. These attitudes are reinforced by the narrator's memories of his own youth, including moments of intense nostalgic identification with his own pastoral dream. Nor has the narrator in his middle age fully abandoned activism. He creates for himself an astonishing variety of heroic roles in the poem, some of which have already been discussed: pursuer of knowledge, satirist, moralist, rebel, and revolutionary quester in poetry like Newton in science ("I have shunned the common shore, / And leaving land far out of sight, would skim / The Ocean of Eternity" [10.4]), courageous and innovative artist (comparing himself to "my Hero," Napoleon [11.55–56]). The list is probably far from complete. These roles, in turn, are often mocked in the very context of their creation, and, in any case, none of them is sustained with any rigor or conviction throughout the length of the poem. They are, in short, simply the heroic gestures of maturity or the partial continuation of "youthful" impulses (the passionate moment) into the ironic dimension of "age"—the middle age of mock-heroic sensibility, the age of Wallace Stevens's later "man of fortune greeting heirs."

In spite of these heroic asides, the primary identification of the middle-aged narrator remains with the figure of Cervantes and a "half-serious" art in which reality and noble views coalesce only in a jesting riddle, which is the artifact of the poem and ultimately a metaphor of life. Poetry is a game of the self, "in-between" like the self,

> A paper kite which flies 'twixt Life and Death,
>   A shadow which the onward Soul behind throws:
> And mind's a bubble, not blown up for praise,
> But just to play with, as an infant plays.   [14.8]

The only "direction" (or resolution) in poetry and life is the onward movement to "the end" of death. Structure, imagery, diction, all the important elements in *Don Juan* reflect its lack of direction, that it involves simply the endless and irreconcilable encounter of conflicting attitudes and points of view. As the narrator explains:

> "The time is out of joint,"—and so am I;
> I quite forget this poem's merely quizzical,
>   And deviate into matters rather dry.
> I n'er decide what I shall say, and this I call
>   Much too poetical: men should know why
> They write, and for what end; but, note or text,
> I never know the word which will come next.
>
> So on I ramble, now and then narrating,
>   Now pondering. . . .   [9.41–42]

To an earlier epic formula, he has, like Cervantes before him, added the important but muddling ingredient of truth to actual life in time. He brags at the end of Canto Eight that he has written

> An *Epic*, if plain truth should prove no bar;
>   For I have drawn much less with a long bow
> Than my forerunners. Carelessly I sing,
> But Phoebus lends me now and then a string,
>   with which I still can harp, and carp, and fiddle.   [8.138–39]

Such truth saves the epic for the present day, but at the cost of clarity and a coherent and sustained heroic theme.

In the same stanzas above, Byron aptly describes his poem as a "grand poetic riddle." But this, after all, is significant. The writer himself is the ultimate mock-hero—commonplace, absurd, yet still committed like his protagonist to a dream of adventure. As Byron phrases it in a splendid mock-heroic exhortation to the Muse:

> We'll do our best to make the best on't:—March!
>   March, my Muse! If you cannot fly, yet flutter;
> And when you may not be sublime, be arch,
>   Or Starch, as are the edicts statesmen utter.
> We surely may find something worth research:
>   Columbus found a new world in a cutter,
> Or brigantine, or pink, of no great tonnage,
> While yet America was in her non-age.   [15.27]

I have already noted that the writer in the mock-heroic mode transforms at every level the epic quest for consummate vision into a sustained drama of effort toward no clear or perhaps possible end: march on one way or another, make the best of it, something "worth research" *may* be found. The act of writing mirrors as well as incorporates the performances of its various voices. For Byron poetry is the ultimate, all-encompassing passion, albeit finally quixotic like all the others:

> As on the beach the waves at last are broke,
>   Thus to their extreme verge the passions brought
> Dash into poetry, which is but Passion,
> Or, at least, were so ere it grew a fashion.   [4.106]

But Byron's final line also hints at a darker possibility: that quixotism itself will become corrupt or impossible under the general tide of banality. We have, in effect, reached one of those limits of the mock-heroic whose nature and significance I shall explore briefly in the final chapter.

Through the Looking Glass: Literature of Regionalism and Childhood

Don't part with your illusions: when they are gone you may still exist but you have ceased to live.

MARK TWAIN
Pudd'nhead Wilson's New Calendar

But the great difficulty is that *adventures don't happen!* Oh, how *am* I to make some happen, so as to have something to tell my darling Enid?

LEWIS CARROLL
to a young correspondent

"Leda" was done at the same time as "Lethe." Lotus-land, all this. It is nostalgia for a lost land. I call it Hellas. I might, psychologically just as well, have listed the Casco Bay Islands off the coast of Maine.

HILDA DOOLITTLE
"A Note on Poetry"

Pudd'nhead Wilson's aphorism suggests the ambivalence with which illusions are viewed by the mock-heroic writer: on one hand, they are an emotional and spiritual necessity; on the other, they are clearly known and labeled as "illusions" in contradistinction to something with the prior ontological status of "reality." The aesthetic problem for the mock-heroic writer has always been to find an objective correlative for feelings and beliefs that are at once morally and imaginatively compelling and realistically absurd. In the later nineteenth century such correlatives were often found close at hand in the materials of so-called literary regionalism and in literature about childhood (by no means the same as "children's literature," though in some cases absolute distinctions are difficult if not impossible to draw). Both of these subgenres of prose narrative could be justified within the larger ethos of literary realism, and both tended to share common characteristics, so that they often came together easily in the same vehicle. The work of Mark Twain represents the supreme example of this confluence. Before dealing with Twain directly, however, I want to explore separately and with reference to others the mock-heroic implications of each of these two important strands of his imagination.

Children in Wonderland: Kenneth Grahame and Lewis Carroll

As I have already pointed out, the quixotic figure is always youthful, in spirit if not in fact; his posture involves a combination of ardency, imagination, naive belief, and imprudence that is impossible to disassociate from childhood. From the nineteenth century, as Julien, Fabrizio, and Don Juan demonstrate, Quixote is often literally a child or adolescent, thanks both to the romantic mystique of childhood innocence and spiritual potency and (they are not, of course, unrelated) to the association of growth and adulthood with a banal, boring, and corrupt middle-class world. On this occasion at least, value-laden literary images reflect in their own complex fashion personal experience and cultural process. I have noted also in Stendhal and Byron the consciousness of historical discontinuity with its accompanying sense of personal anachronism and psychic displacement. Later nineteenth-century writers in many cases felt even more strongly and categorically the problem of change, of alienation from the past, of spiritual and psychological disinheritance. In America the Civil War came to mark a break as sharp as the Napoleonic Wars for the earlier European and English generation. Charles Dudley Warner and Twain wrote in *The Gilded Age* that "the eight years in America from 1860 to 1868 uprooted institutions that were centuries old, changed the politics of a people, transformed the social life of half the country and wrought so profoundly upon the entire national character that the influence cannot be measured short of two or three generations." War, of course, was only the most dramatic form taken by the political and industrial revolutions of the century. Writers whose lives straddled the period tended to feel at some point superannuated like Henry Adams, or, as Henry James put it, "ruptured" from their own biography. In later years, John Ruskin spoke of himself as "of the old race—few of us now left—children who reverenced our fathers . . . few of us now standing here and there, alone, in the midst of this yelping, carnivorous crowd, mad for money and lust." Tennyson wrote to a friend: "To me the far-off world seems nearer than the present, for in the present is always something unreal and indistinct, but the other seems good solid planet, rolling round its green hills and paradises to more steadfast laws."[1]

An important by-product of such feelings was the Victorian and Edwardian cult of childhood: the development of children's literature and, more important, the development of literature about childhood written primarily for adults. Although most of the former were heavily didactic, moralizing the child into adulthood and reducing or denying his claims to autonomy, many of the latter went beyond romantic works in their vision of childhood as the embodiment of a different, more innocent, more imaginative, more ideal and heroic state of being. Living in a disorienting present, the Victorian writer found it easy to idealize his own past and create a fiction on that basis.[2] Mark Twain wrote to Thomas Bailey Aldrich late in life after he had read *The Story of a Bad Boy:* "By the time I had finished it, at three in the morning, it had worked its spell and Portsmouth was become the town of my own boyhood— with all which that implies and compels: the bringing back of one's youth, almost the only time of life worth living over again, the only period whose memories are wholly pathetic—pathetic because we see now that we were in heaven then and there was no one able to make us know it, though no doubt many a poor old devil tried to." The child's world clearly involves an ideal dimension missing from adulthood. The writer is emotionally and imaginatively drawn to this dimension but, as an adult, knows its insubstantiality, knows that it is really a child's "game" briefly played and pertinent only to nostalgic memory—or perhaps simply a creation of memory. His ambivalent vision must span the gap between the heroic child adventuring in the past and an adult author living in the present who has objective and realistic awareness of the literal absurdity or irrelevance of childish claims. The child world, paradoxically, represents, not growth, but everything hostile to change. Kenneth Grahame states as a fundamental premise that "the innate conservatism of youth asks neither poverty nor riches, but only immunity from change." The adult point of view is an almost Kafkan paradox of its own: immunity is of central importance but never granted. From such ironies and double vision emerges the mock-heroic mode of much nineteenth-century literature about childhood.[3]

For Kenneth Grahame in *The Golden Age* (1895) and *Dream Days* (1898), his two adult books recounting the adventures of childhood, child life is both the last refuge of heroic man—free, magical, imaginative, intimately responsive to a natural rather than a social order—and also inevitably lost and irrecoverable. "A saddening doubt, a dull suspicion, creeps over me," writes Grahame in the Prologue. "*Et in Arcadia ego*—I certainly did once inhabit Arcady. Can it be that I also have become an Olympian?" (*GA*, 22). The ironic awareness in this passage and the explicit evocation of Vergilian nostalgia (compare Mark Twain: "we were in heaven then") suggest the characteristic tone and attitude of the entire book, and the irredeemable dualities of time and space mentioned locate the source of its ambivalence. The so-called Olympians are the inhabitants of the adult world who hedge in the children with harsh discipline and social duties. They represent, in Grahame's words, the "right and social" mind, the world of "fact," which has completely usurped the mature life of this culture to the exclusion of what he calls "the higher gift of imagination" (*GA*, 25, 45).

The heroic environment is the child's world of dreams: literal dreams, daydreams ("slipping the husk and passing, a careless lounger, through a sleepy imaginary world all golden and green" [*GA*, 35]), and, in particular, the willed, arbitrary, creative dimension of games—"let's pretend." In this "quaint inconsequent country" of dreams, according to Grahame, you "meet your own pet hero strolling down the road, and commit what hare-brained oddities you like, and everybody understands and appreciates" (*DD*, 144). Episode after episode involves a mock-heroic adventure in which the child imaginatively tries to duplicate the feats of antique heroes only to be "awakened of a sudden to the harshness of real things and the unnumbered hostilities of the actual world" (*DD*, 188). Comic anticlimax follows hard on the heels of momentary transformation. One episode, for example, describes the child with his picture-book journeying in fantasy over the sea with a crowd of knights and ladies toward a "happy island" only to "stumble out of an opalescent dream into the broad daylight" with the fingers of an angry aunt holding him "tight by the scruff of the neck" (*DD*, 188). In another story children duplicate the voyage of the Argonauts, until an irate farmer intervenes to seize their stolen boat. A third significantly links the child with an artist he meets by the roadside. They communicate their longings to each other, so that the child thinks the artist may be a vanished knight from the Golden City. Both are wanderers; both admire the heroic life. "I'm a sort of Ulysses," says the artist, "—seen men and cities, you know. In fact, about the only place I never got to was the Fortunate Island" (*GA*, 94). Only the child and the artist, in other words, continue their quixotic search for values irrevocably lost to their society. Grahame mourns them while recognizing fully their romantic absurdity.

The last story in *Dream Days*, called "A Departure," is at once a final celebration of this absurdity and, by extension, a little allegory of the role of the mock-heroic writer. The tale describes the removal of toys by adults and the children's response of salvaging a few and burying them in a moonlit garden to preserve them from being "spoiled." Grahame, like others before and after him, suggests that the mock-heroic writer is his own Quixote, that the act of salvage, however undertaken, is only another game in the framing context of even wider ironies. By casting himself as the White Knight in *Through the Looking-Glass*, Lewis Carroll had already given vivid and pointed expression to this crucial insight.

In one other important fashion Grahame's work echoes that of his great Victorian predecessor. In *The Golden Age* and *Dream Days* the child is associated with the garden world of pastoral, and both, in turn, are related to non-sense. In one scene in particular the child responds to the passion of the morning with a song:"I ran sideways, shouting . . . I hurled clods skywards at random; and presently I somehow found myself singing. The words were mere nonsense—irresponsible babble; the tune was an improvisation, a weary, unrhythmic thing of rise and fall: and yet it seemed to me a genuine utterance, and just at that moment the one thing fitting and right and perfect. Humanity would have rejected it with scorn. Nature, everywhere singing in the same key, recognized and accepted it without a flicker of dissent" (*GA*, 27). The point of view here is significant and one I have repeatedly tried to define: nominally that of the child, actually that of an adult who is projecting himself ambivalently into both worlds at once. Equally significant, however, is the concept of nonsense utterance as a characteristic and meaningful style of mock-heroic being—"irresponsible," improvisatory, creating an "unrhythmic" counterrhythm that invokes a value-laden world of adventure and simultaneously subverts its authenticity. In any case, *non*sense constitutes an alien order "rejected with scorn" by the *common*sense realities of adulthood. This concept Lewis Carroll exploits in *Alice in Wonderland* and *Through the Looking-Glass*, books in which "disorder" (as an alternate order) constitutes the very ground of heroic experience and nonsense is its primary language.

The fall down the rabbit-hole in *Alice in Wonderland* has lent itself to a great deal of rigorous and imaginative interpretation. Among other things, it invokes echoes of the Underworld Journey of the Hero (Cervantes uses the same action in the Cave of Montesinos episode), and critics are to be pardoned if they treat Carroll's version as if he were merely updating myth. But even less than with Cervantes is the issue one of straight mythic invocation or, alternatively, direct satiric attack. Rather, Carroll's imitation is mock-heroic parody, a transformational device that recontextualizes the world of adventure—making adventure possible at the cost of relentlessly stripping it of teleological significance. Alice's fall down the rabbit-hole translates her instantly from a commonplace environment on a boring day ("sitting by her sister on the bank and having nothing to do") to an exciting, unruly, unpredictable, metamorphic world that tests courage, intelligence, and imagination and quickly brings into question the very assumption of conventional identity. In talking to herself, Alice emphasizes the real point of what has happened: " 'Dear, dear! How queer everything is to-day! And yesterday things went on just as usual. I wonder if I've changed in the night? Let me think: was I the same when I got up this morning? I almost think I can remember feeling a little different. But if I'm not the same, the next question is "Who in the world am I?" Ah, *that's* the great puzzle!' "[4] To a very great extent, this temporary freedom or release from conventional (adult-imposed) identity in a conventional world constitutes in and for itself the fundamental mock-heroic adventure in Carroll's novels.

Similar though even more obvious in its immediate effects is the transformation caused by the looking-glass in the later book after Alice's childish invocation of "let's pretend." The looking-glass inverts reality ("things go the other way" [LG, 110]), only in this case inversion is, in fact, subversion. In the looking-glass room, the fire is warmer because, says Alice, "there'll be no one here to scold me away from the fire." She immediately senses her liberation: "Oh, what fun it'll be, when they see me through the glass in here, and ca'n't get at me!" The objects in the old room she has left are "quite common and uninteresting"; from her new point of view "the pictures on the wall next to the fire seemed to be all alive, and the very clock on the chimney-piece (you know you can only see the back of it in the Looking-glass) had got the face of a little old man, and grinned at her." The new room is not "so tidy as the other" (LG, 112–13). Tidiness, of course, is only the most blatant manifestation of the constriction of the "adult" reality from which Alice is escaping. Huck Finn describes the experience explicitly in commenting on his own escape from the world of Widow Douglas: "The Widow Douglas she took me for her son and allowed she would sivilize me; but it was rough living in the house all the time, considering how dismal regular and decent the widow was in all her ways, and so when I couldn't stand it no longer I lit out. I got into my old rags and my sugar-hogshead again, and was free and satisfied" (13:2). His later nakedness on the raft completes his transformation into another environment.

Nonsense is Carroll's particular device for creating an environment that simulates heroic freedom. In his version of mock-heroic, parody imitates the actions of earlier heroes not directly or literally, but largely insofar as Carroll's subversive imitation of Victorian "sense" creates in its own fashion the bizarre and chaotic landscape of romance in which the hero tests the quality of his selfhood and struggles to understand, to survive, and (perhaps) to restore or find order. Occasionally, of course, more conventional mock-heroic parody and Carroll's own method coalesce. There are splendid scenes—for example, Alice's "combat" with the monstrous puppy (AW, 32) or her desperate swim in the pool made by her own tears—which are at once imitations of the ritual trials of the hero and (since with both puppy and tears proportion and thus relationship and perspective have been reversed) parodic inversions of contemporary norms of substantiality. On the whole, it is these inversions (in effect, subversions) which concern him most. Wonderland is a "mad," chaotic parody of "dull reality" (AW, 98), the "underworld" of insanity repressed or denied by Victorian sanity. Alice undergoes the experience or "trial"—

liberating, fearful, exciting—of moral anarchy, indeterminism, psychological and linguistic irrationality, and the disappearance of fixed forms.[5]

The specific literary forms parodied by Carroll are the didactic children's story and the fairy tale. Alice is quite conscious of herself as a literary figure. In one of her early ponderings she thinks: "I do wonder what *can* have happened to me! When I used to read fairy tales, I fancied that kind of thing never happened, and now here I am in the middle of one! There ought to be a book written about me, that there ought!" (*AW,* 29). In more general literary terms, nonsense involves a systematic parody of realism and all that it represents. Fracturing or disruption of empirical reality, temporal rearrangement where effect comes before cause, destruction of logical communication in favor of non sequitur and pun are Carroll's methods, and they are nothing but the tenets of realism turned upside down. For the Victorian writer, however, the nonsense world remains ultimately one of nostalgic "play." Only a later literary generation, less intimidated by empirical criteria and more openly responsive to symbolist and modern linguistic and philosophical influences, would use nonsense outside the mock-heroic frame to suggest the nature of reality itself.

Although her world is transformed by parody from that of sense to a wholly new dimension of heroic nonsense, Alice is less a parodist (unlike other mock-heroes we have observed) than a more or less willing recipient of the environment created for her by the will and imagination of the author. John Hinz has noted that the *Alice* books reverse the formula of *Don Quixote:* the protagonist is sane in the midst of an insane world. To be sure, this distinction (as Hinz is well aware) is not without serious qualification. Obviously Alice's dreams and her "let's pretend" may be considered in literal and orthodox terms as the manifestations of repressed desires. Carroll's own view of dreams even encourages us to link fantasy closely with the protagonist: "When we are dreaming," he wrote in a diary entry, "do we not say and do things which in waking life would be insane?"[6] In any case, Alice seems to be clearly a familiar of the world that she discovers. Its materials are those of a little girl's imagination, and it is in large part sustained by the quality of acceptance and naive belief that she brings to it. According to the Cheshire-Cat, everyone is mad down the rabbit-hole or through the looking-glass. "You must be," he tells Alice, "or you wouldn't have come here" (*AW,* 51).

Nevertheless, granted Alice's substantial involvement, Carroll's own role as mad fantasist remains striking and important. He is, in fact, knight errant to little girls, providing them with an adventurous world (sometimes an arduous task, as the letter quoted in the epigraph to this chapter suggests) and guiding them on their way through it—both the White Knight helping Alice to complete her game and the creator of the game who has arranged it all to begin with, a creator, one should add, with his own obsessive need for a more perfect system than the world about him could provide.[7] In any case, the emphasis on Alice's experiences as a game is particularly strong in *Through the Looking-Glass*. There it gives her quest a certain arbitrary order and resolution and provides a secure and sufficient metaphor for the landscape over which she passes. Early in the novel she is taken (like the traditional hero) to the top of a hill and given a vision of a countryside divided into squares, a vision to which she responds ecstatically: "'I declare it's marked out just like a large chess-board!' Alice said at last. 'There ought to be some men moving about somewhere—and so there are!' she added in a tone of delight, and her heart began to beat quick with excitement as she went on. 'It's a great huge game of chess that's being played—all over the world—if this *is* the world at all, you know. Oh, what fun it is! How I *wish* I was one of them!'" (*LG*, 125–26). And so she becomes, of course, transformed by the imagination of her creator from "pawn" to "queen" or, as Carroll puts it schematically: "*White Pawn (Alice) to play, and win in eleven moves*" (*LG*, 104).

But Carroll is both White Knight and mature ironist: the mock-heroic mode presupposes such a merger of roles. In the first place, as an "adult" he shares in the sense of temporal loss so common to his century. The *Alice* books include sharp dualities of time and attitude. In Wonderland the nominal child's point of view is carefully framed and limited by the nostalgic sensibility of the author. The tone and backward vision of Carroll's books are instantly set in the dedicatory verses to the earlier volume:

> Alice! A childish story take,
>   And, with a gentle hand,
> Lay it where Childhood's dreams are twined
>   In Memory's mystic band.
> Like pilgrim's wither'd wreath of flowers
>   Pluck'd in a far-off land.   [*AW*, 4]

Alice and the narrator have changed, and the experience of Wonderland is, in fact, "dead" except insofar as it exists within the adult dream of nostalgic memory. The ironies of nostalgia are complex and, when they are exploited, become the stuff of mock-heroic. On one hand, nostalgia lays bare temporal discontinuity and thus, from a wider perspective, exposes the "unreality" of events in times past, however much these events constitute a unique spiritual shrine ("where Childhood's dreams are twined / In Memory's mystic band"). On the other, because of the value-laden power of this shrine, the nostalgic self remains obsessively committed to the hopeless yet still compelling task of its redemption. The White Knight reveals the absurdity of memory (of "then" having significant relation or relevance to "now") in his parody of Words-worth's "Resolution and Independence" as set to a sentimental song by Thomas Moore. After describing the ridiculous adventures of the "aged aged man" told to him "that summer evening long ago," the narrator of the song concludes:

> And now, if e'er by chance I put
>   My fingers into glue,
> Or madly squeeze a right-hand foot
>   Into a left-hand shoe,
> Or if I drop upon my toe
>   A very heavy weight,
> I weep, for it reminds me so
> Of that old man I used to know—[LG, 189]

Carroll here mockingly deconstructs his own nostalgia—both the possibility of vital and heroic truth in the past and even our nonsense rituals of recovery.

Beyond the complexities of nostalgia, moreover, there are other ironic dimensions to the *Alice* books. The heroic experience of Wonderland is additionally qualified at the very moment of its existence, certainly by the adult storyteller, probably even by the children themselves. The same dedicatory verses from which I have already quoted contain Carroll's revealing description of the process of storytelling and listening:

> Anon, to sudden silence won,
>   In fancy they [i.e., the Liddell girls] pursue
> The dream-child moving through a land
>   Of wonders wild and new,
> In friendly chat with bird or beast—
>   And half believe it true.   [AW, 3]

Mock-heroic narrative, as I noted explicitly in connection with Byron, is always only "half" true or "half" serious. The other half is in some sense untrue or cannot or should not be taken seriously. Among the children at least, the raison d'être of adventures (whether we think of them as primary dream or vicarious story) is what Alice aptly calls "fun" in her response on the hill to the vision of the chess-board. These adventures are motivated by the need for distraction and entertainment, they are more absurd than menacing (Alice is constantly stifling smiles or laughter), and they are terminated at will or when the story has "drained / The wells of fancy dry" (AW, 3). Alternately, in her dreams disorder disappears at the first assumption of her "real" (waking) size. Wonderland, in short, is fanciful parenthesis, the Victorian "play" world of conventional children destined for conventional maturity. Nonsense in this context, at least, entails a carefully controlled and limited adventure. Concerning its use in the *Alice* books, Elizabeth Sewell has noted "that although nonsense plays on the side of order, its aim and method is to defeat disorder with disorder's own weapons. It allows disorder in the mind a certain amount of selected material apparently suitable to dream purposes (images and so on), and in this way draws the disordering faculty into play, but manages never to let it gain control."[8] In real life, Carroll complains to his young correspondent, *"adventures don't happen";*[9] in the face of this categorical fact, he can only "make" some—make some, that is, with his imagination in complete awareness that they could not be fully true or seriously relevant to the routine world in which he lived. He may have had a psychological or spiritual need to play White Knight, but in his case the role could not rise above that of entertainer.

The *Alice* books involve not authentic heroism but heroic artifice. A critic from the counterculture once compared Alice's journey down the rabbit-hole to an LSD trip, a facile and absurd comment, perhaps, if taken too literally but at least suggestive of the provisional, arbitrary, illusory, and ultimately limited quality of the experience, whatever the motivation, intense or frivolous, behind it.[10] Down the rabbit-hole or through the looking-glass are directions of escape from all-pervasive reality to an induced heroic dimension. There one can linger briefly during periods of one's childhood. "I'm *not* going in again yet," says Alice at one point. "I know I should have to get through the Looking-glass again—back to the old room—and there'd be an end of all my adventures!" (*LG,* 120). The petulant child's determination to play a little longer is balanced carefully in the sentence by the inexorable adult "yet."

Don Quixote in the Provinces: Daudet's Tartarin

In the nineteenth century a feeling of separation in discontinuous time from childhood was often accompanied by a literal separation in space; the writer was born in one place and lived his mature life in another—the most familiar pattern then as now being, of course, movement from rural area or provincial town to big city. So-called regional or "local color" writing tends to be a particular product of this migration (as opposed to the authentic native literature of a region), a literature of discontinuous space which complements and often incorporates a children's literature of discontinuous time. The double vision of the one (child/adult in ambivalent balance) is only reinforced by the conflicting attitudes implied in the multiplication of spatial perspectives. During this period, to be sure, literary treatment of the "provinces," small towns, or distinct "regions" isolated from urban life occasionally explored extremes of idyllic pastoralism and mean and mongrel landscapes of the sort created by Flaubert in *Madame Bovary*. But such polarization, though examples of each can be found, does not adequately suggest the real complexity in attitude of much regional writing, which is often done by someone who has left the region and looks back on it (through time and space) with a combination of nostalgic identification and the objectivity of distancing, maturity, and greater sophistication. Nostalgia celebrates the heroic possibilities of the region; objectivity records not only the general anachronism and isolation of provincial life (in a culture where change, on the whole, sweeps all before it), but realistic details of the region: local manners, types of people, and scenery, the actual limitations of constricted area, opportunity, and outlook. Regionalism too often is associated simply with the latter point of view and treated as an adjunct to literary realism, though, in fact, like other manifestations of the mock-heroic mode, many of its characteristic documents finally resist placement in unitary terms and seem anomalous.

The largest claim made by the regionalist for his regional setting is that it offers his protagonist at least the possibility of powerful imaginative experience. The protagonist in a regional novel may perhaps exist lonely in an isolated area, left in a situation that encourages subjectivity to encroach on external reality. Hjalmar Boyesen's Gunnar, for example, lives far up in the Norse mountains in an isolated valley under the snow-line, and Boyesen describes him as follows: "The boy had lived so long in a world of his own imagination, and had had so very little to do with the world of reality, that he was not able to distinguish the one from the other."[11] As I shall have occasion to point out, this is the situation of much American regional writing, the Americans often (certainly Mark Twain) adding the dimension of moral imagination to its aesthetic counterpart.

Imagination may also simply be characteristic of the region, encouraged by its folkways, part of the temperament of its people. "The Tarascon imagination," writes Alphonse Daudet, "defies all considerations of time and space."[12] The Southerner, according to Daudet, under the warm sun and vivid skies, lives in "a kind of mental mirage"; to understand him "you have only to look at that Lucifer's own country, where the sun transmogrifies everything, and magnifies it beyond life-size" (*TT*, 16). Transformation, in other words, especially gigantism or heroic illusion, is inherent in the psychic life of the region. Everything seems to take on heroic size: the local hills (450 to 600 feet high) have been "supplied with fabulous and characteristic names, such as *le-Mont-Terrible, le Bont-du-Monde, le Pic-des-Geánts*, etc." (*TA*, 103); games are elevated to the status of myth (a "mad" passion for shooting hats perpetuates the ancient pastime of killing dragons [*TT*, 3–5]); and, above all, the self is everywhere aggrandized to the role of its dreams or the romantic roles of the occasion. Tartarin, for example, asked to pose for a fresco of William Tell, *becomes* William Tell. As Daudet describes the scene:

> Tartarin was going to be painted as he stood, a dumpy, round-backed man, wrapped in his muffler to the chin; fixing the terrified *famulus* [the artist's as- sistant] with his flaming little eye.
>
> Imagination, oh what magic power you possess! He believed himself stand- ing in the market-place of Altorf, facing his son—he who had never had one—a bolt in his cross-bow, another in his girdle to pierce the heart of the tyrant. More than that, he communicated the conviction to the spectators! [*TA*, 129]

The systematic lying and bragging of the Southerner, says Daudet, are pri- marily acts of self-deception (*TT*, 16); Tartarin himself describes the Tarascon- nais at one point as "liars in imagination" (*TA*, 222).

Tartarin, of course, is the embodiment of the Tarascon spirit: "If Tarascon epitomised the South, Tartarin epitomised Tarascon" (*TA*, 104). Even when physically older (in *Tartarin on the Alps*), he "conserved that extraordinary imagination which brought near and enlarged objects with the power of a telescope" (*TA*, 104). He possesses, in addition, a "warm heart . . . an ardent soul" (*TA*, 120), and naive and infantile qualities (*TA*, 168). But he is, in many other ways, a far from simple personality, and Daudet's attitude toward him is far from uncomplicated. He is not a unitary figure at all, but schizoid, engaged in perpetual dialectic with himself—in Daudet's metaphor, not one rabbit, but two: "For in Tartarin, as in all the Tarasconnais, there is a warren and a cabbage breed, very clearly marked. The rabbit of the warren is a rover—an adventurous animal; the cabbage-rabbit is domesticated—a stay- at-home, having an extraordinary horror of fatigue, of draughts, and of all the contingencies which may bring death in their train" (*TA*, 104). In Daudet's Tarascon world, the will to heroism is implacably countered by the ground of the commonplace: the two coextensive, inseparable, linked only in absolute and unresolved tension. Even within the individual self the spiritual yearning for adventure exists in perpetual counterpoise with commonplace sensuality. Sancho Panza, in other words, lives within the Knight as well as forever rid- ing along beside.

Such an incorporation is Daudet's emendation of Cervantes. His pro- tagonist becomes a total reflection of the conflicting possibilities of the re- gional image and Daudet's own need to straddle the alternatives. The emen- dation was done explicitly, and Daudet acknowledges his general indebtedness to Cervantes in a passage significant also for the view it gives of a writer self-consciously discovering the relevance of mock-heroic to the cre- ation of regional literature:

We are afraid we must make a clean breast of it: in our hero there were two very distinct characters. Some Father of the Church has said: "I feel there are two men in me." He would have spoken truly in saying this about Tartarin, who carried in his frame the soul of Don Quixote, the same chivalric impulses, heroic ideal, and crankiness for the grandiose and romantic; but, worse is the luck! he had not the body of the celebrated hidalgo, that thin and meagre apology for a body, on which material life failed to take a hold; one that could get through twenty nights without its breast-plate being unbuckled off, and forty-eight hours on a handful of rice. On the contrary, Tartarin's body was a stout honest bully of a body, very fat, very weighty, most sensual and fond of coddling, highly touchy, full of low-class appetite and homely requirements—the short, paunchy body on stumps of the immortal Sancho Panza.

Don Quixote and Sancho Panza in the one same man! you will readily comprehend what a cat-and-dog couple they made! what strife! what clapperclawing! Oh, the fine dialogue for Lucian or Saint-Evremond to write, between the two Tartarins—Quixote-Tartarin and Sancho-Tartarin! Quixote-Tartarin firing up on the stories of Gustave Aimard, and shouting: "Up and at em!" and Sancho-Tartarin thinking only of the rheumatics ahead, and murmuring: "I mean to stay at home." [*TT*, 13–14]

At this point Daudet breaks up the dialectic into two parallel columns on the page, and what he calls the "duet" continues until the maid enters with food and Quixote-Tartarin (temporarily, at least) lapses into silence and defeat. He has called for a battle-ax but settles for chocolate and grilled steak.

Such a comic anticlimax is characteristic of virtually every episode in the Tartarin series, but it is by no means solely attributable to the internal gap between high aspirations and basic animal drives. Quixote-Tartarin is equally vulnerable to the invincible banality of the external world. Tarascon itself is tame, boring, and pedestrian, and the childish games of its inhabitants do not suffice Tartarin: "This life in a petty town weighed upon him and suffocated him" (*TT*, 9). Heroic fantasy, first reactive to emptiness, then becomes self-generating. As Daudet describes the process: "In vain did he cram with romances, endeavoring like the immortal Don Quixote to wrench himself by the vigour of his fancy out of the talons of pitiless reality. Alas! all that he did to appease his thirst for deeds of daring only helped to augment it!" (*TT*, 9). The "madness" of the quixotic figure, as I have indicated elsewhere, is an index not only of the distance between his illusions and reality but of a need to believe so intense that it feeds on itself and approaches paranoia. Tartarin at night, armed to the teeth, roams the "vile, paltry alleys" of Tarascon hoping that cutthroats will leap out at him, but nothing ever happens. His situation is reminiscent of the side of Lewis Carroll which despaired that "adventures don't happen." Tartarin's cry of anguish on one occasion after waiting fruitlessly for the villains to appear—"Nothing, nothing at all! there never is nothing!" (*TT*, 12)—is as shrill as anything in Flaubert, though Daudet characteristically undercuts the solemnity with a further, more distinctly comic anticlimax and persistent ironic distancing of tone and diction: "Upon which double negation, which he meant as a stronger affirmative, the worthy champion would walk in [to his clubhouse] to play his game of bezique with the major" (*TT*, 12).

From a world without adventure there is no authentic escape. When Tartarin moves beyond Tarascon to the apparently more promising environments of Algeria and Switzerland, he discovers only variants of the same "nothing" he has left behind. "Nothing," in effect, gradually stands revealed as lying at the very center of his quests, descriptive of both vehicle and ends, though not of the ardent spirit behind them. In episode after episode the "mirage" of imagination (Daudet's metaphor alone suggestive of the attenuation of romantic heroism) dissipates in the flat, dead light of commonplace reality. But after each scene, including the final anticlimax, the shimmering haze returns, and the stuff of disillusion becomes the building block of new illusions.

The episodic structure of the major *Tartarin* novels involves another of those complex parodies so common to mock-heroic, in this case a parody of chivalric adventure which is more immediately a parody of the nineteenth-century travel book. Daudet could the more easily blend his parodic materials because of the traditional relation of travel to epic experience. Not only have they been associated from the earliest times, but real travel and the literature of travel have always tended to function as a naive parody of romance—a way of imitating and legitimizing the spirit of romance in a dimension closer to actual human experience. In the landscapes of early travel literature fantasy and empirical reality often mingle indiscriminately. By the nineteenth century, however, genuinely exotic landscapes are far more remote (if, indeed, after scientific examination or colonization they remain exotic at all) and the empirical sense far more highly developed, whereas the opportunity for individual travel expands enormously. Travel literature caters increasingly to the craving for adventure by self-consciously searching out and stressing the bizarre or even by rhetorically heightening the illusion of strangeness and excitement at the expense of truth. In other words, travel and travel literature come to constitute (particularly with the advent of guidebooks and organized tours) another version of the momentary, artificial, and induced adventures of those who live essentially in a tame and commonplace world. It is in these circumstances that the form and content of the travel book finds itself vulnerable to satiric debunking (for example, *The Innocents Abroad*) and exploitation as a medium for mock-heroic narrative.

Tartarin's first journey (in *Tartarin of Tarascon*) is to North Africa, where he believes he can fulfill his desire for heroic combat by killing lions. Characteristically, he models himself on the great African tourists, by reading their books, trying to imitate their habits, and assembling their equipment; then he dresses elaborately for his role in what he thinks is Algerian costume. Once on the way, he finds momentary confirmation of his dreams in the sights, sounds, and smells of the harbor at Marseilles. Reality here, for the first and only time in the novel, approaches heroic romance. "The poor fellow believed he was dreaming," writes Daudet, with his usual mixture of sympathy and distance. "He fancied his name was Sinbad the Sailor, and that he was roaming in one of those fantastic cities abundant in the *Arabian Nights*" (*TT*, 30). But the "fall" from illusion soon begins. Crossing the Mediterranean Sea, the hero in full costume is subject to violent seasickness (and subjected by Daudet to harsh, slapstick comedy). Algiers only confirms the direction of what have now become his misadventures. The city resembles Tarascon: "Beforehand he had pictured it as an Oriental city—a fairy one, mythological, something between Constantinople and Zanzibar; but it was back into Tarascon he fell. Cafés, restaurants, wide streets, four-storey houses, a little market-place, macadamised, where the infantry band played Offenbachian polkas" (*TT*, 38). Algiers is simply a French provincial city, colonial version. Among the many ironies of travel is the fact that the traveler may never really go anywhere. This is one of the insights of Leopold Bloom during the course of his own parodic journey: "Think you're escaping and run into yourself. Longest way round is the shortest way home.[13]

Tartarin's first lion-hunting expedition involves a night trip outside Algiers to what seems to be "a great wilderness, bristling with odd plants of the Oriental kind which look like wicked creatures" (*TT*, 41). In this Wonderland world he follows the approved ritual (as his books have informed him) for hunting lions and eventually shoots at a black mass looming in the dark. But Wonderland vanishes with the light of day, and Tartarin finds himself actually "in a field of artichokes, between a cabbage-garden and a patch of beets. His Sahara grew kitchen vegetables." He is astonished by "the commonplace and kitchen-gardenish aspect of this sleep-steeped country" (*TT*, 43). His "lion" is a poor little ass dying in a pool of blood; his heroic reward, a comic beating from its enraged female owner. Throughout the rest of the novel his ardent dreams continue to be betrayed by the fundamental banality of his environment, the deceptions of others preying on his gullibility, and his own sensuality—all the detritus of reality from which escape is impossible. In the end he returns home, leaving "on the Moorish strand his guncases and his illusions," North Africa now only a "sham Arabia . . . a ridiculous Land of the East, full of locomotives and stage coaches" (*TT*, 85). Back among the Tarasconnais, however, with the skin of a tame lion he had finally shot, his failure is interpreted as triumph, and the mirage gathers around once again. As hero of the imagination, Tartarin achieves limited and local apotheosis.

In *Tartarin on the Alps* Daudet works a significant variation on the pattern he had set up in *Tartarin of Tarascon*. Switzerland in the later novel is not merely a commonplace country transformed by the illusions of its viewer (themselves shaped by the rhetoric of travel literature). In addition, it stimulates and encourages these illusions by actively participating in their apparent fulfillment, a role similar, perhaps, to that of the Duke and Duchess in their support of Don Quixote's fantasies. In the case of Switzerland, it plays heroic games for profit. It is the creation of guidebook writers, full of sham visions and sham adventure, "nothing more than an immense Kursaal," as one of Tartarin's friends tells him, adding that "when you penetrate a little farther into the country, you will not find a corner which is not fixed up and machined like the floor beneath the stage in the Opera" (*TA*, 135–36). Switzerland tries to be the fairy-tale world of tourist dreams; everyone is gamesman in the book, native and foreigner alike. Daudet even includes among the dramatis personae a group of young Russian émigrés playing a brutal game of anarchist revolution to their own set of illusions. The mood of *Tartarin on the Alps* is drier, darker, more mordant than that of *Tartarin of Tarascon*, the gap between reality and illusion more uncompromising, the polaric alternatives more unattractive even on their own terms. [14] The weather is always bad in Daudet's Switzerland—a cold, dreary, blinding rain or snow that comes down steadily throughout the entire book.

The first episode on the Rigi epitomizes the tone, setting, and characteristic action of the novel. The parody is set in motion by the opening lines: "On the 10th of August, 1880, at the fabled hour of sunset, so much belauded by Joanne's and Baedeker's Guide-Books, a thick, yellow fog, rendered more puzzling by a whirling snow-storm, enveloped the summit of the Rigi (*Regina Montium*)" (*TA*, 91). Tartarin suddenly appears from below, an apparition from the storm with "a cross-bow on its shoulder, and the casque of an archer of the middle ages on its head" (*TA*, 92), carrying, in addition, full Alpine equipment, although there is a railway to the summit and a luxury hotel once there. He is, naturally, astonished at coming upon the huge hotel, where tourists wait in boredom for the glorious view that seems forever blocked. After dinner, through sheer warmth and energy of personality, he gets the guests to dance, and boredom, isolation, and inhibition momentarily drop away from them. The next morning they all awake eagerly to see the sunrise on the Rigi, but the "thick, opaque yellow fog" persists and vision never comes. They themselves, however, constitute an absurd and pitiful spectacle:

> They were obliged to give up all hope of seeing the beautiful effects described by the guide-books. On the other hand, the heterodox costumes of the dancers of the night before, hurriedly aroused from sleep, were displayed as in a magic lantern, ludicrous and eccentric; for shawls, counterpanes, even the curtains of the beds which they had occupied were worn. Beneath the varied head-dresses —silk or cotton caps, hoods, toques, night-caps—were scared, puffed faces, the heads of shipwrecked people on an island in the open sea, on the watch for a sail in the offing with all the intentness of gaze of which their widely open eyes were capable.
>
> And nothing—all the time nothing!
>
> Nevertheless, some of them in an access of good will made believe to distinguish the peaks from the belvedere. [TA, 119]

On this occasion, at least, Tartarin gets the point of the scene quicker than most: "A regular humbug, qué this Rigi sunrise!" (TA, 120). His own earlier cry of "nothing" is now the anticlimactic revelation shared by everyone, including the author.

Among all the gamesmen in the novel, Tartarin remains the noblest figure; he is more genuinely imaginative, courageous, warm, and vivacious than the rest of the tourists, more decent and human than the fanatical anarchists. Nevertheless, to him as much as anyone else Daudet persistently denies heroic fulfillment. The ironies of his situation are unremitting: the first climb up the Rigi is ridiculous; during a second expedition, this time up the Jungfrau, he displays great coolness in awaiting rescue while hanging in a crevasse, but only because he is under the delusion that the accident is another fake adventure stage managed by the Swiss. On this occasion he again achieves ironic apotheosis. As he sits on the summit, "[Tarascon] flag in hand, superb, facing the public [tourists in the hotel below] . . . without his perceiving it—by one of those spectral images frequent at the tops of mountains, the result of sun, and of mist which was rising behind him—a gigantic Tartarin was outlined on the sky, enlarged and shortened, the beard bristling out of the comforter, like one of the Scandinavian deities, which tradition presents to us as enthroned in the midst of the clouds" (TA, 191). The protagonist here achieves the gigantism of heart's desire but, at the same time, never escapes from Daudet's mocking frame of reality, which provides a relentless duality of point of view. Elsewhere he describes Tartarin and a friend watching a Swiss fête from the bay of a road tunnel overlooking the scene and comments pointedly: "A truly fairy scene it was, framed in the cold, smooth granite of the tunnel walls" (*TA*, 135).

Tartarin undertakes a last expedition up Mont Blanc in full awareness that the climb is "real," but now, at the crucial moment, "in the agony of fear" (*TA*, 226), cuts the rope when he thinks his companion has fallen and will drag him to his death. His companion also cuts the rope, which is, in fact, wedged between two rocks, both men slide down the mountain on their backsides, leave the area in shame, but return to Tarascon and brazen it out with the help of imagination. In short, the culminating episode of the book (Daudet entitles this chapter portentously—albeit ambiguously—"The Catastrophe") is nothing more or less than a scene of wild farce. The mountain-climbing tales, like the rest of Tartarin's adventures, never finally move beyond parody.

What Daudet denies to Tartarin he is, in effect, denying to himself. Regardless of the specific parodic content of individual adventures, Tartarin remains a regional figure, reflecting Daudet's ambivalent view of his own region, his own past, and, inevitably, his own self as a creation of both. Murray Sachs has noted that Daudet's quality of simultaneous engagement and distancing began very early in life. He quotes Daudet's recollection of himself on the occasion of his brother's death, when his father cried out dramatically, "He's dead, he's dead!": "My first self wept and the second thought: 'What a perfect cry! How fine it would be in the theatre!' I was fourteen years old. That horrible duality has often set me to thinking. Oh! that terrible second self always calmly seated while the other is up, acting, living, suffering, struggling! That second self I have never been able to get drunk, or make cry, or put to sleep! And how well he does see! and how he does mock!"[15] Something of this mockery may be attributable to the general nature of Provençal personality. Tartarin himself has moments (for example, his dual reaction to the assertion that the William Tell story is fraudulent) when he alternates rapidly between committed belief and "the comic side of the question" (*TA*, 131). Daudet speaks of "Provençal eyes, always retaining in their facile emotion a trace of farce or raillery" (*TA*, 133). Clearly his ambivalence had its origin early and from complex causes, but it was reinforced by his movement to Paris from his regional home. This move enhanced the inevitable distancing of change and dislocation and heightened the already conflicting attitudes in the encounter between boulevard sophistication and memory of the lost world of childhood, whose naive ardor and vivid dreams nostalgia made even more intense. The *Tartarin* series is the important literary by-product of this encounter. Like much of the best regional writing, it finds in the mock-heroic mode the only possible vehicle for incompatible values and feelings in sharp and unresolved tension. The region, in turn, constitutes a setting in which heroic illusions can be dramatically "placed," given credible and substantial existence within an ironic frame of physical remoteness and authorial distance. Regional writing is a particularly important strand of American literature, and it is to it that we must now turn to pursue further its identification with mock-heroic narrative.

Heroics in a Lost Land: Mark Twain and American Regionalism

One of the most perceptive criticisms of Mark Twain's work is that of his lifelong friend William Dean Howells in the *North American Review* of February 1901. In this essay Howells describes Twain as a writer of the American West, a creature of conditions. "He found himself placed in them and under them," writes Howells,

> so near to a world in which the natural and primitive was obsolete, that while he could not escape them, neither could he help challenging them. The inventions, the appliances, the improvements of the modern world invaded the hoary eld of his rivers . . . and while he was still a pioneer, a hunter, a trapper, he found himself confronted with the financier, the scholar, the gentleman. They seemed to him, with the world they represented, at first very droll, and he laughed. Then they set him thinking . . . and he thought over the whole field. . . . When they had not their answers ready, without accepting the conventions of the modern world as solutions or in any manner final, he laughed again, not mockingly but patiently, compassionately. Such, or something like this, was the genesis and evolution of Mark Twain.

This laughter Howells describes elsewhere as tinged "with a suggestion of that resentment which youth feels when the disillusion from its trust and hope comes."[16]

This paragraph is rich in implications. In the first place, Howells is describing the central scenario of Mark Twain's writing: the sharp confrontation of one society, one set of values, one point of view with that which is markedly different. The plot of a Twain book almost always involves a militant invasion: the innocent goes to Europe, the tenderfoot travels west, the older man returns to a changed Mississippi River, Huck goes down the river into the slaveholding South, the Duke and Dauphin board the raft, the Yankee violently attacks medieval England, the freethinking Pudd'nhead Wilson comes to Dawson's Landing, Joan of Arc enters the venal world of French politics, and, of course, the Mysterious Stranger drops in on Eseldorf—one could extend the list almost indefinitely.

Equally important, Howells, in his *North American Review* essay, puts his finger on the duality of point of view or double vision in Mark Twain's writing. In its primary form this double vision manifests itself in the differing points of view of the invader and the world he invades. In a more complex fashion it involves an ambivalent relation between the author and even his most sympathetic characters. In Twain's boy stories, for example, the point of view of boyhood is rendered with great fidelity yet we are never allowed to forget the fact of adulthood. Indeed, it is our awareness of adulthood that gives these stories their full meaning. As he himself said in a well-known comment: "I have never written a book for boys; I wrote for grown-ups who have *been* boys."[17] Involved in two worlds, Twain, as Howells notes, can fully subscribe to neither and becomes the most ambiguous figure in his own fictions.

We have not, however, exhausted the implications of Howells's comment. In linking Twain with a remote area of America, Howells implies that he is a regional writer. According to Howells, the regional writer is emotionally and imaginatively involved with a natural and primitive world whose obsolescence he intellectually acknowledges and may, indeed, even approve. *Life on the Mississippi*, for example, celebrates the earlier years of the river in the first part of the book and glorious nineteenth-century civilization in the second. Double vision is endemic to the regional impulse. The regionalist describes with loving attention to fact and detail—with, indeed, a desire to *re*-create for an ignorant present—a time and age which he well knows cannot and does not any longer exist. As Twain wrote concerning his articles on piloting later incorporated into *Life on the Mississippi:* "I am the only man alive that can scribble about the piloting of that day . . . it is about the only new subject I know of."[18] Twain implies that, paradoxically, the newness of his subject is the very measure of its obsolescence; its appeal is not to our sense of the present but to our desperate need to remember things past. He turned to writing about the Mississippi for the same essential reason that Carroll turned to nonsense, Kenneth Grahame to the English country house environment, and Daudet to Provence. The subject could be made into something viable as a contemporary literary form and, at the same time, it could be used to reflect his profound involvement with the heroic myths closest to his own background and imagination.

Twain and other American regionalists respected the aesthetic standards of literary realism and shaped their work in accordance with these standards. They prided themselves on their faithful rendering of actual experience and carefully distinguished their own point of view from that of the romantic sentimentalist, which they used to reinforce the reader's sense of actuality. Mary N. Murfree, for example, in one of her stories of the Tennessee mountains, describes a cultivated outsider who looks at the backwoods community from "an ideal point of view." "He looked upon these people and their inner life only as picturesque bits of the mental and moral landscape," says Murfree: "It was an aesthetic and theoretical pleasure their contemplation afforded him." The outsider misses both the primitive savagery of the mountaineers and the moral purity of the heroine. In Twain's "Old Times on the Mississippi" the "outsider" is the youthful protagonist himself, initiated into the life of the river at the expense of his romantic point of view. He discovers the "very real and worklike" nature of piloting; he discovers, too, that empirical knowledge of the "signs" of the river destroys its picturesqueness. "No, the romance and beauty were all gone from the river," Twain wrote of his education. "All the value any feature of it had for me now was the amount of usefulness it could furnish toward compassing the safe piloting of a steamboat" (12:47, 80). In *Roughing It*, as critics have noted, a similar process initiates the greenhorn into the hard realities of western living. While Twain was writing "Old Times," Howells admonished him to "stick to actual fact and character in the thing, and give things in *detail*."[19] During his fifteen years with the *Atlantic Monthly* Howells was to give similar advice to many regional writers.

At the same time, Howells, Twain, and others found in regional literature a repository of feelings and values that they could not locate in the contemporary world. The regional setting, for all its fidelity to factual detail, is still the magic wonderland of dream transformation, full of moral, spiritual, and imaginative possibilities for the protagonist. Howells defined with great precision the regionalist strategy in his comments on what he called the "spiritual" realism of the Norwegian writer Bjornstjerne Bjornson: "The facts are stated with perfect ruggedness and downrightness when necessary, but some dreamy haze seems still to cling about them, subduing their hard outlines and features like the tender light of the slanting Norwegian sun on the craggy Norwegian headlands."[20] The regional setting (if not a distinct provincial scene such as Daudet's Tarascon) is usually isolated and remote, located in the past or a vestige of the past in the present, in any case free from the Victorian burden of time: Bjornson's Norwegian fiords, Murfree's Tennessee mountains, the rural New England of Sarah Orne Jewett or Alice Brown, or the small town, the raft, and the river of Mark Twain. These regional settings are versions of pastoral, incorporating many of the qualities of the more general Victorian symbols of garden and island so familiar to idyllic poetry of the period—Tennyson's Avalon or Land of the Lotos-Eaters, the Innisfree of early Yeats or the retired haunts of Arnold's Scholar Gipsy, again to mention but a few examples. In America regionalism comes at the end of a long tradition of pastoralism so ably traced by Leo Marx in *The Machine in the Garden*.

The characters who inhabit this regional world are by no means all good, noble, and true; most, in fact, are limited, narrow-minded, often cruel and vengeful, and they are treated with unsparing severity by the better writers. Nevertheless, it is the habitat of the quixotic hero just as surely as through the looking-glass is the habitat of Alice; it is the place where he finds freedom and adventure, the place where the qualities he embodies can be made literally conceivable and, what is more important, imaginatively compelling. At the same time, these qualities can be ironically limited not only by the nature and actions of the other characters in the fiction but also by the adult, responsible point of view of the author, who, as I have already noted, has left the region and identifies, in part at least, with the larger world beyond its boundaries.

Regionalism, in other words, has many of the qualities of nostalgic play that I have previously associated with Kenneth Grahame and Lewis Carroll. Though it is full of the particularity so dear to literary realism, it is nevertheless a partial turning away from what the Victorian writer knows to be mature realities. Alice Brown admits this with unusual candor in her introduction to *Meadow-Grass: Tales of New England Life*, a volume of short stories published in 1895. She writes that "we who are Tiverton born, though false ambition may have ridden us to market, or the world's voice incited us to kindred clamouring, have a way of shutting our eyes, now and then, to present changes, and seeing things as they were once, as they are still, in a certain sleepy yet altogether individual corner of country life."[21] Nostalgic pastoralism seems to originate, as Leo Marx has pointed out, "in a recoil from the pain and responsibility of life in a complex civilization."[22] The passage from *Meadow-Grass* describes this recoil with great precision, but it also suggests how the spasmodic and fugitive nature of recoil leads to the double vision of the regional writer: backward into the past with the momentarily shut eyes of memory; present and forward with the open eyes of empirical knowledge, eyes that are only too well aware of the changing surface of the world and the limited nature of man. The regional impulse, in short, like its concomitant mood of nostalgia, is complex in its "irresponsible" turning away from present truth. The best regionalists mock themselves as well as their protagonists by careful isolation of the object of nostalgia ("a certain sleepy . . . corner of country life") and by self-conscious authorial interventions and control of point of view.

Within their magic landscape the heroic protagonists of regional fiction fall into two rough categories: so-called "shiftless" figures, young people and occasionally adults who refuse to conform to the mores of the community; and older people who exist as lonely, misunderstood, and functionless anachronisms in a changing society, Rip Van Winkles who remember the values, traditions, and adventures of an earlier and more exciting time. The shiftless figures reject adult responsibility in favor of freedom. In *Meadow-Grass* Alice

Brown remarks about one of them that "such as he should never assume domestic relations, to be fettered with requirements of time and space. Let him rather claim maintenance from a grateful public, and live, like troubadours of old, ministrant to the general joy." Whatever their age, they are committed to the spirit of adventure in the face of relentlessly encroaching banality. Brown invokes the resultant conflict in a first story that clearly operates to keynote the rest of the volume. "We knew everything in those days, we aimless knights-errant with dinner pail and slate," she writes of her own childhood,

> the dry, frosty hollow where gentians bloom . . . the sunny banks where violets love to live. . . . At noon [school recess], we roved abroad into solitudes so deep that even our unsuspecting hearts sometimes quaked with fear of dark and lonesomeness; and then we came trooping back at the sound of the bell, untamed, happy little savages, ready to settle, with a long breath, to the afternoon's drowsy routine. Arrant nonsense that! the boundary of British America and the conjugation of the verb *to be!* Who that might loll away the hours upon a bank in silken ease, needed aught even of computation or the tongues? He alone had inherited the earth.[23]

The commitment to the lyric wanderings of childhood in this passage is characteristically undercut by an adult sensibility aware of the absurdity of the point of view it is espousing. These dual perspectives, however, do nothing to blur the central significance of the conflict described: the symbolic encounter of the free and natural child with school, his first and most benign engagement with an organized adult society that will impinge on him ever more threateningly. The passage from *Meadow-Grass* suggests immediately the mischievous games and controlled melodrama of *Tom Sawyer*, but it implies also the action of *Huckleberry Finn*, in which the shiftless figure is brought into fundamental confrontation with the most destructive cruelties of the adult world.

Central to all of Twain's work is the image of the child as heroic figure—child as *king*, we might say. The "prince and pauper," identical children playing both roles interchangeably—the prince as pauper, the pauper as prince—is a paradigm of Twain's fiction. There are echoes of it in all the pairings so characteristic of his work: cub and pilot; Tom and Huck; Huck and Jim; King Arthur and Hank Morgan; Joan of Arc the country girl and Joan the national leader (or Joan and the boy narrator in the novel); even Judge Driscoll, the social leader of Dawson's Landing, and Pudd'nhead Wilson, the maverick lawyer. The latter two, of course, like Arthur, Hank Morgan, Jim, and the river pilots, are not actually children, but they do embody the freedom and independence—the heroic possibilities—that are found at the top and bottom of society, among the all-powerful and the powerless, and nowhere in between. Driscoll and Wilson, significantly, are the only two members of the local freethinkers' organization. According to Twain, "Judge Driscoll could be a free-thinker and still hold his place in society, because he was the person of most consequence in the community, and therefore could venture to go his own way and follow out his own notions. The other member of his pet organization was allowed the like liberty because he was a cipher in the estimation of the public, and nobody attached any importance to what he thought or did" (16:40).

Even in its special regional setting, heroic activity exists only at the peripheries of society, never at its center, and such location limits its expression largely to gesture and games rather than actions that can in any way shape or redeem the world. Heroics are more affective and theatrical than socially *effective* efficacious, a fact that limits the moral claims of Twain's most sympathetic characters and should allow us to put some of his most contentious fictional episodes—the supreme example being the final chapters of *Huckleberry Finn*—in a more secure critical context.[24] For Twain there is a certain identity of role-playing among the most disparate forms of alienation. Critics have pointed out, for example, how in *Huckleberry Finn*, Colonel Sherburn's long speech attacking the cowardice of the average man is a violation of the thematic indirection forced on Twain by the dominant first-person point of view of the book. This, however, is scarcely the point; rather, a technical violation conceals a larger truth, namely, that in their courage, their personal integrity, and their vivid, energetic selfhood Sherburn and Huck are in a class by themselves—even though Sherburn has committed a vicious murder and Huck is a moral innocent.

To be sure, Twain longs for an environment in which the shiftless king will prevail. This is, in fact, the situation of *The Prince and the Pauper*, a book in which temporal remoteness and the fantasy of children's story serve as the magic looking-glass that restores the hero to his rightful place. Though not literally regional fiction, *The Prince and the Pauper* employs the central strategy of regionalism by creating an accurately rendered but remote past time in which heroic values can operate credibly. Although early manuscript fragments indicate that Twain first attempted to place the story in the late nineteenth century and then changed to a specific date in the 1530s, the final text simply begins: "In the ancient city of London, on a certain autumn day in the second quarter of the sixteenth century" (11:1). Elsewhere in the manuscript Twain made every effort to blur the exact age of his child heroes at the time of their adventures by similar elimination of precise temporal references. One invokes them and their world by neutralizing the temporal question, by avoiding the "real" world of present time. The child hero, like Alice in Wonderland, grows larger or smaller as the particular adventure demands; he exists as symbol before he lives in fact.

Having introduced his identical heroes from either end of the social spectrum, Twain first involves them in the purgation of false romance (that is, sentimental heroics) through an initiatory process similar to that which takes place in other works such as *Roughing It* and *Life on the Mississippi*. But this is initiation not into resigned acceptance of commonplace reality (some sort of worldly "maturation") but into more genuine and fundamental forms of heroic activity. At the beginning of *The Prince and the Pauper* both Tom Canty and Edward Tudor have absurdly romantic and inaccurate conceptions of how the other lives. One has wild fantasies about the princely life; the other longs for the freedom of the poor. They change clothes to realize their fantasies, and almost instantly the process of disenchantment begins. By the end of the first day Edward has been beaten and tormented by mobs. Tom learns that he will be shut up forever in a "gilded cage" where men are executed on the slightest whim of a ruthless king. "Turn where he would," writes Twain, "he seemed to see floating in the air the severed head and remembered face of the great Duke of Norfolk, the eyes fixed on him reproachfully. His old dreams had been so pleasant; but this reality was so dreary!" (11:33).

Such disillusionment, however, is by no means the final insight of the book; it is actually a beginning and involves only the early episodes. The bulk of *The Prince and the Pauper* takes place on the roads of rural England and describes the adventures of the unrecognized little king and his adult companion Miles Hendon as each of them fends off the cruelties of society and attempts to affirm his heroic identity. The child's claims are not even acknowledged by his friend, who thinks him mad. Hendon is a gay, brave, chivalric young man who has returned a penniless scarecrow from overseas wars to reclaim his title to ancestral estates. Both boy and youth are disinherited, both are, in effect, knights errant whose claims are derided by the world at large, and, most important, both display courage and moral decency in a world characterized chiefly—as it so often is in Twain—by savage laws and mob action. Meanwhile, in London the beggar boy Tom Canty demonstrates equal independence on the throne of England.

In the end, everything works out happily as personal and public fortune coalesce; the disinherited are restored to the social order, the kingdom freed of iniquity and left in the hands of the just and merciful. Nevertheless, in spite of all the historical apparatus Twain brings to bear, we are left with little doubt that the book is a fairy tale. "Lo, the lord of the Kingdom of Dreams and Shadows on his throne," says Hendon when he first sees his little friend in state (11:267). He has used this phrase earlier in the novel to describe what he thought was the fantasy world of his companion. It is now no longer literally applicable. Yet, like Hendon's astonishment, it lingers in the reader's mind, for we have been on a journey through "the Kingdom of Dreams and Shadows," a play world in which goodness and freedom not only exist but prevail. In contrast, Twain's other child knight errant is Joan of Arc, and she is burned at the stake for her claims, albeit compositional notes suggest how much Twain would have liked to save her by incorporating her, also, within a protective frame of fantasy.[25]

In the earliest manuscript fragments of *The Prince and the Pauper* Tom Canty is called Jim, the name of the Negro slave in *Huckleberry Finn*. The two books were written more or less together and clearly grew out of the same imaginative nexus.[26] When we first meet Huck, he is playing Sancho Panza to Tom Sawyer's Don Quixote—that is, he responds to Tom's bookish romanticism with a practical, pragmatic realism.[27] Huck's own journey begins with a withdrawal from society, but it also involves the abandonment of Tom's more superficial games. As Huck puts it after he has tried in vain to rub a genie out of an old tin lamp: "So then I judged that all that stuff was only one of Tom Sawyer's lies. I reckoned he believed in the A-rabs and the elephants, but as for me I think different. It had all the marks of a Sunday-school" (13:20). Here Twain, from Huck's strongly empirical point of view, explodes the entire play world of his earlier novel and, indeed, equates it with the adult conventions it was supposed to contravene. But Huck is purged of false romance only to enter a realm of more profound games where nostalgia encounters the central moral dreams of man.

In *Huckleberry Finn* the imaginative possibilities of childhood so often described by Victorian writers find ultimate realization in the creative moral imagination of the hero as he gropes toward the articulation of pity and love in the face of hostile society and even his own conscience. On the island, under the stars, down the river on the raft, time seems to stop, the burden of history to ease. From these retreats the heroic child, now a more authentic Quixote, armed with only the ultimate illusions, ventures forth to encounter the worst in society and in himself.

At the same time, we are always aware that Huck is a child. The first-person point of view is a far more subtle instrument than the heavy-handed commentary of Kenneth Grahame or Alice Brown, but, by its very authenticity, it continually reminds us of the inevitable limitations of Huck's perception and understanding. It is obviously more limited than that of the author, who treats Huck in many scenes with considerable irony. Even Huck's famous decision to "go to Hell" rather than turn Jim in to the authorities is a quixotic absurdity. In the light of our more sophisticated "adult" knowledge, he is jousting with windmills, though they are for him very real, his courage very touching, and his moral instincts sound. Certainly the characteristic ambivalence of mock-heroic makes resolution between fact and value almost impossible. In *Huckleberry Finn* Twain avoids the question by returning to the "boy's" world of historical romance from which Huck has escaped early in the novel. At this less profound level of play, the child is almost literally king, and fact and value can be reconciled as they are in the final pages of *The Prince and the Pauper*. But the reappearance of Tom Sawyer, the obvious gamesman, reminds us equally of the limited possibilities of this child's world in the larger context of reality.

A notebook entry made during the time Twain was writing his stories about children suggests that Cervantes's great hero had very different possibilities for him. He wrote in 1880: "Don Quixote is defended against Arabian Nights Supernaturals by Telephone Telegraph etc. & successfully."[28] Here, of course, is the germ of the *Connecticut Yankee*: the isolated, independent hero as an adult, the Victorian realist and believer in social progress who invades and attempts to destroy the "child's" world of an Arthurian England located somewhere in the vague past. Quixote in this case is not an anachronism but a progenitor. The initial pattern of the *Connecticut Yankee* is similar to that of the travel books such as *Innocents Abroad* and the second part of *Life on the Mississippi*, in which the brash outsider, representing a more advanced technological culture, challenges the pretensions of the past and celebrates present and future. Arthur and his fellow countrymen are everywhere described as "big children," "great simple-hearted creatures," who live in a vivid and imaginative but brutal nonsense world. "They were a childlike and innocent lot," says the Yankee, "telling lies of the stateliest pattern with the most gentle and winning naivete. . . . It was hard to associate them with anything cruel or dreadful; and yet they dealt in tales of blood and suffering with a guileless relish that made me almost forget to shudder" (14:19, 21, 111).

The Yankee, on the other hand, is the practical man of affairs, the inventor of "anything a body wanted," the rationalist who, as he himself admits, is "nearly barren of sentiment, I suppose—or poetry, in other words," the advocate of sound laws and good education (14:5). He has every hope of taking over and instituting vast changes in short order. The book, of course, turns out very differently, and, as its direction begins to waver, so does the role of the Yankee. There is an ambivalence from the very beginning: the Yankee is glib, overconfident, aggressive, aesthetically and intellectually limited; Arthur, Launcelot, and Galahad have "manliness . . . noble benignity and purity . . . majesty and greatness . . . and high bearing" (14:22). Most important, the opening description of what Twain called in a subtitle the

"Lost Land" is an invocation of the isolated and serene regional setting so common to the imagination of the age: "It was a soft, reposeful summer landscape, as lovely as a dream, and as lonesome as Sunday. The air was full of the smell of flowers, and the buzzing of insects, and the twittering of birds, and there were no people, no wagons, there was no stir of life, nothing going on" (14:10). As a Quixote of progress, the Yankee wants to transform or destroy this landscape, but this idea turns out to be even more absurd than anachronistic preservation. In fact, he ends up its victim, disillusioned in his plans for mankind and longing for the past that has been denied him. After his return to the nineteenth century, he describes himself as "a stranger and forlorn in that strange England, with an abyss of thirteen centuries yawning between me . . . and all that is dear to me, all that could make life worth the living" (14:449). He has, in other words, finally become the anachronistic Quixote, the nostalgic spokesman for a lost golden age in which love, illusions, and heroic activity are a possibility.

What he really yearns for is the world found so often in Twain's fiction. In the bulk of the novel, the Yankee and King Arthur play the conventional role of Twain's child heroes; they wander unrecognized through the countryside, persecuted by a cruel society, but attempting to aid other victims of that society. They act with courage, independence, and moral concern, though the king is hampered by corrupt aristocratic habits just as Huck is hampered by conscience. The shattered Yankee of the final scenes has, in effect, "grown up" by being forced to leave the past and come back into the present, and he is destroyed by his maturation. Beyond the looking-glass is the dimension of vital and heroic selfhood, but the journey back, transformation in reverse, may lead only to spiritual disaster. In the *Connecticut Yankee* Twain set out, with an adult hero, to affirm a real and positive present; by the end of the book his adult looks obsessively backward toward a more "youthful" state, and Twain has revealed to himself and the reader the despair that lurks just beyond the delicate balance of the mock-heroic mode. Like *Joan of Arc*, the *Connecticut Yankee* makes explicit some of the darker implications of the regional world of *Huckleberry Finn*.

The *Connecticut Yankee* violated the regional world in the name of progress and uncovered despair; *The Mysterious Stranger* violates the same world directly and blatantly in the name of despair. The drowsy and isolated little village, the "paradise . . . for boys," still sleeps "in peace in the deep privacy of a hilly and woodsy solitude where news from the world hardly ever came to disturb its dreams" (27:3–4); but the town is called "Eseldorf"—"Assville" it might be translated—and its children are craven rather than heroic in the face of the familiar social persecution. In *The Mysterious Stranger* transcendent power is achieved but only at the expense of moral vision—the "king" figure is not Don Quixote but Satan, who creates and destroys indiscriminately and at will. Eseldorf is, in fact, the play world of the Victorian imagination in ruins. With the later work of Mark Twain the limits of mock-heroic have again been reached.

More Recent Mock-Heroic
Narrative

Joyce's Epic Forgeries

The artist, he imagined, standing in the position of mediator between the world of his experience and the world of his dreams.

JAMES JOYCE
Stephen Hero

What do you think Vulgariano did but study with stolen fruit how cutely to copy all their various styles of signature so as one day to utter an epical forged cheque on the public for his own private profit.

JAMES JOYCE
Finnegans Wake

The Contexts of Mockery

James Joyce began his career under the influence of two still imaginatively potent but (from his point of view at least) failed or failing heroic traditions: a European romanticism, which he shared with Stendhal, Flaubert, Byron, and Henrik Ibsen, among others, and an Irish cultural and political mythology, which was the central dimension of his own particular nativity. Neither tradition could be dismissed as trivial, meaningless, or irrelevant; yet neither, he quickly became aware, could any longer be taken "straight" by someone with pretensions to becoming a serious "modern" writer. To salvage them (and the moral and imaginative values they represented) for personal and literary use required that they be recast within a new and more credible context. Like other writers we have examined in analogous situations, Joyce turned to the mock-heroic mode and, with his own special rigor and relentlessness, pursued its implications to the furthest dimensions of high art.

As early as his student essay "Drama and Life" (1900), Joyce had firmly in hand most of the basic assumptions that constitute the mock-heroic sensibility. These may be briefly summarized as follows: the banality of modern life provides no medium for heroic experience; time is a record of spiritual diminution and loss; simple nostalgia for the past is sentimental, foolish, and futile; empirical reality must be accepted as the basis of art; and some basis for a heroic dimension to life still exists and, in a proper context, can still be celebrated.[1]

The passage in Joyce's version pivots on the word "still" just as so many of Wallace Stevens's poems or Byron's *Don Juan* stanzas center on the word "yet." Beyond a certain point, Joyce refuses to follow the logic of his reductionism but rather, in his own fashion, turns back toward the partial recapture of what had seemed irrevocably lost, a recapture credible only within the full logic of the position already established—a logic that Joyce spent a lifetime exploring. Gone is a direct treatment of what he calls here "the world of faery"; gone, too, is "mistaken insistence" on the religious, moral, beautiful, and idealizing tendencies of art. The writer remains, nevertheless (in the phrase I have used as an epigraph to this chapter), in some very significant sense a "mediator between the world of his experience and the world of his dreams."[2] Mediation implies distancing from both, yet action inclusive of both toward some larger totality (not necessarily involving resolution) of point of view.

For Joyce, the most palpable model of the mediative artist was the later Ibsen, whom he describes in another early essay as uniting "with his strong, ample imaginative faculty a preoccupation with the things present to him" (CW, 101).[3] This same essay ("Catilina") argues that "the romantic temper, imperfect and impatient as it is, cannot express itself adequately unless it employs the monstrous or heroic" but that this attitude is no longer appropriate because "the breaking up of tradition, which is the work of the modern era, discountenances the absolute" (CW, 100). Joyce's Ibsen, in effect, is an ironist ("a method so calm, so ironical" [CW, 101]), and Joyce's attempt to reestablish "classicism" as an alternative to romanticism represents his own first important theoretical effort toward a comprehensive ironic method centrally focused around the notion of a classical temper "ever mindful of limitations" (SH, 78).

From Joyce's encounter with romanticism there emerges very early the outline of a complex position based upon a rage for order and primary form that, nevertheless, categorically refuses to move beyond the dimensions of material reality. Increasingly, he will both explore the possible limits of the empirical position and exploit its inherent ironies. For the romantic concern with "absolute types" (CW, 100), Joyce begins to work toward a concept of prototype in which the inexorable given of sensible figuration seems to be an imitation or copy of prior or primary forms. In his hands, however, this concept mocks itself on at least two levels: primary form can be experienced only through imitative manifestations so transformed as to be parodic; conversely, such form can be merely hypothesized from the classification and analysis of concrete particulars—it is a supreme fiction, in other words, without absolute validity. It is, in fact, as much the ironies of prototype as prototype itself that Joyce will reveal in the major novels, although finally and most important we are left with the simple fact of their coexistence.

Joyce's complex response to the problem of romanticism in the modern world was reinforced by the lessons he drew as a young man from Irish culture and what he called significantly the "sad comedy" of Irish politics (*CW*, 190). Irish history and literature in general revealed the same gap between hope, dream, vision, and reality and the same failure to effect some sort of reconciliation. Within a larger decline from the heroic period of the eighteenth century, Irish history manifested a relentless pattern of anticlimax: cycles of failure, disappointment, bungled schemes—"vicious cicles" as Joyce called them in *Finnegans Wake*, his later pun reflecting the corroborative insights into world history gleaned from a reading of Giovanni Battista Vico.[4] Irish heroes regularly betrayed their promise, not simply their heroic dreams or projections of themselves, but their very being or destiny as heroes. Oscar Wilde betrayed both. Even Charles Stewart Parnell, for Joyce the most authentic Irish hero, "falls" from his destined role, betrays and is betrayed (see *CW*, 223–28). Obvious enough, perhaps, but also worth mentioning is Joyce's immediate personal situation: the compelling but failed father, the repeated family moves in a cycle of declining prosperity and defeated hopes—a rhythm Joyce exploits when writing of the anticlimactic adventures of Stephen Dedalus.

His most searching comments, however, are reserved for fellow writer, the poet James Clarence Mangan, a personality in whom, like Wilde, the romantic temperament found expression within an Irish cultural context. Joyce's description of Mangan is explicitly tinged with comic irony; he becomes a figure both Rip Van Winkle and Chaplinesque: "In his strange dress—the high conical hat, the baggy trousers three times too big for his little legs, and the old umbrella shaped like a torch—we can see an almost comical expression of his diffidence" (*CW*, 181). As artist and as individual, Mangan represents for Joyce the supreme example of the failure to accommodate heroic dreams with reality. In him the chivalric tradition ends in pure subjective fantasy. Maturing only into comic eccentricity, he remains a vulnerable child who can neither fulfill nor abandon his dreams. Mangan's is the representative message of Irish culture and later nineteenth-century romanticism: "Love of grief, despair, high-sounding threats—these are the great traditions of the race of James Clarence Mangan, and in that impoverished figure, thin and weakened, an hysterical nationalism receives its final justification." Joyce goes on to make final summary judgment concerning Mangan and what he represents: "He is a romantic, a herald manqué, the prototype of a nation manqué, but with all that, one who has expressed in a worthy form the sacred indignation of his soul cannot have written his name in water" (*CW*, 186).

This final judgment, built around the syntactical balance of the compound sentence (again the ubiquitous "but" or "yet") adds a dimension of ambivalence to Joyce's portrait of Mangan that up to this point I have not sufficiently stressed. Even toward Irish political follies Joyce never directs the simple scorn that characterizes his response to the mere commercialism of modern English and Continental life. Certainly toward Mangan's quixotic position and all that it represents personally and culturally, Joyce has become a Cervantes: on one hand, well aware that the temporal present no longer accommodates traditional heroes, equally aware that the tempting heroics of solipsism offers no real solution to the problem of authenticity; on the other, celebrating Mangan's integrity, imagination, and spiritual nobility. Indeed, at moments in the essay of 1907 Mangan soars in Joyce's rhetoric to become an authentic hero-as-artist: "He was one of those strange abnormal spirits who believe that their artistic life should be nothing more than a true and continual revelation of their spiritual life, who believe that their inner life is so valuable that they have no need of popular support, and thus abstain from proffering confessions of faith, who believe, in sum, that the poet is sufficient in himself, the heir and preserver of a secular patrimony, who therefore has no urgent need to become a shouter, or a preacher, or a perfumer" (*CW*, 184). Seen from this point of view, Mangan almost resembles those other (earlier and non-Irish) heroes that Joyce celebrates in his critical writings, Giordano Bruno and William Blake. Indeed, the artist hero as "heir and preserver of a secular patrimony" has apparently assumed the failed father figure role or potentially might assume that role under the proper circumstances.

Does, then, such an assumption of role mean that the artist may be uniquely exempt from the pattern of decline and fall, absurdity and failure that Joyce saw everywhere as characteristic of modern life, exempt from the heroism "manqué" that Joyce was to make the substance of his own work? The exemption of the artist is, one imagines, the last temptation of the postromantic mind. The early critical writings do not adequately resolve this issue, and we can assume Joyce's own uncertainty at least through his rewriting of *Stephen Hero* into *A Portrait of the Artist as a Young Man*. Beyond the *Portrait* he simply refines and expands upon the implications of the mock-heroic mode he has established. Nevertheless, as *Dubliners* and many episodes in the later novels suggest, the failure of Irish history did, at the very least, sensitize Joyce to the problem of rhetoric—the potential or inevitable gap between language and reality—and this awareness of the vulnerability of the writer's primary tool or mode of action was in its own turn reinforced by his observations on the practice of romanticism. He describes the young Ibsen of *Catilina*, for example, as "an ardent romantic exulting in disturbance and escaping from all formal laws under cover of an abundant rhetoric" (*CW*, 99). The possible ironies of this position have steadily increasing resonance for Joyce and lead us inexorably to the predicament of Stephen Dedalus.

Stephen's "failures" in the *Portrait* and in *Ulysses* (if, indeed, they can be called failures, although it is scarcely more relevant to turn him into a humanistic success story) have been subject to wide discussion and some misinterpretation. They are not the signs of a sterile aesthete, albeit his language and attitudes are given by Joyce an Edwardian gloss appropriate both to the important dramatic context of *fin de siècle* and the larger theme of language itself in the novels. Nor are they something particular to him but not to Joyce; nor are they essentially attributable to his youth, however much his basically naive and youthful role is particularly relevant to the form of at least the *Portrait*. Rather, his abortive actions and inability to free himself from a sordid, banal, petty environment, his anticlimactic movement from experience to experience, and his endlessly vulnerable rhetoric are all manifestations of the context of mockery within which Joyce now securely places his heroic figure—in this case, his primary hero in specimen and prototype, the artist as God/creator, father/son. All three of Joyce's major novels return to the same problem first broached in his early critical essays: how to celebrate this prototype (and, in so doing, salvage the imaginative and spiritual possibilities of heroic experience) while avoiding violence to that intractable reality without which modern serious art is impossible. In the excellent phrase of a recent critic, Joyce's aesthetic task was to create "un absolu de possibles."[5] Each of the major novels offers an increasingly sophisticated solution to this problem as Joyce responds more and more comprehensively to its full implications. In other words, as the claims of the artist hero expand to fill all space, like God, so must the dimensions of mockery (on which, paradoxically, the heroic depends for its authentication) become steadily more inclusive.

Like all mock-heroic fictions, *A Portrait of the Artist as a Young Man* is "about" the problem that it has already "solved" (a better word is perhaps "contained") within the form of its own aesthetic presentation. This form—a modal modification of the boy's adventure story—was readily available to Joyce; it experienced wide popularity in the nineteenth century from Stendhal and Byron to Conrad. Fitzgerald would pick it up, and still later Wallace Stevens also used it effectively in "The Comedian as the Letter C," as I will demonstrate in commenting on that problematic poem. More recently, Nabokov has exploited its potential in *The Gift*, his own "portrait of the artist as a young man."

Central to the form is its categorical duality of perspective: a mature, detached narrator remains at an ironic distance from a youthful, ardent, and idealistic protagonist with whom he, nevertheless, strongly identifies, who may indeed represent (with *The Life of Henry Brulard* and *Portrait* the identification is obvious) an important version of his own self with selections from his own biography. In the *Portrait* the mature narrator no longer plays so explicit a role. Between *Stephen Hero* and the later book obvious editorial intrusions have been excised or complexly blended with Stephen's voice, and the narrator is apparent largely by inference in those dimensions of the novel which suggest a wider perspective than that of the protagonist—apparent, that is, only insofar as the novel aesthetically contains or holds in tension that duality which the protagonist cannot adequately resolve. Or, as the best critic of Joyce's narrative methods puts it: "The last—that is, most recent—stage of Stephen's development as an artist is presented through the narration, not in the narrative."[6] Such a carefully crafted duality invites us to avoid any thematic resolution that involves only one pole of the duality or even some one compromised point "in between." Rather, our reading must incorporate both at once as the meaning of the fiction, a total view of experience unresolved and unresolvable—"between" here as in *Don Juan* implying only a mediative stance that limits the claims of both. In other words, Joycean irony, like the irony of the mock-heroic mode in general, is fundamentally inclusive rather than exclusive. L. A. Murillo has described the irony of the *Portrait* as "directed more to the balance our apprehension is to achieve between the elements offered for our contemplation than a contrast between what is expressed and what is implied."[7]

From the opening chapters of the *Portrait*, the relentless quest of Stephen Dedalus for heroic authenticity is counterbalanced with equal rigor by the mockery generated by two important dimensions of his experience: the unyielding opacity to heroics of empirical reality, the medium of actual life in present time; and the even larger problem, especially for the prospective artist hero, of the inauthenticity of language as an ordering principle, the fact that language is no more an absolute or a path to absolutes than any other human construction. This is not to say that Stephen, as we observe him in the course of two different novels, is not partially successful in a process of self-realization—in his imaginative quest, so to speak, for fundamental identity as the expression of personality and type. But mockery remains a constant dimension of experience. Thus Stephen moves from a less to a more comprehensive realization of role, yet even his serial movement reveals the parodic nature of role as Joyce, by this time in his life, has come to conceive of it. In other words, his movement toward authenticity remains always within contexts of irony which legitimize the heroic quest while destroying its absolute basis. Only within a larger inauthenticity can Stephen achieve authenticity as a hero.

Stephen's problem in the *Portrait* and *Ulysses* (of which he becomes more and more self-consciously aware) is not simply one of vocation, although vocation is its immediate and obvious manifestation. It is, in fact, the more basic one (at least for the potential writer hero) of finding an absolute relation between words and things or, assuming there is no such relation, of finding within language, the medium of his work, some means of acknowledging the claims of both. His personal failures, based largely on the persistent failure in actual life of heroic roles self-consciously played from social and literary models, are entwined from the beginning with the larger issue of the authenticity of language. For the young Stephen, a gap opens quickly between a world of imagination and words—expansive, comforting, orderly—and the empirics of pain, weakness, sordidness, and banality.

Indeed, the pattern of the *Portrait* is set in its first few lines; a fairy-tale opening ("Once upon a time and a very good time it was") is immediately and implicitly mocked by the "hairy face" of the father telling the tale.[8] Should we, in this case, have missed the mockery of juxtaposition, Joyce offers us in *Finnegans Wake* more explicit versions: "Eins within a space and a wearywide space it wast" (*FW*, 152); or the even more devastating: "Once upon a drunk and a fairly good drunk it was and the rest of your blatherumskite!" (*FW*, 453). Always for Stephen the gap between imaginative and actual experience is at the center of his youthful life. His passionate desire for Mercedes, which makes him different from others—his desire "to meet in the real world the unsubstantial image which his soul so constantly beheld" (*PA*, 65)—has far more significance than its dramatic context as the romantic yearnings of a schoolboy might suggest; it is the major issue of the novel, indeed of all Joyce's major novels. Mercedes is Stephen's Dulcinea, the goddess (albeit mock or fictive) who activates the heroic quest and represents its spiritual center.

Rhetoric is the domain of value, order, mastery, expansion, and grandiosity; life, the place of disorder, smallness, timidity, and fear. Through the words he has written on the flyleaf of his geography, Stephen expands into "*Ireland/Europe/The World/The Universe*," while at the same time feeling "small and weak" (*PA*, 15–17). The dichotomy is clearly symbolic of his unresolved and unresolvable problem as human being and artist. His more fundamental encounters with both the promise and the vulnerability of language come, however, when he begins seriously to audition for those heroic roles which form the basis of the rhetorical systems of his inheritance. These roles are, respectively, the redeemer of wrongs ("that was what Peter Parley's Tales about Greece and Rome were all about" [*PA*, 53]), the romantic lover and adventurer on the Dumas or Napoleonic model, the priest or follower of Saint Francis Xavier, and, most important, the artist or Dedalian figure, Stephen's encounter with the implications of his own name. I do not mean to suggest that this list is inclusive. After he wins the prize money, for example, Stephen plays the heroic father as a way, similar to the strategy of rhetoric, of trying "to build a breakwater of order and elegance against the sordid tide of life without him and . . . the powerful recurrence of the tides within him" (*PA*, 98). And, obviously, the role of Irish cultural and political leader is always present, if only in the strength of Stephen's rejection and the vehement debates with his friends as to its absurdity. A certain absurdity is the point about all these roles; they are all less ways of ordering reality than of denying its claims. "Useless" is Stephen's important insight after the prize money fiasco (*PA*, 98). Reality pours over the "breakwater" of order, dissolving heroic pretensions and laying bare the limitations of the imaginative and verbal structures on which the heroics have been based.

Joyce's treatment in the *Portrait* of the heroics of Catholicism can perhaps be taken as exemplary of all the roles for which Stephen auditions. Significantly, we experience these heroics largely as a self-contained and internally perfect system of rhetoric. At the center of the novel, for page after page through the entirety of Chapter 3, we are exposed, like Stephen, to the syntactical rhythms and intricate logic of the retreat sermons. On Joyce's part, these sermons constitute one of those extraordinary, self-conscious rhetorical imitations which in the later novels become explicitly parodic. Stephen's response is to attempt to create in life a ritual of order parallel to the verbal structure on which it is based: "Sunday was dedicated to the mystery of the Holy Trinity, Monday to the Holy Ghost, Tuesday to the Guardian Angels, Wednesday to Saint Joseph, Thursday to the Most Blessed Sacrament of the Altar, Friday to the Suffering Jesus, Saturday to the Blessed Virgin Mary" (*PA*, 47). This is life lived imaginatively, heroically, on the pattern of literary and religious models—and, in the process, made unreal.

Joyce, we must observe, here as elsewhere, carefully shapes his own rhetoric into an imitation or mirror of Stephen's moods and, in so doing, further emphasizes the subjectivity of verbal structures. Even though the *Portrait's* occasional naturalism mocks the varieties of fine writing that abound in the book, it is in turn largely used self-consciously by Joyce as a mark of Stephen's periodic encounters in bitterness and disgust with his immediate environment. Like the later novels, the *Portrait* is already, in effect, a mere stylistic compendium in which Joyce himself authenticates the act of using language only by the ceaseless exposure of its inauthenticity as the record of final truth.

The rhythm of plot in the *Portrait* is from anticlimax to anticlimax, each one exposing the vulnerability to life of heroic roles on which particular imaginative structures have been based. Face to face finally with its actual life-denying qualities, which he refuses to accept, Stephen has sharp insight into the fictionality of the priestly role, indeed, into its seductive appeal to him precisely on that basis: "How often had he seen himself as a priest wielding calmly and humbly the awful power of which angels and saints stood in reverence! His soul had loved to muse in secret on this desire. He had seen himself, a young and silentmannered priest, entering a confessional swiftly, ascending the altarsteps, incensing, genuflecting, accomplishing the vague acts of the priesthood which pleased him by reason of their semblance of reality and of their distance from it" (PA, 158). As the last line of this passage makes clear, heroic power is not really wielded; the priestly role, its implications reinforced in Stephen's imaginary version, is an extension of childhood fantasy games and shares in their essential isolation and impotence: "If ever he had seen himself celebrant it was as in the pictures of the mass in his child's massbook, in a church without worshippers, save for the angel of the sacrifice, at a bare altar and served by an acolyte scarcely more boyish than himself. In vague sacrificial or sacramental acts alone his will seemed drawn to go forth to encounter reality: and it was partly the absence of an appointed rite which had always constrained him to inaction whether he had allowed silence to cover his anger or pride or had suffered only an embrace he longed to give" (PA, 159).

Taken together and in addition to their immediate dramatic context, these passages tell us a good deal about the essential nature of heroic role as it manifests itself in the figure of Stephen Dedalus: in particular, its rootedness in childhood needs (the self's early "desire of omnipotence" in the face of actual weakness) and those vaguer and even more basic expressions of personality whose manifestations in fiction have been explored by Marthe Robert;[9] its realization as an act of the imagination; and especially its divorce from any authentic vehicle in the external world, whose characteristic, rather, is the "absence of an appointed rite." In his own awareness, on this occasion at least, of "their semblance of reality and their distance from it," Stephen makes the crucial distinction between heroic acts and acts in life, and this distinction, enormously elaborated but scrupulously upheld, remains the fundamental constant of Joyce's work. Equally significant is Stephen's awareness that loss of role means loss of language. As the priest talks to him about the possibility of a religious vocation, he recalls from the past the conversation of other priests and his own growing sense of their inadequacy as role models: "Lately some of their judgements had sounded a little childish in his ears and had made him feel regret and pity as though he were slowly passing out of an accustomed world and were hearing its language for the last time" (PA, 156).

In rejecting a specific call to the Catholic priesthood, Stephen does not, of course, abandon his will to godlike power or his fundamental commitment to "sacrificial or sacramental acts." By the end of the novel, he has simply become convinced that he can better realize the role of priest hero in the person of the artist, a figure whom, in euphoric fantasy, he now explicitly conceives of as "a priest of eternal imagination, transmuting the daily bread of experience into the radiant body of everliving life" (*PA*, 221). As the rhetoric associated with him here (and elsewhere in the later pages) suggests, however, Stephen's final and correct choice of heroic vocation in no way exempts him from the irony with which Joyce insistently treats such vocation. If anything, as the heroic claims grow more inclusive, so do the possibilities of substantial counterstatement. In this case, the very ambiguities of the Dedalian prototype—the "artificer," the builder of self-contained and containing labyrinths—will reinforce the ironies that Joyce has already located in other heroic models and that hover tantalizingly around the concept of "transmutation." Nor can we ignore Stephen's growing and increasingly self-conscious identification with fallen Satan, that other priestly artificer who engages in the gallant absurdity of playing God. In his assumption of the mantle of Satan, Stephen is perhaps an imitation of an imitation, a fraudulent version of a fraud, himself worthy of the name of Shem (Sham) that Joyce bestowed on a later artist hero. Nevertheless, at the end of the *Portrait* it is under Dedalian and Satanic aegis that Stephen seeks "new adventure" toward fated destiny, "the end he had been born to serve and had been following through the mists of childhood and boyhood" (*PA*, 169).

I will defer a full analysis of the possible ironies in the role of artist as hero until my discussion of Joyce's later novels, where the question can be pursued in the light of Joyce's own developing insights and his aesthetic response to them. Let me only add at this time, as a final comment on the *Portrait*, that the problem of linguistic authenticity, broached, as we have noted, on the opening pages, is treated by Joyce with further complexity later in the novel. I refer not simply to the fact that Stephen's awareness of new vocation comes to us clothed (as critics have often pointed out) in the rhetoric of Edwardian romanticism, or that Joyce continues rigorously to juxtapose such rhetoric with its deliberately vulgar and coarse counterpart so that language remains associated with self-excluding environments or "worlds," or that he uses such Sancho Panza mockers as Lynch (later Buck Mulligan in *Ulysses* and Shaun in *Finnegans Wake*) to puncture brutally Stephen's poses and rhetorical flights. These are significant points, but I want rather to draw attention to the paradox of language in which Stephen is caught without resolution. On one hand, there is his dependence on language as human being and especially as artist, indeed, his almost intoxicated commitment to language as a pure structure of internal relations, with aesthetic and psychological but only the most meager empirical reference. While walking toward the strand, Stephen makes this point himself, first drawing forth "a phrase from his treasure" to describe the day, then ruminating in general about his fascination with words—their "rhythmic rise and fall, the poise and balance of the period itself" (PA, 166). His thoughts on this occasion express something of the compensatory power of language as an ordering principle. Stephen's "treasure" is abundant and, in its way, potent and coherent.

On the other hand, Stephen's thoughts also expose a contrary dimension of the language paradox: the divorce of language from external reality, its life-denying quality. They reflect the message that Joyce drew from romanticism and Irish history concerning the seductiveness of rhetorical systems and their distance (more or less) from reality, both the "sensible world" and something totally opaque to language, the "infrahuman." In the later pages of the Portrait, Stephen occasionally wearies of his endless attempts to fictionalize life (at one point he has a style for every neighborhood during his walks around Dublin) and momentarily becomes aware that he walks "in a lane among heaps of dead language" (PA, 176–80). As an Irish writer, moreover, he senses that English in whatever style can, for him at least, never be authentic nor, in its Irish version, anything but debased. The statue of the national poet of Ireland seems to him merely a droll imposture ("a Firbolg in the borrowed cloak of a Milesian" [PA, 180]), his friend Cranly's Irish drawl simply "an echo of the quays of Dublin given back by a bleak decaying seaport, its energy an echo of the sacred eloquence of Dublin given back flatly by a Wicklow pulpit" (PA, 195). In other words, even regardless of the theoretical limits of language, Stephen, as an alien figure living in a cultural twilight, largely rattles around in the graveyard of its forms. His own various rhetorical flourishes are as anachronistic (at the very least) as the "monkish learning" from which he doggedly tries to build an aesthetic theory (PA, 180). Already in the Portrait the figure of the artist as the Quixote of language begins to emerge sharply.

The paradox of language leads only to another with even wider implications for Joyce's work and, in general, much nineteenth- and twentieth-century literature: the paradoxical role of the artist hero. Attempting, as he does, to enforce the most visionary of claims with the most problematic of weapons, the artist is vulnerable to the full mockery of reality, while remaining the single figure in modern culture who might credibly at least seem to order reality in heroic terms, a figure, one might add, who (if only in default of others) has not been hesitant to arrogate to himself such a role. As the subject of literature, the paradox of authorship can be fully dealt with only in the ironic mode, particularly in some version of the mock-heroic that I have been examining. In the later pages of the Portrait, Stephen begins to show flashes of an ironic point of view, his most useful insight being the well-known response he makes to Cranly's suggestion that he might become a Protestant: "I said that I had lost the faith . . . but not that I had lost selfrespect. What kind

of liberation would that be to forsake an absurdity which is logical and coherent and to embrace one which is illogical and incoherent?" (*PA*, 243–44).
The role that Stephen wants to play is that of a "being apart in every order"
(*PA*, 161), a definition (more than he realizes) of the fully committed ironic
stance. In any case, we must, at this point, move to a consideration of the
logical and coherent absurdities that Joyce himself goes on to create after his
first important work in the mock-heroic mode had both celebrated and chal-
lenged the possibility of a heroic art. Joyce's problem is essentially that of
Stephen: the creation of a credible rhetoric of escape, freedom, adventure,
and new order. In more than one way, such a creation would be the supreme
act of artifice, the prototypal task brought up to date.

Stephen as Lapwing

Having followed Stephen so far into his young life, it is critically tempting to
pursue him through one further adventure in another novel. I refer to his
encounter in *Ulysses* at 2:00 P.M. on 16 June 1904 with the Platonists in the
National Library of Ireland. As well as any in *Ulysses*, the episode suggests, in
general, Joyce's developing sense of the nature of human role and, in particular, the status of what Wallace Stevens will call the "central man" or hero, the
artist as father/creator/God. In accordance with the practice of *Ulysses* as a
whole, the episode is modeled on an equivalent adventure in *The Odyssey*, in
this case, Odysseus's navigation of the gap between Scylla and Charybdis. Its
style is that for which *Ulysses* is best known: stream-of-consciousness, in-
terspersed with monologue, dialogue, and occasional brief narrative interventions.

First, however, a general word about stream-of-consciousness is probably
in order. It has been too exclusively associated with *Ulysses*, and recent criticism is correct in directing our attention to Joyce's intrusive rhetorical parodies, which make up much of the bulk of the book and, on occasion, shape
the streams themselves into explicit parody.[10] Nevertheless, these distinctions can be overstressed. I speak of "explicit parody" because Joyce finds in
the overall technique of stream-of-consciousness an extraordinarily subtle
and comprehensive method for displaying the self's imagined roles and
dreams as a reflection of some prototypal original, with the moment-by-moment existential situation of the self remaining at a further imitative distance
from the original—distant, that is, even from dreams. In effect, Joyce's explicitly parodic streams (Gerty MacDowell's romantic vaporings are the most
obvious example) only make explicit what is implicit in the apparently more
naturalistic and "authentic" streams of Stephen and Bloom in the early chapters. In other words, at the empirical or "real" human level, the self, in Joy-

cean terms, constantly puts on a "performance," a comic imitation, conscious and unconscious, of imagined models and, even more expansively, of fundamental prototype. Although the emphasis may change in Joyce's later books from the willed ego games of the *Portrait* to the rhythm of prototype in *Finnegans Wake*, the fact of imitation does not change nor does an important corollary: the inauthenticity of certain (nevertheless) crucial dimensions of human experience. Joyce's inclusive mind merely moves from imitation as romantic and nostalgic role-modeling (his nineteenth-century inheritance from realism) to imitation as it is a function of human "being." Such a shift, however, creates the need for new devices of mockery, lest the ontological thrust turn toward straight mythology and, in so doing, violate the truth of his vision. Within the Joycean canon, the parodic stream-of-consciousness of *Ulysses* constitutes the crucial bridge between Stephen's self-conscious role-playing in the *Portrait*, recorded by a detached and "older" narrator, and the prototypal, encyclopedic world of *Finnegans Wake*, recorded by means of a special language in which double or triple entendre exists at the level of virtually every word—the word itself thus finally spatialized into the conflicting perspectives that express Joyce's mock-heroic vision.

In short, it is a constant of Joyce's work that our existence remains a perpetual and inevitable parody of our fictions and our essence—essentiality itself being without absolute existence in what is finally a void or "chaosmos" and, in fact, the supreme fiction of Joyce the author. In his hands, stream-of-consciousness lays bare the self's performance as a collage of mutually mocked and mocking games; it internalizes the multiple perspective that was characteristic of earlier mock-heroic, including Joyce's own *Portrait*. Similarly, the even deeper hallucinatory materials of the Circe chapter in *Ulysses* all the more blatantly reinforce our sense of relentless juxtaposition: bringing into sharp dramatic form the self's heroic prototype while reminding us that psychic obsessions are also (like Stephen's overwhelming sexual needs in the *Portrait*) the internal equivalent of life's external physical limitations. Basic psychological drives and needs are, at once, central, monumental, spiritually and imaginatively creative and comic, banal, limiting, and degrading. Concerning Leopold Bloom, Joyce wrote to Frank Budgen: "I see him from all sides, and therefore he is all-around in the sense of your sculptor's figure."[11] Joyce's comment reminds us again that the only final perspective in *Ulysses* (indeed, in all his major works) can be a totality of perspectives, an aggregate (not a resolution) of juxtapositions.

Extending beyond the sharply localized physical selves of the main characters in *Ulysses* are the metaphysical fictions of these selves: their willed and imaginative performances (what we might call their aesthetic existence, including the possibility of actual artistic composition) and their prototypal referents, which are simply further abstractions, also derived, in their own fashion, from the willed organization of particulars into formal categories. The chapter involving Stephen and the Platonists in the National Library to which I have already alluded is only the most obvious episode in which the entire substance of the material explores the nature and significance of performance. Marilyn French has noted that Scylla and Charybdis is strongly dramatic in texture, with Stephen as much as Joyce the dramatist. According to French, "In this chapter Stephen is so busy composing, watching, and manipulating that it is possible to imagine him composing the chapter itself in which he appears, making himself his own grandfather or at least creator."[12] In a book of performances, it is his greatest, comparable in its own way to Bloom's later encounter in the tavern with the Cyclopean citizen. Stephen, in effect, directs, writes, and plays the principal role in a dramatic production which involves, on one level, himself and those with whom he is immediately speaking, on another, Shakespeare as person, player, playwright—the central performer in his own extended life performance, now offered to us secondhand by someone who identifies with him in complex ways and sees himself as imitator.

What we might call Stephen's "Hamlet" (character and play) is, in fact, a mock-heroic version of the two romantic Hamlets invoked early in the Scylla chapter—that of Goethe ("the beautiful ineffectual dreamer who comes to grief against hard facts") and that of Mallarmé (*"il se promène, lisant au livre de lui-même"*).[13] Stephen's Hamlet at once sharpens the quixotic encounter between dream and fact and exploits beyond Mallarmé the concept of selfhood as a book to be written as well as read. The opening pages quickly set in motion a performance taking place simultaneously on several levels:

—It is this hour of a day in mid June, Stephen said, begging with a swift glance their hearing. The flag is up on the playhouse by the bankside. The bear Sackerson growls in the pit near it, Paris garden. Canvasclimbers who sailed with Drake chew their sausages among the groundlings.

Local colour. Work in all you know. Make them accomplices.

—Shakespeare has left the huguenot's house in Silver street and walks by the swanmews along the riverbank. But he does not stay to feed the pen chivying her game of cygnets towards the rushes. The swan of Avon has other thoughts.

Composition of place. Ignatius Loyola, make haste to help me!

—The play begins. A player comes on under the shadow, made up in the castoff mail of a court buck, a wellset man with a bass voice. It is the ghost, the king, a king and no king, and the player is Shakespeare who has studied *Hamlet* all the years of his life which were not vanity in order to play the part of the spectre. He speaks the words to Burbage, the young player who stands before him beyond the rack of cerecloth, calling him by a name:

Hamlet I am thy father's spirit

bidding him list. To a son he speaks, the son of his soul, the prince, young Hamlet and to the son of his body, Hamnet Shakespeare, who has died in Stratford that his namesake may live for ever.

—Is it possible that that player Shakespeare, a ghost by absence, and in the vesture of buried Denmark, a ghost by death, speaking his own words to his own son's name (had Hamnet Shakespeare lived he would have been prince Hamlet's twin) is it possible, I want to know, or probable that he did not draw or foresee the logical conclusion of those premises: you are the dispossessed son: I am the murdered father: your mother is the guilty queen. Ann Shakespeare, born Hathaway? [*U*, 188–89]

Stephen's monologue is directed here both to the aggressive manipulation of his immediate audience ("make them accomplices") and to his larger though equally pressing need to play Shakespeare, whose dress, on this occasion ("the castoff mail of a court buck"), suggests not only the crucial existential fact of his isolation and alienation but the immediacy of Stephen's identification with him (Stephen is himself wearing Buck Mulligan's castoff shoes). Shakespeare, in turn, has conceived of *Hamlet* and now plays in it (or such, at least is Stephen's conception of him) in imaginative response to the primary fact of isolation and defeat in life. *Hamlet*, in effect—and Stephen later in the chapter includes Shakespeare's other plays—represents the final and most complex assertion of personality against the narrow and inexorable limits of its worldly condition.

With regard to the chapter's Homeric symbolism, we can say that Scylla or the terrible attrition of mockery is the price of creative personality, paradoxically its very context, the authenticating basis of its forms. Charybdis, however, represents pure romantic and Platonic essence, Fatherhood without the temporal intrusion of the usurping, destroying (and creative) son. In the appropriately mocking thoughts of one such son, Charybdis is the "formless spiritual. Father, Word and Holy Breath. Allfather, the heavenly man. Hiesos Kristos, magician of the beautiful, the Logos who suffers in us at every moment. This verily is that. I am the fire upon the altar. I am the sacrificial butter" (*U*, 185). Such "suffering" or "sacrifice" does not involve pain, limits, necessity, death; rather, it is simply "the willingness of the Logos to circumscribe 'His infinite Life in order that he might manifest,' but the circumscription is without loss of infinitude."[14] For Stephen as for Joyce himself, on the contrary, the primary ground of experience is the poison poured in the ear of the sleeping king. In other words, the banal vulnerability of the finite self denies it heroic potential; it is impossible for the self *in life* to exist otherwise than within a reductive context of "fall," some absurd failure or defeat delivered in addition to the larger defeat and humiliation of mortality. In this chapter and in *Ulysses* in general, Stephen's own sense of failure and defeat is acute. Significantly, he now identifies with Icarus (and Christ on the cross) more than with Daedalus and, beyond Icarus, finally with the lapwing: "Fabulous artificer, the hawklike man. You flew, Whereto? Newhaven—Dieppe, steerage passenger. Paris and back. Lapwing. Icarus. *Pater, ait.* Seabedabbled, fallen, weltering. Lapwing you are. Lapwing he" (*U*, 210). The mingled allusions suggest that Stephen's responses on this occasion are an attempt to establish (in his imagination and in actual performance) a new heroic role—in effect, now a mock-heroic role—which will affirm the power of creativity and "undiminished personality" within some radically limiting context of worldly weakness and failure.

Certainly in the Scylla chapter poisoning is ubiquitous, Claudius's deed simply prototypal of human experience. Stephen has been poisoned and continues to be; he, in turn, poisons and describes the poisonings in Shakespeare's life and art: "Belief in himself has been untimely killed. He was overborne in a cornfield first (ryefield, I should say) and he will never be a victor in his own eyes after nor play victoriously the game of laugh and lie down. Assumed dongiovannism will not save him. No later undoing will undo the first undoing" (*U*, 196–97). This passage continues as a hodgepodge of Stephen's thoughts, his self-consciously "prepared" and rhetorical presentation, overt and more concealed literary allusion, and (with the entering voice and figure of Mulligan) explicit verbal mockery—all reinforcing the theme of poisoning, goring, wounding, ravishing, which represents the universal mockery engulfing the chapter and, indeed, the entire novel from beginning to end. In Stephen's version, however, within this context of mockery, Shakespeare's "undiminished personality" survives, even prevails ("loss is his gain"). Given similar knowledge and insight, the son can, in his own turn, become consubstantial with the father and assume the father's now complex role of victim and articulate ghost.

To put it another way, father and son both survive their wound only in their articulation of it, an articulation that does nothing to deny or even assuage the wound but nevertheless has a valuable existence of its own as personality, speech, "acting," and, in the hands of genius at least, the most highly wrought and morally profound formal orders. Stephen's response to loss, guilt, loneliness, and aggression in the Scylla chapter combines masochism and narrow self-pleading with something potentially more creative. "Acting" in its full dual or punning sense involves both the mean obsessions of personal destiny (Stephen has a constant sense of himself in a cell or prison) and "performance," the heroic extensions of imagination into language and other structures. As lapwing, the weak bird who survives by performance, he is inexorably committed to both:

> Lapwing.
> Where is your brother? Apothecaries' hall. My whetstone. Him, then Cranly, Mulligan: now these. Speech, speech. But act. Act speech. They mock to try you. Act. Be acted on.
> Lapwing.
> I am tired of my voice, the voice of Esau. My kingdom for a drink.
> On. [*U*, 211]

"Act speech" is the type of heroic action, forever "tried" not only by the very limits of speech, but by the ubiquitous mockery of internal and external voices. Stephen associates this same totality made from duality explicitly with Shakespeare. After agreeing with John Eglington's for once helpful summation that Shakespeare in *Hamlet* is "the ghost and the prince. He is all in all," Stephen continues to pursue the point: "—He is, Stephen said. The boy of act one is the mature man of act five. All in all. In *Cymbeline*, in *Othello* he is bawd and cuckold. He acts and is acted on. Lover of an ideal or a perversion, like José he kills the real Carmen. His unremitting intellect is the hornmad Iago ceaselessly willing that the moor in him shall suffer" (*U*, 212).

In the experience of selfhood, the dream and its perversion are simply complementary dimensions of an inclusive whole. Another of Stephen's characteristic ruminations interweaving Shakespeare's life and art describes the complex and indissoluble totality of "doing": "Do and do. Thing done. In a rosery of Fetter Lane of Gerard, herbalist, he walks, greyedauburn. An azured harebell like her veins. Lids of Juno's eyes, violets. He walks. One life is all. One body. Do. But do. Afar, in reek of lust and squalor, hands are laid on whiteness" (*U*, 202). The phrase "thing done" in the above passage probably refers not only to the prior fall or poisoning that subverts all later actions but, more specifically, to the line from George Meredith's *Ordeal of Richard Feverel* sent by Stephen in a telegram to Buck Mulligan and reading (in Stephen's version) as follows: "The sentimentalist is he who would enjoy without incurring the immense debtorship for a thing done" (*U*, 199). Mulligan has this telegram with him when he joins the group in the library. Meredith's aphorism implies that sentimentality can be avoided only by acknowledging the "cost" in reality of life's nobler roles, attitudes, and dreams.

For Joyce the price paid as debtor to the relentless claims of reality is precisely the dimension of irony or mockery that pervades every aspect of his work. Like Stephen's, Joyce's creator/god/father ("the playwright who wrote the folio of the world and wrote it badly") is "lord of things as they are . . . *dio boia*, hangman god . . . doubtless all in all in all of us" (*U*, 213). In other words, the modern "bad" artist, a mere imitator of a faulty progenitor, has no alternative but to embrace "all in all in all"; such "allness" is at the very center of being, experienced as a simultaneous rhythm of construction and deconstruction. "All events brought grist to his mill," argues Stephen about Shakespeare and almost immediately thinks to himself: "You're getting on very nicely. Just mix up a mixture of theolologicophilological. *Mingo, minxi, mictum, mingere*" (*U*, 205). In addition to the tonal mockery here, his pun on the Latin word *mingo* (which means "to urinate") suggests again the poisonous elements in his mixture and the double nature of creation (or "mixing"). The use of the pun here, moreover, reminds us of its significance to Joyce's work as that linguistic device which systematically incorporates two or more meanings, often contradictory, within "one"word.

"Do you believe your own theory?" Stephen is asked finally and promptly answers "No" (*U*, 213–14). He has staged a creative performance, an expression of personality with no absolute or final meaning beyond the context of personality itself—a brilliant rhetorical structure, an aggressive "con game," a cry of guilt, pain, and loneliness. As Michael Seidel puts it aptly, for Stephen as for Shakespeare "movement becomes personality becomes aesthetic design."[15] Significantly, Stephen quickly turns to mockery of belief itself and transforms it also into a punning duality: "I believe, O Lord, help my unbelief. That is, help me to believe or help me to unbelieve?" (*U*, 214).

Joycean mockery might be described in the broadest sense as the recognition and constant acknowledgment of death or "void" in life—a mockery that, appropriately enough for a writer playing God, is his rendition of the voice of "improvidence." In the language of the *Wake:* "Gricks may rise and Troysirs fall (there being two sights for ever a picture) for in the byways of high improvidence that's what makes life-work leaving and the world's a cell for citters to cit in" (*FW*, 11–12). The complex punning makes clear that mockery is fundamental to cosmos, historical time (Greek and Trojans), and human psychology (the sexual "fall"—pricks and trousers—symbolic in Joyce of all human fall and failure); it is also one basis for a necessarily complete and final duality of point of view ("there being two sights for ever a picture"), in art presumably as in life itself. For mockery, in turn, is "hopelessly" resisted (Stephen self-consciously battles hopelessness, as does Bloom) by other dimensions of "undiminished personality." The material, psychological, and spiritual limits of the self are inexorable, yet they do not preclude noble performances of will, energy, imagination, and even, on occasion, visionary power, with art the ultimate heroic performance of selfhood. In the words of the *Wake*, the world's a cell to "cit" (sit, sing) in.

Critics of Joyce, at least until recently, have had a difficult time dealing with his mockery, preferring either to treat it as the voice of cynicism and dark despair (Flaubert reborn, Samuel Beckett anticipated) or, alternatively, to play it down until Joyce's work becomes merely a recent expression of the "classical temper," the aesthetics of reason and moderation brought up to date. But Joycean mockery is categorical, complete, and uncompromising, its inclusiveness extending even to its own attributes. For example, after the quaker librarian observes that "the mocker is never taken seriously when he is most serious," the narrative voice intones: "They talked seriously of mocker's seriousness" (U, 199). The last line is as much Joyce's intrusion as it is a record of Stephen's thinking, part of the universal mockery, verbal and otherwise that permeates the Scylla chapter and Ulysses in general. At the same time, mockery is only part of Joyce's primary dualism; heroism remains its complement. His mock-heroic is both relentlessly limiting and powerfully liberative into spiritual and imaginative adventure and freedom. The fictions of life (constantly acknowledged as such) can be built into systems of extraordinary complexity and order. With this in mind, a few more general comments about Joyce as performer are now in order.

Vulgariano as Performer and Plagiarist

In his later work, it is Joyce himself who is the primary artificer, the builder of labyrinthine structures that both invite and withhold meaning, both invoke the experience of freedom and adventure and remain a prison. He becomes his own chief performer, the putative characters in his novels increasingly relegated to the status of composite forms (albeit their endless local guises) in a field of relationships whose organization is almost entirely beyond their control—explicitly, elaborately, self-consciously a contrivance of their creator. Joyce's punning term "masterbilker" (FW, 111) for HCE, his Father/Creator prototype in the Wake, suggests not only creativity (Solness, Ibsen's Master Builder, combines artistic talent with guilt-ridden impotence and failure), but solipsistic self-involvement (masturbator) and outright fakery, deception, or "bilking."

The Joycean performance involves an extraordinary attempt to "play" author, one that is modeled on (or should we say "plagiarized from"? Shem's is called the "pelagiarist pen" [FW, 182]) the authentic synthesizers and protean visionaries: Homer, Dante, Shakespeare, Blake, Vico, Bruno, Milton, and God's prophetic interpreters in the Bible, to mention only the most obvious. It is Stephen's act raised to the most grandiose scale, first a mock epic, then, in the Wake, what can best be termed a mock Bible, complete with prototypal deaths and awakenings, generational conflicts, epic battle, historical references, lyric interludes, parabolic stories, riddles, prophetic speeches, and sacred inscriptions of the law—in Joyce's own phrases "his farced epistol to the hibruws" (FW, 228) or "epical forged cheque" (FW, 181).[16] It is, in fact, the act of authorship as a deceptive copying or stealing of Holy Writ that is at the heart of one of Shaun's accusations in the *Wake* against Shem, the mocked and mocking writer figure: "Every dimmed letter in it [Shem's "perfect" or "root" language] is a copy and not a few of the silbils and wholly words I can show you in my Kingdom of Heaven. The loquacity of him! With his threestar monothong! Thaw! The last word in stolentelling!" (FW, 424). Since Shaun is himself a false prophet and empty Messiah, only a particularly pretentious and bombastic pretender to fatherhood, the irony, as so often in Joyce, cuts in both directions and, in effect, turns mockery into a kind of first principle, the appropriate voice and language of God or anyone taking his part. Holy Words in this context are simply and solely ("wholly") words, and language as the expression of metaphysical truth is "dimmed" (attenuated, damned, doomed).

This stance, what we might call the heresy of plagiarism (Shem is, after all, a "pelagiarist"), constitutes the most important dimension of Joyce's later mock-heroic art, one with strong roots in his earlier work but now expressed with a categorical intensity in which plagiarism becomes the very basis of style. Or perhaps it is the style. This is the argument advanced by Stephen Heath: "A la place d'un style, le *plagiat:* Joyce ne se définit pas comme le sujet plein d'un style; il parcourt une multiplicité de styles, ouvert plagiastique-ment à toute une gamme de formes dont s'empare l'écriture dans une frag-mentation perpétuelle."[17] Heath's comment is apt enough if we keep steadily in mind (as I think Heath does not) that parodic imitation in Joyce's hands involves construction as well as deconstruction. Joyce's invocation of epic forms and materials—his sustained effort to play the role of epic and vision-ary writer—represents a profound and heroic commitment to creation and order, a commitment that can, nevertheless, be legitimized only by relentless subversion of the truth of both. Under such conditions, the epic task is ob-viously hopeless, but the mock-heroic writer and his protagonists remain committed, in one way or another, to hopeless and impossible tasks. That they are "lowquacious" figures, finally, singing a stylish but isolated and empty "nothing" song (a "threestar monothong"), in no way detracts from the human impulse to order (the "audacity" and "loquacity" in "lowqua-city"), which is represented by the commitment itself.

In his story "The Analytical Language of John Wilkins," Borges reminds us (after describing the problems of someone committed to the formation of a language that "would organize and contain all human thought") that "ob-viously there is no classification of the universe that is not arbitrary and con-jectural. The reason is very simple: we do not know what the universe is. . . .

We must go even further; we must suspect that there is no universe in the organic, unifying sense of that ambitious word." But Borges adds: "The impossibility of penetrating the divine scheme of the universe cannot dissuade us from outlining human schemes, even though we are aware that they are provisional."[18] Such a situation of intense commitments at odds with coexistent awareness of provisionality is central to the mock-heroic mode and particularly relevant to Joyce's massive final constructions, the last one, in fact, literally inventing the kind of inclusive language that Borges describes. Certainly there can be no question of Joyce's commitment to epic and encyclopedist vision. Richard Ellmann quotes John Joyce as saying of his son at age seven: "If that fellow was dropped in the middle of the Sahara, he'd sit, be God, and make a map of it."[19]

Classification toward the description of a fixed and final system is the basis of epic art and, appropriately, the primary focus of Joyce's mediative parody, although in due course I will note briefly his parodic treatment of two other related and fundamental epic concerns—message and rhetoric. Marthe Robert has written: "Viewed from any perspective, the epic always exhibits the same energy in its purpose. Its parts, its material, its composition, the verbal form of its narration, the stereotypicality of its formulas—all of these converge in the articulation of order that is its first and perhaps its only objective. Written in the ideal preterite, the tense of a past eternally present and eternally resumed, it rehearses—that is, it recalls, commemorates, celebrates—primordial events that, once achieved, must be perpetually repeated by men."[20] Joyce's prototypal sense is well known; it is obviously his most enduring response to the epic desideratum of static order that Robert describes in the passage above. Conflation of character and event in time and space can already be found in his earliest work and steadily increases in density until ontology and cyclic time exist alone in the *Wake*, with particularized naturalistic detail, as such, disappearing almost entirely. Because of this density and in the light of the tradition he is invoking, it is tempting to view these prototypal structures in Joyce's work as absolute, a final and definite limning of time and space, with Joyce the new Godhead combining the best features of Freud, Vico, and James Frazer. Such was the position of Joyce's earlier critics, who, on the whole, simply threw themselves into the role of exegetes. Actually, however, in the larger context of its overall treatment, generic structure is as much an imaginative construct of the author playing God as are the results of Stephen's various roles in the *Portrait* and *Ulysses*. Thus an apparent movement in Joyce's work away from nineteenth-century mock-heroic toward a dimension of heroic vision that seems constituted of something more enduring than imaginative energy represents only a final supreme manifestation of imaginative energy in the service of artifice, with the author now more

patently the principal hero yet simultaneously the vehicle for his own mockery, because of his awareness that the ultimate extension of his role is not
Godhead but sham and farce.

The Joycean system is mocked by both microcosm and macrocosm. I have
already discussed at some length the extent to which his prototypes are reduced by their meager and banal manifestations in the actual human world of
his novels. Equally important to Joyce's work is his explicit awareness of the
cosmic void that (as Borges suggests) mocks all human systems and their
creators. *Finnegans Wake* involves an enormous act of playing God that both
creates a cosmos, demonstrating in the process an extraordinary zest for
order, and mocks its own constructions in systematic verbal and rhetorical
ambiguity, incompletion, anticlimax, irrelevance, incertitude, and human de-
basement (guilt, murder, hidden and forbidden desires, defecation, voyeurism, jealousy, to list only the more obvious). Joyce's final cosmos is complete in its basic forms, organized to the most minute details, relentlessly
banal in its human manifestations, and ultimately "a mere matter of ficfect"
(*FW*, 532). It constitutes encyclopedic creation in the context of total doubt;
thus the mocking accusation directed against Shem, in effect, elucidates the
entire basis of Wakean mockery: "Anarch, egoarch, hiresiarch, you have
reared your disunited kingdom on the vacuum of your own most intensely
doubtful soul" (*FW*, 188).

From Joyce's point of view, creation is not only patricidal but suicidal, not
only murderous to the Absolute Father of cosmic order but to the artistic son
of imagination and visionary dreams. In both cases, the masculine figure lies
damaged, with implications that go beyond psychology to metaphysics (if we
need to make such distinctions; as I have noted in discussing Joyce's work,
human psychological and social failure reinforces the mockery of its cosmic
equivalent). In her important book on the *Wake*, Margot Norris has spelled out
these implications: "The Wakean vision of a universe ever hurtling toward
chaos is based on the theme of the fallen father. He is named rather than
namer. He is uncertain of name and identity, unlocatable rather than a center
that fixes, defines, and gives meaning to his cosmos. He is a lawbreaker
rather than lawgiver. As head of the family, he is incestuous rather than the
source of order in the relations of his lineage." She comments specifically on
his uncertain name: "He is called 'Cloudy father! Unsure! Nongood! (500.18);
and he resides, via initials, in the phrase '*Haud certo ergo*' (263.28), 'nothing
certain, therefore.' "[21] "Nothing certain" is, indeed, one ruling principle of
the book, countered only by the equally compelling principle that everything
can be brought into an appropriate relationship with everything else.

In the *Wake*, Joyce's massive game of resemblances—verbal, geographical,
historical, mythical, and psychological—deconstructs its own metaphysical

substance while affirming the power and energy of imagination and, to some extent, the limited and limiting patterns of human life and death. Whatever the affirmations, a mocking dimension of cosmic distance "frames" the *Wake* (and *Ulysses* also) just as the sensibility of author or mature narrator encompasses the experience of ardent hero in more traditional mock-heroic (Joyce's own first formula in the *Portrait*). Even his well-known affirmation of the life process itself—Molly's yeses, the flowing Liffey, "livesliving" as "the one substance of a streamsbecoming" (*FW*, 597)—must finally take its place within the larger context of "chaosmos." Joyce makes this point categorically: "every person, place and thing in the chaosmos of Alle" (*FW*, 118). Or, as he puts it elsewhere in a mockery of process (the context here being the mob's proclamation of the guilt and death of "Mocked Majesty," HCE): "In the buginning is the woid, in the muddle is the sound-dance and thereinofter you're in the unbewised again, vund vulsyvolsy" (*FW*, 378). We must assume that Joyce's meaning embraces the full dualism of the punning in this passage. Any presumed cycle of cosmos (assuming—incorrectly, of course—that we can speak of cosmos in these or any other terms) involves merely biological and chemical interaction ("*buginning*"), cacophonous muddle (the Tower of Babel is invoked throughout the *Wake*), and a return to the unknown and unprovable. Yet the context or void that makes "the Word" only a "word" does not destroy its possibilities as such ("buginning" probably alludes also to primal man—"Earwicker"), nor does it deny the more positive connotations of "sound-dance."[22]

In the *Wake* a verbal order parodies the forms of cosmic order (God as man). In *Ulysses* a verbal order parodies the forms of heroic humanism (man as God), and more emphasis is put on the bumbling attempts of individual characters to realize their prototypes in the actual surroundings of 1904 Dublin. Nevertheless, even if not so obviously, the earlier novel shares with the later the same cosmic mockery, which, in the case of *Ulysses*, simply adds a final dimension of absurdity to the systematic parody of epic convention undertaken throughout the book. Like everything else, Joyce was careful to give it an appropriate place. "I am writing *Ithaca* [the penultimate chapter in *Ulysses*] in the form of a mathematical catechism," he wrote Frank Budgen in 1921: "All events are resolved into their cosmic, physical, psychical etc. equivalents . . . so that the reader will know everything and know it in the baldest and coldest way, but Bloom and Stephen thereby become heavenly bodies, wanderers like the stars at which they gaze."[23] Again Joyce assumes the role of author as God, the central mock-hero of his own fiction, albeit the questions and answers are nominally presented as a description of the actions, thoughts, and feelings of Stephen and Bloom.

In addition to its obvious parallels with religious catechism, the Ithaca chapter is a parody of the traditional editorial role of the writer, who alone knows the order and meaning of events, structures his fictional world in accordance with this knowledge, and, finally, tells the reader "in the baldest and coldest way" the meaning, message, or truth of his story. And we do, indeed, in this chapter receive much useful expository information about Stephen and Bloom that the rest of the novel has offered us only indirectly, if at all. But this practical function, however welcome in such a technically difficult book, is the least of Ithaca's significance. Rather, Joyce's catechism of the Father/Author/Creator mocks the more substantial and significant explanations it is supposed to furnish; such "answers" as are given constitute, in effect, a denial of answer. Cosmos, Joyce makes clear, ultimately sets everyone and everything adrift in a wilderness of fictions—not the purposive wanderings of the epic hero but the illusory orbit of stars. Or such, at least, is Bloom's "logical conclusion" to his thoughts on interstellar space: "That it was not a heaventree, not a heavengrot, not a heavenbeast, not a heavenman. That it was a Utopia, there being no known method from the known to the unknown: an infinity, renderable equally finite by the suppositous probable apposition of one or more bodies equally of the same and of different magnitudes: a mobility of illusory forms immobilised in space, remobilised in air: a past which possibly had ceased to exist as a present before its future spectators had entered actual present existence" (U, 701).

The lesser corollaries to this general conclusion are almost equally sweeping. Both the evolutionary movement of stars and the biological subdivision of organisms lead only to mathematical infinities which simply dissolve human time and order ("if the progress were carried far enough, nought nowhere was never reached" [U, 699]). Any hope for social and moral redemption is absurd also in the light of the vanity of men of whatever shape and form, on whatever planet we might suppose them. Higher forms of life would "there as here remain inalterably and inalienably attached to vanities, to vanities of vanities and all that is vanity" (U, 700). Perhaps the heavens may at least still have value for the imagination? To this question Bloom's response is more positive, although Joyce's tone of comic irony does not waver for a moment.

> Was he more convinced of the esthetic value of the spectacle?
> Indubitably in consequence of the reiterated examples of poets in the delirium of the frenzy of attachment or in the abasement of rejection invoking ardent sympathetic constellations or the frigidity of the satellite of their planet. [U, 701]

Joycean irony deconstructs even the answer that there are no answers; indeed, the very action of answering becomes a mere "act" or rhetorical performance, however brilliantly detailed and explicit. Here as elsewhere in

Ulysses the parodic style is as significant as any ideas that it may express, the two intimately related. In the Ithaca chapter the individual catechistic unit is sometimes trivialized by its use as a device that relentlessly conveys the irrelevancy of much naturalistic description (for example, concerning the door to the garden at Eccles Street: "For what creature was the door of egress a door of ingress? For a cat" [*U*, 698]). Sometimes, however, the answer begins in sense and then lapses into a nonsense of fantastically elaborated scientific jargon or factual detail mindlessly and mechanically pursued, an infinitude of verbiage equivalent to the cosmic infinitudes that constitute the ultimate framing perspective of this chapter and *Ulysses* as a whole. Since language in such a context cannot "mean" anything, individual words have no final substance and need not have even immediate referents. Thus we are told of an advertisement for Plumtree's Potted Meat: "Manufactured by George Plumtree, 23 Merchants' quay, Dublin, put up in 4 oz. pots, and inserted by Councillor Joseph P. Nannetti, M. P., Rotunda Ward, 19 Hardwicke street, under the obituary notices and anniversaries of deceases. The name on the label is Plumtree. A plumtree in a meatpot, registered trade mark. Beware of imitations. Peatmot. Trumplee. Montpat. Plamtroo" (*U*, 684). The final nonsense words could presumably go on indefinitely, or at least until all possible letter combinations were exhausted. Although the misplaced advertisement invokes the theme of rebirth and life continuity so prevalent in *Ulysses*, the style suggests dimensions of void which, in the end, mock all such attempts at simple thematic statement. As the ad says, "Beware of imitations."

If the answers given in Joyce's work are ceaselessly mocking and mocked, there remain, nevertheless, no lack of questers for the tantalizing grail of meaning and no lack of hints—riddles, "Mamafestas," mysterious figures, rumored events—that such a grail might possibly exist. Its pursuit remains everyone's essential business (including, above all, that of Joyce himself)—the pattern of the small boy's experience in "Araby" or "An Encounter" repeated again and again throughout Joyce's fiction. Thus Bloom, as he is getting ready for bed at the end of the day, has a final encounter with his own enigmatic ghost:

> What selfinvolved enigma did Bloom risen, going, gathering multicoloured multiform multitudinous garments, voluntarily apprehending, not comprehend?
> Who was M'Intosh? [*U*, 729]

In this case the "answer," though puzzling enough in substance (it refers to the thirteenth mourner unknown to anyone, "the chap in the macintosh" [*U*, 110], who turns up at Dignan's funeral), is in fact stylistically simply another question.

In spite of such answers, however, and in spite of other banal limitations on their lives, the various seekers retain a residue of heroic commitment and energy in their very act of seeking. Bloom (mocked, to be sure) believes in "the necessity of order, a place for everything and everything in its place" (*U*, 709). He is described explicitly by Joyce as "a conscious reactor against the void incertitude" (*U*, 734), and this point is reiterated in another catechism involving both the male principals of *Ulysses*. The context here is Bloom's depression over his failure to redeem man's moral and social condition:

> Did Stephen participate in his dejection?
>
> He affirmed his significance as a conscious rational animal proceeding syllogistically from the known to the unknown and a conscious rational reagent between a micro- and a macrocosm ineluctably constructed upon the incertitude of the void.
>
> Was this affirmation apprehended by Bloom?
>
> Not verbally. Substantially.
>
> What comforted his misapprehension?
>
> That as a competent keyless citizen he had proceeded energetically from the unknown to the known through the incertitude of the void. [*U*, 697]

Everything (above all, Joyce's fiction itself) is "ineluctably constructed upon the incertitude of the void." Such a context denies the end but not the act of "proceeding energetically"—the act, so to speak, of acting, of being a "re-agent."

Even the mock-professorial commentator (who is probably Shem) on ALP's "Mamafesta" pursues his hopeless dream of interpretation with manic intensity, and, in his pursuit, specifically includes the reader of the *Wake*: "You is feeling like you was lost in the bush, boy? You say: It is a puling sample jungle of woods. You most shouts out: Bethicket me for a stump of a beech if I have the poultriest notions what the farest he all means" (*FW*, 112). Such an appeal suggests that the reader's role, too, in Joyce's work is to be that of mock-hero, energetically pursuing, with complex schemes in a complex pseudo-order, a meaning that never exists. The reader becomes a figure within the labyrinth of language (here a Dantesque "jungle of woods") who has taken on the coloration of the labyrinth-maker. We learn, moreover, from the professor that what is required for survival in the labyrinth is not merely energy but a quality we have previously observed in Stephen—the courage of angry desperation—another quality that exists independent of the farce of actual performance. In one of the *Wake*'s most brilliant comic passages, the professor exhorts the reader (with regard to the "scrap of paper" remaining from ALP's Mamafesta) to "cling to it as with drowning hands, hoping against hope all the while that, by the light of philophosy, (and may she never folsage us!) things will begin to clear up a bit one way or another within the next quarrel of an hour and be hanged to them as ten to one they will too, please the pigs, as they ought to categorically, as, stricly between ourselves, there is a limit to all things so this will never do" (*FW*, 199). Joyce and his protagonists are finally comic Ahabs in their mad rebellion against disorder. All the while, however, their reason steadily mocks their foolish commitments; they know very well that "stricly between ourselves, there is a limit to all things."

Joyce's own mad pursuit of order extends beyond his prototypal and conflationary instincts, beyond his overall plagiarized structures of epic and bible, beyond even the messages, riddles, and catechisms that he scatters in our path to the most concrete particulars of style. Classification, for example, whose broader manifestations and metaphysical significance I have been discussing, is undertaken incessantly in the form (still, of course, appropriate enough to epic convention) of every variety of catalog. Included are lists of book titles (most notably the three-page list of titles of ALP's Mamafesta), of personal names associated with individual events, of Irish heroes, of places, of groups in a mob or parade, and, in addition, lists of variations on verbal formulas. These latter, especially, give a clue to the significance of the entire classification process in Joyce's work. Aside from the absurdity of individual inclusions or the triviality and irrelevance of an entire class of items taken as a whole or the occasional specific mockery of epic pretensions (in, let us say, the Cyclops chapter of *Ulysses*), such catalogs mock their own potential function as descriptive celebrations of a meaningful system by their very excess of internal proliferation. In a fashion similar to the dissolution of the catechism answers, sense becomes nonsense as verbiage accumulates and we become conscious of systems not only infinitely open-ended but essentially without substantive reference to anything beyond the imaginative wit and energy of their verbal surfaces. Here as elsewhere in Joyce the act of ordering serves to deny the possibility of ultimate order.

One illustration of this cataloging must suffice: Joyce's notorious textual intrusion just after Bloom, facing the chauvinistic citizen in the tavern, courageously defends the "life" principle of love against what he terms "force, hatred, history, all that." Predictably, he is mocked by the citizen; less predictably (since we know how much he personally detested loutish values) by Joyce himself:

Love loves to love love. Nurse loves the new chemist. Constable 14 A loves Mary Kelly. Gerty MacDowell loves the boy that has the bicycle. M. B. loves a fair gentleman. Li Chi Han lovey up kissy Cha Pu Chow. Jumbo, the elephant, loves Alice, the elephant. Old Mr. Verschoyle with the ear trumpet loves old

Mrs. Verschoyle with the turnedin eye. The man in the brown macintosh loves a lady who is dead. His Majesty the King loves Her Majesty the Queen. Mrs. Norman W. Tupper loves officer Taylor. You love a certain person. And this person loves that other person because everybody loves somebody but God loves everybody. [*U*, 333]

Bloom's personal and particular moral statement is taken up by Joyce and "systematized" in a way perfectly appropriate to his authorial role. But his descriptive list is, in fact, simply a comic extension of the tautological and circular verbal formula from which the statement springs, and it "leads" only to a final generalization, which, in spite of the inclusion of pseudo-causality, is essentially also a repetition of the initial formula. In other words, as an expression of truth, the final affirmation of cosmic moral order ("God loves everybody") is the equivalent merely of the first purely reflexive statement, "love loves to love love." Such equivalency, moreover, goes well beyond a mock of moral absolutes to include Joyce's entire colossal enterprise of relating "this" to "that." He no more denies Bloom as moral reagent than he denies Stephen or himself the role of imaginative and intellectual reagents. He does, however, steadily deny the consequences of reagency that are everywhere the implications of its function and certainly the hope of its human actors. His own relentless classification of motifs suggests both the promise of classification and its despair. In discussing various techniques in *Ulysses* that "point toward a unity that transcends the reality of the individual," F. R. Jameson has noted that "there rises up, behind the finite, realized work itself, the mirage of some more perfect totality, to which the former makes allusion at every moment as to its own ultimate meaning, but to which we as readers can never accede."[24] Nor, we must add, can Joyce; that is the crux of his mock-heroism.

Jameson's comment should also remind us again of the fundamental scope and significance of Joycean parody. At every level of his novels, it creates and sustains the duality that Jameson describes—never more so than at the basic stylistic level of rhetorical imitation. Joyce tells us in *Finnegans Wake* that he is not so much the authentic "inventor" of writing as "the poeta, still more learned, who discovered the raiding there originally," not so much one who "coded" as one who "decorded" (*FW*, 482). Decoding/recording or reading/writing/raiding—these terms suggest the fundamental constructive/deconstructive rhythm of Joyce's work. In *Ulysses* Joyce tends to "raid" the language of others; in the *Wake*, he creates an entire pseudo-language (now based on the borrowing of fragments and their recombination) appropriate to the "biblical" function of the later book. [25] Insofar as it shares in the larger role of parody in Joyce's work—that of furnishing the crucial stylistic mechanism for mediation "between the world of his experience and the world of his dreams"—his rhetorical parody has the special purpose of forcing our attention back on the nature and function of language. In so doing, it removes from Joyce's mock-heroic stance (whatever its origins and in spite of the later influence of Vico) the last traces of historical nostalgia. His treatment of language makes clear that for him "dreams" are not finally the children of time but ontological, part of the permanently unfulfilled condition of man, both approached and mocked by the process of language.

Thus in *Ulysses* Joyce's specific and incessant parody of various rhetorical styles serves to reveal them as endlessly generated fictions of selfhood and culture—performances in space and time which are both models of the imaginative effort toward coherence and lessons in absurdity. Appropriately enough, this revelation reaches its climax in the Oxen of the Sun chapter (Bloom and Stephen at the lying-in hospital), where the major themes of *Ulysses* and the particular events of the moment are cast and recast in the verbal molds of major English prose models. Parallel to the systematic parody of the English language on Joyce's part is the fictional action of an ordinary birth taking place at the hospital, the birth itself mocked by the irreverent and obscene conversation of the medical students (including Buck Mulligan, the incarnation of mockery) as much as it is celebrated through the usual moral concern of Bloom and, obviously, through the new mother's commitment to life.

But the major mocker remains Joyce himself; it is he as much as anyone who slays the Oxen of the Sun in the very process of bringing them to birth— or perhaps, rather, to a rebirth of continuity and immortality. Joyce's parodies are, in effect, abortions of a sort. What he called in this chapter "the crime committed against fecundity by sterilizing the act of coition" [26] surely refers as much as anything to the fact that one does not and cannot move beyond the act of verbal creation or, for that matter, the physical creation of individual life to a birth of genuine evolutionary movement toward some eventual "heaventree." Not only are all the literary styles and their creators dead, but whatever development we may think of as having taken place within the language as a whole (if, indeed, we are disposed to think of language in such terms) is framed by Joyce, here as always, within the larger dimensions of chaos.[27]

Almost every passage in Oxen of the Sun deals with the purgation of disorder and the establishment of heaventree through the imaginative ordering of language. But Joyce's rhetorical parody makes clear here and elsewhere in his work that the process of dream fulfillment through the creation of linguistic or any other system is an act of artifice, not a reality, a record finally of living and vital desire, not of metaphysical truth. As we yearn to play the father, so do we create him in imagination—that was both the example and the moral of Stephen's performance in the National Library and that remains Joyce's larger moral in *Ulysses* and the *Wake*.

In this context, the acknowledged "chaos" at the end of Oxen of the Sun is scarcely different in kind from that implied by the multiple parody of the earlier passages. Once more the Father is invoked but now in the explicitly prophetic voice of contemporary evangelism:

> Elijah is coming washed in the Blood of the Lamb. Come on, you winefizzling ginsizzling booseguzzling existences! Come on, you dog-gone, bullnecked, beetlebrowed, hogjowled, peanutbrained, weaseleyed fourflushers, false alarms and excess baggage! Come on, you triple extract of infamy! Alexander J. Christ Dowie, that's yanked to glory most half this planet from 'Frisco Beach to Vladivostok. The Diety ain't no nickel dime bumshow. I put it to you that he's on the square and a corking fine business proposition. He's the grandest thing yet and don't you forget it. Shout salvation in king Jesus. You'll need to rise precious early, you sinner there, if you want to diddle the Almighty God. Pflaaaap! Not half. He's got a coughmixture with a punch in it for you, my friend, in his back-pocket. Just you try it on. [*U*, 428]

Bloom, we must remember, has already put on an inglorious performance as Elijah at the end of the tavern scene, and the American evangelist John Alexander Dowie (who called himself Elijah II and turned out to be a fraud) wanders in and out of the novel as a leitmotif of harebrained prophecy. Obviously this last passage is precariously close to lapsing into pure nonsense such as we have encountered before in Joyce. But then, so (though less obviously) are his imitations of Charles Dickens, Thomas Carlyle, and medieval romance— that, after all, is the point he is trying to make.

As the Carlylean voice says in Oxen of the Sun, *Ulysses* is, indeed, a "chaffering allincluding most farraginous chronicle," the best bargain perhaps that Joyce could make between his heroic vision and his actual experience, but necessarily one heavily made up of chaff, chatter, and the borrowed bits and pieces of various stylistic traditions, a mosaic of comic approximations, in part the performance of his characters, in larger part the transformations of Joyce himself. He clearly emerges in *Ulysses* as his own most relentless player of heroic roles, the imitator of Homer, Dante, and Blake in an age of iron, yet "Vulgariano" also, the new Sancho (or "Sin Showpanza" in Joyce's inspired pun [*FW*, 234]), travestying the heroic performance in the process of its realization. In whatever form, Joyce's rhetoric involves games of analogy which create elaborate verbal structures, while simultaneously mocking their own substance. The irony thus generated, like his twin framing perspectives of existential banality and "chaosmos," is categorical and eventually finds its most complete expression in the fully synthetic language of the *Wake*, a language whose extreme "plurisignification" (as Norris aptly terms it) destroys any lingering possibility of assigning a single evaluative meaning to the Joycean quest.[28] Joyce explicitly disavows unitary reference in his well-known description of the style of the *Wake:* "Every word will be bound over to carry three score and ten toptypsical readings throughout the book of Doublends Jined" (*FW*, 20).

At the vital center of this "toptypsical" style is the pun, Joyce's most perfect, most radical device for the expression, at the basic syntactical level, of the constructive, deconstructive vision that characterizes, in one form or another, his high art. Joyce's puns allow him (as Bernard Benstock has noted) "to include various concepts, overlapping themes, and levels of meaning in compressed form" and to expand easily upon the thematic implications of things (thus "Sin Showpanza" illuminates the "fall," which, at the human level, comically limits heroic intention).[29] But most important, Joyce uses puns as "double talk," simultaneous assertions and denials, conflicting points of view within a single entity ("two thinks at a time" [*FW*, 583] or "counterpoint words" [*FW*, 482]), the perfect verbal equivalent of the unresolved dualism between protagonists or between protagonist and narrative point of view so characteristic of earlier mock-heroic fiction. Along with those I have already borrowed from the *Wake*, one last illustration of Joyce's particular ironic punning must serve for all. He refers to his final work at one point as his "book of kills" (*FW*, 482), and this pun on the splendid Irish illuminated copy of the gospels illuminates, in its own characteristic fashion, the entire contradictory landscape of Joyce's mock-epics: gorgeous structures of imaginative range, depth, and complexity, yet, at the same time, testaments to inexorable limits, failure, and death. Not surprisingly, Vulgariano in the end is more than a little like the great copulating Father, HCE himself: "The galleonman jovial on his bucky brown nightmare" (*FW*, 583).

Romantic Personae in the Work of
William Carlos Williams

The air changes, creates and re-creates, like strength,
And to breathe is a fulfilling of desire,
A clearing, a detecting, a completing,
A largeness lived and not conceived, a space
That is an instant nature, brilliantly.
WALLACE STEVENS
"Chocorua to Its Neighbor"

There is nothing in literature but change
and change is mockery.
WILLIAM CARLOS WILLIAMS
Kora in Hell

Isaiah among the Butterflies

William Carlos Williams's description of Maxwell Bodenheim in *Kora in Hell* suggests two characteristic stances of the modern romantic sensibility. Cast in the mock-heroic formula of an obsessively committed hero observed by a strongly sympathetic yet equally skeptical narrator, the passage looks immediately backward to Joyce's treatment of Mangan and directly forward to Bellow's version of Delmore Schwartz in *Humboldt's Gift* (see Chapter 9). I mention only the more literal parallels because the formula, as I have repeatedly noted, is (romanticism aside) a central characteristic of all manifestations of the mock-heroic mode. Bodenheim, writes Williams,

> pretends to hate most people . . . but that he really goes to this trouble I cannot imagine. He seems rather to me to have the virtues of self-absorption so fully developed that hate is made impossible. Due to this, also, he is an unbelievable physical stoic. I know of no one who lives so completely in his pretenses as Bogie does. Having formulated his world neither toothaches nor the misery to which his indolence reduces him can make head against the force of his imagina-

tion. Because of this he remains for me a heroic figure, which, after all, is quite apart from the stuff he writes and which only concerns him. He is an Isaiah of the butterflies.[1]

This portrait both indicates the direction of modern romanticism and, at the same time, reveals the complex attitude of major romantics such as Williams and Stevens (as opposed to minor figures such as Bodenheim) toward what has happened. Bodenheim in Williams's treatment represents, in effect, the attenuation of romantic heroics and suggests by implication the necessary transformation of the hero that must be undertaken in the light of this attenuation by those most seriously concerned with salvaging something of the romantic visionary stance.

Joseph Riddel has noted that the direction of romanticism in the last hundred years has been from a sense of "privileged consciousness" to "dislocated self-consciousness."[2] Like heroes before him, the romantic hero has increasingly been denied an environment commensurate with his will and vision, in this case a transcendental realm or dimension of power coextensive with the imagination. To be sure, even at its point of highest expression in the nineteenth century, romanticism offered its heroes only a precarious identification of self and energized object—an identification tentative, in need of constant renewal, more involved with process than end, and already finding consummations largely in and through the artifice of art.[3] From the beginning, moreover, the sterile but tempting alternatives of solipsism and Platonism lurked as too easy alternatives to the full dynamics of the romantic vision.

In the work of a later generation of romantics, however—Byron's experiment in the mock-heroic mode, of course, foreshadowing some of these later developments—the transcendental dimension disappeared completely, leaving us with the continuing claims of willful selfhood and its expression through imagination and feelings as *the* source of value, but claims now in active confrontation with material reality. This reality may remain a positive and attractive vehicle for the imaginative tracings of the self or it may be more negatively felt as what Williams calls in *Paterson* "a pustular scum, a decay, a choking / lifelessness."[4] In any case, the concept of a noble self persists, but the locus of heroism necessarily shifts drastically from the quality of ends to the quality of means, from results to effort. As Wallace Stevens puts it, "the heroic effort to live expressed as victory."[5] Heroism becomes the pursuit of desire in the existential immediacy of a world that has only (at best) a casual relation to its fulfillment. Maxwell Bodenheim in Williams's sketch achieves the status of stoic and romantic hero through the sheer rigor of self-absorption, a rigor whose power source is simply "the force of his imagination." Yet

Williams's strong and sympathetic identification with Bodenheim is balanced by an equally persistent counterrhythm of irony. Williams, significantly, has the strong sense of the world and its claims that the other poet refuses to acknowledge. Bodenheim in Williams's splendid phrase is an "Isaiah of the butterflies," "a heroic figure," perhaps, but only in a context so sharply limited as constantly to threaten (though it does not destroy) the very premises on which the heroic claims rest.

Alternatively, we might describe Bodenheim from Williams's point of view as a hero of authentic illusions (he lives "completely in his pretenses"), or what I have been calling a "mock-hero" in the intellectual and formal tradition of Cervantes, a tradition with strong and continuing relevance to romanticism but with far earlier roots in Western culture. In a seminal essay on the Spanish writer, Américo Castro notes that "Cervantes, a Christian and a stoic, relates to a Semitic tradition nine hundred years old; his art consisted of resolving the concept of life as an alternation of 'insides' and 'outsides' purely phenomenological (like a linear arabesque, without volume and open), with the Stoic-Judaic-Christian idea of man raising himself upon the rock of his will and upon the conscience of intimate freedom. Feeling 'one's own self' is achieved at the cost of the uninterrupted effort of sustaining one's self, without paying attention to circumstances: 'Nay has as many letters as aye'."[6] Self-realization, in other words, is an endlessly renewed process of being; the experience of Don Quixote and Sancho, as we have already noted, is a continual adventure, a pursuit of "wonders," open-ended, subject to a ceaseless rhythm of climax/anticlimax, fragmentary, vulnerable largely to exhaustion and death.

Castro goes on to point out that "according to the author of the *Quixote*, the reality of existence consists of being receptive to that impact of whatever can affect man from outside of him and continually transforming such impressions into visible processes of life. The illusion of a dream, the clinging to a belief—yearning in whatever form—introduce themselves into the existence of the one who dreams, creates or yearns, and thus what was an unarticulated externality of the process of living will become a real and effective content of life."[7] Of course, even the Knight (not to mention Sancho) has occasional doubts; more significant is the elaborate and almost total context of doubt within which he operates to create his own particular "reality of existence." The distinction between full heroic vision and Cervantine mock-heroic consists precisely in this dimension of doubt, a doubt in balance with commitment and its equal in intensity.[8] The mock-hero is, by and large, an ardent and receptive believer; his creator is both believer and doubter. From the perspective of Cervantes, complex narrative devices introduce not only commitment to self-realization as its own justification but strong doubts about the final efficacy or end of selfhood *beyond* itself. The Knight exists in a medium that at the same time offers him the possibility of imaginative transformation and mocks those transformations. The author, in turn, of a fiction of significant illusions becomes his own Quixote; indeed, any fundamental distinction between author and protagonist finally collapses in a mockery inclusive of both. Joyce brilliantly exploits this conflation in his work, and it is a point also emphasized by Borges. His creative artist Pierre Menard has the same manic determination as Don Quixote and is just as involved in an ultimately "useless" exercise. For Williams and Stevens, likewise, the roles of author and protagonists—in their transparency I prefer now to call these protagonists "personae"—are particularly close.

In short, Williams shares with Bodenheim a common romanticism and a common absurdity, differing only in his awareness of this absurdity and a concomitant willingness to incorporate it systematically into the forms of his art. Such an awareness shapes his treatment of romantic heroism as surely as Cervantes's similar awareness signals his aesthetic departure from the forms of medieval romance. A study of other personae will shed further light on Williams's transformation of romanticism and the function of mock-heroic in this transformation.

Minor Personae

I have stressed that the mock-heroic mode is a way of preserving the concept of nobility during a historical period that threatens otherwise to polarize into empty and obsolescent conventions and banal reality. In his well-known essay "The Noble Rider and the Sound of Words," Wallace Stevens makes this essential point by comparing Andrea del Verrocchio (for whom nobility "was an affair of the noble style") and Cervantes, to the obvious advantage of the latter: "With Cervantes, nobility was not a thing of the imagination. It was a part of reality, it was something that exists in life, something so true to us that it is in danger of ceasing to exist, if we isolate it, something in the mind of a precarious tenure." Yet today, he goes on to note, "we may derive so much satisfaction from the restoration of reality as to become wholly prejudiced against the imagination." It is a question, rather, Stevens says, of "precise equilibrium."[9]

For Williams, also, nobility involves a continuing and "precarious" encounter between the imagination and reality, in which claim and counterclaim are in complex and ineluctable balance—in some sort of "equilibrium," perhaps, but not in resolution. "In front walks Don Quixote; Sancho follows" (*I*, 64, 291): Williams's reiterated statement suggests his self-conscious awareness of Cervantes and the crucial duality set up by the Spaniard, regardless of who walks "in front." Williams's own stoicism—the strong capacity of his dramatic selves to "bear" reality—comes, like that of Cervantes, squarely from the certain sufficiency of the mock-heroic compromise. The efficacy of the imagination, that is, for art and for self-realization within life is not canceled by its absurdity in other equally compelling contexts. In fact, the full acknowledgment of these contexts—or, more important, the creation of art forms that incorporate these contexts—protects the heroic claims by fully testing them at every vulnerable point by ironic counterstatement. Mock-heroic is a mirror art; heroic and absurd selves stand face to face. "We look, we pretend great things to our glass—rubbing our chin," writes Williams in *Kora in Hell*, adding: "This is a profound comedian who grimaces deeds to slothful breasts" (*I*, 78). Here both by image and tone the dramatic self incorporates mockery into its various "profound" stances.

Unlike many mock-heroes we have observed, Williams's personae respond to loss not by pursuing abstract, obsolete ideals and social conventions, but by their equally determined commitment to the new, the fresh, the improvisational, dissonant, and existential. He has noted the difference: "There are no sagas—only trees now, animals, engines: there's that" (*I*, 148). On rare occasions this commitment may result or may have resulted (such occasions are usually in the past) in true heroic consummation. Daniel Boone, for example, "lived to enjoy ecstasy" by a "descent to the ground of his desire," where the power so central to the romantic vision was fully released.[10] Or there is Williams's description of the life of the Aztecs, with its strong echoes of D. H. Lawrence's romanticism: "Here it was [in their "monstrous" stone and wood imagery] that the tribe's deep feeling for a reality that stems back into the permanence of remote origins had its firm hold. It was the earthward thrust of their logic; blood and earth; the realization of their primal and continuous identity with the ground itself, where everything is fixed in darkness" (*IAG*, 33). To be sure, even on these occasions history has acted as ultimate mocker; the Aztecs are destroyed, and Boone, like Huck Finn, keeps only one step ahead of the settlements. When Hilda Doolittle accused him of "flippancies" in his poetry, of mocking his own song, Williams replied in a line which I have used as an appropriate epigraph to this chapter: "There is nothing in literature but change and change is mockery" (*I*, 13). Time and history, in other words, are basically movement and, as such, inherently anticlimactic: new becomes old; stability and "ends" are an illusion of the moment.

Usually Williams stresses the element of anticlimax even in dealing with the experience of those historical figures whom he can conceive of as having approached consummation more closely than any contemporary persona.

The process of time, indeed, involves not only the simple fact of change but a darker quality of "emptiness" at the heart of things or, as Williams also describes it, "the spirit of malice which underlies men's lives and against which nothing offers resistance" (*IAG*, 27). Men may be "possessed by beauty," according to Williams, but heroic commitment to imaginative vision can be celebrated only as an end in itself since empirical ends are inevitably disastrous. Celebration, if possible at all, can take place only in a context of "perennial disappointment." Desire and the failure of desire are endemic to the experience of Williams's personae, a rhythm/counterrhythm in an almost perfectly balanced and endless tension, as his epic invocation to Sir Walter Raleigh makes clear: "Of the pursuit of beauty and the husk that remains, perversions and mistakes, while the true form escapes in the wind, sing O Muse" (*IAG*, 59).

It is Christopher Columbus, however, who for Williams as for Hart Crane remains the touchstone of possibility, the figure seeking new forms and new freedom in a *Nuevo Mundo*, the persona closest to Williams's own heroic dream of himself. But even in the strong polemical context of *In the American Grain*, Columbus's experience is described by Williams as one of almost complete dislocation between dream and fact, pursuit and capture, conception and growth—a duality inherent in the deepest rhythms of life. As Williams puts it, "The Western land could not guard its seclusion longer; a predestined and bitter fruit existing, perversely, before the white flower of its birth, it was laid bare by the miraculous first voyage. For it is as the achievement of a flower, pure, white, waxlike and fragrant, that Columbus' infatuated course must be depicted, especially when compared with the acrid and poisonous apple which was later by him to be proved" (*IAG*, 7). The aesthetic ("pure, white, waxlike") flower of imaginative vision exists apart from the rank growth of reality in time. Columbus's passion is both noble and foolish ("infatuated") as he rigorously pursues his dream ("the illusive bright future") toward personal and social catastrophe; the greatest hero is the greatest illusionist. In *In the American Grain*, nevertheless, for many of the heroes of history the mockery is muted, and they approach genuine tragic significance, where the heroic will simply encounter its final limits in the overriding predestined plans of the gods. As I have noted elsewhere, the mock-heroic mode is invariably tragicomic, within the exact mixture of larger generic elements varying from work to work.

Elsewhere in Williams's work the comic dimension is clearer and the mockery more harsh. In *The Great American Novel*, for example, Hernando De Soto is obviously viewed as a Don Quixote wandering in weird costume over the plains of, in this case, Alabama instead of La Mancha: "The Spanish stand still. What an ass a man will make of himself in a strange country! In armor De Soto wandering haphazard over Alabama. The Seminoles for guides. Buried him in the Mississippi. . . . The cat-fish ate it [his body]" (*I*, 192). Or there is the great historic pratfall of Aaron Burr, a pratfall both described and imitated in the violent rhetorical switch of the narrative voice: "What chit of a girl could have appreciated you, my darling boy, as I do. A man of your personality, so fresh in wit, so brimming with vigor and new ideas. Aaron my dear, dear boy, life has not yet begun. All is new and untouched in the world waiting . . . for you to pluck it. . . . For you everything is possible. Bing! and Hamilton lies dead" (*I*, 191). In the earlier book even Columbus is seen as someone whose sound business sense quickly mitigates his visionary excesses: "For a moment Columbus stood as if spell-bound by the fact of this new country. Soon however he regained his self-possession and with Alonzo Pinzón ordered the trunks of trifles to be opened which, being opened, the Indians drew near in wonder and began to try to communicate with these gods" (*I*, 185). As an adventurer, with his "trunks of trifles," Columbus is, in effect, a harsh parody of his dream, in life a pretend god with fake wonders.

    The Great American Novel is, of course, the *new* American novel, and its difference of tone from *In the American Grain* reflects Williams's sense of the particularly pressing contingencies within which the contemporary explorer of new forms acts and has his being. In the full context of his own existential drama, the Williams persona is more sharply aware of the possible ironies involved in seeking out models (even new models who are models of the spirit of the new) from the American past. The very act of modeling deepens his sense of parody—his awareness not only of the self-parody involved in the actions of his historical figures (as they "imitated" their own dreams), but, most important, of himself as secondhand imitator of an imitation or perhaps as someone who can only *desire* to imitate. Williams shares with many of his contemporaries a sense of historical "lateness" or diminution. Progress is out of the question—dismissed as "damn foolishness . . . a thieves game" (*I*, 165). He attempts to substitute a theory of "involution" for that of "evolution": "We struggle to comprehend an obscure evolution . . . when the compensatory involution so plainly marked escapes our notice." Invoking the great historical names, he goes on to propose writing "the natural history of involution," but this proposition trails off in mockery as he describes the "return" of great heroes:

> Borne on the foamy crest of involution, like Venus or her wave, stript as she but of all consequence—since it is the return. See they return! From savages in quest of a bear we are come upon rifles, cannon. From Chaldeans solving the stars we

have fallen into the bellies of the telescopes. From great runners we have
evolved into speeches sent over a wire.

But our spirits, our spirits have prospered! Boom, boom. Oh, yes, our spirits
have grown— [*I*, 215]

Involution might suggest that time, if not consequentially redemptive, offers at least a cycle of continuing human spiritual possibility. In fact, its invocation by the narrator is simply an aspect of the mock-heroics of loss and
desire. Elsewhere he wonders "if it were too late to be Eric" (*I*, 182). The
season of *The Great American Novel*, moreover, is autumnal, and spring is no
longer a matter of founded hope but of unfounded desire, even of nostalgia:
"Sometimes it seems it [spring] would still be possible. And this is romance:
to believe that which is unbelievable. This is faith: to desire that which is
never to be obtained, to ride like a swallow on the wind—apparently for the
pleasure of flight" (*I*, 180).

Williams's faith, moreover, exists in contexts of mockery more fundamental even than the past and present disappointments of history. His measure-
ment of potential as a "new" writer in a "new" world with a "new" American
language leads him to a consideration of language, the particular medium of
the writer, but, in larger terms, the medium through which all human beings
encounter and formalize their relationship with reality. In this case, as with
the meditations on history, the form of *The Great American Novel* remains the
very expression of its subject: desire is affirmed concretely through the continuing willed commitment to expression of a self-conscious monologist
whose dual perspectives express endlessly in complex antiphony both the
will and the limits of will. His "romantic" commitment to the swallow's flight,
for example, quoted just above, is immediately followed by an empirical examination of the metaphor, then by a test of its immediate relevance to himself. He notes first that "the swallow's bill is constructed in such a way that in
flying with his mouth open tiny insects that enter are ensnared in hair-like
gills so that he is fed." Obviously for the swallow, although the medium of air
may give pleasure, it is also practically sustaining; the self survives on its
actual encounters with objects. The human parallel, as the narrator describes
it, is more purely solipsistic and more incomplete. His medium is simply
imagination and its formalization in words. He thinks: "Here are a pretty pair
of legs in blue stockings, feed. Yet without the thought of a possible achievement." He imagines an encounter with the girl: "There is one word you must
hear." Yet he does not keep his appointment and is left "thinking, thinking of
the words he will make, new words to be written on white paper but never to
be spoken by the lips to pass into her ear" (*I*, 180).

At best he is left with words, which he calls elsewhere his "poetic sweet-heart" and occasionally mocks harshly: "Ugh. Poetic sweetheart. My dear Miss Word let me hold your W. I love you. Of all the girls in school you alone are the one—" (*I*, 166). In his mock-heroic encounter with language, the monologist is, of course, reflecting one of the great philosophical themes of this century: the disassociation of language from any necessary or effective relation with reality. The Austrian Fritz Mauthner argued in 1901 that "lan-guage is only a convention, like a rule of a game: the more participants, the more compelling it will be. However, it is neither going to grasp nor to alter the real world."[11] For twentieth-century writers as diverse as Joyce, Borges, Nabokov, Stevens, and Williams (to mention only a few prominent names) the most fundamental mock-heroic commitment is the artist's commitment to language. The narrator-monologist of *The Great American Novel* is obsessed with the problem: "I am a writer and will never be anything else. In which case it is impossible to find the word. But to have a novel one must progress with the words. The words must become real, they must take the place of wife and sweetheart. . . . Am I a word? Words, words, words—" (*I*, 166). He realizes he is imitating Joyce—and mocks not only his own imitation but Joyce, an "epicurean of romance," someone mistaking his art for "Rosinante" (*I*, 168–69). The hero of new words is as ironically limited by the very process of change as were the earlier explorers of new worlds: "Words are not perma-nent . . . words progress into the ground. . . . Now I am not what I was when the word was forming to say what I am" (*I*, 158). Word-making, in short, is an exercise that never gets beyond itself: "If I make a word I shall make myself into a word" (*I*, 160).

Within the context of mock-heroic, nevertheless, irony, however cate-gorical, only establishes the context of belief. It does not reduce the narrator's commitment to believing, but simply turns him into a pretender. "Hans An-dersen didn't believe," he notes at one point, "he had to pretend to believe" (*I*, 160). "Deeply religious" (as he describes himself), this mock or pretend Columbus, in the face of almost total doubt, resolutely pledges himself again and again to the quest—or at least the process or game of questing since the absolute end of the quest remains concealed or is determined by purely arbi-trary means: "Somehow a word must be found. . . . A novel must progress toward a word. Any word that—Any word. There is an idea" (*I*, 165). Williams suggests (and struggles in *The Great American Novel* to achieve) what Joyce the year before in *Ulysses* had so convincingly demonstrated: that the "new" novel, like its protagonists, would be a parody of traditional forms, that a concept of life as parody was itself the meaning of the new forms.

Heroics must exist, in short, solely in the quality of means used to no discernible end—in life *style*, so to speak—desire courageously pursued but intensifying only into self-realization. This is the quality apparent in Williams's star, for example, described in the early poem, "El Hombre":

> It's a strange courage
> you give me ancient star:
>
> Shine alone in the sunrise
> toward which you lend no part![12]

Or there is his elegy to D. H. Lawrence, whose "unfading desire" is betrayed by the abortive hopes of the seasonal cycle, Lawrence "worn with a fury of sad labor / to create summer from / spring's decay" (*SP*, 96–98). The persona of the early experimental prose is himself a figure of "unfading desire," who engages in an endless quest for a sustaining theory of art and the imagination. This quest, however, is largely reflexive, a reiterated "activation" of the mind, whose only results are the released and manifest energy of self-assertion, in Williams's terms, the "dance" or "design" of self-assertion. As the form and actual title of *Kora in Hell: Improvisations* make clear, the self can engage only in discrete "improvisations": "*the sad truth is that since the imagination is nothing, nothing will come of it*" (*I*, 36). In another of his glosses, the narrator of *Kora in Hell* reiterates that improvisations are (and can only be) their own justification: "*One may write music and music but who will dance to it? The dance escapes but the music, the music—projects a dance over itself which the feet follow lazily if at all. So a dance is a thing in itself*" (*I*, 47).

In *The Great American Novel* the ultimate balance to its heavy mockery is the narrator's assertion (that is, his argument but, more important, his immediate, improvisational claim or demonstration) of the "flamboyant" self created by an imagination which, he says, "must adorn and exaggerate life, must give it splendor and grotesqueness, beauty and infinite depth." Williams's celebrated concern with "things" (for example, "no ideas but in things") involves more than an existential demand for concreteness and newness; it should remind us also that his positive theme always affirms the primary thrust of identity. Both the self and its objects "live" in the intensity of their realization—in what amounts to a demonstration of energy. His discussion of flamboyance to which I have already alluded goes on to make this point: "The imagination demands for satisfaction creative energy. Flamboyance expresses faith in that energy—it is a shout of delight, a declaration of richness" (*I*, 200–201). The flamboyant self creates what Williams calls elsewhere "the enlivening scurry" (*I*, 280), an extraordinarily vivid and apt phrase that describes at once the form, narrative substance, and essential meaning of most of his poetry and prose. For the writer, the enlivening scurry is possible in an extravagant freedom of language. The language of the surrealists, for example, makes "words into sentences that will have a fantastic reality which is false." To the inevitable falsity of fantastic reality Williams opposes the avoidable "falseness of the piecemeal," in which language is subservient to material and conventional ends (*I*, 280–81). Even conversation (in writing and in life) is "actual" only to the extent that it is an expression of "singleness," of the self as pure design: "It must have only the effect of itself. . . . It must have no other purpose than the roundness and the color and the repetition of grapes in a bunch, such grapes as those of Juan Gris" (*I*, 286–87). Such a thematic statement, of course, exists primarily in a dramatic context; in addition to whatever inherent ironies it may contain, it takes only a momentary place among all the other fragments of associative and disassociative memory, narrative, and exposition that make up the "scurry" of the personae of *The Great American Novel* and the rest of the early prose pieces. As the monologist reminds us at one point, such fragments are "particles of falling stars, coming to nothing" (*I*, 208).

Ends are either complex or nonexistent, the ceaseless mockers of desire. Nevertheless, gestures of desire are central to all of Williams's personae. They are all, in Paterson's phrase, "flagrant in desire" (*P*, 71), and desire seeks to move toward the intensified expression of itself in heroic gesture, design, and dance. Or we might say simply that the self seeks to become articulate; scurryings, that is, are the moment-by-moment articulations of the self, leading perhaps to an aggregate of moments but to no end or resolution. In his "Overture to a Dance of Locomotives" Williams notes that train wheels "repeating / the same gesture remain relatively / stationary: rails forever parallel / return on themselves indefinitely" (*SP*, 19). The artist hears and records these articulations (as Williams describes the process in "Desert Music") in a way that intensifies and finally authenticates them: the verbal self (kinetic, energized, seeking self-realization) becomes the "verb" of the "made poem."[13] Art is both the prototype and the apotheosis of self-realization, and the illusionist paradox is complete: the fictions of the self (including the self of the artist) achieve their fullest "reality" in the fiction of art. The artist "fixes" (designs, articulates, intensifies) the energized moment in an act that is an intensification of his own desire and a general affirmation of life. According to Williams, "It isn't what he says that counts as a work of art, it's what he makes, with such intensity of perception that it lives with an intrinsic movement of its own to verify its authenticity."[14]

"Intrinsic movement" which is self-authenticating is what Williams strives to create, both in those works in which the persona is the self-conscious monologist and in those in which the personae are more objectively drawn and dramatized. Many of the short lyrics deal with an action, or, even more

often, a *poise* for action in which kinesis is momentarily arrested in form.
Williams's "Bird," for example

> with outstretched
> wings poised
> inviolate unreaching
>
> yet reaching
> your image this November
> planes
>
> to a stop
> miraculously fixed in my
> arresting eyes   [PB, 41]

Here the bird's own self-realization, its movement toward articulation of energy (qualified, to be sure: "unreaching / yet reaching / your image") is explicitly augmented by the intense imaginative perception of the artist;
aesthetic "fix" or arrest, in other words, takes place on at least two levels. Or
there is Elaine (in one of three dramatic sketches significantly called
"Stances") "poised for the leap she / is not yet ready for / —save in her eyes"
(PB, 18); or the blue jay "crouched / just before the take-off / caught / in the
cinematograph— / in motion / of the mind." This blue jay, Williams adds, is
"serving art / as usual" (PB, 48–49); or in "The Bitter World of Spring" the red
elms "that lift the tangled / net of their desires hard into / the falling rain" and
the shad ascending "water-headed, unrelenting, upstream" (CLP, 74). At the
center of such poems is literally the articulating verb. In life as in poetry art is
"the agony of self-realization" (as Williams calls it in "Desert Music") actu-
alizing itself in form.

Actualization, it must be emphasized, is far more the form of desire than
the form of consummation; it is tenuous, ephemeral, a "cinematograph" at
best, finding its source in pain as much as in pleasure. It is simply whatever
"measure" we make or find in the arduous, hopeless pursuit of our dreams.
In the later poetry particularly, Williams focuses strongly on the traditional
qualities of stoic heroism—courage, acceptance of suffering, and relentless
commitment to effort in the face of nonexistent ends and sure failure—the
qualities of the elms and shad described above. In Book Four of *Paterson* it is
effort, of course, which emerges as the central theme: "*La Vertue est toute dans
l'effort*" (P, 184). There is also the effort of the music teacher and his pupils in
Williams's poem "Lesson from a Pupil Recital." He remains "blinking from
his dream" as his gross and awkward pupils attempt to release the music
within them. Pupils and teacher (the "creator" of the pupils just as the arrest-

ing eye "miraculously fixed" the bird) fail to achieve anything commensurate with the dream, but the very desire for music takes a certain form, creates a certain music of its own, "cleansing from each / his awkwardness for him to blossom / thence a sound" (*CLP*, 83).

I have already noted Williams's identification with birds; it reflects his mock-heroic commitment to the sheer act of flight as passionate pursuit of the unknown in a void of nothingness. "To seek what?" he asks rhetorically in another poem, "The Woodpecker," and the answer, as we might expect, is that "there is nothing / there." Even the unknown, he notes, if known, is no longer the unknown. Our only relevant "knowledge" is of falling, pain, the consummation of failure: "We never knew the earth so solidly as when we were / crushed upon it." Or there is perhaps the formal knowledge of desire itself, so palpable as to be sustaining. As Joseph Riddel, one of Williams's best critics, puts it, "creative acts, efforts toward virtue, become in themselves the only virtue."[15] Williams's comment on the woodpecker's pursuit of beetles sums up the mock-hero's most optimistic possibilities (which, in his earlier treatment of the swallow in *The Great American Novel*, were themselves mocked):

> Flight
> means only desire and desire the end of flight,
> stabbing there with a barbed tongue which *succeeds!*   [*CLP*, 122]

Paterson

Paterson brings together Williams's tendency in his other poetry to create dramatized personae who are avatars of the poet hero with the use of a self-conscious monologist that was characteristic of the experimental fiction. Even the monologist is here given more prototypal reference (presumably Williams reflects the influence of Joyce, T. S. Eliot, and Ezra Pound) and thus is kept at a somewhat greater dramatic distance from the author. In any case, he remains Williams's central version of the epic quester "walking" the landscape in search of wonders, someone who (as he describes those he represents) "craved the miraculous" (*P*, 10). Or, to state the case more accurately, this is the role Paterson tries to play in an age of iron which yields wonders grudgingly if at all. Critics have noted that he is not "pater" but "pater-son," but this distinction is not simply a sign that he represents rebellion, youth, hope, and renewal. Its ironic dimension suggests diminishment, attenuation, a less than fully adequate version of the father, someone who perhaps essentially models himself on a memorialized ideal—someone whose basic role (not necessarily his approach to that role) is foreign and anachronistic to the environment in which it must be realized. Clearly Paterson's desire to be a romantic quester is heroic, but the context of reality mocks its fulfillment. His own awareness of his precarious situation and thus his self-mockery are acute. From the beginning his intentions are stated in the most tentative terms, his personal "defectiveness" made clear: he is *"hard put to it"*; his major hope, less action itself than *"an identification and a plan for action"*; he is "just another dog / among a lot of dogs"—a lame one at that (*P*, 2–3). Significantly, as dog he is not even allowed by the city to wander "at large" in the park, which is the only natural landscape available to the modern hero (*P*, 61). Paterson's middle name, "Faitoute," describes the fundamental quality of the epic hero in his world, but its ironic echoes in Williams's poem are as insistent as its hint of possibility. Paterson, in fact, does almost nothing; even his walking is largely aimless strolling in a sterile void, "foot pacing foot outward / into emptiness" (*P*, 63).

Of the three other personae in *Paterson* who are the most obvious avatars of the poet hero, two are even more ineffectual than Paterson. Corydon, for instance, is the mock-heroine of what is explicitly a mock-pastoral, the parody (or perhaps travesty) in this case so savage as to reduce both Corydon and her environment to a monochrome of despair and death. Attenuation has resulted in almost total loss of substance. "No more woods and fields. Therefore / present, forever present": this is the refrain of Corydon's modern pastoral of a "pterodactyl"-like helicopter searching the Hellgate current for a corpse while the gulls circle in "vortices of despair" (*P*, 161). But even her message, like her entire modern pastoral, indeed, like Corydon herself, is an imitation of an imitation—bad T. S. Eliot and worse Dante. "It stinks," she admits candidly in one of those moments that reveals simply her pain and her futile but continuing struggle to give some sort of coherence and articulation even to her despair, not to mention any possibilities that a "new" present might have. Her authentic language (or, more precisely, the authentic language of her inauthenticity) is the barest "chatter," as Paterson elsewhere describes the nature of his own voice (*P*, 39). In Book Four her identification with Paterson is substantial and deliberate (they are both made inept lovers of the same person). Cress is another chatterer, and she also reinforces our sense of the poet hero as failure, not only by her revelation of her own personal misfortunes but, of course, in the accusations she makes against Paterson.

At the other positive extreme as model of the poet in *Paterson* is Madame Curie (Allen Ginsberg, a promising beginner, is also paired with her in a positive sense). Like Daniel Boone, Curie experiences the consummation of the romantic hero insofar as she finds and releases (brings to form) in matter a power commensurate with her will and imagination. Her success is a paraphrase of Ralph Waldo Emerson's classic formulation of the transcendental quest and goal: "That which was unconscious truth, becomes, when interpreted and defined in an object, a part of the domain of knowledge—a new weapon in the magazine of power."[16] But as a historical figure she is something of an anomaly, perhaps a lingering echo of the great heroes of the past, more probably a genuine saint, authentically miraculous, essentially out of time. Williams emphasizes her uniqueness by drawing an amusing but significant comparison between the French couple and Mary and Joseph.

Paterson is, in effect, defined by the other personae of the poem, and he, in turn, articulates their natures as dimensions of himself. Together these personae constitute a scale of heroic possibility ranging from the extremes of Corydon's situation to that of Madame Curie. The first two sections of Book Four juxtapose these extremes: an opaque present as the ultimate despairing mockery of hope or the continued possibility of "a luminosity of elements, the / current leaping" (P, 176). Section three then characteristically "resolves" them by returning to the full tension of the mock-heroic mode as it manifests itself in the main body of the poem—by putting the focus neither on final failure or major achievement but on unremitting *effort*. I have already alluded to Williams's major theme as it finds expression here:

> Virtue is wholly
> in the effort to be virtuous.
>   This takes connivance,
>   takes convoluted forms, takes
>   time!   [P, 189]

Despair is simply loss of will to effort. It is not a question of consummations; a steady commitment to effort is itself the heroic task, a failure even of effort the major peril:

> Weakness,
> weakness dogs him, fulfillment only
> a dream or in a dream. No one mind
> can do it all, run smooth
> in the effort: *toute dans l'effort*   [P, 191]

Walking—steady walking—is the articulating verb of the poem and the "design" of its hero. A description of the "form" of walking ("The body is tilted slightly forward" [P, 45]), quoted by Williams from the *Journal of the American Medical Association*, makes this clear from the beginning. Book Five strongly reiterates the centrality of the poet's walk in the world but now in a context in which it is seen as a sufficient and sustaining design, the highest possibility for the modern hero. For Paterson, a continuum of heroic gesture will be his closest approach to formal order, the only possible "measured dance" (*P*, 239) on the ground of his desire.

As I have already noted, Paterson dreams of being an epic explorer of the wonders of the New World. His dream is as impossible of fulfillment as it was for the great explorers before him—as impossible, in fact, as Don Quixote's attempt to perpetuate the Age of Chivalry and Pierre Menard's to write Cervantes's novel. He is a defective hero in a defective world, or perhaps a world simply "gone," as he describes it at one point (*P*, 79), and without renewal: "Who is it spoke of April? Some / insane engineer. There is no recurrence" (*P*, 142). Not only is this quester without an adequate environment for his quest, he is without any real sense of direction:

> There is no direction. Whither? I
> cannot say. I cannot say
> more than how. The how (howl) only
> is at my disposal (proposal). . . .   [*P*, 18]

He has some sense of the proper method of questing, but even this method is less fixed plan than existential cry of pain and need (howl), less under his present control (disposal) and thus some sort of end mastered, than what he calls elsewhere a "plan" (proposal). The irony in Williams's major poem is insistently limiting and inherent in every dimension of its form. *Paterson*, in short, involves a futile quest relentlessly pursued, its structure that of the blocked quest. Williams, of course, realizes this; as his persona says at one point: "Blocked. / (Make a song out of that: concretely)" (*P*, 62).

More precisely, a song in the mock-heroic mode is one of both freedom and blockage, in fact of freedom and blockage in irreconcilable, complex tension. Anticlimax is endemic to the poem—in the structural movement from section to section, even passage to passage, and in the individual actions of the personae. Sam Patch's great dive is a metaphor of the whole: he plunges boldly toward the stream, his body wavers in the air, he disappears in the water and the following spring turns up frozen in an ice cake (*P*, 17). Paterson's monologue, like that of the earlier personae of the experimental prose, alternates between hope and despair, possibility and denial, visions of renewal and of wasteland (or marriage and divorce), between willed commitment to self-realization—"I must / find my meaning and lay it, white, / beside the sliding water" (*P*, 145)—and bitter mockery of himself and others: "Give up / the poem. Give up the shilly- / shally of art" (*P*, 108). But he does not surrender his will and imagination and resigns himself, on the whole, to paying what he calls the "cost" of loving; one recalls Paterson's vision in Book Five of the Jew in the extermination pit, smiling and comforting his companions as they are sprayed with machine gun fire (*P*, 223).

We are left in the end with the living ("concrete") shapes of desire in defeat. This is what Paterson articulates in himself and others. Cress, for example, takes this shape in her letters; so does the evangelist in the park; so even does Corydon. For Williams, this is the shape of Maxwell Bodenheim, of Edgar Allan Poe, of all his various personae. In this sense, desire is fulfilled in the form of its own expression or self-realization. For Williams as for Cervantes the environment still offers some dimension of adventure, some opportunity for the pursuit of dreams in which the pursuit at least allows the self to create (live) its fictions and the poet to give them further shape in naming. This is the most optimistic hope of mock-heroic narrative, the one expressed by Stevens through the towering figure of Chocorua: "The air changes, creates and re-creates, like strength, / And to breathe is a fulfilling of desire." At the same time, Chocorua is simply the "singular" spokesman ("megalfrere") of the "common self," the latter called by Stevens a "political tramp with an heraldic air" (*CP*, 300–302). His punning on "air" reminds us of the fragility of the mock-heroic environment, of the degree to which it offers at best only the opportunity for play or pretense. We cannot possess dreams but they can perhaps possess us. This at least is where Paterson has come out in Book Five:

> Dreams possess me
>   and the dance
>   of my thoughts
>   involving animals
>   the blameless beasts   [*P*, 224]

Wallace Stevens's Improvisations

Perhaps it's the lunch that we had
Or the lunch that we should have had.
But I am, in any case,
A most inappropriate man
In a most unpropitious place.
STEVENS
"Sailing after Lunch"

No spring can follow past meridian.
Yet you persist with anecdotal bliss
To make believe a starry *connaissance*.
STEVENS
"Le Monocle de Mon Oncle"

The point of vision and desire are the same.
It is to the hero of midnight that we pray
On a hill of stones to make beau mont thereof.
STEVENS
"An Ordinary Evening in New Haven"

Dislocation

One crucial dimension of the mock-heroic mode is clearly its expression of dislocation, of alienation from one's own time and culture, of being, as Wallace Stevens puts it bluntly in "Sailing after Lunch," "a most inappropriate man / In a most unpropitious place" (*CP*, 120). At the same time, Cervantine mock-heroic is characteristically self-conscious about its own dislocation. It mocks the nostalgia that it so acutely feels; it acknowledges the claims of "reality" (time present) against the pain of loss (time past). In effect, assertions of reality and the commitments of feeling are expressed simultaneously—or as simultaneously as the essential seriality of writing will allow. The mock-heroic mode involves literary collage, various kinds of spatial structuring, invariably, in one form or another, a superimposition of attitudes experienced at once and without resolution, except insofar as we think of the fictional "dance" as resolution of sorts.

In "Sailing after Lunch," Stevens makes plain that his specific imaginative and emotional commitments are to the heroics of romanticism, even in the face of a rational awareness that this tradition, in a literal, historical, "straight" sense was dead and, perhaps more than that, "wholly the vapidest fake" in any empirical context at any time and place. "It is the word *pejorative* that hurts," he says in the poem, but the word is essentially self-inflicted (that is, going beyond whatever point of view the critics of this period might have taken toward his work) and a basic dimension of a more complex total attitude. Significantly, after the strong mockery of pure and historical romantic sailing, a counterrhythm returns with an appeal to the "way one feels" about wind and water as the only "slight transcendence" possible—in effect, a feeling of transcendence in the face of the literal impossibility of the fact or, to put it another way, a transcendence of feeling seen as a fact, an imitation, a surrogate clearly recognized as such.

In Harold Bloom's useful phrase, Stevens is a "belated" romantic, and it is this belated romanticism in all its ramifications that is the key to his work.[1] The mock-hero is by definition a belated hero, born too late, with his deepest emotional commitments rooted in a dead mythology or historical period, an exiled figure forced to make do in a generation or environment hostile to the possibility of heroically defined selfhood. Don Quixote's willed anachronism is at once the particular expression of his essential displacement and the key to its nature. The mock-heroic sensibility assumes a lack of meaningful temporal continuity: the death of gods and heroes, a sharp sense of historical diminution, the outright rupture of present from past, or the mere sterile "red-in-red repetitions never going / Away" of cyclical time as Stevens describes it in "Notes toward a Supreme Fiction" (CP, 400). The structural anticlimax endemic to the mock-heroic mode is predicated on a pervasive sense of spiritual and cultural anticlimax; nothing (least of all time) "leads to" anything that is resolved, permanent, or absolute.

For Stevens the only "real" time is time present, a moment that momentarily becomes the unreality of time past. He reminds his alter ego in "Sunday Morning" that the "old catastrophe" of Christ's crucifixion can come to her "only in silent shadows and in dreams" and celebrates a "mythy" age (also lost) when man and gods commingled (CP, 67–68). In a later poem, "Dutch Graves in Bucks County," he is even more explicit, on this occasion reminding his ancestors that in "the total / Of remembrance" they "share nothing of ourselves" and bluntly telling them further to "know that the past is not part of the present." Ends involve neither inheritance nor significant individual consummations but simply death in a cycle of repetition: "This is the pit of torment that placid end / Should be illusion, that the mobs of birth / Avoid our stale perfections, seeking out / Their own . . ." (*CP*, 292–93). With Stevens as with Williams, the fact of ceaseless change, the continuity of discontinuity, offers us the cruel freedom of possibility at the expense of ends.

The mockery of time, moreover, involves an additional sense, so acute in Stevens, of present man as a historically diminished figure, a "parody" of the figures of heroic myth in his past. In "Academic Discourse at Havana" Stevens describes what had been (the poem is written from the even more desolate temporal point of view of a present "grand decadence") the civilized order of a public park in Havana as "a peanut parody / For peanut people." He carefully sets this parody in the context of its heroic prototypes:

> Canaries in the morning, orchestras
> In the afternoon, balloons at night. That is
> A difference, at least, from nightingales,
> Jehovah and the great sea-worm. The air
> Is not so elemental nor the earth
> So near.
> But the sustenance of the wilderness
> Does not sustain us in the metropoles.   [*CP*, 142–43]

A parody order of some sort, one must emphasize, is what modern man can look forward to at best. At worst are grander decadences, blankness, deadness, the Snow Man world of a few of Stevens's poems, where even the mock-hero is reduced to despair and silence.

"All history is modern history," Stevens writes in *Adagia*.[2] Although his aphorism scarcely suggests the psychology of disinheritance, it is actually remote (though not entirely divorced) from the confident assertions of Emerson and Henry David Thoreau that man is reborn every morning. It records the fact of loss, possibly the opportunities of newness, but not the pain of loss or the divided sensibility with which one is left. "These days of disinheritance," he calls the present in "Cuisine Bourgeoisie," a poem whose description of psychological mood resonates to include that of a larger psychic dislocation in time. As Stevens describes this dislocation:

> It is like the season when, after summer,
> It is summer and it is not, it is autumn
> And it is not, it is day and it is not,
> As if last night's lamps continued to burn,
> As if yesterday's people continued to watch
> The sky, half porcelain, preferring that

To shaking out heavy bodies in the glares
Of this present, this science, this unrecognized.

This outpost, this douce, this dumb, this dead, in which
We feast on human heads, brought in on leaves,
Crowned with the first, cold buds. On these we live,
No longer on the ancient cake of seed,
The almond and deep fruit. This bitter meat
Sustains us . . . Who, then, are they, seated here?
Is the table a mirror in which they sit and look?
Are the men eating reflections of themselves?   [CP, 228]

The season after summer is the season of parody, described in Stevens's favorite parodic formulas (denial—"It is . . . it is not"—as the mirror double of affirmation and "as if," the conditional of pretension). The dual reference of this particular parody simultaneously directs the self backward in nostalgic memory of a lost feast ("the ancient cake of seed, / The almond and deep fruit"), noble and truly sustaining, and forward into the present moment or "outpost" of time where it must now find sustenance. In this particular poem, the sustaining "bitter meat" remains only a savage travesty of the parodic strategy central to Steven's most characteristic work: the creation of a solipsistic hero (his heroics sustained only by and within the context of himself) in some way imitative in spirit, if unequal in substance, to the heroes of the past. In "Cuisine Bourgeoisie," however, the solipsism is mere cannibalism, the sterile perversions of Salome, dead eating dead in a dumb and dead present.

Certainly the delicate equilibrium that the mock-heroic mode tries to maintain is constantly threatened by an imbalance of its internal tensions, the scales tipping on occasion either toward straight invocation of heroic vision or toward bitter mockery and the simple expression of blank despair. These extremes mark the polarities of Stevens's work and can be identified in individual poems. I am concerned, however, rather with his obsessive quest (or mock-quest, since its recurrent pursuit is a manifestation of the ironies it explores) for equilibrium, specifically, for an adequate poetics of duality in balance, a poetics, as I have already termed it, of heroic parody. As much as that of any writer examined on these pages, Stevens's best work locates meaning in the complex and unresolved dialectic between an acknowledged "real" and an "ideal" passionately desired. I have already mentioned in connection with Williams Stevens's identification with Cervantes over Verrocchio, an identification that accepts Cervantine instability and complexity of attitude in return for poetic truth, indeed, in return for the simple preservation in some form of nobility as human attribute ("it is in danger of ceasing to exist, if we isolate it"). For Stevens Don Quixote is clearly the model figure for the poet of the present day, a figure whose example in one form or another must be followed without reduction or oversimplification: "Don Quixote will make it imperative for him to make a choice, to come to a decision regarding the imagination and reality; and he will find that it is not a choice of one over the other and not a decision that divides them, but something subtler, a recognition that here, too, as between these poles, the universal interdependence exists, and hence his choice and his decision must be that they are equal and inseparable."[3] Stevens saw William Carlos Williams in this same quixotic tradition, as his well-known comment in a review of *Collected Poems, 1921–1931*, suggests: "What, then, is a romantic poet now-a-days? He happens to be one who still dwells in an ivory tower, but who insists that life would be intolerable except for the fact that one has, from the top, such an exceptional view of the public dump and the advertising signs of Snider's Catsup, Ivory Soap and Chevrolet cars; he is the hermit who dwells alone with sun and moon, but insists on taking a rotten newspaper" (*OP*, 256).

These comments suggest that such dual vision as he ascribes to Cervantes and Williams and reserves for himself, however much it may stem from an acute sense of disinheritance and loss, involves for Stevens an attitude far more creative and complex than the mere expression of nostalgic memory and bitterness. To be sure, such feelings do occasionally find simple expression, and they clearly constitute the raw emotional force behind a continual commitment to the "ivory tower," to a dimension of experience that no longer *by and in itself* has a basis in reality, assuming it was ever more than the "vapidest fake." But today at least, some basis has to be found beyond nostalgic need if romantic heroism is to remain a credible subject for the major artist; the function of the dump is to supply such a basis. Like other writers in the mock-heroic mode, Stevens recognizes that the ironies of dual vision need not lead only to deconstruction; rather, these deconstructions can provide in themselves a potential environment for new constructions. It cannot be emphasized enough, particularly in the light of continuing critical debate, that irony in Stevens's career as in individual poems is not something he "works through" to vision. In fact, it constitutes the very foundation and context of vision, a context that deconstructs while allowing the simultaneous possibility of construction. Here as elsewhere, the mock-heroic mode generates its positive implications from the very context of its negations: by severely limiting heroic claims in time and substance, it makes possible a new and vital expression of freedom and "adventure" so the self can at least experience the feeling of being a hero. As Stevens might have phrased it, mock-heroic makes the possible possible. The modern romantic poet hero must willingly become "the hero without heroics" (*OP*, 84), the hero who is validated only by his encounter with those ironies which finally deny him in reality. In short, authenticity resides squarely and fully in the very duality that denies truth other than the status of fiction.

For Stevens the artist, the problem from the beginning was to create an aesthetic "tough, diverse, untamed" (as he describes it in "The Comedian as the Letter C" [CP, 31]), and adequate to the literary expression of this crucial duality. Later in life he noted explicitly that "in an age of unbelief, when the gods have come to an end . . . men turn to a fundamental glory of their own and from that create a new style of bearing themselves in reality. They create a new style of a new bearing in a new reality." Such a style will "supply the satisfactions of belief" (OP, 206–9)—an aim, we must keep in mind, rather different from supplying belief itself. But even early in his career Stevens already recognizes the necessity of transposing nostalgic feelings into some form of ironic comedy; the discovery of an adequate mode becomes critical to the development of his work. In "The Weeping Burgher," for example, the poetic voice is "tortured for old speech, / A white of wildly woven rings" and "weeping in a calcined heart," while trapped in the "sorry verities" of a banal present. His response to this situation, however, begins with a characteristic "yet," that word as important to Stevens's poetic structures as it is to those of Byron in Don Juan and for the same reason: its function as fulcrum for the movement of counterstatement:

> Yet in excess, continual,
> There is cure of sorrow.
>
> Permit that if as ghost I come
> Among the people burning in me still,
> I come as belle design
> Of foppish line.   [CP, 61]

The ironic ghost here emerges as the tenuous "spirit" of the romantic visionary and manifests itself in what will become the significant and enduring role of actor, player, clown, dandy, and mocker. In short, the rhythm of even this early poem (in structure more complicated than my sketch of it) is an antiphony of elegy, bitterness, and ironic hope.

In "Sad Strains of a Gay Waltz," to cite a somewhat later example, Stevens announces far more bluntly that one must turn from mourning old music to a search for new form, what he calls a new "mode of desire":

> The truth is that there comes a time
> When we can mourn no more over music
> That is so much motionless sound.

> There comes a time when the waltz
> Is no longer a mode of desire, a mode
> Of revealing desire and is empty of shadows.
>
> Too many waltzes have ended.

Stevens adds that even for "mountain-minded Hoon," the figure of the high romantic visionary who lingers on in his poetry, the "forms have vanished." The poem goes on to express the sense of chaotic disorder that Stevens felt so painfully in the 1930s and then turns on its feelings of loss with another "yet":

> Too many waltzes have ended. Yet the shapes
> For which the voices cry, these, too, may be
> Modes of desire, modes of revealing desire.
>
> Too many waltzes—The epic of disbelief
> Blares oftener and soon, will soon be constant.
> Some harmonious skeptic soon in a skeptical music
>
> Will unite these figures of men and their shapes
> Will glisten again with motion, the music
> Will be motion and full of shadows.   [CP, 121–22]

By this time in his life, Stevens's description of the forms of lost order is qualified by the same ironic context that must be characteristic of any present song; these forms were not truth, not even belief in the truth, but modes of the desire to believe. And that is what the new poetry can and must be—a "skeptical music" composed by a "harmonious skeptic," presumably in some new mode appropriate to the expression of harmonious skepticism.

Critics of Stevens have tended to shy away from full acknowledgment of the complex formal ramifications of this skeptical music, most of them finding it easier (and more satisfying to their own preconceptions) either to seek out the harmonies or catalog the ironic deconstructions. Stevens himself gropes constantly and self-consciously for a genre label that will adequately describe his work, but this groping is more a drama of desire than a record of achieved ends. In "Like Decorations in a Nigger Cemetery," for example, he tries to pinpoint a variant of one of the traditional genres, noting that "the comedy of hollow sounds derives / From truth and not from satire on our lives" (CP, 154). Or there are the elaborate invocations of tragedy and comedy in sections 16 and 17 of "An Ordinary Evening in New Haven," invocations full of qualifications and culminating in a disclaimer: "The serious reflection is composed / Neither of comic nor tragic but of commonplace" (CP, 476–78). These traditional genres, of course, are among the "too many waltzes" that have ended. Albeit they may have been modes of desire, even in this they are too pure for present circumstances, which require a mode more immediately of the present, more tentative, more mixed, more fully deconstructive of its implications, a mode, in short, that reaches full maturity in the significantly entitled "Notes toward a Supreme Fiction," a work that generates its own unstable form from the very complexities of definition. Likewise, the personae of this mode will be imperfect, "addicts / To blotches, angular anonymids / Gulping for shape" (CP, 371), always in some vital (though not simple) sense clowns in Chaplinesque "old coat" and "sagging pantaloons" (CP, 389), not heroes but "imaginary" heroes in both senses of the word "imaginary"—contrary, that is, to fact and, at the same time, heroic in imagination, heroic in their heroic construction of themselves.[4] With Stevens, as with other writers discussed here, a psychology of dislocation and historical anticlimax produces an equivalent literature whose systematic dissonance is, paradoxically, an attempt to preserve without sentimentality or other distortions the commitment to heroic experience which is at the heart of the sense of loss.

The mock-heroic mode preserves nobility, let me emphasize again, at the expense of fictionalizing both its manifestations and its ends. According to Stevens, "The final belief is to believe in a fiction, which you know to be a fiction, there being nothing else" (OP, 163). Or, as he puts it better in "The Pure Good of Theory":

> To say the solar chariot is junk
>
> Is not a variation but an end.
> Yet to speak of the whole world as metaphor
> Is still to stick to the contents of the mind
>
> And the desire to believe in a metaphor.
> It is to stick to the nicer knowledge of
> Belief, that what it believes in is not true.   [CP, 332]

The "desire to believe"—the "act," so to speak, of believing in a fiction—is as fictional as the metaphorical constructs of belief. The central significance of Don Quixote, we must remember, rests in his heroic commitment to fictions: his fictionalization of himself (and his encounters with other fictionalizations) in addition to his general insistence that all fictions are valuable and worth preserving. Quixote's antagonists in one way or another are destroyers of fictions, from those concerned with his personal rehabilitation, to book burners, to ignorant lower-class mockers, to sophisticated proponents of the classical position that the truths of history are superior to those of poetry. He is, to be sure, mad, but Cervantes, like Stevens, accepts his madness while being fully aware of its implications. In the modern age, as Michel Foucault has noted, poet and madman join in a common quest for resemblance ("the whole world as metaphor"), both insisting on order, unity, authentic identities where, in fact, none exist.[5] What we might call Stevens's "ironic madness" leads him, appropriately enough, to "The Comedian as the Letter C," his first explicit, major experiment in the mock-heroic mode, and then beyond that significant model to the later long poems, which still incorporate the mode but in more subtle and original ways.

Pedagogues in Pantaloons

"Unless we believe in the hero, what is there / To believe?" asks Stevens in his important poem, "Examination of the Hero in a Time of War," a poem whose wartime setting gives particular immediacy and poignancy to Stevens's sense of the "death" of the hero—his physical extinction in cold and darkness ("Death is my / Master and, without light, I dwell") and his decadence in forms "of a still life, symbols, brown things to think of / In brown books" that have lost their potency as credible invocations of heroism (CP, 273–76). The poem as a whole makes clear his awareness that belief in the hero must be contained within the same authenticating irony as any other. Late in life, in a valedictory context that suggests the earlier poem's importance to him, Stevens described it as "about the credible hero" (OP, 117). For a writer committed, however "belatedly," to the preservation of a heroic tradition, the search for such a credible hero is the central problem of his work—with Stevens the search beginning in his earliest poems and remaining an obsession. From the beginning, also, credibility was sought principally by various experiments in the ironic distancing of romantic feelings and attitudes. Critics of this early work have carefully documented his various borrowings from the ironic models available to him: Baudelaire, Jules Laforgue, Ben Jonson, Voltaire, Pope, Byron, Commedia dell'arte, among others.[6]

Stevens's most useful discovery (in effect culminating his early studies in irony and leading directly to several poems, whose major exemplar is "The Comedian as the Letter C") was one which some of his major critics still find anomalous to his work and others have not sufficiently explored—the possibilities of mock-heroic.[7] My point, let me emphasize, is not that Stevens tried to learn to write like Pope as the literal basis of a future style but rather than he sensed behind the satirical surface of traditional mock-heroic the ironic structuring needed for his poetry and thus, naturally, was attracted to the mode in its received form as a point of departure. Like Byron, he saw in mock-heroic the full, complex possibilities which Cervantes had opened up but which the eighteenth century with its strong satirical bias had done much to obscure. As Stevens tries to make clear in the passage I have already quoted from "Like Decorations in a Nigger Cemetery," his comedy derives "from truth and not from satire on our lives." His comment reminds us again of the distinction between satire and quixotism that writers such as Byron intuited as they worked to restore the full implications of the mode and that critics such as Marthe Robert have brought to our attention.

"The Comedian as the Letter C" is, in effect, Stevens's first major "imitation" (to borrow Robert's useful word).[8] The title is correct in suggesting that the poem involves the essential Stevens, one that is fundamentally perpetuated in the more subtle, individual, and sophisticated forms of his later poetry. Stevens's description of his poem as "rudimentary" is more apt than his own disparaging use of that word might imply: in fact, it contains all the basic elements of what will constitute his ironic romanticism.[9] It is, to be sure, stylistically still too narrowly derivative, appropriate enough in its own way but only an initial or imperfect response to an enduring need. As a poet committed to heroes, Stevens had to learn to write an epic poetry; as "harmonious skeptic," he was equally committed, in one form or another, to a particular kind of epic termed by himself "the epic of disbelief."

In this connection, the most obvious fact about "The Comedian"—obvious probably because it is the only one of Stevens's long poems to attempt the use of narrative plot—is that it involves a parodic or "imitation" quest. On one hand, its resonances are such that critics have had little trouble in establishing various levels of heroic reference: cosmological journeys of the great mythic prototypes; cultural journeys of the American Adam to a "new" world; romantic journeys in search of the self such as those undertaken by Walt Whitman, Byron, Wordsworth, Shelley, and others. On the other hand, as Stevens made clear to one of his correspondents, "The Comedian" is an "anti-mythological" poem about an "every-day man who lives a life without the slightest adventure, except that he lives it in poetic atmosphere as we all do."[10] Stevens's exception defines the very nature of adventure in his work and the substance of Crispin's experience: adventure in this context meaning the self's attempts (in an environment that offers us the freedom not of fulfillment but of possibility) to create a formal order "truly" consonant with reality. The constructions of the authentic hero (including his imaginative creation of himself) are, even in the case of tragic experience, to some substantial extent synchronous with a sympathetic environment that shapes or is shaped by them. The mock-hero, however, exists in a state of perpetual dissynchronization that denies unity but not desire.

Stevens describes Crispin as "a clown, perhaps, but an aspiring clown" (CP, 39). Another of Stevens's clown heroes, we must remember, will be called with superb punning irony "the Canon Aspirin" in "Notes toward a

Supreme Fiction." Crispin's aspiration is clearly that of poet and madman in the modern age: to unite the words of things (the mind's constructions of things) with the things themselves:

> He could not be content with counterfeit,
> With masquerade of thought, with hapless words
> That must belie the racking masquerade,
> With fictive flourishes. . . .   [CP, 39]

It is this aspiration, we are told, "that first drove Crispin to his wandering," and it is at the core of any heroic dimension he may have. He is a clown, in turn, not simply because of his repeated failures or his sophomoric enthusiasms or his pedantry but, most important, because of his banality, his absurdity within a cosmic or absolute context, within, that is, a context of the same external reality he tries hopelessly to master.

Stevens makes clear that the tragic note (a possibility if one has created a protagonist who fails) is inappropriate to Crispin's final resigned acceptance "of shall or ought to be in is":

> Was he to bray this in profoundest brass
> Arointing his dreams with fugal requiems?
> Was he to company vastest things defunct
> With a blubber of tom-toms harrowing the sky?
> Scrawl a tragedian's testament? Prolong
> His active force in an inactive dirge,
> Which, let the tall musicians call and call,
> Should merely call him dead? Pronounce amen
> Through choirs infolded to the outmost clouds?
> Because he built a cabin who once planned
> Loquacious columns by the ructive sea?
> Because he turned to salad-beds again?
> Jovial Crispin, in calamitous crape?
> Should he lay by the personal and make
> Of his own fate an instance of all fate?
> What is one man among so many men?
> What are so many men in such a world?
> Can one man think one thing and think it long?
> Can one man be one thing and be it long?
> The very man despising honest quilts
> Lies quilted to his poll in his despite.
> For realist, what is is what should be.   [CP, 41]

In Stevens's terms, the "tragedian's testament" is the same absurd fiction as any other in the context of the "mere" fact of death and change. "The only emperor is the emperor of ice-cream" is his harsh judgment on the possibilities of transcendence in the best known of those occasional brutal short poems that heavily mock the elegance of most of his work (*CP*, 64). Beyond the existential lie only its fictions, quantitative, and qualitative, which even as fictions have no long duration. In his later poetry, Stevens may seem to move closer to tragedy, but it is more a matter of tone than substance, essentially a sharper tone of elegy and loss, which is only one important dimension of the mock-heroic mode. As he himself was aware, his quest for an adequate genre involved identification of a form that would incorporate a complex mode of conflicting and juxtaposed perspectives.

Banality remains the crucial context of adventure, and in "The Comedian" it is reinforced by Stevens's final brutal reduction of Crispin to mere salad-picker and doddler of ludicrous children. We should be reminded again of Cervantes's calculated ridicule and systematic humiliation of Don Quixote—the beatings, the curds on the head, the sitting in his own feces. "So may the relation of each man be clipped" (*CP*, 46) reads the carefully set-off line in "The Comedian" that literally and thematically ends the poem, a line bluntly reminding us of a dimension of quixotism that its more sentimental commentators like to ignore. Poems, illusions, life itself are harshly "clipped" or trimmed by the very conditions that foster their existence. In "the end," to use one of Stevens's favorite words, is "nothing"—"illustrious nothing" possibly, as he calls it in "Description without Place" (*CP*, 339), but still nothing.

Stevens's other poem involving Crispin, "Anecdote of the Abnormal," seems to mute the reductiveness and stress the heroic counterrhythm. It emphasizes new possibilities in life and ends with a vision of Crispin's apotheosis:

> Crispin—valet, Crispin—saint!
> The exhausted realist beholds
> His tattered manikin arise,
> Tuck in the straw,
> And stalk the skies.   [*OP*, 24]

But the fact remains that Crispin is, to use Robert's formula, valet *and* saint, Crispin seen from a dual perspective that denies resolution, indeed, one whose viability and meaning rest on sustained irresolution, complete abandonment of what Robert calls "the categorical either/or."

Certainly the "alternative ending" that Stevens hints at for Crispin in "The Comedian" involves options more apparent than substantial:

> Crispin as hermit, pure and capable,
> Dwelt in the land. Perhaps if discontent
> Had kept him still the prickling realist,
> Choosing his element from droll confect
> Of was and is and shall or ought to be,
> Beyond Bordeaux, beyond Havana, far
> Beyond carked Yucatan, he might have come
> To colonize his polar planterdom
> And jig his chits upon a cloudy knee.
> But his emprize to that idea soon sped.   [*CP*, 40]

Not only is possibility here syntactically hedged around with Stevens's celebrated panoply of conditionals; tone and language also suggest that nothing finally would have come from such emprize but more elegant fictions and philosophical doddling. That Crispin succumbs to his environment, that his "prickling" realism dissipates as he lapses into entrapment ("day by day, now this thing and now that / Confined him" [*CP*, 40]), is only a matter of sooner rather than later. Stevens's choice of sooner merely emphasizes the narrative anticlimax—what he calls "haphazard denouement" (*CP*, 40)—which is endemic to the mock-heroic quest and, here as in other works I have examined, reinforced by the episodic nature of the action.

We are dealing in "The Comedian" with one action endlessly repeated. The poem begins, as *Don Quixote* begins, with the protagonist leaving his village to encounter reality. In neither work does anything actually "happen" beyond this prototypal movement, which in Stevens's poetry is the movement from an "old" world of effete and obsolete conventions and attitudes—a world of "too many waltzes," in effect, "lost" to reality—to a "new" environment that promises fresh illusionary possibilities among the endlessly vivid and obdurate realities encountered. This essential movement is obviously symbolized in Crispin's journey as immigrant from Europe to America. But the initiation of ocean experience once over, new quickly becomes old, and the journey must be repeated until the "end" I have already described takes place. This movement is also reflected in the two basic dicta that frame the action of the poem: from "man is the intelligence of his soil" to "his soil is man's intelligence" (*CP*, 27, 36). In the latter dictum and all its implications reside whatever meaning is to be found in the poem. For Stevens as for other writers in the mock-heroic mode, the cruel test of reality accredits the romantic visionary process while steadily denying its fulfillment.

Finally, we must keep in mind that Crispin is brought within the enabling frame of irony not simply by the action, structure, and denouement of "The

Comedian," but, in addition, by Stevens's use of a narrative voice complexly involved with Crispin, yet mocking him in a sustained sardonic commentary. In Stevens's later poetry, the unresolved dialectic manifests itself in the dramatic modulations—what I will call the various dramatic "roles" or personae —of one voice. In "The Comedian," however, he uses the device of paired characters so typical of earlier mock-heroic: in particular, the young and ardent quester, the "greenhorn" or "sophomore" or "annotator" (as Crispin is variously called [*CP*, 28, 32, 36]), observed and commented on by the mature realist. The immediate model here is probably *Don Juan*, but the original pair are, of course, Don Quixote and Sancho Panza, a pairing which in itself virtually signaled a new mode of narrative. Howard Mancing scarcely exaggerates when he observes that "the most important single event in Cervantes's novel, after the original exposition, is the introduction of Sancho Panza. Once Sancho with his nonchivalric reality rides beside Don Quixote, the latter can never again be the same."[11] Joyce's work takes the same direction. A. Walton Litz has noted an analogy between Joyce's revision of *Stephen Hero* into *A Portrait of the Artist as a Young Man* and Stevens's own reworking, in the summer of 1922, of an earlier "From the Journal of Crispin" into the present "Comedian." As Litz points out, "The Comedian" should be read as "a modern novel, with a complex *persona*-hero qualified by the author's ironic point of view."[12]

Behind this "middle-aged" point of view and exploring its implications more directly lies Stevens's earlier mock-heroic poem, "Le Monocle de Mon Oncle," in which the poet urges himself "in verses wild with motion, full of din," to "come, celebrate / The faith of forty" (*CP*, 16). Middle age is the psychological breeding ground of mock-heroic; Janus-faced, it remains involved (if not obsessed) with the commitments of youth but no longer believes in the literal possibility of their realization. A sense of time and death has intruded to mock the fulfillment but not the desire for visionary experience and the qualities of youth now lost. "Like a dull scholar," Stevens has only in middle age achieved a new perspective: "I behold, in love, / An ancient aspect touching a new mind. / It comes, it blooms, it bears its fruit and dies" (*CP*, 16).

Stevens also compares his situation with that of a red bird who "seeks out his choir" in the spring:

> I am a man of fortune greeting heirs;
> For it has come that thus I greet the spring.
> These choirs of welcome choir for me farewell.
> No spring can follow past meridian.

> Yet you persist with anecdotal bliss
> To make believe a starry *connaissance*.   [*CP*, 13]

The self of this passage is triadic in its perspectives: blunt acknowledgment of the fact of time; continued pursuit of visionary experience; and self-conscious awareness (suggested by the change in person to "you") that the nature of the pursuit and its goal have been radically altered. As usual, the conjunction "yet" takes us in Stevens from a world of fact to a world of fictions. Punning on the French *faire connaissance*, he reduces the visionary hope of having knowledge of the stars, to making their acquaintance, to "making-believe" any relationship at all—"make-believe" being, of course, that same "nice knowledge of / Belief" in which Stevens locates poetic meaning. His poems, in turn, are mere "stories" around which cluster (absurdly) quasi-religious feelings, what he calls elsewhere in "Le Monocle de Mon Oncle" "doleful heroics" (*CP*, 17). In the last stanza of the poem, he makes explicit the various roles that inform it and returns to a definition of the compromised heroics of middle age:

> A blue pigeon it is, that circles the blue sky,
> On sidelong wing, around and round and round.
> A white pigeon it is, that flutters to the ground,
> Grown tired of flight. Like a dark rabbi, I
> Observed, when young, the nature of mankind,
> In lordly study. Every day, I found
> Man proved a gobbet in my mincing world.
> Like a rose rabbi, later, I pursued,
> And still pursue, the origin and course
> Of love, but until now I never knew
> That fluttering things have so distinct a shade.   [*CP*, 17–18]

Crispin obviously is or tries to be the youthful "mincer." The narrator is aware of the gross failure (I say "gross" because we are dealing only with degrees of failure) of such pure heroics or at least their impossibility to him in the present personal and cultural circumstances. His, rather, will be the more tenuous pursuit of "fluttering things," the heroics of impermanence, of stance, style, and "shade"—the latter image taking us ahead to the mock-heroic world of Nabokov.

In this context the mocking narrator of "The Comedian" shares in the mockery directed at his protagonist. Stevens's earlier poem is again useful in explicitly alerting us to the possible reflexivity of the mockery. "Le Monocle de Mon Oncle" begins with the poet's elaborate invocation to his muse and

then immediately raises the critical question: "And so I mocked her in magnificent measure. / Or was it that I mocked myself alone?" (*CP*, 13). For the
narrator of "The Comedian," Stevens creates an even more "magnificent
measure," a style that represents an extraordinary attempt to infuse comic
mockery into the very texture of language. As he explained, with careful
illustration, to his correspondents, "the letter C is a Comedian"; "what was in
my mind was to play on that sound throughout the poem."[13] But the most
significant thing about the style of "The Comedian"—and this is true, though
in different ways, of Stevens's later stylistic experiments—is that it calls attention to itself simply *as style*. In other words, it deconstructs its own pretensions while destroying those against which it is directed. The learned narrator
is the same "nincompated pedagogue" as Crispin, with Stevens's splendidly
punning "nincompated" suggesting not merely folly but, more specifically,
Crispin and the narrator's "barber" role (the shaper and clipper who is himself "clipped"), the priest or rabbi role associated with that of pedagogue,
and, finally, perhaps, the sense of role as the costumed "act" of an actor ("this
same wig / Of things, this nincompated pedagogue" [*CP*, 27]).

Like Crispin, too, the narrator is an "annotator" (*CP*, 32), but annotations
do not lead collectively to thesis (the message, vision, or program that is the
end result of the teacher's role), only back upon themselves as manifestations
of role. At the end of the poem, indeed, his "doctrine" ("Seraphic proclama-
tions of the pure / Delivered with a deluging onwardness" [*CP*, 45]) is a parody of the moral instruction of traditional epic. He first offers us Crispin's
formulation ("as Crispin willed," that is, Crispin's desire to formulize), which
claims that the world, however momentarily "daubed out," remains "the
same insoluble lump" (*CP*, 45)—a formulation that, in effect, denies the possibility of formulation. Then the narrator suggests alternatively that the "anecdote" and moral (such as it is) may be false, with Crispin "proving what he
proves / Is nothing." Finally he concludes with a comment which, in spite of
many of his critics, is, from Stevens's perspective, more factual than cynical:
"What can all this matter since / The relation comes, benignly, to its end" (*CP*,
46). Here, paradoxically, we have perhaps arrived at a doctrine of sorts: the
anecdotes of the self prove nothing except that nothing can be proved. They
do, however, both describe and manifest the imaginative energies of the self.
We are back to that "illustrious nothing" about which I have already commented in discussing action and structure. Stevens denied even any concept
of a developing meaning from this poem to later ones, for developing implies
a more fixed and stable structuring of the poet's journey in time than reality
will bear. To a correspondent who saw such a "development" in comparing
"The Comedian" with the apparently more affirmative "Idea of Order at Key
West," Stevens replied: "I never thought that it was a fixed philosophic prop-

osition that life was a mass of irrelevancies any more than I now think that it is a fixed philosophical proposition that every man introduces his own order as part of a general order. These are tentative ideas for the purposes of poetry."[14]

"The Comedian," in short, is both record and manifestation of Stevens's first important encounter with his "necessary angel" of reality—who, for all practical purposes, is the enabling angel of irony. Likewise, his well-known realistic oriole—"From oriole to crow, note the decline / In music. Crow is realist. But, then, / Oriole, also, may be realist" (CP, 154)—is, in fact, the ironic oriole of romantic singer performing in a context of comic absurdity, singing in the mock-heroic mode. As Stevens describes himself and his situation elsewhere in "Like Decorations in a Nigger Cemetery":

> XXXV
> Men and the affairs of men seldom concerned
> This pundit of the weather, who never ceased
> To think of man the abstraction, the comic sum.
>
> XXXVI
> The children will be crying on the stair,
> Half-way to bed, when the phrase will be spoken,
> The starry voluptuary will be born. [CP, 156]

Like so many of his poems, "Decorations" begins by invoking an authentic hero (in this case, Walt Whitman) and his environment, both no longer extant. Then it attempts to create a parodic version from the "half-way" or "in between" world, which, Stevens says, is the sphere of his fortune (CP, 151). What remains of heroism (here the parody of high romanticism is particularly sharp) lingers on in the sense of quest as its own end, the mere occasion of momentary expansions of the self:

> If ever the search for a tranquil belief should end,
> The future might stop emerging out of the past,
> Out of what is full of us; yet the search
> And the future emerging out of us seem to be one. [CP, 151]

Harold Bloom has noted that Stevens's "true idea of order is the Emersonian-Whitmanian Self-Reliance, in which the Self accepts an expansiveness with all its attendant dangers," but, in Stevens's case (pace Bloom), these dangers are of a kind only neutralized by the relentless qualifications of an irony which, to be sure, poses new dangers of its own.[15] Stevens is, in effect, the ironic solipsist; he learned as a poet various methods of containing his solipsism within a secure and complete context of mockery where seem is the finale of being and desire leads only to personal freshenings.

Stevens's solipsism is consistently self-conscious of itself as solipsism in a poetry that develops a variety of mechanisms for recording self-consciousness, ranging from certain characteristic verbal devices, to metaphor, to entire structures. Among the shorter poems, there is, for example, his other well-known exercise in explicit mock-heroic, "Bantams in Pine-Woods," with its Chaucerian rooster persona brought to attention by an external mocking voice:

> Chieftain Iffucan of Azcan in caftan
> Of tan with henna hackles, halt!
>
> Damned universal cock, as if the sun
> Was blackamoor to bear your blazing tail.
>
> Fat! Fat! Fat! Fat! I am the personal.
> Your world is you. I am my world. [CP, 75]

We might say of the so aptly named chief that he both "can" and "can't," or that his name invokes both a condition of fact and a condition of longing (Stevens's conditional "if it were possible"), or that it contains both heroic echoes and a suggestion of Stevens's ubiquitous dump (at least the "ash-can" headed there). The claims of the personal are dazzling but merely reflexive and thus limited, the "fat" self at once heroic and comically absurd in its pretensions—nonetheless so if Iffucan is, as he is described later in the poem, a "ten-foot poet."

Occasionally, Stevens's personae seem to exist free of mockery, like his splendid rabbit enjoying a pure moment of being:

> To be, in the grass, in the peacefullest time,
> Without that monument of cat,
> The cat forgotten in the moon;
>
> And to feel that the light is a rabbit-light,
> In which everything is meant for you
> And nothing need be explained;
>
> Then there is nothing to think of. It comes of itself;
> And east rushes west and west rushes down,
> No matter. The grass is full
>
> And full of yourself. The trees around are for you,
> The whole of the wideness of night is for you,
> A self that touches all edges,
>
> You become a self that fills the four corners of night.
> The red cat hides away in the fur-light
> And there you are humped high, humped up. . . . .   [CP, 209]

The rabbit, however, remains contained not only by the delicate comic tone of the poem, but, in this case more important, by the crucial syntactical parallelism of being and feeling. The statement that moonlight is "a rabbit-light" is a description of the feelings of a self momentarily responsive to the moon, not an empirical statement about the moon. Although the rabbit gradually expands to heroic proportions, he turns himself only into a work of art ("black as stone— / You sit with your head like a carving in space" [CP, 210]), whose artifice is as apparent as its beauty. He exists, we might say, in a "through the looking-glass" world of heroic make-believe which, even as make-believe, will end when the cat (now "a bug in the grass") reasserts his own personal form and becomes, once again, the "fat cat" of daylight, a "monument," whose description begins the poem. To dispel any lingering doubts we may have concerning the relativity of the rabbit's experience, Stevens pairs the poem on facing pages with another called "The Dwarf," in which the self is described in its most shrunken or minimal phase, a winter world as compared to the expansive August of both rabbit and cat. In short, "A Rabbit as King of the Ghosts" deals simply with the same "undulations" of personality as does the rest of Stevens's work, whether one, two, or more personae are involved. As he puts it in another poem, "let the place of the solitaires / Be a place of perpetual undulation" (CP, 60).

The place of the solitaires, it must be emphasized, is both prison-house and romantic landscape of possibility. The expansions of the self with their attendant sense of freedom can legitimately occur only in the context of confinement. Stevens uses the metaphor of prison in another poem, "Montrachet-le-Jardin," in which tonal mockery is addressed almost entirely to the heroic conventions of the past, and the present moment (again moonlight) is greeted with ecstasy:

> To-night, night's undeciphered murmuring
> Comes close to the prisoner's ear, becomes a throat
> The hand can touch, neither green bronze nor marble,
>
> The hero's throat in which the words are spoken,
> From which the chant comes close upon the ear,
> Out of the hero's being, the deliverer
>
> Delivering the prisoner by his words,
> So that the skeleton in the moonlight sings,
> Sings of an heroic world beyond the cell,
>
> No, not believing, but to make the cell
> A hero's world in which he is the hero.
> Man must become the hero of his world.   [CP, 261]

Here the moment of heroic possibility is intensely alive (not the false or dead heroics of the "bronze" and "marble" statues that Stevens scatters throughout his poetry), and the hero remains, in some sense, valid heir to tradition. "He hears," we are told elsewhere, "the earliest poems of the world / In which man is the hero" (*CP*, 261). At the same time, because of the way the central metaphor is worked out, the ironic frame remains in place. Whitman's "song of myself" is now clearly an act of make-believe, an assertion of nothing but itself as heroic song—the imagination "delivering the prisoner" solely in and through the very process of its expression. Singing "of an heroic world beyond the cell," the self, in fact (again that crucial qualification), affirms its heroism only *within* the cell.

Sometimes in Stevens's work the inherent duality of the mock-heroic mode will surface as the explicit dialogue one finds in his "Colloquy with a Polish Aunt":

> *Elle savait toutes les légendes*
> *du Paradis et tous les contes de*
> *la Pologne.*
> Revue des Deux Mondes

SHE

How is it that my saints from Voragine,
In their embroidered slippers, touch your spleen?

HE

Old Pantaloons, duenna of the spring!

SHE

Imagination is the will of things. . . .
Thus, on the basis of the common drudge,
You dream of women, swathed in indigo,
Holding their books toward the nearer stars,
To read, in secret, burning secrecies. . . .   [*CP*, 84]

The woman in this poem responds to the man's mockery by noting that he, too, is a Quixote creating his own Dulcineas "on the basis of the common drudge"—an act that affirms the heroic will to imagination, though not the reality of its visionary products. At the same time, his mockery of her illusions (undulations again of the self in its "spring" or summer phase) probably involves a response more mixed than her accusation of mere spleen might suggest. His epithet, "Old Pantaloons," invokes the same clown or tramp developed in "The Comedian," a figure who receives even more substantial definition in the first section of "Notes toward a Supreme Fiction" as (once again) Stevens's basic persona, his "idea of man" complexly both heroic and commonplace.

This section of "Notes," indeed, concludes with the parodic apotheosis of the hero as clown. "Who is it?" asks the monologist of the poem, and he responds with more questions and some answers:

> What rabbi, grown furious with human wish,
> What chieftain, walking by himself, crying
> Most miserable, most victorious,
>
> Does not see these separate figures one by one,
> And yet see only one, in his old coat,
> His slouching pantaloons, beyond the town,
>
> Looking for what was, where it used to be?
> Cloudless the morning. It is he. The man
> In that old coat, those sagging pantaloons,
>
> It is of him, ephebe, to make, to confect
> The final elegance, not to console
> Nor sanctify, but plainly to propound. [CP, 389]

The comic incarnation here parodies both God and heroic man. The mock-hero steps forth complete in his solitude ("beyond the town"), his nostalgic desire ("Looking for what was, where it used to be"), and, of course, his pratfalling, Chaplinesque absurdity. Less apparent, perhaps, is that even this apparition is as much a manifestation of desire as an emblem of its fulfillment, however limited. He is raised up through questions, he is seen (possibly) by viewers in passionate need of vision and themselves probably "looking for what was or used to be"; the referent of this participial phrase seems deliberately ambiguous. Finally, he is the creation or attempted creation of the pedagogue, lecturer, monologist, whose "propounding" is really a "making" or "confecting" similar, one must assume, to the confections of cat, rabbit, Chieftain Iffucan, the prisoner in his cell, or the Polish lady and her critic.

It is this comic pedagogue who emerges in Stevens's longer poems as the major persona: an amalgam of ardent, note-taking Crispin and his skeptical observer, both, however, still vestigially present occasionally in the situation of an "ephebe" addressed, presumably, by an older teacher. This amalgamate figure is the undulating solitaire whose movement Stevens defines as "the motion of thought / And its restless iteration" (CP, 60). He is also the belated American Scholar or Man Thinking, liberated by the act of imaginative questioning, defeated in his attempts to answer, "gulping for shape" like the bathers in "A Lot of People Bathing in a Stream":

> We bathed in yellow green and yellow blue
> And in these comic colors dangled down,
>
> Like their particular characters, addicts
> To blotches, angular anonymids
> Gulping for shape among the reeds.   [*CP,* 371]

"Blotching" in the clown's motley of vivid but haphazard "comic colors" is the most that "angular anonymids" can hope for in the yellow sunlit world of reality. The term suggests ambiguously both crude and provisional shapes and loss of shape. Crispin, too, we should remember, begins his initiation with a similar primary blotching—in his case, the naive illusion of a simple heroics "blotched out beyond unblotching" (*CP,* 28) by the sea. As bather-lecturer, Stevens is forever trying to "get straight" that which is insubstantial, irrational, and untrue.[16]

Clearly at the end of "Notes toward a Supreme Fiction" the pedagogue mocks his own situation after struggling toward one last definition of heroic experience and finding it in the moment when feeling seems to coalesce into form, the eccentric nuance of pleasure amid "mere repetitions" (the temporal context which the hero in some fashion must redeem). Such, apparently, is the thematic conclusion of the poem, and the lecturer, in gratitude and relief (the pleasures of the pedagogue), reaches to encapsulate theme in aphorism:

> That's it: the more than rational distortion,
> The fiction that results from feeling. Yes, that.
>
> They will get it straight one day at the Sorbonne.
> We shall return at twilight from the lecture
> Pleased that the irrational is rational,
>
> Until flicked by feeling, in a gildered street,
> I call you by name, my green, my fluent mundo.
> You will have stopped revolving except in crystal. [*CP,* 405–7]

Lecturing remains, in effect, an open-ended task and formulations, simply a mode of pleasure, fictions of feeling whose heroic substance lies only in the *spirit* of their manifestations, in the continued willingness of the self to respond to a world of repetitions, even if the response is repetitive (creating, that is, nothing unique or transcendent).

In the penultimate stanza of "Notes," Stevens compares such a response to the whistling of birds and comments that "these things at least comprise / An occupation, an exercise, a work, / A thing final in itself and, therefore, good . . . (*CP,* 405). "Perhaps," he adds (even such slender claims are made only tentatively), "the man-hero is not the exceptional monster / But he that of repetition is most master" (*CP*, 406). But this whistling is also "whistling in the dark," and elsewhere in the "Notes" Stevens savagely mocks the fatuity of solipsistic song:

> Bethou me, said sparrow, to the crackled blade,
> And you, and you, bethou me as you blow,
> When in my coppice you behold me be.
>
> Ah, ké! the bloody wren, the felon jay,
> Ké-ké, the jug-throated robin pouring out,
> Bethou, bethou, bethou me in my glade.
>
> There was such idiot minstrelsy in rain,
> So many clappers going without bells,
> That these bethous compose a heavenly gong.
>
> One voice repeating, one tireless chorister,
> The phrases of a single phrase, ké-ké,
> A single text, granite monotony. . . .   [*CP*, 393–94]

From its perspective of mockery, the mock-heroic mode, as I have pointed out before, is particularly direct and brutal in its denial of temporal redemption— freedom from the empirical world—as a real or true possibility. Reality and truth are, in fact, just the opposite. Time is the remorseless oppressor of individual spirit, a "granite monotony" whose only end is death—an end that mocks the possibility of other ends: "Bethou him, you / And you, bethou him and bethou. It is / A sound like any other. It will end" (*CP*, 394). Stevens's lecturer continues ceaselessly to aspire, but, as the name of his exemplary persona, the Canon Aspirin, suggests, aspiration is as much a palliative to despair as it is a program of positive hope. The pathos or will to vision—the "huge pathetic force" (*CP*, 403)—that the Canon manifests "numbs" or counters emptiness while remaining, at the same time, a comic delusion, a parody, almost a travesty of the Emersonian, transcendental encounter with power.

Virtually every stanza of "Notes" deconstructs itself in one fashion or another or is deconstructed by a following stanza. Like the generality of Stevens's long poems, "Notes" ceaselessly mocks its own driving impulse toward some sort of romantic vision. As a result, we get not so much achieved vision as "romantic intoning" (*CP*, 387), not sustained aphoristic wisdom but "endlessly elaborating" (*CP*, 486) notes that undercut their own prior formulations and manifest only the energy of what Stevens calls in "An Ordinary Evening in New Haven" "the swarming activities of the formulae / Of statement" (*CP*, 488). Or as he says (aphoristically) elsewhere: "Life consists / Of propositions about life" (*CP*, 355). Helen Vendler has observed how "the experience of energetic free feeling flaunts its own truths," and she has also accurately described the relentless rhetorical irony of most of the poetry: the suppositions, the hypotheses, the syntactical uncertainty, the creation of a "realm of 'as if'" which is shadowy, ephemeral, barely perceived, heavily qualified, and paradoxically circumscribed.[17] The pedagogue's is the ultimate quixotism of trying to create a theory of life

> As it is, in the intricate evasions of as,
> In things seen and unseen, created from nothingness,
> The heavens, the hells, the worlds, the longed-for lands.   [CP, 486]

"Created from nothingness," this is essentially the same shadowy "wonderland" or "through the looking-glass" world that Lewis Carroll built for his children, the same also that we will encounter later in the paranoid visions of Nabokov's madmen.

From the fundamental irony of such a position and the smaller ironies of the "intricate evasions," with the various commitments that they represent, comes the mock-heroic sensibility and its attendant mode. Like many other modern scholars, Stevens's pedagogue must depend solely on a certain freedom of the mind's response to phenomena if he is to be reconciled with the prison-house of reality. He speaks in "An Ordinary Evening in New Haven" of

> Inescapable romance, inescapable choice
> Of dreams, disillusion as the last illusion,
> Reality as a thing seen by the mind,
>
> Not that which is but that which is apprehended,
> A mirror, a lake of reflections in a room,
> A glassy ocean lying at the door,
>
> A great town hanging pendent in a shade,
> An enormous nation happy in a style,
> Everything as unreal as real can be,
>
> In the inexquisite eye.   [CP, 468]

In the phrase "as unreal as real can be," the evasive and childish "as" of possibility is delicately balanced by the mature "as" of limitation. The previous stanza contains Stevens's description of the soothing cold of autumn as "a children's tale of ice." This ambiguous realm, he goes on to imply, offers some common ground, some dimension compatible with duality, to the self divided in its commitments between "common earth" and the visionary search for "such majesty as it could find" (CP, 468–69). Among the parodic elements of Stevens's mock-heroic is its echo of Emersonian compensation, the essential unity of opposites within a larger order, what Stevens calls in

"An Ordinary Evening" "a matching and mating of surprised accords" (*CP*, 468). At the very least, the pedagogue, in the quality of his utterances and in the energy and imagination with which they are pursued, can legitimately affirm both the reality and the humanistic value of illusion. In Stevens's terms, this is a "possible," the only "possible" remaining for the would-be visionary. The creator of mock-heroic struggles simply to sustain some concept of nobility in circumstances when a literal belief in the noble hero no longer remains an option. As Stevens explains in "The Noble Rider and the Sound of Words" (in effect, his essay on quixotism): "For the sensitive poet, conscious of negations, nothing is more difficult than the affirmations of nobility and yet there is nothing that he requires of himself more persistently, since in them and in their kind, alone, are to be found those sanctions that are the reasons for his being and for that occasional ecstasy, or ecstatic freedom of the mind, which is his special privilege."[18]

Heroism as Theater

Stevens's pedagogue simply "goes on asking questions," and the question, not the answer, is "in point." That, at least, is the picture of lecturing he gives in "The Ultimate Poem Is Abstract":

> This day writhes with what? The lecturer
> On This Beautiful World of Ours composes himself
> And hems the planet rose and haws it ripe,
>
> And red, and right. The particular question—here
> The particular answer to the particular question
> Is not in point—the question is in point.
>
> If the day writhes, it is not with revelations.
> One goes on asking questions. That, then, is one
> Of the categories.   [*CP*, 429]

This mocking picture of the pompous lecturer preparing to deliver romantic platitudes conceals within its punning a larger truth about alternatives: that even authentic lecturing can now involve, as its essence and end, only a process of composition, the self "composing itself," endlessly assuming the stance or preparatory rituals of vision without, however, the possibility of revelation.[19] We can say of Stevens's lecturer as we can of his rabbit or cat (or as we can of Don Quixote and other mock-heroes) that he insists on formally realizing himself. Such action is, indeed, simply an "act," a theatrical performance, but it remains, nevertheless, the sole residue of heroic experience.

In "The Ultimate Poem Is Abstract" Stevens also explicitly expresses his sense of loss, his nostalgic awareness of having fallen away from some heroic center:

> It would be enough
> If we were ever, just once, at the middle, fixed
> In This Beautiful World of Ours and not as now,
>
> Helplessly at the edge, enough to be
> Complete, because at the middle, if only in sense,
> And in that enormous sense, merely enjoy.   [CP, 430]

Toward the end of the passage, the nostalgic vision begins to deconstruct ("if only in sense"), but, on this occasion at least, a phenomenal centrality is just as unattainable as genuine transcendence; the mock-hero is left merely with tenuous games "at the edge." Nevertheless, "questions" or fresh and imaginative encounters with reality in one form or another are all we have. In a charming late poem about his grandson, another pedagogue, "the expert aetat. 2" who is asking questions, Stevens comments:

> His question is complete because it contains
> His utmost statement. It is his own array,
> His own pageant and procession and display
> As far as nothingness permits. . . .   [CP, 462–63]

Questioning is questing in Stevens's work, with no end beyond the desire, freedom, and imagination manifest in or released by the question/quest itself and the aesthetic forms that are its momentary shape. In a systolic rhythm of expansion and contraction, the self comes to form, and, in its repeated forms, so to speak, is its performance—"pageant and procession and display." As he explains carefully in "An Ordinary Evening in New Haven" after the apparent fixity of the aphorism that begins the poem:

> Of this,
> A few words, an and yet, and yet, and yet—
>
> As part of the never-ending meditation,
> Part of the question that is the giant himself. . . .   [CP, 465]

In its endless excursions into nothingness, Stevens's heroic question must self-destruct just as relentlessly as it expands; its process is a continual mockery of its possibility.

Theatrical metaphor is pervasive in Stevens's poetry. His personae are "actors" in the full punning sense of that word: not only (as he describes them in "Notes" [CP, 383–84]) displaced parodists or "mimics" of authentic heroes but (in particular mockery of the romantic hero) reflexive figures, formal creations of their own will and imagination, perceivers whose perceptions essentially create the perceiver. "The hero," writes Stevens in "Examination of the Hero in a Time of War," "acts in reality, adds nothing / To what he does. He is the heroic / Actor and act but not divided" (CP, 279). In *Adagia* he emphasizes that "authors are actors, books are theatres" (OP, 157). The self is both the creator and creation of words; as Stevens explains in "Certain Phenomena of Sound": "There is no life except in the word of it. / I write *Semiramide* and in the script / I am and have a being and play a part" (CP, 287). At one point in the "Notes," he locates the poet pedagogue sitting in the park, where "a bench was his catalepsy, Theatre / Of Trope" (CP, 397).

It is in "The Man with the Blue Guitar," however, Stevens's major attempt between "The Comedian" and "Notes" to define (and "play," in this case as musical performer) the comic hero, that he most explicitly "evolves" this hero finally as masker and figure of theater:

XXIX

In the cathedral, I sat there, and read,
Alone, a lean Review and said,

"These degustations in the vaults
Oppose the past and the festival,

What is beyond the cathedral, outside,
Balances with nuptial song.

So it is to sit and to balance things
To and to and to the point of still,

To know that the balance does not quite rest,
That the mask is strange, however like."

The shapes are wrong and the sounds are false.
The bells are the bellowing of bulls.

Yet Franciscan don was never more
Himself than in this fertile glass.

XXX

From this I shall evolve a man.
This is his essence: the old fantoche

Hanging his shawl upon the wind,
Like something on the stage, puffed out,

His strutting studied through centuries.
At last, in spite of his manner, his eye

A-cock at the cross-piece on a pole
Supporting heavy cables, slung

Through Oxidia, banal suburb,
One-half of all its installments paid.   [CP, 180–82]

In lines I have not included, the tonal mock of suburbia deepens until the stanza ends with mock apotheosis: "Oxidia is the soot of fire, / Oxidia is Olympia" (CP, 182). Slightly further on, Stevens describes himself at this moment in the poem as a "blunted player" (CP, 182). The entire poem, like all his longer poems, has been a "balancing act," an endless trying on of masks, "to and to and to the point of still." Again the punning is crucial; stability (the still point) is never really reached, but we can approximate (imitate) it in what is an ever or still continuing process.

The mockery of the evolved "puppet" hero (not to mention the pedagogue, appropriately enough here reading his "lean Review," his own major mask) is heavy, yet ("in spite of his manner") he remains, in some fashion, "still" a seeker after vision; the claims of Oxidia are, after all, not quite nonsense, its banality perhaps not quite opaque to heroic pretensions. The theatrical metaphor delicately "balances" the creativity and energy of the mock hero with the true emptiness or nothingness of his expansions ("fatness" becomes, in this context, clothing "puffed out" with air) in a meager world and the pompous absurdity of his repetitive roles. After further stanzas reiterating in *Paterson*-like terms the brutal opacity of modern life to any heroic song, "The Man with the Blue Guitar" concludes with lines emphasizing the positive significance of play as our only possible option: "The moments when we choose to play / The imagined pine, the imagined jay" (CP, 184). Such creative role-playing constitutes the very core of Stevens's poetic position, a position essentially stable throughout his career but built on a notoriously unstable, complex, and delicate balance of opposites. To accommodate formally such a paradox is precisely the function of the mock-heroic mode.

Even "Credences of Summer," the poem of Stevens that comes closest to an unbridled celebration of "the heroic power" (CP, 375) manifest in the persona's consummation with the vital center of reality, becomes self-conscious of itself toward the end as an emotional performance, another drama of desire. In the penultimate stanza, Stevens notes that "a complex of emotions falls apart" (CP, 377), a mood passes, ephemeral as the temporal moment of summer. The last stanza describes summer as a cosmic drama in which, however, the individual characters "speak because they want / To speak":

The personae of summer play the characters
Of an inhuman author, who meditates

With the gold bugs, in blue meadows, late at night.
He does not hear his characters talk. He sees
Them mottled, in the moodiest costumes,
Of blue and yellow, sky and sun, belted
And knotted, sashed and seamed, half pales of red,
Half pales of green, appropriate habit for
The huge decorum, the manner of the time,
Part of the mottled mood of summer's whole,

In which the characters speak because they want
To speak, the fat, the roseate characters,
Free, for a moment, from malice and sudden cry,
Complete in a completed scene, speaking
Their parts as in a youthful happiness. [CP, 377–78]

Images of motley, fatness, youth, and a certain freedom come together in this drama of summer. Of course, even the title of Stevens's poem makes clear to the alert reader the essential contextuality of his "credences."

At the opposite pole from even such limited credences as those just described stands the passage in "The Auroras of Autumn" which constitutes Stevens's most bitter mockery of the implications of his theatrical metaphor:

The father fetches pageants out of air,
Scenes of the theatre, vistas and blocks of woods
And curtains like a naive pretence of sleep.

Among these the musicians strike the instinctive poem.
The father fetches his unherded herds,
Of barbarous tongue, slavered and panting halves

Of breath, obedient to his trumpet's touch.
This then is Chatillon or as you please.
We stand in the tumult of a festival.

What festival? This loud, disordered mooch?
These hospitaliers? These brute-like guests?
These musicians dubbing at a tragedy,
A-dub, a-dub, which is made up of this:
That there are no lines to speak? There is no play.
Or, the persons act one merely by being here.   [CP, 415–16]

The great heroic role of romanticism—the self as God/Creator/Poet—a role, in one form or another, consistently parodied in Stevens's work and coming to its sharpest ironic focus in his use of theatrical metaphor—stands here revealed in its final appalling and grotesque emptiness. "Dubbing at" presumably puns on both "making a thrust or 'stab' at" and "investing with dignity" (often, according to the *OED*, used mockingly), but, in any case, it amounts substantially on this occasion to the "rub-a-dub" of nonsense rhyme. Just as the earlier Stevens had "dubbed at" comedy, so the later, in his dramatic meditations, is inclined to strain toward tragic roles. As he finally makes clear in "An Ordinary Evening in New Haven," however, neither comedy nor tragedy per se constitutes the authentic mode of his art.

Even in "The Auroras," Stevens quickly moves away from a completely reductive concept of theater (a reduction that does, indeed, describe the dimension of "fact" or "truth" in theater) toward one more characteristic of his work in general. In the next stanza, theater becomes fluid and metamorphic:

> It is a theatre floating through the clouds,
> Itself a cloud, although of misted rock
> And mountains running like water, wave on wave,
>
> Through waves of light. It is of cloud transformed
> To cloud transformed again, idly, the way
> A season changes color to no end,
>
> Except the lavishing of itself in change. . . . [*CP*, 416]

The fact of "no end" remains in addition to lack of coherent direction (transformations are "idle"), but change becomes its own end as display, "the lavishing of itself," the parodic end toward which the mock-hero moves. Stevens, in short, begins himself to move, to "contrive" something else from his metaphor, and, by the end of the poem, he has contrived himself again as pedagogue (or, in this case, "rabbi"), with, appropriately enough, a message essentially about himself as contriver:

> Read to the congregation, for today
> And for tomorrow, this extremity,
> This contrivance of the spectre of the spheres,
>
> Contriving balance to contrive a whole,
> The vital, the never-failing genius,
> Fulfilling his meditations, great and small. [*CP*, 420]

Again we are largely conscious of a balancing "act," a contrived meditation "contriving balance to contrive a whole." It is all makeshift, a plasterboard theater of appearances, at best "actual seemings" (to borrow a phrase from another poem, *CP*, 340), a Chinese box of fictional contrivances where parodic approximation never ends.

The "meditations, great and small" of Stevens's persona are his willed "compositions" of himself as hero. Like Don Quixote, the most that he can hope to make of himself is a work of art. This is the sense of Stevens's short poem, "The Pastor Caballero":

> The importance of its hat to a form becomes
> More definite. The sweeping brim of the hat
> Makes of the form Most Merciful Capitan,
>
> If the observer says so: grandiloquent
> Locution of a hand in a rhapsody.
> Its line moves quickly with the genius
>
> Of its improvisation until, at length,
> It enfolds the head in a vital ambiance,
> A vital, linear ambiance. . . .   [CP, 379]

The locus of heroics is clearly not in the achievement of transcendent ends, but in the quality of the observer's performance ("grandiloquent / Locution of a hand in a rhapsody" is Stevens's splendid and significant phrase). Grandiloquent, of course, suggests a style both impressive, appropriate to a grand theme, and pompous, artificial, and absurd. Although the irony does not vitiate the "vital ambiance" generated, neither does it invite us to see such vitality as more than (what he calls later in the poem) a "human evocation." As Stevens makes clear in an important modification, the ambiance is linear, in and from the line or gesture.

In "The Pastor Caballero," heroic gesture or stance is caught in a moment of apparent stability, but in fact the "improvisations" of the self, as the word implies, are a "making do," without larger plan, without completion or closure, a try for order within a larger disorder. Stevens notes elsewhere that "The law of chaos is the law of ideas, / Of improvisations and seasons of belief" (CP, 255). I have already noted in discussing William Carlos Williams that both Stevens and he attempt to reimagine heroism and its attendant literary forms as an index of freely willed effort, not victory. The terms of their reimagining make failure inevitable and even necessary; indeed, to paraphrase a line from "Esthétique du Mal," that which rejects heroism saves it in the end. In one of his later, autumnal poems, "The Plain Sense of Things," Stevens observes that with the decline of summer "a fantastic effort has failed, a repetition / In a repetitiousness of men and flies" (CP, 502). "Fantastic" punningly implies both "strongly willed" and an "act of fantasy or fancy." Effort so conceived remains, on one hand, relentlessly negated by cosmic nothingness; on the other, as a particularly human act, it has, for a limited period, qualities beyond those that a fly can muster. In the same poem Stevens points out that, at the very least, there is a certain freedom, autonomy, and power in the phenomenological priority of the imagination to the *ding an sich:* "Yet the absence of the imagination had / Itself to be imagined" (*CP*, 503). Again a timely "yet" (reacting to a heavy awareness of a death-haunted world) contrives balance for a point of view that refuses unitary resolution.

Aside from the continuing presence of the pedagogue, it is Penelope in the later poetry who represents the supreme example of heroic make-believe. As the epigraph to "The World as Meditation" suggests, she lives in *"un rêve permanent"* (*CP*, 520). Endlessly committed to consummation with heroic Ulysses, she remains limited to the composition and recomposition of herself as some sort of imaginary equivalent:

> She has composed, so long, a self with which to welcome him,
> Companion to his self for her, which she imagined,
> Two in a deep-founded sheltering, friend and dear friend.   [*CP*, 521]

From the sun of the morning, Penelope can only improvise Ulysses (and herself). Finally she becomes aware, at least intuitively, of the delicate balance of illusion and reality that constitutes the actuality of her world:

> But was it Ulysses? Or was it only the warmth of the sun
> On her pillow? The thought kept beating in her like her heart.
> The two kept beating together. It was only day.
>
> It was Ulysses and it was not. Yet they had met,
> Friend and dear friend and a planet's encouragement.
> The barbarous strength within her would never fail.
>
> She would talk a little to herself as she combed her hair,
> Repeating his name with its patient syllables,
> Never forgetting him that kept coming constantly so near.   [*CP*, 521]

Power of will and energy ("barbarous strength"), the emotional commitment of elegiac memory ("Never forgetting him"), the imaginative possibilities of words, and a world not totally hostile to adventure ("A planet's encouragement"), all combine to bring Penelope a make-believe Ulysses who is simply a mirror of those qualities in herself.

"The beings of the mind," Stevens writes in "The Owl in the Sarcophagus," are "the children of a desire that is the will" (*CP*, 436). What is manifest in Penelope's dramatic stance and what lingers in Stevens's work from beginning to end is the quixotism of desire, a self-conscious commitment (whose alternative is despair) to the parodic possible as a substitute for the authentic impossible. Or, in the urgent language of "An Ordinary Evening in New Haven," the tone itself here an incantation of desire:

Say next to holiness is the will thereto,
And next to love is the desire for love,
The desire for its celestial ease in the heart,

Which nothing can frustrate, that most secure,
Unlike love in possession of that which was
To be possessed and is. But this cannot

Possess. It is desire, set deep in the eye,
Behind all actual seeing, in the actual scene,
In the street, in a room, on a carpet or a wall,

Always in emptiness that would be filled,
In denial that cannot contain its blood,
A porcelain, as yet in the bats thereof.   [CP, 467]

Desire in these categorical terms seeks to become a metaphysical substitute for consummations. Like Joyce, Stevens has his own mock-Ulysses, now a hero of desire, still retaining a certain potency, still able to create his own mode of adventure:

The bud of the apple is desire, the down-falling gold,
The catbird's gobble in the morning half-awake—

These are real only if I make them so. Whistle
For me, grow green for me and, as you whistle and grow green,

Intangible arrows quiver and stick in the skin
And I taste at the root of the tongue the unreal of what is real.   [CP, 313]

Nabokov: Reassembling Zembla

> I leaf again and again through these miserable memories, and keep
> asking myself, was it then, in the glitter of that remote summer,
> that the rift in my life began.
>
> VLADIMIR NABOKOV
> *Lolita*

> (I wonder, Van, *why* you are doing your best to transform our poet-
> ical and unique past into a dirty farce?)
>
> VLADIMIR NABOKOV
> *Ada*

I have already noted the relationship between mock-heroic, a literary mode
marked in part by constant narrative anticlimax, and a culture of broken continuity and anticlimax which it usually reflects and often directly comments
upon: Spain after Lepanto, post-Napoleonic Europe, bourgeois and ur-
banized England and America of the later nineteenth century, Ireland in 1900,
and the modern wasteland that constitutes the ground of Williams's and Stevens's belated romanticism. With none of the writers under discussion, however, is the cultural break more obvious, more dramatic, and more crucial
than with Vladimir Nabokov. In their treatment of Nabokov's career, critics
quickly discerned the personal and literary significance of exile. I too want to
deal further with the nature and situation of the hero in exile, focusing briefly
on *Invitation to a Beheading*, a particularly stark description of this situation
and its implications for life and death. I will follow these comments with an
extended analysis of *The Gift*, Nabokov's own "portrait of the artist," the work
of his which most completely explores the rhetorical options open to the exiled artist from the aesthetic perspective of the exploration successfully resolved. Like Joyce's *Portrait*, *The Gift* is "about" what its style everywhere
formally enacts. The argument of *The Gift*, in turn, finds full realization in the
great novels of Nabokov's maturity, *Pale Fire, Lolita*, and *Ada*.

Lost Fathers

My epigraph from *Lolita* should remind us that central to Humbert Humbert's consciousness is an awareness of a "rift" in his life, which he shares with most of Nabokov's protagonists and, in fact, with Nabokov himself.[1] Such an awareness expands into the conviction that life is divided finally and categorically into two entities, which might be described variously as youth and maturity, past and present, timeless idyll and death-haunted mortality, a lost "kingdom" of heroic values and a gained environment grotesquely incommensurate with dreams, expectations, indeed, one's entire lifestyle. As the terms of this division suggest, moreover, the sensed reality of a rift is coupled with an equally intense commitment to one of its dimensions. Nabokov's protagonists are displaced persons, politically and otherwise, anachronisms, ghosts, shadows, unreal people (the words are those used again and again by Nabokov himself), who are imaginatively and emotionally pledged to a childhood wonderland divorced from any dimension of temporal continuity with the "wrought-iron world" (*L*, 23) or "witherland" (*L*, 159) of their later experience as adults. Humbert Humbert, for example, writes "never grow up" (*L*, 23)—a statement that is both fact and imperative. Van Veen describes himself as "ever-adolescent";[2] Cincinnatus in *Invitation to a Beheading* is everywhere called child, childlike, childish, boyish; Pnin's most passionate dream is of "a Russian wildwood . . . traversed by an old forest road," which "emerged into the romantic, free, beloved radiance of a great field unmowed by time."[3] In *The Defense* Luzhin's story is a parody version of the perpetual childhood (or life without rift) characteristic of the Victorian boy heroes in his father's books for young people: "the image of a fair-haired lad, 'headstrong,' 'brooding,' who later turned into a violinist or a painter without losing his moral beauty in the process."[4] And Nabokov's comment about his own past is well known: "The nostalgia I have been cherishing all these years is a hypertrophied sense of lost childhood, not sorrow for lost banknotes."[5]

As Nabokov describes it in *Speak, Memory,* his was "the harmonious world of a perfect childhood" destroyed by the "cataclysm" of the Russian Revolution (*SM*, 24–25). The events of 1917 severed him at once from his first great romantic love and "the wildwood grading into old gardens" of his youth (*SM*, 249–50). Reflected in Nabokov's experience, however, are cultural responses that have implications beyond the shock and disorientation of political exile common to a generation of upper-class Russians. As he himself recognized, his childhood was "English" not only in many of its substantial components, but, more important, in its particular emotional and spiritual resonances—specifically, in its invocation of the enchanted garden world of the late Victorian imagination. Even the English word "childhood" had· "magic" connotations for Nabokov; he tells us that wandering later in life over the rocks at Abbazia on the Adriatic, he kept repeating the word "in a kind of jestful, copious, and deeply gratifying incantation," that it got mixed with fairy stories in his mind, and that his muttering of the word cast "certain spells" over the tidal pools (*SM*, 26). In other words, that "trite *deus ex machina*, the Russian Revolution" (*SM*, 229) was only the proximate cause of those strong nostalgic feelings for the past which were an important theme of Anglo-American culture from the 1870s to World War I and beyond.

Though it informs much of his early work, simple lyric nostalgia was not to become the literary stance of the mature Nabokov. Every major writer in one way or another indicates the minor writer he is not, and it is in this context that we must read Nabokov's description in *Pnin* "of those literary soirées where young *émigré* poets, who had left Russia in their pale, unpampered pubescence, chanted nostalgic elegies dedicated to a country that could be little more to them than a sad stylized toy, a bauble found in the attic " (*PN*, 392). I will analyze Nabokov's own sophisticated literary response to nostalgia—a mock-heroic art of great complexity—at length. First, however, I want to describe more fully the nature of these two worlds that exist on either side of the rift: their moral and spiritual substance; their range of possible symbolic reference; their crucial role in defining the immediate existential situation of Nabokov's protagonists.[6]

As Alfred Appel, Jr., puts it categorically, exile for Nabokov becomes "a correlative for all human loss" (*L*, Introduction, xxi). His local version of the personal and cultural fall of man presupposes a transcendental and timeless Eden in the nineteenth century that has been supplanted by the brutal, death-ridden reality of the contemporary world—"the decaying corpse of actuality" in Nabokov's vivid phrase.[7] Politically, Nabokov is referring to the totalitarian environments of the Soviet Union and Nazi Germany; they constitute a much more pervasive and significant context of his work than has been generally acknowledged. But however specific the political references, one quickly realizes that politics is ultimately only a metaphor of life lived in the shadow of the headsman of time and death. In the short story "That in Alleppo Once . . .," for example, the narrator, fleeing with a young woman from the arrival of German troops after a brief, passionate romance in Paris, comments retrospectively on the refugee exodus by pointing out that the "farther we fled, the clearer it became that what was driving us on was something more than a booted and buckled fool with his assortment of variously propelled junk—something of which he was a mere symbol, something monstrous and impalpable, a timeless and faceless mass of unmemorial horror that still keeps coming at me from behind even here, in the green vacuum of

Central Park" (*PN*, 147). Later in the course of their wanderings, they come upon a group of refugees sitting around the corpse of a family member who had died on the road. Among them is a little boy, who "crouched on his haunches, his thin, eloquent neck showing all its vertebra to the headsman" (*PN*, 147).

Reference to an implacable executioner is even more blatant in an earlier short story, "Cloud, Castle, Lake." In this case, a nostalgic exile is forced to go on an excursion to the German countryside with a group led by a monstrous and brutal young Nazi. The exile finds in the course of the trip a "pure, blue lake," which, in its harmony, beauty, and innocence, is the very consummation of his dream of happiness. He wants to remain by the lakeside permanently but is told by the leader that "there can be no question of anyone—in this case you—refusing to continue this communal journey." His reply to the Nazi penetrates to the heart of the issue between them and echoes the title of the novel that Nabokov at that time (1937) had just written on the same theme: "Oh, but this is nothing less than an invitation to a beheading" (*PN*, 105–7).

Forced relentlessly to live within the confines of a monstrous reality ("this pellet of muck," as Van Veen describes the world [*A*, 529]; Nabokov remains true to this theme throughout his career), his anachronistic protagonists, who remember another world in which love and visionary experience were present and whose style and beliefs have been shaped by that memory, struggle to experience some modicum of spiritual life in the present. Their role has no legitimacy and no chance of substantial success; a character in another early story refers to his "fragile, illegal life" (*PN*, 119). Nabokov's decaying corpse of actuality is a world without genuine heroes and without the authenticating environment that might make true heroics possible, but the problem for his protagonists remains, nevertheless, how to pursue heroic commitments. "Can't you even now remain within legitimate limits?" Cincinnatus's lawyer implores him in prison.[8] He can't; even there he quests for alternate values and alternate worlds.

Cincinnatus's position in *Invitation to a Beheading* remains Nabokov's starkest description of the protagonist fundamentally displaced by the rift between the environment of his memory and imagination and that of his waking life. The novel presents a situation in which all positive value is identified with the sensibility of Cincinnatus, all reality with the prison in which he is forced to live while awaiting an arbitrarily determined death—merely the most blatant version of the "prison of life" that permanently incarcerates all of Nabokov's protagonists. As the executioner reminds Cincinnatus bluntly: "Only in fairy tales do people escape from prison" (*IB*, 114). The "cold ochre" of the prison cell walls "smelled of the grave, it was pimply and horrible," and Cincinnatus himself is well aware that "the only real, genuinely unquestionable thing here was only death itself, the inevitability of the author's physical death" (*IB*, 124). In this case, he is referring to another writer, who has produced a gigantic novel depicting a vast and complex catalog of time and history, with the author himself distantly "spying" on the people and events he has created. But Cincinnatus knows the executioner is right; such imaginative distancing may in one sense create and control time, but in fact ("Matterfact Street" is a principal road in the town where Cincinnatus lives), no one escapes the horror of the prison cell. The present time of the novel incorporates the death of both flesh and spirit; it is a world without love and without vision. A graffito near a high barred window in Cincinnatus's cell mocks the spiritual question: "You cannot see anything. I tried it too" (*IB*, 29).

The prison allegory in *Invitation to a Beheading* has significance that goes beyond a political statement about totalitarian rule (Nabokov, in the Foreword, scornfully rejects identification with George Orwell) or a social statement describing the general banality and nastiness of modern wasteland culture, though both of these elements are important dimensions of the iron age in which the protagonist finds himself compelled to live. The largest implications, however, are metaphysical; Nabokov's protagonists (and Cincinnatus as much as any) must struggle to pursue their individual values and dreams in a context of "nothing." In a word, it is the *soul* that the headsman mocks most obscenely: "I am ashamed, my soul has disgraced itself," Cincinnatus laments during a moment of fear (*IB*, 192). Nabokov's own description of his novel could not be more to the point: "It is a violin in a void" (*IB*, Foreword, 7), with the principal violinist Cincinnatus himself, perpetual child of the nineteenth century.

The double denouement of the book—Cincinnatus apparently both does and does not escape execution—still leaves this void intact. Although one Cincinnatus walks away finally to the larger, more humane domain of Nabokov's imagination, another Cincinnatus still remains behind to die in the hands of M'sieur Pierre, his obscene, mocking, clown double. Even the surviving Cincinnatus, however, merely traverses another circle into Nabokov's own more spacious prison. The epigraph to *Invitation to a Beheading* probes at the book's deepest level of meaning: *Comme un fou se croit Dieu, nous nous croyons mortels*. Nabokov has taken this sentence from an invented book significantly entitled *Discours sur les ombres*, and it suggests that the central commitments (however irrational) of "shadow" men are to belief and desire. The madman believes he has the power and creativity of God, and we make the same claims for selfhood, the artist most of all. From Nabokov's perspective, both ironic and committed at once, such claims (including his own) are the very essence of quixotism.

For all their absurdity, these claims represent our one escape from metaphysical horror: the death of consciousness in and out of life, the gaping "nonnon" of emptiness, banality, and nonbeing. In the world of Nabokov's fiction, against despair there is essentially only the self's heroic resolve to pursue glimmers, to be creative and independent (that is, to preserve something of freedom, integrity, "style"). But self-consciousness includes self-mockery, an awareness of the absurdity against which all efforts must be measured. Freedom, in other words, is possible only within the inexorable prison of life. Obviously, trapped protagonists such as Krug or Cincinnatus may be liberated into the larger consciousness of their actor, but he himself is omnipotent only within a closed system, a crippled or damaged omnipotence, which is reflected in the various perversions, solipsisms, and madnesses of his protagonists. As with William Carlos Williams, instead of "Pater" we have "Paterson"; instead of the heroes of a lost generation, we have the mock-heroes of the new and the mock-heroic mode that is their appropriate literary environment.

It is *The Gift*, however, which tells us most about the heroic background of Nabokov's art and its metamorphoses through nostalgic lyricism and straight epic recovery to mature mock-heroic form. Like his father before him but now under vastly different circumstances, Fyodor Godunov-Cherdyntsev remains committed to visionary experience. *The Gift* explores the various ways of seeing (the "gifts") still open to him—especially the continued possibility of a perspective that will be in some way transformational.

Fyodor's situation at the beginning of the novel makes explicit and literal what *Invitation to a Beheading* presents in symbolic terms: the protagonist hopelessly split between the lost child's world of his memory and imagination—"the hothouse paradise of the past" (*G*, 92)—and the gross, vulgar, ugly Berlin of the 1920s, where he lives in sordid meanness as a foreigner, a Berlin whose description, according to Nabokov, was further colored by the later "rise of a nauseous dictatorship" (*G*, Foreword, [10]). An early description of Fyodor in his rented room may be taken as representative:

> For some time he stood by the window. In the curds-and-whey sky opaline pits now and then formed where the blind sun circulated, and, in response, on the gray convex roof of the van, the slender shadows of linden branches hastened headlong toward substantiation, but dissolved without having materialized. The house directly across the way was half enclosed in scaffolding, while the sound part of its brick façade was overgrown with window-invading ivy. At the far end of the path that cut through its front yard he could make out the black sign of a coal cellar. Taken by itself, all this was a view, just as the room was itself a separate entity; but now a middleman had appeared, and now that

view became the view from this room and no other. The gift of sight which it now had received did not improve it. It would be hard, he mused, to transform the wallpaper (pale yellow, with bluish tulips) into a distant steppe. The desert of the desk would have to be tilled for a long time before it would sprout its first rhymes. And much cigarette ash would have to fall under the armchair and into its folds before it would become suitable for traveling. [G, 19–20]

For this young, homesick exile in "gray" Berlin, the gift of transformational sight is largely missing. Not only is his environment itself totally opaque (the "blind sun" circulating, the linden shadows promising "substantiation" but dissolving "without having materialized," the "coal cellar" at the end of it all); but, subjective seeing—the crucial view of the "middleman"—proves also to be very difficult. Nevertheless, it remains his essential task: his father has actually walked the "distant steppe" and desert; his son must attempt something of the same with desk and wallpaper. Like all of Nabokov's exile protagonists, Fyodor takes his form (his personal "style," his fundamental moral, spiritual, and emotional commitments) from a previous avatar, which is now no longer real, possibly an illusion to begin with (the protagonist in *The Defense* is bluntly called "Luzhin"), certainly a fiction of mind in the present. His actual substance in the contemporary world is grossly, comically dissynchronous with the "dream" role that obsessively continues to shape his being. With form in place but substance gone, attenuated, or changed, Fyodor is a parodic figure, becomes aware of himself as parody, and gropes toward appropriate self-expression in a parodic art.

Fyodor's initial literary stance, however, is not parody but a nostalgic lyricism dealing directly with memories of childhood. In the first chapter of *The Gift*, he has just published a slender volume opening with a poem called "The Lost Ball," whose title and substance obviously set the theme of the entire collection. A child's ball has slipped away in a darkened room, is found momentarily by probing under furniture, then irrevocably lost when it "promptly goes under / The impregnable sofa" (G, 22). The act of memory does little to disturb the impregnable sofa and, indeed, largely testifies to its vulnerability. After referring to a pretty passage in another of these poems about getting up on a winter morning to a hot stove and "the silence of snow, / Pink-shaded azure, / And immaculate whiteness," Fyodor notes sharply:

It is strange how a memory will grow into a wax figure, how the cherub grows suspiciously prettier as its frame darkens with age—strange, strange are the mishaps of memory. I emigrated several years ago; this foreign land has by now lost its aura of abroadness just as my own ceased to be geographic habit. The Year Seven. The wandering ghost of an empire immediately adopted this system of reckoning, akin to the one formerly introduced by the ardent French citizens in honor of newborn liberty. But the years roll on, and honor is no consolation; recollections either melt away, or else acquire a deathly gloss, so that instead of marvelous apparitions we are left with a fan of picture postcards. Nothing can help me, no poetry, no stereoscope. [G, 29]

Memory apparently offers us the unpalatable alternatives of either absolute losses or the sterility of its picturesque distortions. Besides, nostalgic memory, at least, is too easy; the minor lyricist can scarcely be the heroic artist. "Because I have an innate distrust of what I feel easy to express, no sentimental wanderer will ever be allowed to land on the rock of my unfriendly prose," writes Sebastian Knight, another artist seeking a role appropriate, in this case, to the implications of his name.[9] As the above passage from *The Gift* suggests, the young Fyodor alternates between lyric identification with his poetry and considerable objectivity, even to composing mentally the critical review ("We have before us a thin volume entitled *Poems*" [G, 21]) which, in fact, his stillborn book never gets. A distancing third person "he" alternates with the more subjective "I" from the beginning of the first chapter and represents the narrative point of view toward which the novel increasingly moves, though only to enhance, not destroy, the delicate antiphony between passionate commitment and ironic commentary.

In various ingenious forms, *The Gift* offers essentially internal dialogue, and this dialogue constitutes the most important formal expression of the fundamental duality of the parodic or mock-heroic self: its life in two "time zones" (Fyodor dates his present experience from the "Year Seven"); its split into ideal hero and clownish ghost; its self-consciousness (direct or through surrogate voice) of its own duality, one avatar mocking the other, the irony generated by disparity. We have already noted, for example, Fyodor's denigration of memory. At other moments, however, he affirms its enduring power; somehow it will determine the shape of the future or, rather, it *is* the future. As Van Veen, Nabokov's philosopher of time, puts it: "Time is but memory in the making" (A, 595). In another passage, Fyodor imagines an eventual return to Russia:

> Perhaps one day, on foreign-made soles with heels long since worn down, feeling myself a ghost despite the idiotic substantiality of the insulators, I shall again come out of that station and without visible companions walk along the footpath that accompanies the highway the ten or so versts to Leshino. . . . The day will probably be on the grayish side. . . . When I reach the sites where I grew up and see this and that—or else, because of fires, rebuilding, lumbering operations or the negligence of nature, see neither this nor that (but still make

out something infinitely and unwaveringly faithful to me, if only because my
eyes are, in the long run, made of the same stuff as the grayness, the clarity, the
dampness of those sites), then, after all the excitement, I shall experience a certain satiation of suffering—perhaps on the mountain pass to a kind of happiness
which it is too early for me to know (I know only that when I reach it, it will be
with pen in hand). But there is one thing, I shall definitely not find there awaiting me—the thing which, indeed, made the whole business of exile worth
cultivating: my childhood and the fruits of my childhood. Its fruits—here they
are, today, already ripe; while my childhood itself has disappeared into a distance even more remote than that of our Russian North. [G, 37–38]

The grayness here is not that of Berlin but rather of its symbolic double, that
of another mode of time and seeing, mysterious, not banal. Or "perhaps" (to
use Fyodor's significant qualifier) Russian gray is the gray of imaginative
seeing. The lost ball of childhood will not be found, yet the experience of the
past will be encountered again in the future. Or, must it be found in some
willed, obsessive pursuit? The Nabokov protagonist is, as much as anything,
a Quixote of time. Fyodor suggests that the artist's role ("pen in hand") can at
least absorb the paradoxes of memory and imagination and, in so doing,
furnish "a kind of" visionary experience, "childish" ardency and integrity of
belief and commitment in some later context. The supreme model here of
ecstatic possibility is his father (invoked again by references to steppes and
mountain passes), and we must now examine Fyodor's treatment of that figure to define more precisely those heroic values which the ideal self of the
protagonist affirms. What authentic hero does he mimic? This parodic model
will, of course, partially determine the nature of the parody.

In Nabokov's fiction the reader questing for answers runs into paradox.
The authentic father/hero can be encountered, if at all, only in the fictions of
the inauthentic son. Like Stephen Dedalus, Fyodor must create the prototypal father whom he comically imitates. The elder Godunov-Cherdyntsev
never exists in the present ("Year Seven") time of the novel. He has been
missing since an expedition to Asia undertaken just before the Revolution,
and even his son, whose life is embellished by dreams of his return, is ter-
rified by the thought of the possible "arrival of a live father" (G, 100). Reality
would only make palpable the gap between style and fate and lead finally to
anticlimax. Of his own father's relatively meager role in the revolutionary
events of 1917–18 and his assassination by a "sinister ruffian" in 1922,
Nabokov has written: "History seems to have been anxious of depriving him
of a full opportunity to reveal his great gifts of statesmanship in a Russian
republic of the Western type" (SM, 176). Certainly Fyodor's father belongs

(and must remain) in mythic time. Fyodor remembers at one point an old fairy tale of his father's which began: "The only son of a great khan, having lost his way during a hunt," and he goes on to comment parenthetically: "Thus begin the best fairy tales and thus end the best lives" (*G*, 146).

Fyodor realizes that minor lyrics will not do in rendering the heroic fairy tale of his father; they are too easy and sterile in their nostalgia, too limited in their subjectivity. He turns, therefore, to an obvious alternative, the epic narrative of Aleksander Pushkin, a writer with whom he closely associates his father. Reading the work of the heroic artist, he simultaneously does research on the heroic parent; the two figures fuse together: "Pushkin entered his blood. With Pushkin's voice merged the voice of his father" or, as he describes this imaginative process elsewhere: "Indefatigably, in ecstasy, he was really preparing his work now . . . [he] collected material, read until dawn, studied maps, wrote letters and met with the necessary people. From Pushkin's prose he had passed to his life, so that in the beginning the rhythm of Pushkin's era commingled with the rhythm of his father's life" (*G*, 110). Even Fyodor's grandfather (at one point, a Mississippi gambler, Texas cattle breeder, and duelist) and great-grandfather ("a hero of the Napoleonic War" [*G*, 111]) are caught up finally in the collective portrait.

Fyodor creates an extraordinarily complete and detailed composite of the nineteenth-century hero as soldier, statesman, adventurer, romantic artist, explorer, and scientist—a composite that precisely defines the nexus of Fyodor's own emotional and imaginative commitments, his moral values, and his spiritual goals. The elder Godunov-Cherdyntsev's life represents both the culmination of this heroic period and its last phase before the arrival of what Nabokov has called elsewhere "our disastrous century."[10] Fyodor's father is, in effect, the ideal Victorian: the scientist who is traveler, discoverer, encyclopedic and definitive writer (his colleagues call him significantly "the conquistador of Russian entomology" [*G*, 114]); the godlike, legendary parent (his home museum "smelled as it probably smells in Paradise" and was "a kind of mysterious central hearth" [*G*, 118]); above all, the severe, resolute example of masculine force and power "over everything that he undertook" (*G*, 124).

In his father Fyodor identifies authentic nobility—in the most serious and profound sense of that word. This nobility manifests itself in two different clusters of virtues, which can be labeled loosely as "aristocratic" and "romantic" without insisting necessarily on absolute distinctions between categories. The aristocratic qualities I have suggested already and, in any case, can be quickly summarized: bravery, independence, absolute commitment to a code of honor, freedom from the pragmatic attitudes and perspective of the bourgeois world, aloofness, severity, resolution, familiarity with power and leadership, noblesse oblige, and above all, a certain style. Fyodor remembers how much he liked "that special easy knack [his father] showed in dealing with a horse, a dog, a gun, a bird, or a peasant boy with a two-inch splinter in his back" (G, 125).

Even more significant, however, is his father's ecstatic, visionary romanticism. Power in his hands goes beyond his masculine and aristocratic implications to include vitalistic energy, imagination, the will to measure spaces, God's act of creating the world in its naming: "He was happy in that incompletely named world in which at every step he named the nameless" (G, 131). Significantly, Fyodor's father is a lonely, mysterious, visionary quester moving toward "perfect peace, silence, transparency" in the high mountains (G, 134), the pursuer of beauty at the extremities of human experience, the perfect exemplar of what Fyodor calls "knowledge-amplified love" (G, 144). Behind the nineteenth-century forebears of his father already noted is Marco Polo, the prototype of the visionary explorer, who has seen miracles in the same deserts through which the elder Godunov-Cherdyntsev later progresses. Appropriately, a picture of "Marco Polo leaving Venice" hangs in his father's office (G, 127). In this connection, we must remember that Cincinnatus, living in an imaginary future when the airports are grown over with weeds and there are no more "flights," remembers vaguely that "there was in town a certain man, a pharmacist, whose great-grandfather, it was said, had left a memoir describing how merchants used to go to China by air," (IB, 44). In the year Seven of present time, the Journey to the East, if not forgotten completely, can only be parodied. Sebastian Knight, for example, goes with a futurist poet on "a Marcopolian journey" through Russia, a trip that involves renting halls and giving poetical performances (SK, 29). And much later in Nabokov's career, Van Veen as a young man puts on performances in the guise of a character aptly called "Mascodagama."

Fyodor's biography in its own way is also a performance, and he finally becomes aware of the limitations of such "secondary" imitation. As the author of The Gift, however, he turns these limitations into a crucial dimension of its subject matter. The style of these biographical notes, for example, suggests that what we are reading is as much Fyodor's imaginative projection as any "true" record of his father's expeditions. The visionary role constantly threatens to shift from the object of the biography to its narrator. His father's traverse of the high country is continually punctuated by the phrase "I see" or "this is the way I see it" or, more revealingly, "I can conjure up." At other times, Fyodor will shift to the first-person plural ("our caravan moved east") or a union of first and third ("he and I would take Elwes' Swallowtail" [G, 128–34]).

We are made aware, moreover, that Fyodor can never long escape his exile world; like Stephen Dedalus's environment, it constitutes a perpetual mockery of his reveries. After one ecstatic passage, for example, invoking an imaginary transit of the desert of Lob with his father, during which they hear in the sandstorms the same "whisper of spirits" reported by Marco Polo, Fyodor abruptly switches to a description of himself in the act (and failure) of performance: "All this lingered bewitchingly, full of color and air, with lively movement in the foreground and a convincing backdrop; then, like smoke from a breeze, it shifted and dispersed—and Fyodor saw again the dead and impossible tulips of his wallpaper, the crumbling mound of cigarette butts in the ashtray, and the lamp's reflection in the black windowpane. He threw open the window." But damp, cold air rushes in, and only by closing the window and picking up his "still-warm pen" can he "return to that world which was as natural to him as snow to the white hare or water to Ophelia" (*G*, 136–37).

Still seeking a direct and simple response to loss (a response in which the heroic past is invoked into being by the art form that was its most perfect expression—thus the past not really lost), the earlier Fyodor attempts literally to become "one" with his father. He offers the ardors of desire and the powers of imagination and language as an authentic method of reaching perfect transparency and hearing immortal whispers. The putative author of *The Gift*, however, now writing his own biography in a composite style appropriate to the circumstances, conceives of his persona as two people (the son/father separate from the lonely son), living in two irreconcilable worlds, each with its inexorable claims, each even with a rhetoric expressive of those claims. From such a dual perspective, the strength and intensity of Fyodor's commitment to visionary experience in no way actually transforms or even mitigates the rigors of mean and sordid Berlin. Conversely, the banal climate limits or denies only the absolute end of questing, not its value and necessity as a moral and spiritual imperative. In becoming self-conscious of its own absurdity, the heroic code of values paradoxically survives the dissolution of its circumstances. The fundamental action of *The Gift* involves Fyodor's gradual discovery that he is, in fact, the mock-hero of what will be, at best, his own mock-heroic narrative.

One important dimension of Fyodor's discovery is his growing awareness of the instability of language and imagination as authentic instruments of power and truth. Already in writing poetry he had become aware of this problem; he has even sharper intimations while working on his father's biography. He abandons this second project when he becomes aware that the verbal creation of proximate worlds cannot literally be offered as a simple substitute for or copy of reality, that, in effect, he has become a mere naive imitator of his father's life and career. As Fyodor explains to his mother in a letter:

> You know, when I read his or Grum's books and I hear their entrancing rhythm, when I study the position of the words that can neither be replaced nor rearranged, it seems to me a sacrilege to take all this and dilute it with myself. If you like I'll admit it: I myself am a mere seeker of verbal adventures, and forgive me if I refuse to hunt down my fancies on my father's own collecting ground. I have realized, you see, the impossibility of having the imagery of his travels germinate without contaminating them with a kind of secondary poetization which keeps departing further and further from that real poetry with which the live experience of these receptive, knowledgeable and chaste naturalists endowed their research. [G, 151]

She responds by telling him of her conviction "that some day you shall yet write this book" (G, 151). And, in a sense, she is correct, although Fyodor will write it from the perspective of the self-conscious parodist whose protagonist is now himself as mock-hero, himself the verbal adventurer trying to play some version of his father, and whose style of "secondary poetization" achieves, in this new context, its own legitimation insofar as it becomes its own end—no longer requiring verification with "the real poetry" of some prior "live experience." As Margaret Rose (following Foucault) says of metalanguage in Cervantes, it "offers Don Quixote the chance to be true to himself in Cervantes' text rather than true to the roles given in the Knightly Romance."[11] The heroic or "Pushkin" phase of Fyodor's life ends when he moves his lodgings, a move to which Nabokov gives a literary direction: "The distance from the old residence to the new was about the same as, somewhere in Russia, that from Pushkin Avenue to Gogol Street" (G, 157). In other words, Fyodor travels steadily from lyric to epic to a more direct encounter with ironic realism.

The straight fairy tale, at least, will not do. In a slightly later novel, *The Real Life of Sebastian Knight* (1941), the narrator (V.) is also a potential biographer (in this case, of a famous brother) and also directed initially to create or recreate an authentic romantic hero. His adviser is a nostalgic old governess, who lives wholly in the events of the past and who urges him to "write that book, that beautiful book . . . make it a fairy-tale with Sebastian for prince. The enchanted prince." But V. senses the implications of this advice in the very looks of the governess: "I glanced at her misty old eyes, at the dead lustre of her false teeth" (SK, 23). Andrew Field has pointed out the tension in Nabokov's early poetry between the pull of childhood, couched in the mode of Georgian elegy, and a determination to live and write in a present context. One poem is reminiscent of Stevens's "Sad Strains of a Gay Waltz":

some lady who writes
or ha'penny bard
will bewail the disappearance of former dances;
but for me, I'll tell you frankly,
there is no special delight
in a rude and unwashed
marquis dancing a minuet.[12]

The mock-heroic mode, let me emphasize again, is a strategy for personal and literary survival. Nowhere is this more obvious than in the work of Nabokov. As it did for Joyce, Stevens, and others before them, such a strategy requires that Nabokov come to terms with romanticism and realism, acknowledging these perspectives, finally, in a complex art that includes the claims of both. Since Nabokov had explored the present possibilities of heroic romanticism, it is scarcely surprising that *The Gift* next brings literary realism under scrutiny.

On the face of it, however, Fyodor's next biographical venture, a treatment of the great realist critic Chernyshevski, seems anomalous. It puzzled and disturbed Fyodor's publisher, and he rejected it; so did Nabokov's own publisher, and a complete edition of *The Gift* did not appear until 1952 (as Nabokov reports in his Foreword to the Putnam edition). The fat, dirty, coarse, inept, comic Chernyshevski has apparently little in common with Fyodor's sublime father; nor could his literary theory, with its strong emphasis on empiricism, common sense, and social concerns, be expected to have significance for the romantic artist. In fiction as in life, Fyodor's (or Nabokov's) portrait of Chernyshevski seems an act of gratuitous satire, an aggression against a hero of Russian liberalism at a time when the liberals were already under heavy attack from external enemies.

But Fyodor's biography is, in fact, a complex exercise in ironic perspective, a perspective he has clearly in mind from the beginning. As he explains to Zina, his girl friend and patient auditor: "I want to keep everything as it were on the very brink of parody. You know those idiotic *'biographies romancées'* where Byron is coolly slipped a dream extracted from one of his own poems? And there must be on the other hand an abyss of seriousness, and I must make my way along this narrow ridge between my own truth and a caricature of it" (*G,* 212). Given the anticlimax (the collapse into *roman*) of the earlier Fyodor's own attempt at heroic biography—scarcely "idiotic," to be sure, but nevertheless a failure of aesthetic control, a failure of the artist-hero even in his own "act"—it is appropriate that he turn to the possibilities of parody as a deliberate, self-conscious method of bringing visionary experience and reality into a controlled, comprehensive balance. Fyodor's metaphor of the ridge-walker between describes the same categorical duality, the same perspective "between" two truths and inclusive of both that I have previously associated with the mock-heroic mode. And it is understandable that the claims of reality might be more readily acknowledged in a historically important figure with whom one has no personal, intellectual, or nostalgic connection.

Fyodor is not essentially concerned, however, with the easy irony of demolishing the romantic legend of the chief spokesman of realism. His task, rather, is the more difficult, subtle, and significant one (obviously too subtle for many of Fyodor and Nabokov's critics!) of finding heroic possibility in Chernyshevski's obsessions, comic absurdities, and various misadventures. Fyodor makes clear that he will continue to pursue his own truth—now, however, exploring its embodiment in another mode, an ironic art squarely concerned with the gap between human conceptualizations of reality and the actual opacity of reality to imagination and desire. His version of Chernyshevski's career emphasizes at once aspects of reality darker than the partisans of realism would acknowledge and dimensions of idealism which they chose to ignore or deny. Fyodor's treatment of Chernyshevski turns materialism on its ear as a form of idealism and yet accepts the banal emptiness of reality, an emptiness which, as Erich Heller long ago pointed out, tends to constitute the hidden agenda of the great realists. Incongruity (the explicit models here are Nikolai Gogol and Flaubert) is the stylistic key, the fundamental incongruity of concrete horrors everywhere in tangled juxtaposition with idealistic commitments. The resultant portrait of a "mad," grotesque visionary observed by an apparently "saner" narrator-artist culminates Fyodor's preparatory biographical studies of others (his next protagonist will be himself as young lyricist and biographer) and has wide ramifications for Nabokov's own career.[13]

In his review of Chernyshevski's life, Fyodor everywhere insists that mockery is the voice of destiny. If so, mockery, in turn, must become part of the artist's voice as guarantor of its authenticity—an authenticity that paradoxically achieves its final, full authority only in self-conscious awareness of its own ultimate inauthenticity. For Nabokov, as for other writers examined here, mockery is the true message of realism and one that must be accepted even by those who despise realism. It is mockery that draws down the greatest wrath of Fyodor's imaginary reviewers. According to one, "excessive zeal, and even kindness, in the process of exposing evil is always more understandable and forgivable than the least mockery—no matter how witty it may be—of that which public opinion feels to be objectively good" (G, 317). Or again: "He makes fun, not only of his hero: he also makes fun of his reader." Even satire would represent a clear and understandable position: "It would at least be a point of view, and reading the book the reader would make a constant adjustment for the author's partisan approach, in that way arriving at the truth. But the pity is that with Mr. Godunov-Cherdyntsev there is nothing to adjust to and the point of view is 'everywhere and nowhere'" (G, 318). Here, with some help from behind the scenes, our critic does, indeed, get to the essential point: Nabokov's irony is inclusive, not exclusive, a mode of affirming contradictory truths, not of arriving at *the* truth.

Even parody must always be self-conscious of itself as a parodic style. As another (more sympathetic) imaginary critic tells Fyodor, "You sometimes bring up parody to such a degree of naturalness that it actually becomes a genuine serious thought, but on *this* level it suddenly falters, lapsing into a mannerism that is yours and not a parody of a mannerism, although it is precisely the kind of thing you are ridiculing" (G, 351). In other words, a totality of perspective must be aware of and mock even its own totality as a particular perspective or "mannerism." In all this, Nabokov seeks to define a humanism that includes mockery and places art (the modern road to heroic freedom and adventure) at the center of human experience as opposed to realistic, utilitarian, moralistic humanisms that subtly or grossly denigrate art and thus the possibility of heroic values. Mockery, in short, is the enabling device that makes life and art possible, not a mordant weapon operating at their expense.

With the completion of his biography of Chernyshevski, Fyodor has largely come into his only inheritance, his only possible "gifts" in the face of obvious loss. Not the least of these gifts is his love affair with Zina Mertz (the "real hub" of the Gogol chapter, according to Nabokov [G, Foreword, 10]). Sexual passion, of course, looms large in Nabokov's later work, but even in *The Gift*, where sex is not mentioned and the relationship seldom dwelt on, Zina is both the focus and central manifestation of Fyodor's desire. Human love, characteristically, both mocks and invokes the spiritual love which it imitates, whose shade or shadow it is. Of his encounter, for example, on the street with another young girl who "contained a particle of that fascination, both special and vague," found in Zina, Fyodor notes that "he felt for a moment the impact of a hopeless desire, whose whole charm and richness was in its unquenchability. Oh trite demon of cheap thrills, do not tempt me with the catchword 'my type.' Not that, not that, but something beyond that. Definition is always finite, but I keep straining for the far-away; I search beyond the barricades (of words, of senses, of the world) for infinity, where all, all the lines meet" (G, 341). The passage characteristically moves between the objective "he" and a passionate, lyric, questing "I" that seeks, forever hopelessly, to break out of its prison through the sheer strength of desire. Nabokov's work is characterized throughout by this primary "search . . . for infinity, where all, all the lines meet." Unless we recognize this, we cannot begin to understand his art.

Fyodor and Nabokov never waver in their fundamental motivation. They engage in parody not for metafictional ends but as a means of continuing "the spirit of his father's peregrinations" (G, 347) toward an ideal consummation of ecstasy and love, the only proper goal of the heroic soul. "Ecstasy" and "love" are, indeed, Nabokov's terms, used in Speak, Memory to describe the "timeless" pursuit of butterflies, one of his own methods for achieving "something akin to" the power of the past. "The highest enjoyment of time-lessness," he writes, "is when I stand among rare butterflies and their food plants. This is ecstasy, and behind the ecstasy is something else, which is hard to explain. It is like a momentary vacuum into which rushes all that I love" (SM, 139). Nabokov's parodies, likewise, are only another method of setting protagonists and author free within the confines of their prison to find at least "shimmers" of spiritual truth. He systematically exploits the style toward which Fyodor must painfully grope in The Gift. Many of the more popular and banal literary genres—the detective or "mystery" story, the con-fessional, the exposé or investigative biography (the search for the truth about someone)—are already naive parodies of romantic/heroic narrative and become, in Nabokov's hands, perfect vehicles for more sophisticated de-scriptions of the romantic quest in a banal world. One might say of The Gift that it almost literally describes the dynamics of parody: the invocation of past values and styles; the transcendence of mere imitation; the achievement, finally, of authentic transformation and thus continuity.

The focus, nevertheless, remains always on the "act" (action, perfor-mance) of questing, on whatever spiritual intimations that process itself may furnish. Ends remain illusory, anticlimactic, fatal, even utilitarian. Ecstasy, love, creative "naming" (all those apparent ends associated with the pro-totypal butterfly hunt) are finally human qualities, expansions of the self, emotional and imaginative aggrandizement, rather than dimensions of the absolute. To say as much is to limit whatever claims are made for these qualities, not to denigrate them or make their pursuit less crucial. Nabokov, for example, writes of his mother, who enjoyed searching for mushrooms on the grounds of their country estate, that "her delight was in the quest, and this quest had its rules"—set, of course, by herself (SM, 43). The family, to be sure, ate the mushrooms for dinner, but this is almost beside the point, scarcely the real concern of mother and son. In The Gift, Fyodor, his father, even Chernyshevski have most in common the heroic quality of their seek-ing, their act of pursuit as hunters, not what, if anything, they find. But Fyodor alone becomes the ironist, and in the ironic history of his quest, he finally discovers an adequate vehicle for his heroic theme. It is a lesson Nabokov had already learned, and it is the crucial lesson of his literary career.

Whereas the authentic hero may be tragically tested or tested by the perils of romantic adventure, the mock-hero is essentially tested by irony, by a total immersion in the mockery of fate and banal circumstances which denies final authority to his vision at every level and which, nevertheless, constitutes the environment of his quest. But vital commitments (both protagonist and author if not godlike, at least able to "play" God, the authentic Father), aesthetic and emotional pleasure from patterns of order imposed—these qualities are still achievable, and, indeed, crucially distinguish the soul of the mock-hero from those who would be his jailers. This is certainly the conclusion that John Shade comes to in his poem "Pale Fire," when commenting on his own mock consummations:

> But all at once it dawned on me that *this*
> Was the real point, the contrapuntal theme;
> Just this: not text, but texture; not the dream
> But topsy-turvical coincidence,
> Not flimsy nonsense, but a web of sense.
> Yes! It sufficed that I in life could find
> Some kind of link-and-bobolink, some kind
> Of correlated pattern in the game.
> Plexed artistry, and something of the same
> Pleasure in it as they who played it found.[14]

As a lecturer at the Institute of Preparation for the Hereafter ("or If, as we / Called it—big if!" [*PF*, 52]), Shade speaks with some authority. He suggests that the quests of Nabokov's protagonists are not crowned with absolute vision ("not text") but that neither are they directed toward frivolous ends ("not flimsy nonsense"). In between these two alternatives are heroic games, imitation adventures, performances of Marco Polo which reveal or discover "some kind of" fictive order. Such "correlated pattern" or "plexed artistry" constitutes both human sense and metaphysical absurdity ("topsyturvical coincidence"). It suffices, says Shade, whose name describes his own attenuated status as hero; it gives pleasure (to paraphrase Wallace Stevens's "notes" regarding supreme fictions).

To Shade's defense of "texture," we must add the comment of his mad editor Kinbote, desperately and obsessively seeking to impose his own meaning and order on Shade's poem. In a characteristic tortuous note (where one thing "reminds" him of another and his own imagination begins to create "correlated pattern"), Kinbote mentions reading a book in which "a passage . . . curiously echoes Shade's tone at the end of Canto Three." In this book the author, another man "on the eve of his death," conceives of going to heaven and seeking out Aristotle, the father figure he most admires: "—Ah, there would be a man to talk with! What satisfaction to see him take, like reins from between his fingers, the long ribbon of man's life and trace it through the mystifying maze of all the wonderful adventure. . . . The crooked made straight. The Daedalian plan simplified by a look from above—smeared out as it were by the splotch of some master thumb that made the whole involuted, boggling thing one beautiful straight line" (PF, 261). Kinbote's gloss of Shade emphasizes the yearning for the "beautiful straight line" that informs the work of both men as well as their creator. Exiled from an authentic garden world, Nabokov's children survive (as Shade puts it) by "Playing a game of worlds, promoting pawns / To ivory unicorns and ebon fauns . . . Making ornaments / Of accidents and possibilities" (PF, 630). Kinbote, the pedant, speaks of "lexical playfields" and attempts, by playing elaborate word games with Shade's poem, to "reassemble" his mythical Zembla (PF, 260), his lost kingdom, which, in turn, reminds us of Humbert Humbert's losses and (through echoes of Poe in Lolita) of all the lost kingdoms of the romantic tradition. In such ways is the categorical mockery of Nabokov's parody matched only by its extraordinary spiritual resonance. Nobility lingers on in the capacity of certain individuals to find spiritual adventure in circumstances that deny its actual possibility. Of Clare, the heroine of The Real Life of Sebastian Knight, an admiring V. notes: "She possessed . . . that real sense of beauty which has far less to do with art than with the constant readiness to discern the halo around a frying pan" (SK, 83). This visionary readiness is the real point of Nabokov's aesthetic games.

The Souls of Madmen

Don Quixote's friends constantly question his sanity and, from a position of rational maturity, disclaim his attempts to impose on the real world ideal values from heroic romance or some mythical golden age. However charming and valuable, Clare's readiness to see haloes around frying pans is also a form of insanity. Madness is a central characteristic of all mock-heroes or those who identify with them; Foucault's modern "man of primitive resemblances" is ubiquitous to our study. Nabokov, however, approaches the issue with an explicitness, intensity, and obsessive repetition that can be matched, if at all, only by our primary Cervantine model. Before turning to the perversions of Nabokov's notorious sexual adventurers, therefore, I want to identify more sharply the particular nature of madness in his work. For our specific discussion, Pale Fire can stand as exemplary. As much as any, this novel is directly about madness, and, in Kinbote at least, the protagonist seems readily identifiable as an obvious lunatic. Kinbote himself makes one of the most telling comments on madness, though naturally he excludes his own activities from any of its implications. In an elaborate gloss on a phrase—"The madman's fate"—that Shade has apparently stricken from the final version of his poem, Kinbote comments: "The ultimate destiny of madmen's souls has been probed by many Zemblan theologians who generally hold the view that even the most demented mind still contains within its diseased mass a sane basic particle that survives death and suddenly expands, bursts out as it were, in peals of healthy and triumphant laughter when the world of timorous fools and trim blockheads has fallen away far behind. Personally, I have not known any lunatics; but have heard of several amusing cases in New Wye ('Even in Arcady am I,' says Dementia, chained to her gray column)." He gives a couple of examples, then reports on a party at which he had come up behind Shade just as Shade was objecting to a remark made to him by a Mrs. H.:

> "That was the wrong word," he said. "One should not apply it to a person who deliberately peels off a drab and unhappy past and replaces it with a brilliant invention. That's merely turning a new leaf with the left hand."
>
> I patted my friend on the head and bowed slighly to Eberthella H. The Poet looked at me with glazed eyes. She said:
>
> "You must help us, Mr. Kinbote: I maintain that what's his name, old—the old man, you know, at the Exton railway station, who thought he was God and began redirecting the trains, was technically a loony, but John calls him a fellow poet."
>
> "We all are, in a sense, poets, Madam," I replied. [PF, 237–38]

The exquisite comedy of this footnote is matched only by its significance—the passage given one final, splendid ironic twist because, on this occasion at least, Kinbote feels his note may have been redundant: "I am not sure this trivial variant has been worth commenting" (PF, 238).

At the risk of unwittingly reinforcing the comedy (or spoiling it by heavy-handedness), let me add a few comments of my own. Shade's defense of the old man "at the Exton railway station who thought he was God" constitutes a further gloss on the epigraph to Invitation to a Beheading which I have already briefly discussed: "Comme un fou se croit Dieu, nous nous croyons mortels." He reminds us again that madness in Nabokov's work (the state of mind of his protagonists but also his philosophical theme, essentially even his own role) identifies, indeed precisely describes, the act of expansive and creative selfhood in the face of loss, death, and the banality and horror of the temporal world. The "brilliant invention" that Shade mentions involves playing God, the relentless creation of alternative worlds, poetic or otherwise, so that one "survives death," not physical death (survival of which would rationalize their actions and make them wholly sane), but the death in life of the trim-mers, the "timorous fools," the banal persecutors as well as the tragic death in life of despair, grief, and pain.

At the most minimal level of definition, Kinbote suggests what his "god-like" madmen are not. He notes, for example (reporting a religious discussion he has had with Shade), that "as St. Augustine said, 'One can know what God is not; one cannot know what he is.' I think I know what he is not: He is not despair, He is not Terror, He is not the earth in one's rattling throat, not the black hum in one's ears fading to nothing in nothing" (PF, 227). Or, in even more tentative terms, he reports walking home from church on a cloud-less day: "On such sunny, sad mornings I always feel in my bones that there is a chance yet of my not being excluded from Heaven, and that Salvation may be granted to me despite the frozen mud and horror in my heart" (PF, 258). Obviously this is a pathetic illusion, yet, at the same time, it reflects the spiritual substance behind his lunatic attempt at "reassembling Zembla."

In more positive terms, Nabokov's mock-heroes are heroic survivors. However perverse or perverted by fate and local circumstances, they affirm "a sane basic particle" that expands beyond these circumstances to proclaim triumphantly some sort of spiritual vivacity, power, and freedom, the "tri-umphant laughter" to which Kinbote refers. Like the traditional heroes whom they parody, Nabokov's madmen define the limits, constrained as they may be, of human hope and desire: Kinbote is "King—but"; Shade com-ments that he likes his name ("Shade, *Ombre*, almost 'man' / In Spanish" [PF, 174]); and one alternative to the Institute of Preparation for the Hereafter—the "big if"—is "*L'if*" or "life" as alternative to death. I mean "alternative," of course, in the only context provided by this form of ironic narrative: namely, as one dimension of a punning term that continues to bear its own negation. Kinbote glosses the word by noting that it means "yew" in French and a "weeping willow" in Zemblan (PF, 222). These "almost" men, mad each in his own way, are "almost" heroes or what I have persistently called mock-heroes—the "almosts" the "big ifs," and all the other conditionals and pun-ning double or triple meanings at once denying and making possible their role.

Nabokov's madmen are both solipsistic and paranoic. Like Sebastian in *The Real Life of Sebastian Knight,* they all look into a reflecting pool. As Kinbote proudly admits in his editorial Foreword to Shade's poem, the beholding self is the only begetter, never more the begetter than when engaged in arcane examination of "the underside of the weave" (PF, 14). Earlier, describing an apparently rough canto draft, Kinbote notes that "it turns out to be beau-tifully accurate when you once make the plunge and compel yourself to open your eyes in the limpid depths under its confused surface" (PF, 14). Metaphors of "diving" and looking underneath, the concept of visionary meaning as below the surface of reality, involves a perfectly sound romantic premise which Nabokov's protagonists follow rigorously. Appropriately enough, Humbert at one point becomes a member of "a weather station on Pierre Point in Melville Sound" (*L*, 35). In Nabokov's work, however, this surface actuality never ceases to mock the experiences of the depth; instead of a transcendent monism, we are left with an intransigent dualism. Melville's fears and doubts concerning the subjectivity of meditation find strong reinforcement in the ironies of the later author, though both men still remain very much committed to "diving."

Mentioning his obsessive attempts to make Shade write *his* poem, Kinbote observes that "by mid-June I felt sure at least he would recreate in a poem the dazzling Zembla burning in my brain. I mesmerized him with it, I saturated him with my vision" (*PF*, 80). Shade's poem undoubtedly deals with his own obsessions, but Kinbote's illusion of "saturation" becomes, in turn, an exact description of what he will not be denied and of what, in fact, his editorial apparatus does to Shade's poem in terms of a new "begetting." In other words, we can describe his notes as only a "pale" reflected shadow of the poem which constitutes their apparent basis, or, because of his will to survive and "(re)assemble" order and because of his extraordinary imaginative energy, we can, with equal propriety, describe Shade's poem as only a pale shadow of Kinbote's own massive counterfiction.

In either case, the material and the fictional order created from the material has been, as Humbert claims of Lolita, "safely solipsised" (*L*, 62). On one hand, the matter of reality is substantially pliable to the mind's quest for synchronization and resemblance, the staples of order and meaning; on the other (and this is the source of ironic pathos and comedy in the mock-heroic mode from Cervantes on), matter remains totally opaque and indifferent. Kinbote's "temptation to synchronize" (*PF*, 74) his vision with Shade's poem is heroic as an act of will, imagination, and effort. "I, too" is his most characteristic phrase as he struggles to link the individual lines of the poem to his own role, as he avidly reads every word for sign or clue to the story of his beloved Zembla. The very name Zembla, we are reminded (ironically, by Kinbote), may be "a corruption not of the Russian *zemlya*, but of Semberland, a land of reflections, of 'resemblers.'" And Shade adds that "resemblances are the shadows of differences. Different people see different similarities and similar differences" (*PF*, 265). In other words, "resembling" (which puns easily into "reassembling") is only a dimension of "pale fire," a parody shadow of a reality that forever escapes the true engagement and mastery traditionally brought to it by the authentic hero. Resemblances are, in fact, simply a function of perception: seeing as seeming.

Shade himself, the admitted preterist, "begets" his past and his dead daughter in a poem written in face of the fact that (as he puts it) "we die every day; oblivion thrives / Not on dry thighbones but on blood-ripe lives, / And our best yesterdays are now foul piles / Of crumpled names, phone numbers and boxed files" (PF, 52). He dies finally in ways even beyond his awareness: not only does one "day" bring his actual murder, but he is further assassinated in the counterfiction of his admiring editor. His daughter is the very personification of mortal time (as a child she has appropriately played "Mother Time" in a school pantomine [PF, 44]) in its guise of pathetic defeats, suffering, and final hopelessness. Nor does cosmic time offer much more. Of the beauties of skyscape day and night, Shade notes that "we are most artistically caged"; of their temporal implications, he adds: "Infinite foretime and / Infinite aftertime: above your head / They close like giant wings, and you are dead" (PF, 37). His daughter's suicide is probably a form of rational sanity; his own role as mock-hero of memory and imagination, a form of madness.

Nabokov's lunatic questers can perhaps be best understood as heroic within the desperate and narrow context of other options, limited in this case to three: banal inhumanity (represented in Pale Fire by Gradus, another executioner and mechanical monster: "Mere springs and coils produced the inward movements of our clockwork man" [PF, 152]); despair; and, of course, death itself. Nabokov's questers are mad in their hopeless attempt to escape their cage, mad in their relentless organization of purely subjective worlds, mad in their manic insistence on pursuing and reading spiritual signs or "clues," and mad also (in a darker sense) in their destructiveness, absurdity, and even outright perversions, all a measure of their inauthenticity and their exile from a true heroic landscape.[15] They remain permanently as I have earlier described them—crippled offspring of omnipotent fathers. When Shade asks Kinbote if his name doesn't mean "regicide" in Zemblan, the latter replies: "'Yes, a king's destroyer,' I said (longing to explain that a king who sinks his identity in the mirror of exile is in a sense just that)" (PF, 267). Even the apparently saner Shade makes clear from the beginning of his poem the tenuous and unstable environment of his own spiritual drama. His well-known opening lines also invoke "the mirror of exile":

> I was the shadow of the waxwing slain
> By the false azure of the window pane;
> I was the smudge of ashen fluff—and I
> Lived on, flew on, in the reflected sky.   [PF, 33]

It is as such a shadow figure in a reflected world that the mock-hero must, nevertheless, struggle to make his spiritual gestures. Shade affirms the act of singing itself ("Dead is the mandible, alive the song" [PF, 42]); he can respond positively to the "mad, / Impossible, unutterably weird, / Wonderful nonsense" of life (PF, 40–41); he develops the theory of "texture" about which I have already commented; and he returns again to the power of "invention" at the end of the poem:

> Maybe my sensual love for the *consonne*
> *D'appui,* Echo's fey child, is based upon
> A feeling of fantastically planned,
> Richly rhymed life.
>   I feel I understand
> Existence, or at least a minute part
> Of my existence, only through my art
> In terms of combinational delight;   [PF, 68–69]

In such "combinational delight" Nabokov's mock-heroes come as close as they ever will to apotheosis—as Kinbote puts it, "John Shade perceiving and transforming the world" (PF, 27). That such transformations are limited is suggested again by the poem's anticlimactic end. Shade further writes that "I am reasonably sure that I / Shall wake at six tomorrow, on July / The twenty-second" (PF, 69), but he is, in fact, dead a few minutes later on the twenty-first, shot by a murderous madman, who mistakes him for someone else.

If Nabokov were tempted to exempt himself from the absurd yet gallant lunacy of his mock-heroes (hard to do, in any case, because shortly after *Pale Fire* he was to publish his four-volume translation and commentary on Pushkin's *Eugene Onegin*), the epigraph to *Pale Fire* from Boswell's *Life of Johnson* would seem to argue otherwise. Boswell mentions "the despicable state of a young gentleman of good family," who goes around town shooting cats but who "bethought himself of his own favorite cat, and said, 'But Hodge shan't be shot: no, no, Hodge shall not be shot.'" The young gentleman's actions mock our all too human tendency to make personal exceptions, but they may also reflect the distinction that Nabokov tried to draw for his students between lunacy and artistic inspiration—lunatics merely dismembering a familiar world, without the power (or having lost the power) "to create a new one as harmonious as the old."[16] On a madness scale tied to creativity, any distinction between Nabokov the author and his creations involves simply the quality and range of performance, the magnitude and power of the imaginative world new and transformed (as Kinbote puts it, "immortal imagery, involutions of thought, new worlds with live people" [PF, 289]). Shade is well aware that the writer "dies every day" like everyone else, yet he heroically (and obsessively) attempts resistance: "there was the sleepless night / When I decided to explore and fight / The foul, the inadmissible abyss, / Devoting all my twisted life to this / One task" (PF, 39).

Don Juan as Don Quixote

For Nabokov sexual passion in the contemporary world exists in the same parodic relationship to ideal or transcendental love as art and other formal games of the spirit do to a true metaphysical order. At issue here as elsewhere are not so much the ethics of the Judeo-Christian moral tradition as those aristocratic and romantic qualities I have noted before: style, rigorous commitments, heroic energy, and power. We must constantly keep in mind V.'s comments concerning the ethics of Sebastian: "He would not mind perhaps having a bite at the apple of sin because, apart from solecisms, he was indifferent to the idea of sin; but he did mind apple-jelly potted and patented" (*SK*, 149–50). In *The Gift*, Nabokov puts what will become the plot of *Lolita* into the mouth of Zina's vulgar, garrulous, anti-Semitic father, who tells it as something that happened to a friend and then comments: "Eh? D'you feel here a kind of Dostoevskian tragedy?" (*G*, 198). The point, obviously, is that this is precisely what *Lolita* will *not* become. To see, therefore, Nabokov's most "depraved" and crazy protagonists (Kinbote and Humbert, let us say, and probably Van Veen, that perpetual sexual adolescent) primarily within an ethics of guilt is to miss the point. Their perverted sexuality, indeed physical sex itself, is only a gross and zany imitation of the "knowledge-amplified love" of the authentic hero. As such it reflects the positive qualities of questing (ardor, single-mindedness, imagination, the historical memory of something valuable lost), while expressing fully, brutally, the context of gross mockery that frames the hero's experience in present time.

Incessant and unslaked sexual desire in Nabokov's later work is a powerful and explicit metaphor for all desire, physical and spiritual, that essentially remains without adequate consummation or fulfillment. The reminiscent Humbert describes himself lying on the sand as a young man, with Annabel nearby but with their parents also only a few feet away. "We would sprawl all morning," he writes, "in a petrified paroxysm of desire" (*L*, 14). Their one attempt to escape parental eyes and have intercourse is coarsely broken up by other bathers, and "four months later she died of typhus on Corfu" (*L*, 15). Humbert remains fixed forever in "a petrified paroxysm of desire"; indeed, the phrase describes the essential emotional and spiritual stance, expressed in one way or another, of most of Nabokov's protagonists early and late. The Garden of Eden story involves pure and immortal lovers betrayed into a time- and death-ridden world, and *Ada* only makes explicit a myth whose Georgian version I have already commented on in Nabokov's work. *Lolita*, likewise, merely gives a certain daring, brilliant, and flamboyant dramatization to themes that have been present in his writing from the beginning. More than any of his books, *Lolita* tests Nabokov's commitment to heroic values on the wheel of fire; more than in any other, they are subjected to savage and de-grading mockery, yet retain their integrity within a complex perspective. We are warned from the beginning (John Ray, Jr., Ph.D.'s Foreword) not to over-simplify. On one hand, Ray has been moved by Humbert's "style" ("how magically his singing violin can conjure up a tendresse" [*L*, 7]); on the other, Ray's trite ethical and psychological reading of the story tells us again, as Zina's father has already done, what *Lolita* is not about. And *Ada* reaffirms that a commitment to questing survives its context, however grotesque, of moral and metaphysical horror and curse—damnation into a fallen world, authentic Eden forever lost. In short, the sexual pursuit, hunt, or quest in these novels reflects at least five qualities that I have argued as characteristic of the quest theme in his earlier work: it is one dimension of the rediscovery and redemption of childhood; it is an obvious vehicle for the expression of obsessive commitment and ardency of emotion and spirit; its consummations or attempts at consummation are those of fallen man and parody those of the spirit; it affirms the heroic value of love in a world without love; and, finally, sexual experience may lead to one form of that "stop-time"—"that intangible island of entranced time," as Humbert calls it (*L*, 19)—with which Nabokov, like the great modernists before him, has been so concerned.

Sex, nevertheless, remains only a stand-in or handmaiden for the larger actual and symbolic role of art. Here as elsewhere, Nabokov gleefully re-verses Freud; surely Humbert speaks for his creator when he writes: "It is not the artistic aptitudes that are secondary sexual characters as some shams and shamans have said; it is the other way around: sex is but the ancilla of art" (*L*, 261). In any case, wherever the emphasis, sex and artistic aspiration com-mingle in the modern heroic quest and constitute its only possible basis. Shade speaks of "texture" or aesthetic order as the highest spiritual form to which the mock-hero can aspire; likewise, at the emotional and psychological level, sexual obsession or perversion becomes the closest approximation to-day of ideal love and perfect physical consummation. It stands (parodying the traditional role of sexual love in literature and myth) as at least the human equivalent to, if not a driving force behind, other, more sublime heroic consummations.

That *Lolita* is about loss or attempts to deal with and redeem loss is a commonplace of more recent criticism of the novel. Discussing his stage ad-aptation of *Lolita* in 1981, Edward Albee, for example, commented that "the essence of the book seems to me to be about lost time, symbolized by the image of Annabell [sic], the young Humbert's first love. That's what he's after from then on, a way to re-create that first experience."[17] Much earlier, Alfred Appel, Jr., *Lolita*'s most sensitive and exhaustive commentator, had observed that "Humbert's narrative dramatizes a Shade's effort to capture the essence of a Haze . . . he . . . pursues the illusion that he can recapture what is inexorably lost."[18] But if *Lolita* is about loss, what must be emphasized are the sweeping dimensions of its lost and fallen world and the qualities of spirit embodied in the heroic efforts of Humbert and his creator to redeem loss in some fashion. The novel presents us with a protagonist (or protagonists, if we include the author, whose name is carefully coded into the text) with a soul, or at least something sensitive to the claims of the spirit, struggling to assert these claims against the mockery of the horror within himself and his own acts, but also the horror that constitutes the principal dimension of the external world.

Humbert is another "Shade, *Ombre, almost 'man,'* " a "pseudo" figure, whose very description of himself—"pseudo-Celtic, attractively simian, boyishly manly" (*L*, 106)—consists of phrases, each half of which mocks the other, as does Nabokov's own explanation of Humbert's name: "It is a hateful name for a hateful person. It is also a kingly name, but I did need a royal vibration for Humber the Fierce and Humber the Humble."[19] When he describes Lolita's reluctance to enter his solipsistic world ("my world, umber and black Humberland" [*L*, 168]), Humbert, in effect, describes the narrow range of alternatives open to all the characters in the world of the novel: "To the wonderland I had to offer, my fool preferred the corniest movies and the most cloying fudge. To think that between a Hamburger and a Humburger she would—invariably, with icy precision—plump for the former" (*L*, 168). The choice, in other words, is between the banality, emotional paralysis, and spiritual emptiness of the modern world—the "ice" (or ice-cream) world so often recorded by the writers of this century—and the wonderland of fictions, with its imaginative and emotional possibilities, perhaps, but also with its own deceptions and "humbug." Among other things, *Lolita* is an up-to-date version of *Alice in Wonderland*. While invoking the liberating nonsense world of the earlier book, *Lolita* reveals, at the same time, the element of sexual perversion in the Victorian worship of children—an aspect of the irony behind the idyll which, in this case, the Victorian writer had not explored.[20]

Humbert's description of his wonderland and his defense of that choice ("my elected paradise") regardless of Lolita's attitude expresses the full range of its complex duality:

> Oh, do not scowl at me, I do not intend to convey the impression that I did not manage to be happy. Reader must understand that in the possession and thralldom of a nymphet the enchanted traveler stands, as it were, *beyond happiness*. For there is no other bliss on earth comparable to that of fondling a nymphet. It is *hors concours*, that bliss, it belongs to another class, another plane of sensitivity. Despite our tiffs, despite her nastiness, despite all the fuss and

faces she made, the vulgarity, and the danger, and the horrible hopelessness of it all, I still dwelled deep in my elected paradise—a paradise whose skies were the color of hell-flames—but still a paradise. [*L*, 168]

This passage cannot be dismissed as the rationalizations of a murderer and pervert; nor will psychiatric explanations do, the idea (as "Dr." Humbert mockingly puts it) that he is seeking "release from the 'subconscious' obsessions of an incomplete childhood romance with the initial little Miss Lee" (*L*, 169). As usual, Nabokov tells us how not to read his book. Humbert himself goes on to point out that, far from "seeking release" from obsession, he chooses it and pursues it with every fiber of his being.

Rather, the passage quoted above describes both the continued possibility and the terrible price of contemporary spiritual questing. All of Nabokov's characters are under the shadow of the headsman, but in *Lolita* the doom and horror are particularly pressing, the alternatives particularly tenuous, however significant and necessary. The quest becomes (as Humbert describes one of his frantic trips around the country with Lolita) "our grotesque journey" (*L*, 231). On one hand, the passage emphasizes the vulgarity, nastiness, "horrible hopelessness," and "hell-flames" of life in actual time and experience, including the actuality of Lolita and Humbert's "simian" (physical, corrupted, existential) self. On the other, it hints at spiritual drama, the hero's enduring commitment to beauty, purity, ecstasy, a transcendence "beyond happiness," in "another class, another plane of sensitivity." In his refusal to succumb to despair (he abandons finally any literal attempt to recapture Lolita, only to pursue her in memory, imagination, "words") or to Quilty's vicious cynicism—a depravity unmitigated by ardency and spiritual awareness—Humbert remains Nabokov's heroic quester. In his clownish and destructive perversion—to the degree that Quilty exists as a legitimate dimension of his identity—he becomes Nabokov's darkest symbol of the fate of vision in its context of worldly reality, of life in its brutal mockery of illusions, whatever more positive name we may give them. Regardless of his spiritual yearnings, Humbert's "paradisal philters" (*L*, 186) consist largely of the sexual intercourse which he extracts as often as possible from a reluctant, pathetic, manipulative, and abandoned Lolita.

Lolita herself, with her "lovely, inane, lost look" (*L*, 78), is the central personification in the novel (appropriately given her name for title) of true paradise lost, the shadow of original childish purity existing only in its present temporal corruption. Alexander Welsh has pointed out that "a passion for nymphets is perhaps the neatest expression one could devise of a desire to stop time, to stand on a threshold, and ultimately not to die."[21] But Humbert recognizes that "she it was to whom ads were dedicated: the ideal consumer, the subject and object of every foul poster" (*L*, 150). Lolita's "consumption" mocks his dream of spiritual "consummation," describes the American culture through which the couple pass and repass in their essential entrapment, and, indeed, largely describes Humbert's role as "consumer" of herself.

But for Humbert, in any case, the hero of shades, these shades survive all debasements, including his own, or at least they survive as imaginative projections of "desire and decision," which, Humbert notes tellingly, are "the two things that create a live world" (*L*, 73). In a universe of death, he remains hopelessly committed to life, attuned to the complex landscape of America, which resembles Lolita in constantly hinting at beauty and mystery while actually full of tawdriness, vulgarity, and pretentious simulations such as "Lincoln's home, largely spurious, with parlor books and period furniture that most visitors reverently accepted as personal belongings" (*L*, 160). They are largely spurious, also, like Humbert's own simulations of the past. In describing his search through the Haze family album for pictures of Lolita as a child, he comments that "I tompeeped across the hedges of years, into wan little windows" (*L*, 78). The comment is an adequate metaphor of his entire quest in the novel: the end is wan or "hazy," the visionary impulse corrupted into voyeurism. Yet even in the most negative terms, his quest involves a refusal to surrender to despair, the despair that constantly threatens his original pursuit of Lolita and that later occasionally breaks into the predominantly witty and mocking narrative of his adventures. In language more directly evocative of the role of the traditional hero, Humbert writes of his desperate lovemaking with Charlotte, Lolita's mother (a parody, one might say, of a parody): "It was still a nymphet's scent that in despair I tried to pick up, as I bayed through the undergrowth of dark decaying forests" (*L*, 78–79).

Though "largely spurious" ("boldly simulating the past" [*L*, 157]), Lincoln's log cabin is not completely so. It is another "wan" mirror of the hero and reflects at least the lingering human aspiration to heroic values that Humbert alone can still articulate. Likewise, the witherland "gray" of America (note the "washed-out gray eyes" of Lolita [*L*, 274]) shades off into gray-blue, that of the high mountains, for example ("bluish beauties never attainable" [*L*, 158]), or "a hazy blue view beyond the railing on a mountain pass" (*L*, 159). With an artist's sensibility (or as he puts it elsewhere, "while lost in an artist's dream" [*L*, 155]), Humbert can discern "the delicate beauty ever present in the margin of our undeserving journey" (*L*, 154) or find in a country sunset the very apotheosis of Poe's aesthetic, a sunset in whose imagery sex and spirit finally fuse as one: "Beyond the tilled plain, beyond the toy roofs, there would be a slow suffusion of inutile loveliness, a low sun in platinum haze with a warm, peeled-peach tinge pervading the upper edge of a two dimensional dove-gray cloud fusing with the distant amorous mist" (*L*, 154).

Humbert can occasionally find this same marginal suffusion in people. Lolita's aging, homosexual tennis coach becomes, from his perspective, the very incarnation of the fallen hero, another shadow of the potent past. Humbert observes that "now and then, when in the course of a lesson, to keep up the exchange, he would put out as it were an exquisite spring blossom of a stroke and twang the ball back to his pupil, that divine delicacy of absolute power made me recall that, thirty years before, I had seen *him* in Cannes demolish the great Gobbert!" (*L*, 164). It is while watching Lolita's own tennis game, however, that Humbert most completely feels himself "teetering on the very brink of unearthly order and splendor" (*L*, 232). She too brings art to the point at which it seems a direct manifestation of absolute power. Its "perfect imitation" (*L*, 233) almost closes the parodic gap; sheer style alone creates (or recreates) "a powerful and graceful cosmos" (*L*, 234). But Humbert never does get beyond the brink, and the gap never really closes. From his own mature perspective he makes this point clearly: "Her tennis was the highest point to which I can imagine a young creature bringing the art of make-believe, although I daresay, for her it was the very geometry of basic reality" (*L*, 233).

Even when Humbert sees Lolita for the last time, "hopelessly worn at seventeen" (*L*, 279) and shortly to die in childbirth, he recognizes in her some still significant echo of pure beauty and love, "inutile loveliness." She too is now a parody of a parody but no less cherished as a residue:

> I looked and looked at her, and knew as clearly as I know I am to die, that I loved her more than anything I had ever seen or imagined on earth, or hoped for anywhere. She was only the faint violet whiff and dead leaf echo of the nymphet I had rolled myself upon with such cries in the past; an echo on the brink of a russet ravine, with a far wood under a white sky, and brown leaves choking the brook, and one last cricket in the crisp weeds . . . but thank God it was not that echo alone that I worshipped. What I used to pamper among the tangled vines of my heart, *mon grand péché radieux*, had dwindled to its essence: sterile and selfish vice, all *that* I canceled and cursed. [*L*, 279–80]

Her dwindling reality in life liberates his romantic dream of her and reaffirms at least the power of imagination and love in the dreamer. The ebb of reality in the later pages culminates in the death of Quilty, the sterile and cynical aesthete, another Beardsley figure, the "guilty" side of Humbert which relates him to de Sade ("Sade's Justine was twelve at the start," notes Humbert parenthetically when Lolita tells him about life at Quilty's ranch [*L*, 278]), not the side informed by the spiritual passion and pain of the visionary. This ebbing represents a rhythm counter to the gross intrusion of reality—the ribald swimmers emerging from the waves just as the youthful Humbert is about to make love to Annabel—which constitutes the prototypal event behind the immediate action of the novel. For Humbert, the swimmers come to symbolize all such later episodes in his life. As he puts it: "My romantic soul gets all clammy and shivery at the thought of running into some indecent unpleasantness. Those ribald sea monsters. *'Mais allez-y, allez-y!'* Annabel skipping on one foot to get into her shorts, I seasick with rage, trying to screen her" (*L*, 55). Having lost Annabel, Humbert seeks to incarnate her in Lolita; having lost Lolita, he can only incarnate her in "the melancholy and very local palliative of articulate art" (*L*, 285). Humbert, moreover, seeks to incarnate his own "romantic soul" in his memoir. Indeed, the perception of an "imaginary" Humbert involves the same desperate necessity which he had earlier brought to the pursuit of marginal beauty in the landscape and in other human beings and in which he now hopes to engage even the reader. "Imagine me," he pleads; "I shall not exist if you do not imagine me; try to discern the doe in me, trembling in the forest of my own iniquity" (*L*, 131).

Humbert's plea and the counterrhythm it represents exist, however, within the broader context of irony that is emphasized by the circumstances of posthumous publication. Since he is a character now "dead," surviving in any form only through his memoir and Nabokov's overriding fiction, we can, in one sense, scarcely do otherwise than imagine him. Although the approach of death, in other words, as the waning of reality may liberate the self from the ceaseless mockery of experience, it is, at the same time, our sharpest reminder that the games of the self are not truly transcendent and thus, from a second perspective, brutally emphasizes the limits of imagination. What may seem directional or ebb and flow at one level remains always, at another, within an implacable dualism.

Even the death of Quilty is arbitrary and relative; like the escape of Cincinnatus, it reminds us of both the power and artifice of art. As Humbert puts it (addressing Lolita but speaking almost in the voice of Nabokov): "One had to choose between him and H. H., and one wanted H. H. to exist at least a couple of months longer, so as to have him make you live in the minds of later generations. I am thinking of aurochs and angels, the secret of durable pigments, prophetic sonnets, the refuge of art. And this is the only immortality you and I may share, my Lolita" (*L*, 311). In these sentences, the claims and limitations of art reach their final equipoise in the novel: on one hand, the "gift" of art, its promise to the hero of space for spiritual questing and temporal transcendence ("the only immortality"); on the other, its function as expedient alternative, its compulsions in loss and need more than choice, its essential fakery—only the highest form of make-believe, to paraphrase Humbert on Lolita's tennis game. Alfred Appel has observed that the "remote" tone of this passage is appropriate, "for Humbert's love and Nabokov's labors have become one" (L, 437, n. 311/2). Appel's comment directs us finally to the overall art of the novel.

In his literary role—left, in his misery, with nothing but "the melancholy and very local palliative of articulate art" (a "secondary poetization" similar to the movement in *The Gift* from Fyodor's father to Fyodor)—Humbert embraces an art that will limit, reduce, mock, or otherwise explicitly deconstruct its claims in the very act of their assertion, an art that will celebrate illusions while itself without illusions. In one tag (apparently invented) Humbert quotes an old poet to the effect that "The moral sense in mortals is the duty / We have to pay on mortal sense of beauty" (L, 285). In other words, the artist at least must not deny moral issues, the real consequences of human acts in the world of experience; denial, in fact, is the position of the cynical and sybaritic Quilty and the aesthetes.

Rather, true art, in the pursuit of its own celebration, must constantly "pay the price" of moral awareness; Humbert seeks an art in which "cost" and "gift" are in perfect balance. Fyodor becomes convinced that he must make his way along a "narrow ridge" between his own truth and "a caricature of it"; Humbert, likewise, in his own fashion, seeks to fix a borderline. As he puts it: "I am trying to describe these things not to relive them in my present boundless misery, but to sort out the portion of hell and the portion of heaven in that strange, awful, maddening world—nymphet love. The beastly and beautiful merged at one point, and it is that borderline I would like to fix, and I feel I fail to do so utterly. Why?" (L, 137). The task of art breeds its own hopelessness and failure, nor does it, he makes clear, alleviate the moral horror of his life that he "cannot shake off" (L, 137). Nevertheless, his memoir ends by affirming again the "secret of durable pigments, prophetic sonnets, the refuge of art." Humbert's literary quest "to fix once for all the perilous magic of nymphets" (L, 136) parallels the physical quest he had earlier undertaken using the body of Lolita, but it takes place in the more secure context of ironic awareness. Humbert, so to speak, "resolipsizes" Lolita in his memoir. Reduced to "only words," she becomes more fictional than ever, now perhaps indeed "safely solipsized" or at least, in her very fictionality, a more serious and daring affront to what Van Veen calls the "ardis of time" (A, 197).

In his life experience a parody of the lover, Humbert becomes the parodic writer and an echo, in turn, of Nabokov the master parodist, whose ironic perspective extends beyond Humbert's toward the infinity of contradictory alternatives which constitutes the true nonsense world of mock-heroic art. More than any other literary mode, mock-heroic pays for affirmation in the mirror of nullity that it everywhere holds up to the expression of heroic ardor and imagination. Nullity is the essence of "quilted Quilty, Clare Obscure" (*L*, 308), the prototypal double. In explaining the etymology of the word *cento* (the name of an ancient verse form characterized by the random borrowing and placement of verses from one or more poets), Susan Stewart points out that it means "a cloak made of patches" and that "the form prefigures not only the modernist collages but also the quilt—that simultaneity of fabrics out of time with one another."[22] Temporal dissonance—the simultaneous existence of the contradictory temporal orders of art and life—is the basis of nullity and lies behind all the incessant doubling in *Lolita*, a practice that extends from the most minute details of "double names, initials, and phonetic effects" to the widest range of parodic reference, which includes levels of mythology and literary allusion.[23]

Lolita is about Humbert's ceaseless efforts in his life and memoir to "play" Prince Charming, Odysseus, Dante, Petrarch, Poe, and a host of other romantic lovers. It is also about Nabokov's own passionate and hopeless commitment to the game of spirit, the pursuit in life of its felt but illusory dimension of "semitranslucent mystery" (*L*, 55), mystery that seems always about to reveal itself but never does. The order of art is comparable to Humbert's memory (from one moment in his travels) of the faraway voices of children at play—"a mirage of wonder and hopelessness" (*L*, 309). The certain freedom of the artist, his remaining opportunity for adventures, his ceaseless impulse to defy temporal reality in the face of its iron necessity—the true aesthetic stance, so to speak—is, in turn, reflected in Humbert's act of driving on the wrong side of the road after he has killed Quilty and when any practical possibility of repossessing Lolita in life has clearly passed:

> The road now stretched across open country, and it occurred to me—not by way of protest, not as a symbol, or anything like that, but merely as a novel experience—that since I had disregarded all laws of humanity, I might as well disregard the rules of traffic. So I crossed to the left side of the highway and checked the feeling, and the feeling was good. It was a pleasant diaphragmal melting, with elements of diffused tactility, all this enhanced by the thought that nothing could be nearer to the elimination of basic physical laws than deliberately driving on the wrong side of the road. In a way, it was a very spiritual itch. Gently, dreamily, not exceeding twenty miles an hour, I drove on that queer mirror side. [*L*, 308]

Nabokov's art likewise involves neither social satire nor the fixed abstractions of absolute truth ("not by way of protest, not as a symbol") but, instead, precisely such a drive on "that queer mirror side." In its own way it reflects the persistence of the "spiritual itch" at a time when epic gratifications are no longer possible. In a world without authentic metaphysical sanctions and a true Creator, the artist at best is like McFate, another "synchronizing phantom" (*L*, 1050), supreme shadow among shadows.

Van Veen in *Ada* can also be described as someone who persistently drives, metaphorically at least, on the wrong side of the road. All his roles (which, in their inclusiveness, summarize the parts played by the major characters in Nabokov's earlier fiction) involve an intense commitment to "that queer mirror side." In *Ada* as elsewhere with Nabokov, a structure of retrospective narration (the novel purports to be an autobiographical fiction written by a dying man in his very old age) underlines the ultimate futility and hopelessness of such "reckless" driving by keeping firmly in place the usual frame of doom and death, the space beyond the prison walls, which Van Veen describes as "that meaningless space overhead, underhead, everywhere, the demon counterpart of divine time" (*A*, 80). This is the ubiquitous and circumscribing space that accepts the body of Ada's sister Lucette in her suicide by drowning and later Van Veen's father, falling from sky to sea in a disintegrating airplane (*A*, 535–36); and it is this space that represents all the loss, horror, entropy, and null in the book. As Van Veen, the aphorist of space and time, puts it: "The lost shafts of every man's destiny remain scattered all around him" (*A*, 537). The narrative (both as a creative act in the present and a lifelong record of actions) everywhere assumes a limiting context that is finally a fundamental dimension of consciousness in its paradoxical affirmation of identity and death—what Van Veen calls "the final tragic triumph of human cognition: I am because I die" (*A*, 164).

The fantastic "Antiterra" world in which Van Veen and Ada perform remains less the permissive landscape of heroic romance than Nabokov's usual parodic environment heightened and simplified, its spiritual derivation from nineteenth-century aristocratic and romantic culture clearly located by a crucial time lag that places events some fifty years behind "Terra," its speculative alternative. Ellen Pifer has noted that "the inhabitants of Antiterra, suggestively called Demonia, appear uniquely free of the pressing concerns that both limit and define existence on our planet. An anti-earth, Antiterra is not conceived as a speculative middle ground (occupied by our earth from the beginnings of Judeo-Christian tradition at least) between the symbolic heights of heaven and the depths of hell. The polar extremes of experience which we associate with these regions—heavenly ecstasy and hellish degradation, delight and despair—are no longer kept at safe remove."[24] In other words, Nabokov's mocking dualities are stripped in *Ada* to their essentials and brought into particularly sharp and dramatic encounter. *Ada* is unusually explicit in dealing with the issues I have touched on so far, and to conclude this chapter I want to review these issues briefly, focusing specifically on Van Veen's various mock-heroic roles, all of which closely complement each other

("'Van,' rhyming with and indeed signifying 'one' in Marina's double-you-less deep-voweled Russian pronunciation" [A, 382]) and all, in their several ways, quixotic efforts to redeem time.

The general goal of the questing self is clear enough. "I wish to caress time," writes Van Veen, describing the purpose behind his last major philosophical work, the "difficult, delectable, and blessed" *Textures of Time*. He goes on to explain:

> One can be a lover of Space and its possibilities: take, for example, speed, the smoothness and sword-swish of speed; the aquiline glory of ruling velocity; the joy cry of the curve; and one can be an amateur of Time, an epicure of duration. I delight sensually in time, and its stuff and spread, in the fall of its folds, in the very impalpability of its grayish gauze, in the coolness of its continuum. I wish to do something about it; to indulge in a simulacrum of possession. I am aware that all who have tried to reach the charmed castle have got lost in obscurity or have bogged down in Space. I am also aware that Time is a fluid medium for the culture of metaphors. [A, 571]

"To indulge in a simulacrum of possession": the phrase describes the very essence of parodic questing—both the obsessive commitment of the mock-hero and the sham of ends, even the inauthenticity of means, albeit the landscape of time remains a "fluid medium" of imaginative possibility. Van Veen and Ada, Nabokov's "accursed children" (A, 288), are archetypal in their early loss of Eden and their subsequent hopeless games of recovery. In Nabokov's work, the value of the protagonist's efforts, his defiant stance, his refusal to succumb to pain and despair, are beyond question. Elsewhere Van Veen (and surely the master parodist, the other V. V.) points out that "we must always remember that the strength, the dignity, and delight of man is to spite and despise the shadows and stars that hide their secrets from us" (A, 32). What is possible, he notes in another context, is "not the achievement, but the obstinate attempt" (A, 500). If "all ends are banal," if anticlimax is the fundamental context of life experience, Van Veen, nevertheless, remains committed to the Latin tag he uses in one of his manuscripts: "*Insiste, anime meus, et adtende fortiter* (courage, my soul and press on strongly)" (A, 514). It is this mad and gallant obstinacy whose manifestations need closer examination.

Van Veen's most apparently inconsequential role is richly symbolic, suggesting the meaning of others more substantial. I refer to his undergraduate performance as Mascodagama, a music-hall act in which he appears on stage with his body reversed, walking on his shoe-clad hands, his feet together and covered by a bearded mask and Karakul cap. His stage name in this guise, as I have already noted in my discussion of *The Gift*, relates Van Veen to other characters from Nabokov's work who identify with Marco Polo. As an old man, he still feels delight in his act and is well aware of its significance:

> The essence of the satisfaction belonged rather to the same order as the one he later derived from self-imposed, extravagantly difficult, seemingly absurd tasks when V. V. sought to express something, which *until* expressed had only a twilight being (or even none at all—nothing but the illusion of the backward shadow of its imminent expression). It was Ada's castle of cards. It was the standing of a metaphor on its head not for the sake of the trick's difficulty, but in order to perceive an ascending waterfall or a sunrise in reverse: a triumph, in a sense, over the ardis of time. Thus the rapture young Mascodagama derived from overcoming gravity was akin to that of artistic revelation in the sense utterly and naturally unknown to the innocents of critical appraisal, the social-scene commentators, the moralists, the idea-mongers and so forth. Van on the stage was performing organically what his figures of speech were to perform later in life—acrobatic wonders that had never been expected from them and which frightened children. [*A*, 197]

Questers such as Marco Polo and Vasco da Gama freed Western man from his prison and returned him to the Edenic, visionary East of his origins—Renaissance man becoming godlike again in his new-found power. The fundamental role of the traditional hero is always, in one fashion or another, the redemption of time. Even in fairy tales (a genre, incidentally, strongly echoed in *Ada*) and nineteenth-century popular fiction the formulaic ending of living "happily ever after" precisely records the central significance of the hero's actions.[25] Mascodagama, in turn, the shadow, masked, or pretend hero, the performer of "acrobatic wonders," clown, trickster, magician, works toward the same end—"a triumph . . . over the ardis of time"—but with qualified results, triumph "in a sense" only.

As shadow heroes committed to a shadow world, Nabokov's protagonists seek at least the articulation of "twilight being." In Van's act the performing self comes as close as possible to original creation, to a new order, which, in its defiance of the logic and laws of reality, achieves autonomy and freedom within the limits of its own "nonsense" form. Here as elsewhere in Nabokov's work, we encounter again the transformational role of parody. In her excellent book on nonsense, Susan Stewart notes that such parody appropriates another text, "not to reify that primary text but in order to transform it, to reduce it to a set of elements available to an alternative order or to an order available to an alternative set of elements." Alternative orders invoke an alternative time, what Stewart calls the "play time" of "play worlds," but she also points out that these play worlds constantly "implicate" and "undercut" themselves.[26]

In Nabokov's work at least, they can exist only because of their self-implication. Acknowledgment of the hopeless gap between art and life is, paradoxically, the price we must pay for art. Such surely is the answer to Ada's question, which I have used as an epigraph to this chapter: "(I wonder, Van, *why* you are doing your best to transform our poetical and unique past into a dirty farce?)" (*A*, 121). Her question reminds us again that, in Nabokov's fallen world, purity of act can exist only in and through impurity. When Ada, in another characteristic dialectical parenthesis, mocks Van for doing his *grand Joyce* imitation after his *petit Proust*, he responds significantly within his own interpolation: "(it is pure V. V. Note that lady!)" (*A*, 181). Nabokov here pointedly takes his place with Joyce as another "forger."

At one point in her life Ada has been an actress, and her comments shed more light on the nature and end of mock-heroic performance. As she explains to Van Veen:

> "I seem to have always felt, for example, that acting should be focused not on 'characters,' not on 'types' of something or other, not on the *fokus-pokus* of a social theme, but exclusively on the subjective and unique poetry of the author, because playwrights, as the greatest among them has shown, are closer to poets than to novelists. In 'real' life we are creatures of chance in an absolute void— unless we be artists ourselves, naturally; but in a good play I feel authored, I feel passed by the board of censors, I feel secure, with only a breathing blackness before me (instead of our Fourth-Wall Time), I feel cuddled in the embrace of puzzled Will (he thought I was you) or in that of the much more normal Anton Pavlovich, who was always passionately fond of long dark hair." [*A*, 451–52]

Ada conceives of the actress in a play as assuming not some dead abstraction of personality but the expressive and creative selfhood (the "Will"?) of the playwright. In this secular yet still god-centered world ("I feel authored"), the null of infinite time (all "Pennsylvania and rain," as Humbert would say) gives way to a more humane and vital blackness. Like Van Veen in his comments on Mascodagama, Ada makes clear that the roles of actor, performer, and artist are synonymous. Elsewhere she speaks of "verbal circuses," "performing words," and "poodle-doodles" and argues that they are "redeemable by the quality of brain work required for the creation of a great logograph or inspired pun" (*A*, 234). Van calls their childhood acrostic games "arcrobatics" (*A*, 204).

Van Veen's music-hall performances shade off into and shed light on his later, more substantial roles of philosopher of time and (with Ada's help) autobiographical novelist and annotator of his own life. As philosopher, he pursues a description of the "texture of time" (the title of his major book) with the same combination of commitment and ironic awareness that he brings to his other roles. "It is a queer enterprise," he notes wryly, "this attempt to determine the nature of something consisting of phantomic phrases," yet he adds that he hopes the reader will agree "there is nothing more splendid than lone thought" (A, 574). Here as always in Nabokov (and mock-heroic in general) the rhythm of thought moves away from the tragic possibility of despair to the comic affirmation of effort, however hopeless. What Van Veen relentlessly attempts to define and justify is the time of the performing self, the time of play worlds, the time he labels "individual, perceptual" and distinguishes from "Objective Time" or "the history, in a word, of humanity and humor, and that kind of thing" (A, 570). Elsewhere he describes significant time as "the gray gap between black beats: The Tender Interval" (A, 572). It is in this "gray gap" that the expansions of memory and imagination can take place.

Above all, Van seeks to locate a "Tangible Time" in which the Past "as an accumulation of sensa" (A, 579) commingles with a sensuous present to create "nowness . . . the only reality we know" (A, 585). He describes this "Deliberate Present" as "the time span that one is directly and actually aware of, with the lingering freshness of the Past still perceived as part of the nowness" (A, 586). A telephone call from the long absent Ada becomes for Van a supreme example of the nature of tangible time: "That telephone voice, by resurrecting the past and linking it up with the present, with the darkening slate-blue mountains beyond the lake, with the spangles of the sun wake dancing through the poplar, formed the centerpiece in his deepest perception of tangible time, the glittering 'now' that was the only reality of Time's texture" (A, 592). "Time is but memory in the making," Van goes on to say, adding that it constitutes "that *backbone of consciousness*, which is the Time of the Strong" (A, 595–96). We might add that this is time, like Lolita, "safely solipsised," a "glittering 'now'" whose seizure represents the hero's task and brings him closest to the redemption of loss. Van's speculations end with Ada's antiphonal voice responding that "we can never know time" (A, 599).[27] She reminds us that this "end," like all others, remains unachievable; the dialectic continues, and Van shifts to the role of autobiographical artist.

It is as an artist that Van Veen wishes to be known ("He knew he was not quite a savant, but completely an artist" [A, 501]), and his art is, of course, "Ada," the book that he writes as well as the woman he loves. Like *The Gift*, *Ada* toward the end describes its own future composition; to a greater degree than Fyodor, however, Van Veen is the composite mock-hero, the hero of the senses in all his phases. Whereas the earlier book was more concerned with origins and influence, the later one emphasizes the entire spectrum of present possibility. "Ever-adolescent Van" (A, 414), as he calls himself—the youthful spirit remains intact—moves among the various roles of lover, performer, philosopher, later the memorialist and annotator, finally the bedridden old man "heroically" correcting galley proofs (A, 232). If life is meaningful only insofar as it allows one, in Van's words, to catch "sight of the lining of time" (A, 239), then autobiography (that is, the fiction of one's life) involves the extension of those moments of capture in memory and imagination. As Van puts it, remembering the "hammock and honey" at the center of his emotional and spiritual life, "memory met imagination halfway in the hammock of his boyhood's dreams." He goes on to call such an act of consciousness not a dream but a "recapitulation," and Ada joins him to comment on "the details that shine through or shade through." It is the quality and intensity of these details, she adds, which make Van and herself "a unique super-imperial couple" with an "unnatural history." This last she identifies in the following splendid passage: "Unnatural history—because the precision of senses and sense must seem unpleasantly peculiar to peasants, and because the detail is all: The song of a Tuscan Firecrest or a Sitka Kinglet in a cemetery cypress; a minty whiff of Summer Savory or Yerba Buena on a coastal slope; the dancing flitter of a Holly Blue or an Echo Azure—combined with other birds, flowers and butterflies: *that* has to be heard, smelled and seen through the transparency of death and ardent beauty. And the most difficult: beauty itself as perceived through the there and then" (A, 76–77). What Ada describes is the only possible goal of the contemporary quest—the "Echo Azure" of beauty seen once through the transparency of matter, seen again through the transparency of time. In his role as parody of the Creator, the novelist brings a certain stability and order to such perceptions, in Van Veen's words, "a frame . . . [and] a form, something supporting and guarding life, otherwise unprovidenced on Desdemonia, where artists are the only gods" (A, 553). In such a fashion Van does, indeed, make good his pledge to Ada to "redeem our childhood by making a book of it: *Ardis* a family chronicle" (A, 430).

This final role of Van Veen as artist of the senses only complements his more youthful and yet enduring performance as lover of the body of Ada. From satyr to "crotchety gray old wordman" (A, 129) is a steady progression; Don Juan and Don Quixote are finally one and same. The influence of Byron is acknowledged by Nabokov in the name of the heroine and in other details, and, lest there be any lingering doubt, the quixotic relationship is made explicit in the movie *Don Juan's Last Fling*, which includes one of Ada's performances as actress. The movie involves muddled borrowings from both *Don Quixote* and the Don Juan legend (the traditional version with an "aging libertine" [A, 519], not Byron's romantic youth), leaving the hero "to play an im-

possible cross between two Dons" (*A*, 529–30), with Ada cast as a gypsy dancing girl called Dolores (the name obviously linking her to Lolita) and acting as
agent of vengeance and death as well as desire. For Van viewing this film she
remains his perfect nymphet: "The few brief scenes she was given formed a
perfect compendium of her 1884 and 1888 and 1892 looks" (*A*, 520).

In the two major novels of Nabokov's later period, sexual consummation
(as human experience and as metaphor) most notably represents the self's
ardent quest for creative perception, its closest approach to authentic vision.
A crucial passage in *Ada* makes this clear, and it comes in response to the
obvious question: "What, then, was it that raised the animal act to a level
higher than even that of the most exact arts or the wildest flights of pure
science?" Van (or perhaps Nabokov) proceeds to answer his own query:

> It would not be sufficient to say that in his love-making with Ada he discovered
> the pang, the *ogon'*, the agony of supreme "reality." Reality, better say, lost the
> quotes it wore like claws—in a world where independent and original minds
> must cling to things or pull things apart in order to ward off madness or death
> (which is the master madness). For one spasm or two, he was safe. The new
> naked reality needed no tentacle or anchor; it lasted a moment, but could be
> repeated as often as he and she were physically able to make love. The color and
> fire of that instant reality depended solely on Ada's identity as perceived by him.
> It had nothing to do with virtue or the vanity of virtue in a large sense—in fact it
> seemed to Van later that during the ardencies of that summer he knew all along
> that she had been, and still was, atrociously untrue to him. [*A*, 232]

An added note speaks of the "rapture of her identity" and sees in this rapture
a sensuous order ("a complex system of those subtle bridges which the
senses transverse") becoming also "a form of memory, even at the moment of
its perception" (*A*, 233). Within such a bridging order, another version of the
"prison cell of paradise," reality can be truly pure and one, losing its ironic
"claws."

In the context of larger cosmos, however, those savage claws remain.
"Ardis" suggests ardor and oneness (dis) but also the "arrow" of time; the
name "Ada" contains within it both heaven (da) and hell (ad).[28] Incest in the
novel is identified with defiant freedom but also with sterility (Ada speaks of
her "acarpous destiny" [*A*, 231]); Ada herself is both "Ada in Wonderland"
(*A*, 137) and the legendary betrayer who leads Van into "their much too premature and in many ways fatal romance" (*A*, 158). Here as elsewhere
throughout Nabokov's work, fictions of whatever kind have their own severe
and melancholy limits. "You admit yourself," Ada comments to Van at one
point, "that I am only a pale wild girl with gipsy hair in a deathless ballad, in
a nulliverse, in Rattner's 'menald world' where the only principle is random

variation" (*A*, 441). More immediate and personal is her complaint in a letter responding to the death of her sister: "I cannot express, dear Van, how unhappy I am, the more so as we never learned in the arbors of Ardis that such unhappiness could exist" (*A*, 531). In spite of the mock-hero's efforts, life and cosmos remain everywhere a plot against purity, authenticity, and duration. For Van, resist as he will, "numbers and rows and series—the nightmare and malediction harrowing pure thought and pure time—seemed bent on mechanizing his mind" (*A*, 478). We are left, after all, with "a simulacrum of possession," but we are left also with an enduring capacity for heroic performance. As Van notes in another aphorism: "Eccentricity is the greatest grief's greatest remedy" (*A*, 370).

Bellow's Escape Artists

In her nutty devotion to culture she couldn't have been more Jewish.

BELLOW

Mr. Sammler's Planet

He was not a quixote, was he? A quixote imitated great models. What models did he imitate? A quixote was a Christian, and Moses E. Herzog was no Christian. This was a post-quixotic, post-Copernican U.S.A., where a mind freely poised in space might discover relationships utterly unsuspected by a seventeenth-century man sealed in his smaller universe. There lay his twentieth-century advantage. Only . . . in nine-tenths of his existence he was exactly what others were before him.

BELLOW

Herzog

QUESTION TO BELLOW: "Which of your characters is most like you?"

BELLOW: "Henderson—the absurd seeker of high qualities."

From an interview in *Show*, 1964

The One-Eyed King of the Jews

Relatively neglected in the criticism of Saul Bellow's work (and probably more obvious now that we can view the last five novels as a group) is the issue of temporal loss and nostalgic identification with the past.[1] In fact, however, Bellow's later protagonists have a sense of temporal loss, displacement, and anachronism almost as acute (though not so precisely focused) as those of Nabokov. In the passage I have cited as one epigraph to this chapter, Herzog senses his own quixotism but puzzles over the question of what "great models" he, a Jew, could be imitating. He puzzles also over the problem of how and why he continues to model on the past at a time when all earlier roles have become obsolete.[2] This second problem exposes the very nature of quixotism: its obsessive and irrational commitment to a dead past; its essential alienation from and irrelevance to the mocking ground of the present.

Daniel Hughes, one critic who has noticed the crucial sense of loss in Bellow's work, first invokes Erich Heller's splendid definition of "higher parody" (what I have been calling mock-heroic parody)—"the only thing that is still left when the 'real thing' has become impossible"—and then goes on to link Bellow with both Nabokov and Stendhal. The protagonists of these three writers, he notes, are each involved in a situation where "the external reality in which he finds himself is less real than his sense of himself, is not large or various enough for his completest expression."[3] Bellow's narrator, Charles Citrine, in *Humboldt's Gift* offers us an even more complete description of this typically lost and displaced figure. Talking about his friend the romantic poet Von Humboldt Fleisher, he sharply locates the cause of displacement and, just as important, relates it to madness:

> Being crazy was the conclusion of the joke Humboldt tried to make out of his great disappointment. He was so intensely disappointed. All a man of that sort really asks for is a chance to work his heart out at some high work. People like Humboldt—they express a sense of life, they declare the feelings of their times or they discover meanings or find out the truths of nature, using the opportunities their time offers. When these opportunities are great, then there's love and friendship between all who are in the same enterprise. As you can see in Haydn's praise for Mozart. When the opportunities are smaller, there's spite and rage, insanity.[4]

In a further comment suggesting the possibility of an alternate intellectual and aesthetic response to this situation, Citrine adds significantly: "The agony is too deep, the disorder too big for art enterprises undertaken in the old way" (*HG*, 477). His total comment thus both hints at what is probably the major issue in *Humboldt's Gift* and inferentially directs us backward to the aesthetic form of all Bellow's later novels.

What alternative direction, then, might the writer choose who is still concerned with celebrating heroic experience and the "lost" values associated with such experience but who recognizes the impossibility today of a straight epic art and the sentimental limitations of simple nostalgia? We know Fyodor among others to have also dealt with this problem, and its solution became his own and Nabokov's particular "gift." But whereas Nabokov's novel, in the manner of Joyce's *Portrait*, functions to discard alternatives and point the way ahead for the young writer, *Humboldt's Gift*, covering much of the same ground at a different moment in its author's life, represents a mature and comprehensive rationale for the direction Bellow's later career has taken. Bellow's own groundbreaker and signal of change, of sharply refocused formal articulation, is rather *Henderson the Rain King*, whose publication in 1954 represents, in style and content, a dramatic departure from his till then characteristic work. Indeed, *Henderson* involves a formal breakthrough most meaningfully compared to that which takes place in Stevens's *Comedian*; both writers undertake experiments in the mock-heroic mode which announce the general direction of all their later work. Like the *Comedian*, *Henderson* seems anomalous in its mannered, derivative, and hypertrophic form—a departure apparently from the author's normal style and concerns—yet actually constitutes a crucial and necessary exercise in the development of Bellow's mature version of mock-heroic, a version, incidentally, which, in its improvisatory, meditative, and polemical voice, will continue to have something in common with that of Stevens.

Probably *Herzog's* comment on the apparent remoteness of the Jew from the quixotic role even gives us a clue as to why the protagonist of *Henderson* is so blatantly a gentile. In a new and self-conscious experiment with mock-heroic narrative who more easily or obviously (since "a quixote was a Christian") could one find to use than a Protestant aristocrat of instantly credible noble background and readily available role models? Even the necessary complement of heavy mockery could perhaps be indulged more freely in the context of gentile romance. Sarah Blacher Cohen has noted the degree to which the comic tone in *Henderson*, especially when directed toward the protagonist, gets harsher, more categorically limiting than it had been in Bellow's earlier quest narrative. As she says, in *The Adventures of Augie March* "the gravity of the situation is seldom minimized, its speculative definition seldom undermined and the earnestness of the speaker seldom wavering."[5] This is not to say, of course, that Bellow was not enormously committed to the figure he had created in Henderson. In 1964, at least, Henderson was the character in his work with whom he most personally identified, and his capsule description of the Rain King—"the absurd seeker of high qualities"—remains as splendid a brief definition of the Cervantine mock-hero as one can find anywhere.[6]

What the seeker seeks is already behind him somewhere in the irrecoverable past; such a situation constitutes the major index of his absurdity. Both present and future are of no interest to the mock-heroic writer and his protagonist except insofar as they represent the necessary ground of life and thus may offer the materials for a mock redemption of the past by somehow reflecting a "pale fire" suggestive of its reality. Van Veen, the philosopher of time, is expansive in his scorn for any purely "future" time. In the passage I have previously quoted and elsewhere, Herzog, in turn, gives lip service to the possibility of a brave, new "post-Copernican U.S.A.," but immediately disavows any serious belief in some "twentieth-century advantage." Bellow's later protagonists are all parodies of Lazarus. From a background mythology of purity, power, and love, they experience in the present a flagging or erratic commitment to what has been lost and, as Herzog's comment suggests, a diminished or uncertain awareness even of the heroic models they may be imitating, unlike, let us say, the manic single-mindedness of Nabokov's protagonists. Then at some point they are "reborn," but merely into the same problematic present, where they are at least free to affirm the value of life and free also to perform some perhaps clarified mock-heroic role.

They are reborn obviously into a continuing context of death. Reality's ultimate mockery, the last bad joke epitomizing all the rest, the final loss that ratifies despair, is always in mock-heroic narrative the presence of the headsman. Bellow makes clear in his novels and in talks with interviewers that the nub of his protagonists' search is always for an answer to entropy and death—for something that will reaffirm personal, moral, and spiritual power and continuity, all those "higher qualities" to which the heroic life has traditionally served as witness and which constitute the real end of any authentic quest. In Mr. Sammler's succinct phrase, what the potential hero has lost and may have once possessed is the "power to impart design."[7] Dahfu, Henderson's instructor in the nature of heroism, speaks of "relation" as the key to heroic power. It is one meaning of the lion: "Now you are a lion. Mentally, conceive of the environment. The sky, the sun, and creatures of the bush. You are related to all."[8] Dahfu's words, in effect, articulate the vision of high romanticism; indeed, they point toward the vitalistic landscape of heroic myth that lies behind romanticism and is anterior to it. He goes on to point out that imagination may establish contact with transcendent power ("the mind of the human may associate with the all-intelligent to perform certain work" [HRK, 269]) and, through such connection, may affect reality: "Imagination is a force of nature. . . . It converts to actual. It sustains, it alters, it redeems" (HRK, 271). Henderson gets the point; Dahfu, he says, "was no mere dreamer but one of the dream-doers, a guy with a program" (HRK, 235).

But Henderson's ambitious hopes for the heroic life are premature. As it unfolds in the novel, Dahfu's "program" concerns itself largely with preparations for an encounter with death, preparations he, of course, shares with Henderson, his double and initiate, and preparations that turn out to be futile, if rational judgment is the only yardstick we bring to the novel. Bellow emphasized this concern and its final absurdity in a remark to an interviewer: "What Henderson is really seeking is a remedy to the anxiety over death. . . . All his efforts are a satire on the attempts people make to answer the enigma by movement and random action or even by conscious effort."[9] Henderson's own eloquent statement of aims, written toward the end of his African experience in a letter to his wife, stresses both the urgency and the passion of the quest and avoids Bellow's harsh objectivity, though it is not, as I shall point out, without ironic overtones: "to raise my spirit from the earth, to leave the body *of this death. I was very stubborn. I wanted to raise myself into another world. My life and deeds were a prison"* (*HRK*, 284). The prison or tomb image in Bellow's work symbolizes the fundamental barrier against which the human spirit, in one form or another, organizes all its imaginary escapes. It invokes the same sense of entrapment as in Stevens and Nabokov but suggests less the positive possibilities of solipsism.

I have already indicated that what Henderson's statement lacks in obvious mockery it more than makes up for in ironic overtones. The use of italics on occasion throughout the long letter is curious: intensity is added, of course, but more significant is their hint of a dimension of deeper meditation—not what he is writing to Lily as the best explanation possible of his strange disappearance but what he is simultaneously thinking, thoughts that sometimes affirm, sometimes undermine the surface text. As the past tense of his statement suggests, with its implications of distancing, finality, elegy, the immediate context of its expression is an admission of failure. "I am giving up the violin [he writes Lily]. I guess I will never reach my object through it" (*HRK*, 284). The violin-playing, we must remember, represents Henderson's most important attempt before the African experience to invoke the spirit of his famous, powerful, and eccentric father ("He could not settle into the quiet life either" [*HRK*, 25]). The motive on this earlier occasion parallels that of the African quest:

> I have never been able to convince myself the dead are utterly dead. I admire rational people and envy their clear heads, but what's the use of kidding? I played in the basement to my father and my mother, and when I heard a few pieces I would whisper, "Ma, this is 'Humoresque' for you." Or, "Pa, listen—'Meditation' from *Thaïs*." I played with dedication, with feeling, with longing, love—played to the point of emotional collapse. Also down there in my studio I sang as I played, "Rispondi! Anima bella" (Mozart). "He was despised and rejected, a man of sorrows and acquainted with grief" (Handel). Clutching the neck of the little instrument as if there were strangulation in my heart, I got cramps in my neck and shoulders. [*HRK*, 30]

In this passage, the ludicrous manner of questing mocks the actual quest, a pattern later repeated regularly during Henderson's various African adventures. The larger mocking force, however, is the reality of failure, the sense of potency and love lost and irrecoverable, regardless of their passionate pursuit. To a request for "response," spirit answers nothing—nothing, at least, beyond the ardor and the effort of the questing self.

Henderson's description of himself—"I, Henderson, with all my striving and earnestness" (*HRK*, 140)—survives its touch of comic pomposity (heightened, in this case, by his thinking it while unwittingly carrying another dead king on his back and trying to dispose of him) to serve as a positive description of all of Bellow's later protagonists. The emphasis is always on the noble but absurd struggle of the mock-heroic self against death. On another occasion Henderson thinks of "the last little room of dirt [that] is waiting. Without windows." And he admonishes himself characteristically: "So for God's sake make a move, Henderson, put forth effort. You, too, will die of this pestilence. Death will annihilate you and nothing will remain, and there will be nothing left but junk. Because nothing will have been, and so nothing will be left" (HRK, 40). The last sentence here implies an alternative rhythm of positive cause and effect, but any such implication is actually more nonsense, as finally irrational as the practical possibilities of all other spiritual ideas. Henderson realizes that he is committed to madness and has, indeed, as much insight into this paradoxical heroic style as Charles Citrine: "Of course, in an age of madness, to expect to be untouched by madness is a form of madness. But the pursuit of sanity can be a form of madness, too" (HRK, 25). The nature of the mock-heroic mode—indeed, the crux of its value system— is to offer us simply a moral choice among madmen; in Bellow's art as much as any does this continue to be true.

With Nabokov, the shadows or "shades" of heroic form linger everywhere in the postheroic world, shadows visible only to his protagonists and informing the obsessions of their every moment. Don Quixote himself characteristically "sees" a heroic dimension of reality opaque to those around him. Bellow's protagonists, likewise, are sensitive to what Citrine calls "the idea" of a noble, value-filled reality. Looking around him, for example, in Chicago, he sees "the insignificant Picasso sculpture with its struts and its sheet metal, no wings, no victory, only a token, a reminder, only the *idea* of a work of art. Very similar, I thought, to the other ideas or reminders by which we lived— no more apples but the idea, the pomologist's reconstruction of what an apple once was, no more ice cream but the idea, the recollection of something delicious made of substitutes, of starch, glucose, and other chemicals, no more sex but the idea or reminiscence of that, and so with love, belief, thought, and so on" (HG, 218). To reclaim some substance for the heroic idea constitutes the focus of mock-heroic madness.

Henderson's world is steeped in heroic echoes to which he is painfully attuned: not simply the distinguished family background of statesmen, writers, and soldiers ("I am a soldier. All my people have been soldiers. They protected the peasants, and they went on the crusades and fought the Mohammedans" [HRK, 256–57]), but the heroes of myth and history to which he makes constant, self-conscious reference—Odysseus, Oedipus, Lazarus, Daniel, Joseph ("Believe me, I felt like a dreamer" [HRK, 171]), Gordon of Khartoum, Wilfred Grenfell, Albert Schweitzer, the great English explorers of

Africa, and undoubtedly others. Not surprisingly, Henderson continues to insist that the world *must* have a noumenal dimension. As he puts it: "The world of facts is real, all right, and not to be altered. The physical is all there and belongs to science. But then there is the noumenal department, and there we create and create and create" (*HRK*, 167). Such a statement, however, postulates the duality as much as the reconciliation of idea and substance and, indeed, contains in germ both the possibility and the countervailing mockery of mock-heroic experience. In any case, Bellow at least sets free his hero into a landscape that offers him the possibility of "enchantment" (*HRK*, 98) and spiritual adventure toward the goal, crucial to the hero's continuing existence, of redeeming loss. Within the enchanted landscape exists the possibility of somehow replicating the past. After he has arrived among the Arnewi, Henderson says to himself at one point, "I *knew* that this place was of old" and goes on mentally to gloss his own statement: "Meaning, I had sensed from the first that I might find things here which were of old, which I saw when I was still innocent and have longed for all my life—and without which *I could not make it*" (*HRK*, 102).

Within the context of a make-believe Africa—an Africa of the imagination, his own and Bellow's—Henderson does, indeed, "make it," though even in this artificial medium, his gains are tenuous beyond a renewed commitment to effort itself. At the same time, the mockery of anticlimactic failure and comic pratfall is relentless. What he tells Dahfu about his misadventures among the Arnewi may be taken as a representative description of the narrative rhythm of the book: "King, I had a great desire to do a disinterested and pure thing—to express my belief in something higher. Instead I landed in a lot of trouble" (*HRK*, 188). As critics have often observed, Henderson's clownishness is fundamental; even his enormous and ungainly body is as much a parody of heroic stature as Don Quixote's emaciation—the body, notes Sarah Blacher Cohen, constantly mocking his airborne spirit, duality indigenous at the most basic level.[10]

What we chiefly feel in Henderson's experience, moreover, is the continuing pain of loss and failure. He is very much a "Knight of the Woeful Countenance," his suffering another index of both nobility and absurdity, of heroic effort in its guise as substitute for consummation. Dahfu pointedly reminds him late in the novel that (in Henderson's paraphrase) "suffering was the closest thing to worship that I knew anything about" (*HRK*, 303–4). His constant cry of "I want, I want" is less the complaint of a selfish and undisciplined ego than the tragic sound of loss in its need to recover what is missing. In turn, the state of "becoming" about which he makes so much is really the manifestation of his perpetual state of desire—"becoming," in other words, at best the mere shade of past "being." In a letter to his wife late in the novel he tells her that he "may apply for missionary work, like Dr. Wilfred Grenfell or Albert Schweitzer. Hey! Axel Munthe—how about him?" (*HRK*, 285). The speculations continue in a similar vein, the flippant tone suggesting more lack of conviction as to ends than lack of desire. Authentic heroism fulfills "noble self-conception" (*HRK*, 268) in power and actuality; it breaks the cycle of death and desire which is the common lot. As Dahfu tells Henderson: "Any good man will try to break the cycle. There is no issue from that cycle for a man who does not take things into his hands" (*HRK*, 297). But Henderson knows better than his teacher about true escape from prison. He follows the passage to his wife reporting future plans with a deeper speculation: "*I don't think the struggles of desire can ever be won. Ages of longing and willing, willing and longing, and how have they ended? In a draw, dust and dust*" (*HRK*, 285).

It turns out in the end that even Dahfu's celebrated "being" is as fragile as the tenuousness of his brilliant ratiocination, which, in Henderson's telling description, was "not a secure gift but like [his] ramshackle red palace rested on doubtful underpinnings" (*HRK*, 269). Of course, when Dahfu falls to his brave but futile death from a perch above the lion he has trapped but cannot contain, whatever "underpinnings" he may have had give way completely. In speech, Dahfu defines an authentic heroism irrecoverably lost; in his life, he illustrates whatever mock-heroism may be possible.

Henderson survives Dahfu as his heir apparent, his "royal material" (*HRK*, 315) perhaps heightened and renewed by his encounter with the king, his commitment to nobility and greatness now more expansive than ever, its rhetorical manifestation worthy of Emerson: "Oh, greatness! . . . the universe itself being put into us, it calls out for scope. The external is bonded into us. It calls out for its share" (*HRK*, 318). What is most striking, however, about the end of the novel is not as much its projection of future hopes as the return of echoes from the past: Henderson carrying in his arms the pure child he dreams of having been; Henderson remembering his brother's death and his father's consequent despair, anger with him, and abandonment of his paternal role; above all, Henderson's memory of himself as cast-off adolescent becoming keeper in an amusement park to Smolak, a ruined and aged brown bear. The two of them ride a roller coaster for the entertainment of large crowds, figures linked in a common bond of despair, embracing cheek to cheek while (as Henderson recalls) "all support seemed to leave us and we started down the perpendicular drop" (*HRK*, 338). The two "Ishmaels" together remind us again of the mocking realities of isolation, loneliness, suffering, and the final "drop," which at one time or another takes every human being to inexorable death as it has already taken Dahfu. Nevertheless, the two "humorists before the crowd but brothers in our souls" love each other and, in their relationship, constitute a touching parody of heroic aspirations to an organic connection between the self and nature—"I embeared by him, and he probably humanized by me," as Henderson puts it (*HRK*, 338). Such a meager organicism is at least something—or so Henderson claims: "Whatever gains I ever made were already due to love and nothing else" (*HRK*, 339). He is last seen cavorting in pure joy of life on the tarmac at Gander Airport while his plane is being refueled for the final leg of its journey to New York.

None of these final scenes and statements constitutes a "resolution" of the issues raised in the novel—that aspect of fiction which critics so often complain of missing in Bellow's work. Rather, they are further examples of the ceaseless dialectic of statement and counterstatement that I have noted so often in describing the mock-heroic mode, examples of heroic attitudes, values, style, and role which paradoxically survive their relentless ironic demolition. That is the true meaning and significance of the survival theme in Bellow's art. His protagonists' ritual dying, as versions of Lazarus, involves the full experience and incorporation of mockery—reality, "the facts," life as destructive element. "No, I really believe in reality," says Henderson at one point, after speculating that "maybe every guy has his own Africa" (what we might call after reading a Nabokov, an Africa "safely solipsized"); then he adds emphatically: "That is a known fact" (*HRK*, 276). Rebirth involves the ability of Bellow's protagonists to "live with" the facts, to assimilate idealism into a total context of mockery. For Mr. Sammler, Bellow's prototypal survivor, the message is clear but difficult and bitter: "All postures are mocked by their opposites" (*MSP*, 122).

With the publication of *Herzog* in 1964, Bellow triumphantly integrated the mock-heroic mode into the Jewish context that informs his best work. Before dealing with that book, however, I want to comment at least briefly on *Mr. Sammler's Planet* as a more obvious example of such integration and a more blatant treatment of the issues I have been pursuing in *Henderson*. Presumably the intellectual direction of the late 1960s, which tended to define all problems in the name of a new romantic utopianism, served to nudge Bellow's very different mock-heroic sensibility into an unusually clear and sharp response, a return not in style and tone but in a certain directness and simplification of development and structure to the first of his mock-heroic novels. The times were such as made all "middle age" seem particularly irrelevant. I have noted before the manner in which the mixed feelings of middle age—that period which hovers so precariously between youthful passions and comic impotency, between a sense of engagement with one's culture and pained awareness of obsolescence—so often constitute a significant dimension of the sensibility responsible for mock-heroic art. As Herzog, age forty-seven, is reminded by one of his "reality instructors": "Guys at our time of life must face facts" (*H*, 83). The late 1960s could only have reinforced the inclinations of a writer already acutely conscious of being out of step even with the intellectual generation with which he was most closely identified, a consciousness that, of course, finds consummate expression in *Herzog*. By making the protagonist of *Mr. Sammler's Planet* an old man, Bellow obviously heightens the tensions endemic to age, increasing the alienation, making even more difficult the possibility of substantial commitments, even more tenuous the relevance of affirmations.

In any case, more than Henderson or Herzog it is Sammler who has been most savagely tested by "the facts." Like Nabokov's figures, he is explicitly the victim of a historical catastrophe (one is tempted to say, of the continuing historical catastrophe of the twentieth century) that has categorically broken the thread of his temporal experience by literally wiping out the world of his origins—in Bellow's somber formulation: "Historical ruin. Transformation of society" (*MSP*, 11). A patent anachronism, Sammler is Bellow's version of Nabokov's Pnin, the displaced person from a culture of different style and values who ends his life in an America scornful of, indifferent to, or, at best, tolerantly amused at his eccentricity. Sammler surpasses even Pnin in the degree to which he has been and continues to be threatened by the reality of history: not only the holocaust, which almost destroyed him, but the militant contemporary barbarism of the 1960s, which jeers at everything he represents. Sammler shares Max Weber's view of the entire direction of modern culture: "Specialists without spirit, sensualists without heart, this nullity imagines that it has attained a level of civilization never before achieved" (*MSP*, 58). Certainly Sammler's particular encounters with nullity are as brutal and complete as those of any of the mock-heroes I have examined. Among Bellow's later protagonists, moreover, Sammler's nostalgia is most blatant (though he resists its easy blandishments) and his present role most obviously shaped by a clearly focused, value-laden past. At the same time, compared to the roles of others, his seems most totally divorced from the possibility of vital action in the "spatial-temporal prison" (*MSP*, 57), where it is condemned to play out its search for moral and spiritual redemption.

Sarah Blacher Cohen has noted of Henderson that "his Amadis de Gaul is Sir Wilfred Grenfell. His knight errant is the physician errant, armed with scalpel and stethoscope, setting out to rescue humanity from distress."[11] Sammler's Amadis, in turn, is H. G. Wells, with his heroic vision of nineteenth-century utopian rationalism, of humanism and science joined in the creation of a new human order. By means of this prophetic vision, Wells, according to Sammler, thought he could explain everything; above all, what he explains—or rather attempts to explain away—is death itself. In Sammler's paraphrase of Wells: "As the old filth and gloomy sickness were cleared away, there would emerge a larger, stronger, older, brainier, better-nourished, better-oxygenated, more vital human type, able to eat and drink sanely, perfectly autonomous and well regulated in desires, going nude while attending tranquilly to duties, performing his fascinating and useful mental work. Yes, gradually the long shudder of mankind at the swift transitoriness of mortal beauty, pleasure, would cease, to be replaced by the wisdom of prolongation" (MSP, 76). At its less extreme, Wells's vision represents an affirmation of the power and value of civilization, of the hero as scientist, intellectual, legislator, social visionary; it represents, in Sammler's summary, "faith in an emancipated future, in active benevolence, in reason, in civilization" (MSP, 213). Behind them both is the culture of Bloomsbury, with its high polish of style, civility, and concern for the life of the mind. Behind even Bloomsbury, in turn, are the historical dreams of Victorian and Edwardian society and their promise of orderly and rational progress. Sammler's Polish background is upper middle class, enlightened, Anglophile; he anticipates Bloomsbury before he arrives to take up residence. Once there, he had "written articles for News of Progress [and] for the other publication, The World Citizen on a project based on the propagation of the sciences of biology, history, and sociology and the effective application of scientific principles to the enlargement of human life; the building of a planned, orderly, and beautiful world society" (MSP, 45).

Such as least was the heroic vision of an earlier time. In recounting it years later to students at Columbia University, Sammler, thinking to himself, mocks his own earlier hopes ("feeling what a kindhearted, ingenuous, stupid scheme it had been" [MSP, 45–46]) and finally is himself brutally and tellingly mocked by the students: "His balls are dry. He's dead. He can't come" (MSP, 46). Of course, even during his original habitation of this now lost world, Sammler, the Polish Jew, however anglicized and enlightened, was a less than authentic figure. In its own brutal way, the holocaust only exposed what had from the beginning contained a dimension of artificiality and role-playing. His very name Artus ("at that period not very Jewish . . . the most international, enlightened name you could give a boy" [MSP, 212]) potentially mocks him before the terrible events that confirm the mockery. He was named for Schopenhauer, Sammler explains, "but Schopenhauer didn't care for Jews" (MSP, 212). Wells himself, "tough brave little old fellow" that he was (MSP, 110), ends in depression and failure, his dream mocked first by his grotesque sexual needs, then obviously by the general calamity of World War II, the final and terrible anticlimax of his hopes.

Critics have tended to argue that in Mr. Sammler's Planet the sardonic voice so characteristic of Herzog has given way almost entirely to sententiousness, with Sammler cast as the superhuman spokesman for a crotchety Saul Bellow.[12] Such a criticism, however, takes little account of the terrible contexts of sententiousness in the novel: not simply the cultural anticlimax, which constitutes the social basis of the novel, or the way Sammler's sententiousness often turns back upon its own earlier positions, but the universal madness of the novel's world, the degree to which madness has usurped the reason that sought its banishment, with Sammler's sententiousness, finally, only a form of madness, albeit perhaps a noble one. For Sammler as for the reader the entire experience of the novel is soaked in "the bad literalness, the yellow light of Polish summer heat behind the mausoleum door. It was the light also of that china-cabinet room in the apartment where he had suffered confinement with Shula-Slawa." In Sammler's interpretation, the light represents the loss of coherence, or "punishment for having failed to find coherence," or simply "a longing for sacredness . . . when everyone is murdering everyone" (*MSP*, 96). New York in the spring occupies the same killing ground as wartime Poland, its pervasive smell of sewage a bitter parody of the promise of lilacs: "There was as yet no lilacs, but an element of the savage gas was velvety and sweet, reminiscent of blooming lilac" (*MSP*, 120). The meaning of New York with its smells and crowds is simple and patent enough for Sammler: "That reality was a terrible thing, and that the final truth about mankind was overwhelming and crushing" (*MSP*, 283). But this "vulgar, cowardly conclusion" is quickly rejected by Sammler "with all his heart," a rejection that points us toward the very essence of his mock-heroism—a fundamental unwillingness to accept the acknowledged nullity of reality, a continual obsessive quest for coherence lost.

He is not alone, however, in his refusal to accept nullity; such a refusal also constitutes the basis of the more general madness encompassed by the novel. Indeed, it is the fundamental quality of the human imagination, which Govinda Lal, the novel's other resident philosopher, describes as "innately a biological power seeking to overcome impossible conditions" (*MSP*, 111). The complex irony of the book is generated not so much by Sammler's distance from those he ceaselessly comments on (granted that his own role involves scholarly aloofness and Bloomsbury manners) as from his essential identification with them and the constant mirror of mocking resemblance that is set up as a consequence. In Sammler's encounters with "quivering, stinking Broadway," for example, "the philosophical rambler . . . out inspecting the phenomenon" and the phenomenon in question meld toward a common articulation of meaning:

It was aware of being a scene of perversity, it knew its own despair. And fear. The terror of it. Here you might see the soul of America at grips with historical problems, struggling with certain impossibilities, experiencing violently states

inherently static. Being realized but trying itself to realize, to act. Attempting to
make interest. This attempt to make interest was, for Sammler, one reason for
the pursuit of madness. Madness makes interest. Madness is the attempted liberty of people who feel themselves overwhelmed by the giant forces of organized control. Seeking the magic of extremes. Madness is a base form of the
religious life. [*MSP*, 150]

Sammler mocks the possibility of a rambling "tourist" role ("was there any
land stable enough to tour?" [*MSP*, 149]); obviously, he as much as any is
"attempting to make interest" through his endlessly reformulated meditations, his own attempt "to realize, to act."

Indeed, Sammler goes on to link madness with heroism, the most extreme
manifestation of the imagination's power to mythologize the self. As he puts
it: "To perform higher actions, to serve the imagination with special distinction, it seems essential to be histrionic. This, too, is a brand of madness.
Madness has always been a favorite choice of the civilized man who prepares
himself for a noble achievement" (*MSP*, 151). In ethical terms, we are left only
with a choice among roles: "to accept the inevitability of imitation and then
imitate good things" (*MSP*, 153). In absolute terms, however, roles simply
mock each other, with madness in general finally a parody performance that
manifests unwittingly the reality it would seek to transcend: "a masquerade,
the project of a deeper reason, a result of the despair we feel before infinities
and eternities" (*MSP*, 152).

"Play-acting, originality, dramatic individuality, theatricality in people,"
says Sammler to Lal at one point, are "the forms taken by spiritual striving"
(*MSP*, 234). In this context, the other characters in the novel are parodic doubles of the mock-hero and cast a further ironic light on his role. Some represent virtual travesties of heroic performance, others display considerable spiritual range and power, but all reflect the problem of heroism in one form or
another, and to them Sammler is consciously or unconsciously drawn in mysterious association. An obvious example of such affinity is his fascination
with the black pickpocket, a personage of great masculine style, power, and
mastery. In this case, Sammler can explain his attraction: "Objectively I have
little use for such experiences, but there is such an absurd craving for actions
that connect with other actions, for coherency, for forms, for mysteries or
fables" (*MSP*, 124). Later in the novel, of course, Sammler has to intervene to
prevent this apparently potent figure from being beaten to death.

More obvious still is his interest in Govinda Lal, H. G. Wells brought up to
date, the scientific humanist committed to the new order and freedom of
space travel, mankind's latest "invitation to the voyage" of escape from
prison ("not to accept the opportunity would make this earth seem more and

more a prison" [*MSP*, 222]). Despite superficial disagreements as to means, futurist and memorialist remain essentially one in their commitment to the same impossible end. Both, in turn, are parodied by the harebrained activities of Sammler's daughter Schula, who sees the two men as sharing the same inspiration and who engages in frantic and absurd activities to bring them together. Her vision of her father—"She thought he was Prospero. He could make beautiful culture" (*MSP*, 118)—devastatingly mocks whatever heroic pretensions he may have. His explanation to Dr. Lal of her visionary obsessions, however, locates at least the possibility of spiritual nobility in such claims and commitments: "Everyone grapples, each in his awkward muffled way, with a power, a Jacob's angel, to get a final satisfaction or glory that is withheld" (*MSP*, 132–33).

Further still than Schula toward the pole of heroic travesty are such minor characters as Angela, the voluptuary ("Both low comic and high serious. Goddess and majorette" [*MSP*, 168]); her brother Wallace, the precocious but undisciplined and irresponsible genius, multiple Ph.D. and mad scientist; Eisen, the artist, who tries to make something beautiful from "iron pyrites, belonging at the bottom of the Dead Sea" (*MSP*, 174); and, not least, Feffer, the academic entrepreneur of the 1960s, whose role and speech, echoing Emerson and other romantic sources, mocks the mystery of naming ("knowing the names of things braces people up" [*MSP*, 115]), the power of the imagination to create fresh order and, indeed, the whole problem central to modern culture and the mock-heroic sensibility of going beyond the language act to authentic action. In Feffer's matchless rephrasing of romantic hopes: "When you set up a new enterprise, you redescribe the phenomena and create a feeling that we're getting somewhere. If people want things named or renamed, you can make dough by becoming a taxonomist" (*MSP*, 115).

Sammler finds his darkest reflection, however, in a figure from recent history, Rumkowski, "the mad Jewish King of Lodz," who, with Nazi encouragement, creates his own court and pageantry, while "presiding over the deaths of half a million people." Sammler tells Lal that, in thinking about play-acting, his mind returns again and again to Rumkowski as the supreme example of the "antics of failed individuality," human beings as "horrible clowns" with only "the imaginary grandeur of insects," above all, of the inadequacy of imagination to encompass and transcend the realities with which it must deal and thus create an authentic "king"—what Sammler describes as the "too great . . . demand upon the imagination to produce a human figure of adequate stature." Sammler goes on to note that the Germans found Rumkowski amusing and speaks of "the killers' delight in abasement in parody" (*MSP*, 234–36). His final comment suggests the degree to which Bellow, unlike Nabokov, is uneasy with parody, sensing in it a dimension of self-hatred, tragic bitterness, and moral despair which Nabokov tends to play down (except perhaps in *Lolita*). Certainly in *Mr. Sammler's Planet* the positive possibilities of parody are less celebrated than its inevitability accepted, with a heavy awareness of loss and suffering—of the moral cost of the persistent failure of roles. And there is an equally heavy sense of the emotional waste in clownishness: "Humankind kept doing the same stunts over and over. The old comical-tearful stuff. Emotional relationships. Desires incapable of useful fulfillment. Over and over, trying to vent and empty the breast of certain cries, of certain fervencies" (*MSP*, 177).

Sammler's identification with Rumkowski is as fundamental to Bellow's novel as Humbert's similarly complex relationship with Quilty in *Lolita*. In addition to his obsession with the King of Lodz as symbol, he associates his own present role with some sort of "kingship," even describing himself at one point as comparable to the figure in "the old saying about the one-eyed being King in the Country of the Blind" (*MSP*, 214). Sammler's baptism into death and subsequent arbitrary and doubtful resurrection constitute the background action of the book. The temporal foreground involves the long dying of nephew Gruner, the other character who most sharply manifests a certain nobility, while also covered with the dirt of the grave ("Soil was scattered on *his* face. Look hard. You must see some grains" [*MSP*, 145]). Yet even though the tomb encloses these figures (Sammler's resurrection, such as it is, matched by Gruner's actual death), both never really cease to affirm, in action and statement, at least the desire for moral and spiritual reality. Like that of other artists in the mock-heroic mode. Bellow's point of view pivots finally on his central ambivalence toward desire, its futility and waste, on one hand, its function as the locus of hope, imagination, and moral energy, on the other. Conversing with Wallace, Sammler refers to a scene from *War and Peace* in which Pierre Bezhukov is spared from execution when his eyes catch those of a notoriously cruel executioner. According to Sammler, Tolstoy's moral is that "you don't kill another human being with whom you have exchanged such a look." Asked for his opinion on this idea, Sammler refocuses the entire issue around the more positive aspects of desire: "I sympathize with such a desire for such a belief . . . I sympathize deeply. I sympathize sadly. When men of genius think about mankind, they are almost forced to believe in this form of psychic unity. I wish it were so." And he goes on to attempt a distinction between the certain moral value of noble desire and its probable falsity as a description of reality: " 'Pierre was exceptionally lucky to catch the eye of his executioner. I myself never knew it to work. No, I never saw it happen. It is a thing worth praying for. And it is based on something. It's not an arbitrary idea. It's based on the belief that there is the same truth in the heart of every human being, or a splash of God's own spirit, and that this is the richest thing we share in common. And up to a point I would agree. But though it's not an arbitrary idea, I wouldn't count on it'" (*MSP*, 191–92). As if Sammler's rhetoric here were not tentative enough, Wallace's following comment brutally reminds us of context: "They say you were in the grave once" (*MSP*, 192).

Unlike Rumkowski presumably (although the king of Lodz, we are told, in the end "voluntarily stepped into the train for Auschwitz" [*MSP*, 236]), Sammler remains at least a "one-eyed" king. Destroyed by a German rifle butt, his blind eye reminds us obviously of the power of nullity that denies authentic heroism. But his remaining good eye suggests some possibility of "seeing"—a certain lingering visionary stance and perhaps also, as "half" of total vision (paired with nullity), something of Bellow's more comprehensive dualistic perspective. The world of death has turned Sammler from a dilettantish social critic into a potential reader of signs and metaphysical messages, "who kept on vainly trying to perform some kind of symbolic task" (*MSP*, 95), eaten, as he is, by the "longing for sacredness" already noted. At the same time, Sammler's constant self-mockery regarding the necessity of "short views" identifies what is, on the contrary, a continuous meditative process that never arrives at views either short or final. Like that of other mock-heroes, Sammler's is the courage of effort—Paterson's formulation: "Virtue is wholly / in the effort to be virtuous." Daily he wakes up early, attempting "to get a handle on the situation," apparently a hopeless task: "He didn't think he could. Nor, if he could, would he be able to convince or convert anyone" (*MSP*, 78). Late in the novel, in the full context of the yellow sun (showing "the fury of the world") Sammler is "still thinking things through. Tired, dizzy, despairing, he still thought. Still in touch. With reality, that is" (*MSP*, 301–2).

His courage goes beyond effort, however sustained, to include a willed and self-conscious encounter with the element that will inevitably mock and destroy any potential results of effort. Behind Sammler as heroic prototype in literature lurks not only Prospero, the king of human love, the human bond, and civil order, but, even more significantly, Kierkegaard's Knight of Faith, in Sammler's version, "that real prodigy" who, "having set its relations with the infinite, was entirely at home in the finite" (*MSP*, 66). The Knight of Faith, nevertheless, exists in an essentially monistic environment, and Sammler's heroics are subject to a devastating and irreconcilable dualism, the reductive "finite" everywhere dissynchronous with a potential "infinite." He is a quixote of Jewish humanism (love, compassion, virtuous conduct, acceptance of the "pain of duty," obedience to God), whose own experience has been his most relentless Sancho Panza.

Gruner, in turn, meets the "terms of his contract" (*MSP*, 316) in the face of callous and indifferent children and the reality of the tomb. His dead face reflects finally the same duality that is suggested by Sammler's eyes: "In the lips bitterness and an expression of obedience were combined" (*MSP*, 316). Just as Nabokov invokes an aesthetic order as a parody of ideal forms, so Bellow remains committed to an ethical order (the human bond) as a parody of an adequate civil order (civilization as an ethical construction) and a God of love and justice. What Gruner and Sammler essentially identify in each other is a willingness "to affirm the human bond" (*MSP*, 276) in the context of metaphysical nullity, social collapse, and human depravity. Auschwitz offers the bitterest mockery of Jewish claims in this century and probably ever. Bellow, in *Mr. Sammler's Planet*, gives it the widest possible apocalyptic implications and then pursues his own heroic affirmations in the light of these implications. His resultant mock-heroic art characteristically involves something far more complex than either nostalgia or despair. As Sammler observes, noting on one occasion the green areas of New York City but recognizing that these areas have lost their "association with peaceful sanctuary": "The old-time poetry of parks was banned. Obsolete thickness of shade leading to private meditation. Truth was now slummier and called for litter in the setting—leafy reverie? A thing of the past" (*MSP*, 282).

Meditations on the Sofa

Jewish truth has always been accustomed to a high degree of litter in the setting, and this litter, in turn, generated an indigenous tradition of mock-heroic. Referring to Bellow's comments on the subject, Marcus Klein has noted that "the little man of the Eastern European ghetto, the *stetl* [was] forced by the presence of perils everywhere to ingenious ways of personal survival" and that "one of these ways is in mock-heroism." He points out that Yiddish conversation mingles heroic allusion and banal reference and goes on to comment on the significance of such irreconcilable juxtapositions:

> This manner of living on terms of familiarity with greatness . . . contributed to the ghetto's sense of the ridiculous. It also performed a more delicate feat of irony, and one to which Bellow is sensitive. On the one hand, the mock-heroics of the little man render all conventional heroism absurd. . . . On the other hand, the acts themselves constitute real heroism, a mode of strong self-assertion in a community that disallows the self. Given the prison of restrictive circumstances of the *stetl*, and then those of Bellow's city, it is the only mode by which personal identity can be emphasized.[13]

Pursuing this same theme in his book on Bellow, John Clayton mentions the Jewish tradition of yea-saying "in the face of the grimmest facts" and the simultaneous presence under great tension in Jewish culture and literature of "the world as it is and the world as it will be," the latter, however, really a vision of the past, "not a Heavenly Jerusalem, but the earthly Jerusalem returned." Clayton quotes Isaac Rosenfield to the effect that the Jew "struggles forward to the halls of yesterday."[14] In one sense, Herzog's speculations on the possibility of a Jewish quixote constitute Bellow's clear signal that he has finally brought together the wider European tradition identified and tried out in *Henderson the Rain King* with its relevant counterpart in Jewish culture.

Another function of these speculations, as I have already indicated, is that they raise all the important questions about quixotism, questions whose exploration constitutes the heart of Herzog's quest and the source of the novel's rich complexity and wide significance. Herzog has strong, almost overpowering intimations that he is both "archaic" (his favorite word for himself) and a survivor, but neither to him, his friends, or the reader are the dimensions of his archaism and the manner of his survival immediately apparent. These issues indeed make up the substance of more than three hundred pages of meditation, which, in multiple ways, becomes the central manifestation of the themes it engages. In his apparent assimilation into upper-middle-class liberal culture, Herzog has none of the obvious and immediate anachronism so inherent in Henderson's role as Victorian adventurer and Sammler's as Bloomsbury refugee. Nor is his survival identified melodramatically with escape from lions or German death squads, however important such melodrama may be for its symbolism. But the fact of Herzog's being in many ways a representative American type, if it makes his task ultimately more significant, makes it, at the same time, immeasurably more difficult. This task (and the action of the novel) involves nothing less than the total self-conscious invention of himself as quixote: not simply the articulation of some present function (the focus of Henderson's and Sammler's concerns) but even the prior identification of heroic role or roles to be imitated. Herzog's claims are in the end grander, more complex, and more vague than those of Henderson and Sammler, but they reflect essentially the same issues pursued nobly to the same inevitable failure.

"What models did he imitate?" We must examine Herzog's various responses to his own question. Probably the place to begin, however, is to note that Herzog's sense of a cultural break between past and present—between classic Western culture and modernism, between childhood (his own but also childhood in a more generic sense) and adulthood, between Russian Jewish life and that of North American immigrants—is as strong (if more diffuse) and passionately felt as anything expressed by the obviously exiled Sammler. Herzog's fundamental exile, indeed, can scarcely be emphasized enough: not simply his emotional and intellectual isolation or his family diaspora and its continuation into his own generation, but, at the most literal level, his immediate existence on his Vermont property, an existence that constitutes the present time and setting of the novel and becomes emblematic of his entire situation.

Possibly we should think of this second, later Vermont episode as a version of the traditional pastoral retreat of the hero from which he will return strengthened to energize society with the authentic word. This, after all, is how the first episode was supposed to work and did not. More probably, however, Herzog's later vigil in Vermont represents a continuing pastoral parody, the imaginary climate not of potential success but of desire and failure, of fundamental exile and ultimate sterility and death—a version rather of the prototypal Vermont of American regional literature. Even in the later stages of his meditation, Herzog thinks primarily of his location as "on the fringes of the Berkshires, not the fashionable section." His elaboration of this point is telling: "You couldn't even ski on these slopes. No one came here. He had only gentle, dotty old neighbors, Jukes and Kallikaks, rocking themselves to death on their porches, watching television, the nineteenth-century quietly dying in this remote green hole" (*H,* 322).

Herzog's quintessential role is that of Displaced Person. After his release from jail, tired, dirty, "a lousy lost sheep," he declines a dinner invitation from his brother Will and adds by way of explanation: "I look as if I'd just arrived in this country. A D.P. Just as we arrived from Canada at the old Baltimore and Ohio Station. On the Michigan Central. God, we were filthy with soot" (*H,* 306). Will, engineer, technologist, builder, very much the modern man, has no sympathy for this allusion ("he did not share his brother's passion for reminiscence"), but it precisely locates Herzog both in relation to personal history and to his wider cultural situation.

Herzog's physical exile, in short, is a reflection of his sense of emotional and spiritual anachronism, and both, in turn, echo the more authentic and potent heroic roles he yearns to play. His comparison of himself with Will describes his present situation and locates key heroic prototypes in the background:

> He's a good man, a very good man. But there's a strange division of functions that I sense, in which I am the specialist in . . . in spiritual self-awareness; or emotionalism; or ideas; or nonsense. Perhaps of no real use or relevance except to keep alive primordial feelings of a certain sort. He mixes grout to pump into these new high-risers all over town. He has to be political, and deal, and wangle and pay off and figure tax angles. All that Pape was inept in but dreamed he was born to do. Will is a quiet man of duty and routine, has his money, position, influence, and is just as glad to be rid of his private or "personal" side. Sees me spluttering fire in the wilderness of this world, and pities me no doubt for my

temperament. Under the old dispensation, as the stumbling, ingenuous, burlap Moses, a heart without guile, in need of protection, a morbid phenomenon, a modern remnant of otherworldliness—under that former dispensation I would need protection. And it would be gladly offered by him—by the person who "knows-the-world-for-what-it-is." Whereas a man like me has shown the arbitrary withdrawal of proud subjectivity from the collective and historical progress of mankind. And that is true of lowerclass emotional boys and girls who adopt the aesthetic mode, the mode of rich sensibility. Seeking to sustain their own version of existence under the crushing weight of *mass*. What Marx described as that "material weight." [*H,* 307]

Though not uncharacteristic, the self-mockery in this passage is particularly sharp, reflecting, no doubt, the specific incorporation of Will's perspective into Herzog's own. However decent a man personally, Will is essentially another of Herzog's "reality instructors," an embodiment of the "crushing weight of *mass*" that universally denies authentic selfhood in the modern world. Nevertheless, here as elsewhere in mock-heroic narrative, the heroic image is established in the very process of its reduction. Herzog's reference to himself as a "burlap Moses" "spluttering fire in the wilderness" suggests, of course, his great namesake; the present Moses, who may represent, in his frivolous and "arbitrary withdrawal of proud subjectivity," only the final stages of decadent aestheticism hints, nevertheless, at a more profound romanticism.

The ethical hero of Western culture and the romantic hero of power and imagination exist together without complete reconciliation in Bellow's fiction (indeed, they often cast an ironic light on each other), and, in the novels previously discussed, each takes on a special emphasis: Sammler, obviously representative of moral duty and civic responsibility; Henderson (in spite of his yearnings to take care of the sick like Dr. Grenfell), essentially the figure of expansive selfhood. Herzog is himself, to some extent, consciously aware that his full name—Moses Elkanah Herzog—contains elements of both prototypes: Moses the supreme leader and bringer of the Divine Word as law but also Moses as associated with the Wandering Jew; Elkanah, another God-possessed prophet; Herzog, the lonely explorer of high places (for example, Maurice Herzog, conqueror of Annapurna) and "duke" (see its meaning in German) to the "king" his father.[15] In his endless meditative wanderings through the rubble of Western culture, Herzog identifies the final manifestation of this collective hero with the Renaissance man of ideas. At a later date, the composite Renaissance figure splits into the narrower roles of philosopher (Herzog offers examples here ranging from Alexis de Toqueville to Adlai Stevenson) and romantic visionary—his crucial model, in this case, Emerson.

The historical function of such heroes is the traditional one, and it is the one Herzog explicitly selects for himself. As he puts it, "The progress of civilization—indeed, the survival of civilization—depended on the successes of Moses E. Herzog" (*H*, 125). He is equally clear about the spiritual end of the heroic quest: "The dream of man's heart . . . is that life may complete itself in significant pattern" (*H*, 303).

Herzog is his own Dahfu in obsessively (indeed, masochistically) reminding himself of the nature and specific attributes of the heroic role in its alternate versions. Most attractive to him because of his personal situation, his talent with words, and his sense of the direction of history are the possibilities of romanticism. Its historical significance at least is unquestioned; in one of his imaginary letters he writes "the editor of *Atlantic Civilization*": "*Romanticism guarded the 'inspired condition,' preserved the poetic, philosophical, and religious teachings, the teachings and records of transcendence and the most generous ideas of mankind, during the greatest and most rapid of transformations, the most accelerated phase of the modern scientific and technical transformation*" (*H*, 165). In his romanticism Herzog's intellectual mentor has been Emerson, his text those lines from *The American Scholar* that he first used as high school class orator: "*The main enterprise of the world, for splendor . . . is the upbuilding of a man. The private life of one man shall be a more illustrious monarchy . . . than any kingdom in history*" (*H*, 160).

The potential vulnerability of this position, however, is suggested to Herzog not only by the sterility and chaos of his own "private life" but by his commitment, at the same time, to the attributes of the ethical hero: justice, courage, temperance, mercy, duty, civility, brotherhood, as he variously identifies them—above all, "civil usefulness" (*H*, 161). "The real and essential question," he tells his friend Asphalter on one occasion, "is one of our employment by other human beings and their employment by us" (*H*, 272). The crucial issue of usefulness—the authentication of heroic virtue in action—is that which Bellow stressed in his *Paris Review* interview. "Herzog wants very much to have effective virtues," he observed. "But that's the source of comedy in the book."[16]

Herzog reminds us again of the mock-hero's characteristic role as "actor"—the figure whose "performances" within the walls of an enduring prison are a parody of authentic action in the context of actual freedom. The tendency of literary realism, Bellow points out in the same interview, has been to contrast its protagonists "with aristocratic greatness," a contrast that always "damages" them. He analyzes (as I have noted) the almost inevitable ambivalence that is a result of the realistic impulse: "The realistic tendency is to challenge the human significance of things. The more realistic you are the more you threaten the grounds of your own art. Realism has always both accepted and rejected the circumstances of ordinary life. It accepted the task of writing about ordinary life and tried to meet it in some extraordinary fashion." Concerning one fashion, he is clear enough: "In the end, the force of tradition carries realism into parody, satire, mock-epic—Leopold Bloom."[17] Bellow here suggests another significant reference in Herzog's name (Moses Herzog is a Jewish merchant in the Cyclops chapter of *Ulysses*) and the major novel in the background of his own book. In his meditative auditioning for various heroic roles, Herzog attempts to blend the prototypal attributes of both Stephen Dedalus and Leopold Bloom and, in doing so, sheds further light on their own constant auditioning.

It is, nevertheless, as parody of the Emersonian hero that Herzog achieves his central significance. Bellow, in effect, relentlessly exposes the tendency of *The American Scholar* to vacillate between bland assertions of the inevitable relation of heroic being to significant action ("The great man makes the great thing") and its readiness elsewhere to subordinate action to personal living. In Bellow's novel, the tenuous but potent paradoxes of high romanticism dissolve into dissonance under what Bellow calls the "challenge" of the realistic impulse. Herzog saves some of his sharpest mockery for the implications of his favorite role. To a navy psychiatrist who had in 1942 diagnosed him as "unusually immature" (after an episode at sea during which, as communications officer, he had failed at a crucial moment to "communicate"), Herzog, for example, writes:

> I am really in an unusually free condition of mind. "In paths untrodden," as Walt Whitman marvelously put it. "Escaped from the life that exhibits itself . . ." Oh, that's a plague, the life that exhibits itself, a real plague! There comes a time when every ridiculous son of Adam wishes to arise before the rest, with all his quirks and twitches and tics, all the glory of his self-adored ugliness, his grinning teeth, his sharp nose, his madly twisted reason, saying to the rest—in an overflow of narcissism which he interprets as benevolence—"I am here to witness. I am come to be your exemplar." Poor dizzy spook! [H, 323–24]

"Oneself is simply grotesque," he thinks on another occasion and notes down the obvious corrective: "*Subjective monstrosity must be overcome, must be corrected by community, by useful duty . . . private suffering transformed from masochism*" (H, 219). Another version of this critique is closer to the voice of the author: "A loving brute—a subtle, spoiled, loving man. Who can make use of him? He craves use. Where is he needed? Show him the way to make his sacrifice to truth, to order, peace" (H, 308).

In the most fundamental sense, then, Herzog's retreats to Vermont involve an unresolved paradox (the act of retreat and isolation annulling all its possible justifications) that constitutes the ironic crux of the novel. The first time, "set apart from daily labor for greater achievements" (*H*, 128), he had gone there to develop a grand intellectual scheme that would take modern culture beyond romantic stances, "showing how life could be lived by renewing universal connections; overturning the last of the Romantic errors about the uniqueness of the Self; revising the old Western, Faustian ideology; investigating the social meaning of Nothingness" (*H*, 39). On this occasion, the futile circularity implied by using a romantic stance as the vehicle for overcoming "Romantic errors" is reinforced by the hopelessness of the task to be undertaken, given the chaotic disorder of modern culture—what Herzog calls "the mire of post-Renaissance, post-humanistic, post-Cartesian dissolution, next door to the Void" (*H*, 93)—and given also the nature of the Void—"*the hollowness of God . . . the final multiplicity of facts . . . [the] ultimate distances*" (*H*, 325). His dream of a new intellectual synthesis is comparable to Humbert Humbert's hope of a Lolita "safely solipsized."[18]

Herzog's later return to Vermont allows him to sort through his personal and intellectual failures and achieve, apparently, a heightened intensity of being, but toward what new significance or end? Herzog raises the question but characteristically more as an expression of desire than of genuine puzzlement ("this intensity, doesn't it mean anything?" [*H*, 340]); in fact, he has not really moved beyond the romantic prison of expansive being where he essentially has been all along—"a dazzling acrobat of consciousness, a prestidigitator of his constantly burgeoning selves," as Earl Rovit has called him.[19] The structure of the novel involves no essential linear development, not even patterned cycle, but rather the uncertain rhythms of this performing self in the constant process of its own composition.[20] In other words, beyond the narrower symbolic association of Vermont with anachronism and beyond the fact that most of Herzog's personal and intellectual life there becomes a microcosm of an inner chaos that is itself "next door to the Void" (both dimensions of Vermont relevant enough, of course, to the larger issue), is Vermont finally as a primary metaphor of the mock-hero's perpetual distance from what Bellow calls "effective virtues"—the imposition of the authentic hero in some fashion on the very ground of reality.

Measured by all his more ambitious ends, the failed communications officer remains a paralytic failure; in the context of his creation, he could scarcely be otherwise. At the same time, however, Herzog remains a noble figure in his struggles to affirm value and link it with objective reality ("*Resisting the argument that scientific thought has put into disorder all considerations based on value. . . . Convinced that the extent of universal space does not destroy human value, and that the realm of facts and that of values are not eternally separated*" [*H*, 106]). He remains noble also in his unceasing, fierce desire to communicate; in his sheer ability to survive in the face of death forces as palpably felt (though, to be sure, less literal in their manifestations) as those experienced by Sammler; and, last but by no means least, in his courageous subversion of his own most treasured ideas and attitudes, a quality he, of course, shares with his creator.

With regard to this final point (later to become the central issue in *Humboldt's Gift*), the destructive element of irony, here as elsewhere in mock-heroic narrative, becomes, paradoxically, the special dimension that makes survival and affirmation possible at some level of the fiction. Herzog's complex perspective must be contrasted with the uncompromising romanticism of his childhood friend Nachman, who destroys himself in his quest for purity and whose major charge against Herzog is that he has "learned to accept a mixed condition of life" (*H*, 134). Herzog reminds himself pointedly that "you must aim the imagination also at yourself, point-blank" (*H*, 118) and repeatedly directs his brilliant wit against his roles, his ideas, and his aspirations, generating, in the process, most of the actual mock-heroic rhetoric in the book, including a devastating view of himself as noble hero in Vermont ("I, myself, in Ludeyville, as Squire Herzog. The Graf Pototsky of the Berkshires" [*H*, 76]). Herzog's mockery, like Bellow's, is not fundamentally satiric; it limits while refusing denial, a mockery that goes beyond cynicism, masochism, and self-hatred, while yet incorporating them as part of the reality to be acknowledged. "My balance comes from instability," notes Herzog (*H*, 330), with an insight crucial to his own story and to the mode to which it belongs.

At the same time, from his perspective as perpetual child, Nachman can identify in Herzog an important dimension of his quixotism. Although rejecting Herzog's "mixed condition," Nachman tells him, nevertheless, that he is "a good man . . . a good heart . . . like your mother . . . a gentle spirit" (*H*, 134). Another character describes Herzog even more pointedly as "a real, genuine old Jewish type that digs the emotions" (*H*, 84). In a passage I have already quoted, Bellow speaks of his protagonist as a "loving man," and Herzog himself notes his commitment to the "law of the heart" (*H*, 119) and his concomitant emotional "archaism" ("*Belongs to the agricultural or pastoral stages*" [*H*, 265]). This last description, in particular, reminds us that Herzog's acts of love are, for the most part, acts of memory and imagination. As emotional counterparts to his ideas, they reinforce both his heroic presence as a value-laden figure—his role within the context of what Nabokov calls "perceptual time," the subjective time of the performing self—and his comic impotence beyond this context.

The emotional center of the novel is fixed much less in Herzog's present conflicts than in his crowding memories of a lost and apparently irrelevant childhood ("My ancient times. Remoter than Egypt" [*H*, 140]), memories that reenact the emotional power of his mother (he speaks of his "mother-bound" and "nostalgic" soul [H, 114]) and the even more remote but still compelling claims of his father. The latter, "a sacred being, a king" (H, 147) to his children, wears the tattered remnants of his gentleman's clothing and maintains a "high style" through repeated business failures. His exile presages the more complex alienation of his son. His inauthenticity in Canada mirrors both the certain inauthenticity of his own Russian-Jewish origins ("In Russia, Father Herzog had been a gentleman. With forged papers of the First Guild. But many gentlemen lived on forged papers" [H, 136]) and the elaborate pretensions of the younger Herzog, who would reaffirm kingship on a far more sweeping and categorical basis. As Joyce reminds us in *Finnegans Wake*, the mock-hero always, in one way or another, carries forged papers.

In any case, Herzog's deepest feelings have their origins on Napoleon Street, his childhood neighborhood in Montreal, and it remains their primary source, a place where value and reality seem to have achieved the potent and active coalescence impossible to find again in later life. Herzog remembers this coalescence: "Napoleon Street, rotten, toylike, crazy and filthy, riddled, flogged with harsh weather—the bootlegger's boys reciting ancient prayers. To this Moses' heart was attached with great power. Here was a wider range of human feelings than he had ever again been able to find. The children of the race, by a never-failing miracle, opened their eyes on one strange world after another, age after age, and uttered the same prayer in each, eagerly loving what they found. What was wrong with Napoleon Street? thought Herzog. All he ever wanted was there" (H, 140). Herzog's nostalgic stance, which, we must keep in mind, he intellectually disavows ("He fought the insidious blight of nostalgia in New York—softening, heartrotting emotions" [H, 141]), reflects not only Bellow's sense of the Jew as anachronism in the contemporary world ("Young Jews," thinks Herzog, "brought up on moral principles as Victorian ladies were on pianoforte and needlepoint" [H, 231]), but a more general Wordsworthian commitment to childhood per se as locus of some prior moral and spiritual order that can only be lost by the adult and that becomes Herzog's hopeless task to redeem.[21]

The Jew as "immigrant," in other words, constitutes only the most blatant example of what is, in effect, general adult loss. Charles Citrine in *Humboldt's Gift* invokes generic origins when he thinks of himself and Von Humboldt Fleisher as "banished souls . . . longing for their home-world" (HG, 125). Fleisher, the pure romantic, expresses this idea even more pointedly. According to Citrine, "One of Humboldt's themes was the perennial human feeling that there was an original world, a home-world, which was lost. Sometimes he spoke of Poetry as the merciful Ellis Island where a host of aliens began their naturalization and of this planet as a thrilling but insufficiently humanized imitation of the home-world. He spoke of our species as castaways" (*HG*, 24). Herzog is a "castaway" in Vermont and, in any fundamental sense, will remain so. His heroic childhood takes its place as another significant dimension of what is essentially a long and passionately sustained act of imagination.

At the same time, Bellow's ironic "containment" of nostalgia goes beyond occasional passages of explicit criticism and his use of the Vermont setting. In the present or objective time of the novel, the portrayal of parenting and childhood steadily mocks its imaginative invocation. This portrayal goes beyond the comic ineptitude that characterizes Herzog's relationship with his own child. The child beaten to death whose story Herzog hears about in magistrate's court suggests a more categorical human nullity that renders all human feelings impotent. At least this is the situation in which Herzog, here as elsewhere, finds himself. Bellow puts the problem succinctly: Herzog, he writes, "experienced nothing but his own *human feelings,* in which he found nothing of use" (*H*, 240). The vision of human beings "lying down to copulate, and standing up to kill" (*H*, 240) lingers at the realistic center of the novel and reminds us again of Bellow's comment that realism's tendency "is to challenge the human significance of things"—challenging, in this case, the very moral grounds of his own art.

Like other mock-heroic writers, Bellow sustains the challenge by incorporating it as a major voice in his fiction. Early in the novel Herzog remembers the time when his mother had cleaned his cheek with her saliva-covered handkerchief and then thinks: "These things either matter or they do not matter. It depends upon the universe, what it is" (*H*, 33). The novel as a whole, however, rejects any such simple "either/or" solution (to change Herzog's terms: the novel suggests that things both matter *and* do not matter) and steadily resists what seems increasingly to be the negative judgment of the universe, not to mention the weight of historical evidence. Certainly resistance, effort, desire, and survival characterize both the protagonist and his creator—the latter surviving, as I have already implied, in and through the creation of an ironic narrative that incorporates the fundamental challenge of realism to art. This is the issue that Nabokov deals with explicitly in the content and structure of *The Gift* and that Bellow will himself self-consciously explore in his novel dealing with possible artistic "gifts." Herzog, in turn, in his own passionate but inadequate way ("obstinately, defiantly, blindly, but without sufficient courage or intelligence" [*H*, 93]), never ceases trying to be *"marvelous* Herzog," Herzog the authentic hero. He remains committed to "the dream of man's heart . . . that life may complete itself in significant pattern" (*H*, 303), and he is, as he says, "stirred fiercely by a desire to communicate, or by the curious project of attempted communication" (*H*, 162).

What the novel on the whole records, let me reiterate, are his failed attempts. Herzog's letters strike polemical attitudes (he is, as he says, "a gesture-maker" [*H*, 234]) and constitute, in effect, a disjointed series of polemical performances; his overall meditations resemble those of Stephen Dedalus, which I have previously described as a collage of mutually mocked and mocking games. But these failures, Herzog insists, must be evaluated in the context of alternatives even more meager in moral and spiritual substance and in the context also of what he calls the "intensity" of commitment. Such intensity, he argues, becomes a substitute for meaning: "He [man] does not need meaning as long as such intensity has scope. Because then it is self-evident; it *is* meaning" (*H*, 289). Speaking through his protagonist, Bellow makes explicit what we have already observed in other writers considered: that the central strategy of mock-heroic narrative is to shift the question of value from nonexistent ends to the quality of means. Authentic consummations are impossible. The hero of Western culture in his latest avatar as "communications officer" is mocked not only by the messages he cannot or does not send for reasons of personal inadequacy and the deafness of potential auditors, but, even more categorically, by the nature of language in its precarious relation to reality. Herzog's objectivity includes his awareness of the reflexivity of his major weapon. "Still, what can thoughtful persons and humanists do but struggle toward suitable words?" he asks his friend Luke Asphalter, and adds: "Take me, for instance. I've been writing letters helter-skelter in all directions. More words. I go after reality with language. Perhaps I'd like to change it all into language . . . I put my whole heart into these constructions. But they are constructions" (*H*, 272). The "struggle toward suitable words," in short, ends finally in language constructions that authenticate simply their own internal coherency—their own identity as constructions.

What remains real enough, however, is the effort and intensity of the struggle and, above all, the courage, skill, and tenacity of the mock-hero as "survivor." The act of living becomes principally the continued "act" of asserting form and value, with death the voice finally muted in an already death-ridden world. Bellow's later protagonists are escape artists, and they admire other escape artists such as Willie Sutton and Houdini. Herzog is the Western hero reduced to the role of comic survivor but no less committed to his traditional functions because of such a reduction. As usual, his meditation is to the point: "*Survival!* he noted. *Till we figure out what's what. Till the chance comes to exert a positive influence.* (Personal responsibility for history, a trait of Western culture, rooted in the Testaments, Old and New, the idea of the continual improvement of human life on this earth. What else explained Herzog's ridiculous intensity?) *Lord, I ran to fight in Thy holy cause, but kept tripping, never reached the scene of the struggle"* (H, 128). Even this highly qualified note Herzog characteristically "sees through." Waiting for a "chance" may be either a rationalization for inadequacy or an expression of undue hope. Reality includes failure, but it finally limits survival as well. Herzog also identifies with Robert Falcon Scott (*H*, 314), who first is beaten to the Pole by Amundsen and then does not escape the rigors of the Antarctic. Nevertheless, like the other madmen I have discussed, Herzog remains, in Bellow's words, "a frail hopeful lunatic" (*H*, 106), committed to the continuity of life in the face of natural mortality, the modern mass culture of boredom and genocide, and the hollowness of God. Herzog's second problem in his meditation on Quixote—what could he possibly *do* with the role in the post-Copernican world (assuming he had found appropriate models to imitate)—is, in effect, answered by Bellow through his profound insight into the nature of mock-heroic narrative and its significance to contemporary culture.

Sleepers Awake: The Gift of Mock-Heroic

Humboldt's Gift is essentially another meditation on the couch like *Herzog*, and in dealing with the earlier novel, I have already commented on many elements of the later book. As critics have frequently pointed out, Charles Citrine has a strong family resemblance to Bellow's other scholar-monologuist; Von Humboldt Fleisher, in turn, is an extended portrait of the "pure" romantic (the Nachman type: "I keep my heart with William Blake and Rilke" [*H*, 133]) who refuses, in this case until shortly before the end of his life, the comic perspective that might, paradoxically, have preserved his romantic quest in some fashion. If anything, the issues in the later book are even more sharply drawn.

Citrine accepts as a given that the modern world is filled with "barren idols . . . a world of categories devoid of spirit wait[ing] for life to return" (*HG*, 17); that modern poetry lacks the "sane and steady idealization" possible to Homer or Dante (*HG*, 11); that the modern novel lacks comprehensiveness (*HG*, 73); that the imagination of the American artist "deadens its delicacy in vulgarity and in things attainable" (*HG*, 341); that, finally, the widespread malaise of boredom and passivity is symptomatic of our contemporary awareness of the hopeless gap between "pure expectation" and reality (*HG*, 199). Bellow again involves his protagonist in frantic entanglements with various women, his handy device (as Citrine makes explicit) for keeping them "in touch with the facts of life" (*HG*, 270). The banal world of *Humboldt's Gift* even contains its peculiar "demon" or "agent of distraction" in Cantabile, the petty gangster and confidence man from Chicago; here, too, Citrine provides us with what amounts to an allegorical gloss on this curiously intrusive double: "His job was to make noise and to deflect and misdirect and send me floundering into bogs" (*HG*, 180).

Moreover, Citrine's fascination with Rudolf Steiner's "pure consciousness" (*HG*, 281), the soul free at last "from the weight of death that everybody carries upon the heart" (*HG*, 442), is simply a futuristic version of Herzog and Von Humboldt Fleisher's romantic, Platonic yearning for a past home world and the pure spirit of childhood. Reduced first to improvisation and "a swarm, a huge volume of notions" (*HG*, 21), then violent paranoia and death, Fleisher exemplifies the fate of categorical romanticism in an environment that has rendered it obsolescent. As Citrine puts it: "Orpheus moved stones and trees. But a poet can't perform a hysterectomy or send a vehicle out of the solar system. Miracle and power no longer belong to him" (*HG*, 118). The American literary reference is probably clear enough here, but Bellow reinforces it on the occasion of this meditation with a reference to the weather: "The sun still shone beautifully enough, the blue was wintry, of Emersonian haughtiness" (*HG*, 119).

In the face of all such potential for passivity, madness, and despair, Citrine, like Herzog, nevertheless, retains his ethical commitments, but in the context of a comic sensibility (his own and that of Bellow) that everywhere keeps such commitments within a secure ironic frame made up of insistent self-mockery, the steady mockery of other characters, and life's wayward circumstances. One scene may be taken as representative. Late in the novel, flying toward Spain, where he hopes to meet up with Renata, "enjoy a quiet month," and "begin to set myself straight," Citrine meditates on the future:

> Actuarially speaking, I had only a decade left to make up for a life-span largely misspent. There was not time to waste even on remorse and penitence. I felt also that Humboldt, out there in death, stood in need of my help. The dead and the living still formed one community. This planet was still the base of operations. There was Humboldt's bungled life, and my bungled life, and it was up to me to do something, to give a last favorable turn to the wheel, to transmit moral understanding from the earth where you can get it to the next existence where you needed it. Of course I had my other dead. It wasn't Humboldt alone. I also had a substantial suspicion of lunacy. But why should my receptivity fall under such suspicion? On the contrary, etcetera. I concluded, We'll see what we shall see. We flew through unshadowed heights, and in the pure upper light I saw that the beautiful brown booze in my glass contained many crystalline corpuscles and thermal lines of heat-generating cold fluid. This was how I entertained myself and passed the time. [*HG*, 405–6]

As well as any, this passage defines the nature of Citrine's commitments. At the same time, however, the language moves from the solemn enunciation of moral imperatives straight toward anticlimax—toward self-conscious awareness of itself as stock-in-trade rhetorical performance, as mere "entertainment"—and so does Citrine on the 747. At Madrid airport his bag ("with its elegant wardrobe, its Hermès neckties, its old chaser's monkey-jackets" [*HG*, 406]) is last off the conveyor and prefigures Citrine's own lonely abandonment; instead of Renata at the Ritz, he ends up taking care of her neglected child in a pension.

Citrine's brother Ulick knows him well ("I'd bet you fifty to one you're ass-deep in crank theory this minute. You couldn't live without it" [*HG*, 388]) and reminds him of the crucial necessity of mockery. Senator Everett Dirksen, Ulick points out, "wrote poems for greeting cards" and "had a literary period, too," but "he at least kidded his own hokum" (*HG*, 388). Seldom has the mock-heroic imagination defined its options with more brutal clarity. Citrine, by and large, does kid his hokum constantly, never more so than in his steady acceptance of the role of "Shoveleer"—the pun on his French title of "Chevalier" ("It served the French right, too. This was not one of their best centuries" [*HG*, 283]) suggesting both heroic aims and the endless verbiage that constitutes largely the sum of practical results. If Fleisher is the "Mozart of conversation," the sublime verbal performer ("his monologue was an oratorio in which he sang and played all parts" [*HG*, 13–14]), Citrine is at least its Beethoven. "Citrine the lecturer" is another self-bestowed epithet (*HG*, 188). "Would you talk to me the way you talk to one of your intelligent friends—better yet, the way you talk to yourself? Did you have an important thought yesterday, for instance?" asks an old girl friend, meeting Citrine much later in life and remembering what was already an adolescent propensity (*HG*, 305).

The fact remains that, here as elsewhere, the mock hero continues to pursue his visionary quest within the narrow and unsatisfactory options of his contemporary culture. Referring to his award from the French government, Citrine notes that "the only real distinction of this dangerous moment in human history has nothing to do with medals and ribbons. Not to fall asleep is distinguished" (*HG*, 283). Sleep for Citrine is synonymous with his culture's many modes of death; more even than Herzog, he identifies with Houdini, "the great Jewish escape artist," who "defied all forms of restraint and confinement, including the grave. He broke out of everything. They buried him and he escaped" (*HG*, 435). Sammler has only enacted literally what Bellow's later protagonists rehearse in symbolic terms.

Citrine at least escapes the stasis of boredom, the sterile self-destructiveness of Fleisher, and the pomposities of his "straight" double and fellow editor, Thaxter, who (as Citrine describes him with an irony that constitutes the very mode of escape) "has a terrible weakness for making major statements" (*HG*, 481). "In Chicago," Citrine notes elsewhere, "you became a connoisseur of the near-nothing" (*HG,* 24)—a comment hinting at both the context and continuing possibility of mock-heroic action. Regardless of achievable secular ends or final metaphysical justification (which, of course, continue to be yearned for nostalgically), spiritual discriminations of a sort—at least those between life and death—are still of crucial importance. This is the central point on which the mock-heroic writer (and very often his protagonist) insists. This is the point that Citrine makes late in the novel after he fully realizes that Renata has abandoned him to marry an undertaker: "Oh, that stupid Renata, didn't she know the difference between a corpse-man and a would-be seer?" (*HG,* 442). Fleisher also, according to Citrine, before his death makes "a Houdini escape from the hardened projections of paranoia, or manic depression, or whatever it was. Sleepers do awaken" (*HG,* 373). Here again the vehicle of escape is the return of ironic humor, and it is this same humor that from beyond the grave bestows its final gift on Charles Citrine in the form of an aesthetic model.

With this model we come upon what, in comparison with Bellow's earlier fiction, is new in *Humboldt's Gift* or at least achieves strong new emphasis: its explicit concern with the mock-heroic mode as an aesthetic—the same "gift" that Nabokov had so self-consciously explored in his novel of that name. Although the essential ethical and spiritual concerns of the mock-hero remain, as I have already demonstrated, Bellow shifts the focus in *Humboldt's Gift* to the mock-hero as artist and the rationale and form of a mock-heroic art. The role of the "would-be seer" continues as an alternative to death; the nature of such a seer's art comes in for special attention.

The comment on Dirksen, of course, has already given us a clue as to the necessary attitude of the contemporary artist; it does not, however, suggest the form his art must take. On this latter question, Fleisher's gift of a movie scenario is explicit. In the scenario a writer named Corcoran (modeled, Fleisher notes pointedly, on Citrine) has a brief, idyllic affair in a pastoral paradise, "still quite pure in its beauty," where "life is renewed. Dross and impurities evaporate." He makes a book of "potency and beauty" from the experience but cannot publish it because of his entanglements with a disagreeable wife ("this bitch-affliction") in his other "real" life. Corcoran is thus squarely caught between the claims of a lyric-pastoral art directly expressive of powerful and authentic spiritual experience and the claims of reality until his agent (to be played, says Fleisher, by Zero Mostel) suggests that he exactly reproduce the trip accompanied by his wife, this time with Corcoran reduced to playing the "role" of lover and the agent going on ahead "staging each event." Out of this parody version of the original experience Corcoran does indeed write and publish a successful book, although the compromise still "solves" nothing in his personal life and even exacerbates the previous situation by alienating now both the wife and the original heroine. Fleisher attempts to invoke the meaning of his own parable:

> Thus Corcoran repeats with Hepzibah the journey he made with Laverne. Oh what a difference! All now is parody, desecration, wicked laughter. Which must be suffered. To the high types of Martyrdom the twentieth century has added the farcical martyr. This you see is the artist. By wishing to play a great role in the fate of mankind he becomes a bum and a joke. A double punishment is inflicted on him as the would-be representative of meaning and beauty. When the artist-agonist has learned to be sunk and shipwrecked, to embrace defeat and assert nothing, to subdue his will and accept his assignment to the hell of modern truth perhaps his Orphic powers will be restored, the stones will dance again when he plays. Then heaven and earth will be reunited. After long divorce. With what joy on both sides, Charlie! What joy!
>
> But this has no place in our picture. [HG, 343–46]

In his hopeless attempt to mediate between incompatible worlds, the contemporary artist is reduced to "parody, desecration, wicked laughter." I say "reduced" because the spirit of parody and parodic forms remains for Bellow what they were in *Mr. Sammler's Planet:* more a tragic necessity than attractive in themselves or positively to be desired if the contemporary artist still retained a wide range of authentic options. This point is perhaps always implicit in Cervantine mock-heroic; Bellow's reluctance to accept parodic transformation gives it a particular emphasis and poignancy. Fleisher, his spokesman on the occasion of the Corcoran scenario, is heavily aware of pain and loss; "the farcical martyr" suffers the agony of what Fleisher in another passage calls the comedy of "low seriousness which has succeeded the high seriousness of the Victorians" (HG, 344). However resigned Fleisher may be to the modern condition with the return of his sense of humor, however sharply he can now define the artist's role and medium, he never ceases to dream of redemption—the compelling illusion which, nevertheless, "has no place in our picture," the significant "perhaps" in the passage above, which, alone or in equivalent forms, helps to generate the special ambivalence of the mock-heroic sensibility. In the name of Blake, he admonishes Citrine not to allow "the caricatures to get out of hand," reminds him that "we are not natural beings but supernatural beings," and, finally, views Citrine from the context of a limited secular world already transcended. As Fleisher puts it: "I have a leg already over the last stile and I look back and see you far back laboring still in the fields of ridicule" (HG, 347). To emphasize the agony of "assignment to the hell of modern truth" and the continuing nostalgia for transcendental escape, however, is to oversimplify the full meaning and significance of this episode. Fleisher, at the very least, finds a certain satisfaction in the actual process of creating his scenario. "The fitting together of the parts," he notes, "gave me the pleasure of a good intricacy. The therapy of delight" (*HG*, 342).

Fleisher has, in addition, been involved in a second scenario, this one written with Citrine while both were teaching at Princeton and later, unknown to both, made into the film *Caldofreddo*. Citrine catches up with it finally in Paris and realizes that the producers have successfully exploited the insights of the original script. These insights, in turn, amount to a further commentary by Bellow on the necessary form of contemporary art. If the first scenario deals with the desperate expedients of the writer and features Citrine in the guise of Corcoran, the second reenacts heroic tragedy (Bellow mentions explicitly *Oedipus at Colonus*) as comedy and stars an actor in the role of Caldofreddo who "strongly resembled Humboldt" (*HG*, 462). The film portrays first the farcical heroics of Amundsen and Umberto Nobile ("played by excellent comedians, highly stylized" [*HG*, 461]) in their competition to fly over the North Pole; then the terrible crashes of both men at different times in Arctic waters (of Amundsen's accident, Citrine notes: "I was shocked to see how effective the comic interpretation of this disaster was " [*HG*, 461]); finally, and most important, the complex fate of Caldofreddo, reduced to cannibalism (as a crewman of Nobile) while awaiting rescue on the ice floes and later, in response to his sin, alternating between raging despair and his benign role in a "little town in Sicily where no one knew his sin, where he was just a jolly old man who peddled ice cream and played in the village band." Citrine comments specifically on the significance of Caldofreddo's Sicilian period: "I felt that there was something important about the contrast between his little arpeggios and the terrible modern complexity of his position. Lucky the man who has nothing more to say or play than these easy melodies. Are there still such people around? It was disconcerting also to see, as Otway [the actor in the role of Caldofreddo] was puffing at the trumpet, a face so much like Humboldt's" (*HG*, 461–63).

Citrine's observation and the film in general suggests two different human—and, by inference, literary—responses to the "terrible modern complexity" embodied in the story of Caldofreddo: one obviously involves Caldofreddo's and Fleisher's own sterile and destructive alternations between despairing madness and the "little arpeggios" of a simple affirmative art rooted too much in omission and denial; the other, a duality more integrative, more akin to the complexity it must deal with, more able to embrace radical incompatibility within some large perspective or literary form. Caldofreddo and Von Humboldt Fleisher, in effect, must learn the significance of their own punning names: hot and cold as one irreducible entity; the heroic voyager and explorer in the avatar of comic Jew.

Certainly these names and his obviously parabolic scenarios suggest where Bellow has come out in his own art. Late in the novel Citrine asks Fleisher's widow if he can get a job in a historical film she is working on—appropriately titled *Memoirs of a Cavalier*—as an extra wearing "boots and bloomers . . . a casque, or a hat with plumes." She demurs, suggesting that such an occupation would be "too distracting mentally" in the light of the great work he has to do, but Citrine replies that "if these things I have to do can't find their way around those mountains of absurdity there's no hope for them" (*HG*, 478). His comment makes clear the necessary context of his own mock-heroic quest and that of his creator.

Citrine's comment suggests also Bellow's insight into the nature of mock-heroic narrative and his strong endorsement of its formal acknowledgment and incorporation of reality as the visionary writer's only remaining viable stance. For much of *Humboldt's Gift*, Fleisher becomes the American romantic as tragic Quixote, hopelessly, despairingly, destructively committed to "high dreaming states" even though such "enchantments" always fail him or wear thin. As Citrine puts it: "He could never come up with enough enchantment or dream material to sheathe himself in. It would not cover" (*HG*, 240). Fleisher "wakes up" finally to an awareness of the duality that has, in effect, been inherent in him all along; "below, shuffling comedy," notes Citrine, describing him physically, "above, princeliness and dignity, a certain nutty charm" (*HG*, 11). Citrine's sensibility incorporates Sancho Panza from the beginning, and he is surrounded by other figures such as Renata who relentlessly reinforce that perspective. Bellow embraces them all, his later work collectively finding in irony (however suspect, however itself a symptomatic product of the "moronic infernos" [*HG*, 45] of the present) a "sheathe" more substantial than enchantments within which the modern romantic imagination may seek some sort of covering. "I always had a text to the contrary," Citrine observes at one point (*HG*, 438); Bellow's protagonists tirelessly improvise their visionary desires as much as anything on the sustaining basis of such contrary texts. The heroic goal of desire, however, remains constant: nothing less than "raising the dead" (including their own "dead" selves) or, as writers, completing Whitman's task of writing for democracy "its great poems of death" (*HG*, 376).

In Bellow's work, the self's improvisatory meditations seldom go beyond acts of memory, imagination, and language, but these characteristic mock-heroic "acts" are themselves life-affirming or, to be more precise, affirmations of the adventures of a "found" self in the style of a modern "intellectual comedy" appropriate to the form such adventures must now take. Citrine makes clear that Humboldt's gift is more dimensional than even the scenarios might suggest and, most important, that it complements Citrine's own gift to himself. Explaining the "different kind of imaginative projection" he hopes to create, he points out: "I conceived of it while still a youngish man. It was actually Humboldt who lent me the book of Valéry that suggested it. Valéry wrote of Leonardo, 'Cet Apollon me ravissait au plus haut degré de moi-meme.' I too was ravished with permanent effect—perhaps carried beyond my mental means. But Valéry had added a note in the margin: 'Trouve avant dechercher.' This finding before seeking was my special gift. If I had any gift" (HG, 73). Citrine, to be sure, never abandons the more ambitious dream of linking the "highest degree" of selfhood with some external counterpart. Ideally, his "great poem of death" would literally traverse the same ground as Emerson and Whitman. He can vividly articulate such a dream during moments of what he aptly calls "outer-space feeling":

> I had the strange hunch that nature itself was not *out there*, an object world eternally separated from subjects, but that everything external corresponded vividly with something internal, that the two realms were identical and interchangeable, and that nature was my own unconscious being. Which I could come to know through intellectual work, scientific study, and intimate contemplation. Each thing in nature was an emblem for something in my own soul. At this moment in the Plaza, I took a rapid reading on my position. I had a slightly outer-space feeling. The frame of reference was tenuous and shuddering all around me. So it was necessary to be firm and to put metaphysics and the conduct of life together in some practical way. [HG, 356–57]

For Citrine in particular, however, and in Bellow's novels generally the supreme hope of uniting metaphysics, the conduct of life, and practical reality remains unfulfilled. But Citrine is representative also in that his Emersonian stance survives its comic pratfalls and, in so doing, perhaps achieves a precarious spiritual authority of its own. At least his old girl friend Naomi thinks so. "Well, you are a crackpot," she tells him bluntly, "but you do have a real soul" (HG, 307).

The Limits of Mock-Heroic

Others live for the lie of love;
Echo lives for her lovely lies, loves
for their livening.

JOHN BARTH
"Echo," in *Lost in the Funhouse*

Banalities and Metafictions

Since the mock-heroic mode is so often critically confused with its near relatives, a few final discriminations are in order. The primary source of this
confusion is common lineage, namely, the continuing, varied, and complex
influence of *Don Quixote* on later narrative. In *Moby-Dick*, for example, the
realistic Ishmael may on occasion mock the particular vision of the absolute
entertained by Ahab, but both he and Melville never question the essentially
heroic environment of the sea journey. The result is clearly romantic tragedy.
At the other extreme, the author may be essentially disinterested in the values of heroic commitment—as with Laurence Sterne or John Barth it may not
be his real subject—or mockery overwhelms heroics to the point that even
heroic games are denied value and possibility because the characters lack the
"energies of the self" or the noble sensibility necessary to play them well and
because, most often, the illusions behind the games are enervated, sentimental, and corrupting, themselves an expression of the banality they would sub-
vert. The result in this case is a form of ironic narrative limited in its positive
human claims and saturated with a sense of banal, inert, yet fluxional
materiality.

Here the most significant figure is Flaubert. Victor Brombert has noted that
"the characteristic weather in Flaubert's Paris is a steady drizzle and a de-
pressing fog. At times rain becomes torrential: streets are transformed into
waterways. But most often an almost anesthetizing fog seems to settle."[1] We
are far removed from the more promising and invigorating climate of mock-
heroic, even though of all the writers of his century Flaubert is probably the

one most immediately identified with the Cervantine tradition. Like most, he read and loved *Don Quixote* in his youth; like most, he was caught squarely between the waning claims of romanticism (the cult of childhood; the heroic selfhood of imagination and feeling) and new realistic attitudes—the contemporary dilemma that made Cervantes's novel so relevant and compelling. His entire life and literary career, as Harry Levin and others have pointed out, is a prototype of the new realism in dialogue with romanticism. *Madame Bovary*, moreover, is the most notorious of the several "female Quixotes" in the literature of the age, and *bovarysme* has become a coinage for the psychology of illusional role-playing.[2] This is not to mention Flaubert's brilliant exploitation of those technical devices such as parody and dramatic and rhetorical juxtaposition so central to the mock-heroic mode.

Yet regardless of all the obvious and important relationships between Flaubert's life and work and the Cervantine tradition, *Madame Bovary* and *The Sentimental Education* (not to mention *Bouvard and Pécuchet*) explore a darker vein of nihilism and despair than anywhere suggested in the world of mock-heroic, with its still vital sense of adventure and its persistent, strong, genuine dualities of point of view (or even larger multiplication of perspectives), indicative of ambivalent but value-laden authorial commitments.

Flaubert's mature work is a true fiction of worldly disillusionment, with the author outside of and beyond rather than still ambivalently involved in the illusions of his protagonists. Eric Gans, in his important book on Flaubert's early literary development, has argued that the process of evolution is in the direction of disengagement from these illusions—from participation in the illusions and disillusionment of his protagonist to a sense of the inferiority of this same romantic protagonist to his already disillusioned self, who, as a writer, is and can always remain outside society. In art and in the role of artist Flaubert finds a creative alienation and an adequate and geniune ideal order "outside" the banal world entirely. The artist, then, is the only possible romantic hero, and he is fully authentic, not mock. Flaubert becomes his own authentic hero by discovering the power of style to transform mundane into ideal and thus create an adequate medium for the heroic instincts of the self: the barber's basin really is transformed into Malbrino's helmet. According to Flaubert, "From the standpoint of pure Art one might almost establish the axiom that there is no such thing as subject, style in itself being an absolute manner of seeing things." With duality resolved into monism, art takes on the aspect of truly heroic adventure. It requires faith and freedom, says Flaubert, but it returns in kind what it demands: the hero is on a real journey to a real Grail.[3]

The experience of Flaubert's protagonists, however, is very different. As Gans puts it: "Because, like Flaubert, Emma and Frédéric are Romantics, they are driven to refuse the narrowness of any place in the bourgeois world; yet because, unlike him, they have been condemned to live in this world, the solutions they choose all prove to be valueless at their very core."4 In other words, even mock-heroic is denied them because Flaubert has resolved for himself the incompatible perspectives and the open irony on which the mode is based. The extreme tension between vital illusion and reality is relaxed or collapses completely, and the irony modulates only between delusion and reality, both, on the whole, treated in negative terms. There is a quality of distancing in Flaubert that is missing in writers who fully embrace the mock-heroic mode. They are self-conscious of themselves as artists also, but the awareness gives them only a certain objectivity without freeing them from a sense of the absurdity of all engagement, even the engagement of art. Likewise, they are willing to acknowledge in the creative role-playing of their protagonists some of the dimensions of true art.

Madame Bovary is, to be sure, an artist of sorts; she has qualities of imagination and sensibility beyond the capacity of the rest of her community and inevitably leading to alienation. But hers is the corrupt and corrupting art of concocting a fantasy life modeled on forms debased and banal in themselves and so remote from her own reality as to involve not the heroic (or mock-heroic) realization of self (the attempt, at least, to make the real world, whether or not finally opaque, malleable to the force of heroic energy), but systematic escape from selfhood. In a passage later suppressed as perhaps too abstract and explicit, Flaubert describes her characteristic response to the disappointment of actual events, in this case her marriage. "Like a poet who combines," he says, "she tried to discover in her head those adventures which had not happened, that life which wasn't hers, that husband whom she didn't know."5 Significantly, her attitude here is not even a noble response to banality; rather, it is a banal reaction to the genuine if inarticulate and clumsy passion of her husband. As Flaubert notes in connection with this episode, she was "incapable . . . of understanding what she did not experience or of believing anything that did not take on a conventional form" (MB, 31). By the same token, presented with conventional form, she is, naturally, unaware that it is totally lacking in value.

As a result, the tension between illusions (in mock-heroic the source, however "mad," of value) and fact is too attenuated to sustain the ambivalence so crucial to mock-heroic. Madame Bovary is not a figure of tragicomic absurdity whose illusions, even if ridiculous in fact, are life-sustaining or at least represent the noblest aspirations of the human spirit. Instead, she appears in the course of the novel as largely the exaggerated embodiment of widely shared illusionist tendencies, essentially a representative figure identified increasingly with destruction, disease, and finally the death that overwhelms her so graphically in the end.[6]

Frédéric Moreau in *The Sentimental Education* has a finer sensibility than Madame Bovary, but in him the loss of heroic energy is even more complete, the sense of entrapment no less inexorable. His illusions have a certain moral substance insofar as they are associated with the general hopes and dreams of youth (he is a generic character, as the title makes clear) and, in particular, insofar as they are focused around Madame Arnoux, who is, literally and symbolically, a figure of genuine spiritual value. Nevertheless, his lassitude and passivity—the relative ease and certainty with which banality triumphs over hope—destroys most of the tension and vitality characteristic of the mock-heroic mode. Life for Frédéric is not so much anticlimactic as it is without serious movement toward climax; his imprisonment is and remains categorical. Flaubert's early description of him in a posture of frustrated longing for Madame Arnoux will hold throughout the book: "Incapable of action, cursing God, and accusing himself of cowardice, he turned restlessly about in his desire, like a prisoner in his dungeon."[7] "Looking at this woman," says Flaubert, "had an enervating effect on him, like a scent that is too strong" (*SE*, 78). Even his romantic fantasies involving Madame Arnoux are enervated ("They travelled together on the backs of dromedaries, under the awnings of elephants, in the calm of a yacht among blue archipelagoes, etc." [*SE*, 78]). To be sure, at their final retrospective meeting, there is something of the Stendhalian "game" whereby the ideal dimension is established and preserved by artificial constraints (to lower the barriers would be to make it "real"). But the game now can be played (if this word is any longer appropriate) only by total passivity and seems, in fact, much closer to the thin mask worn by despair. What Flaubert stresses is not quixotic action but incapacity for action because of sterile fastidiousness, emotional blockage, and timidity of spirit—behavior from weakness rather than strength.

In Flaubert's world the gap between real and ideal is too large even to be linked by mediation. Disjunction is no longer conceivable in a situation in which the different dimensions of experience scarcely touch. The dreams of Frédéric have raised Madame Arnoux "to a position outside the human condition" (*SE*, 174). She is, significantly, more a maternal than a sexual figure, echoing faintly and at once both the Virgin "Marie" and the lost mother of a lost nostalgic child. There is nothing in her of the worldly force that Cervantes ironically ascribed to Dulcinea, Stendhal to Clelia, or even Nabokov to Lolita. Instead, she breeds paralysis of the will, and the world is completely given over to prostitutes and various forms of prostitution.[8]

What force there is in the novel operates only as a debased and totally corrupt parody of heroic energy. The figure of Delmar, popular actor and onetime lover of Frédéric's mistress Rosanette (the profane double of Madame Arnoux), may be taken as representative. According to Flaubert,

> a play in which he had taken the part of a peasant who sermonizes Louis XVI and prophesies 1789 had made him so famous that the same part was constantly being reproduced for him; and his occupation now consisted in insulting the monarchs of every country under the sun. . . . Street urchins waited at the stage-door to see him; and his biography, which was on sale in the intervals, depicted him as caring for his aged mother, reading the Bible, and helping the poor, in fact as a combination of St. Vincent de Paul, Brutus, and Mirabeau. People spoke of "our Delmar." He had a mission: he was turning into a Messiah. [SE, 177–78]

The image of heroic role-playing, of creating a "theatre of the self" so important to mock-heroic, is reduced by Flaubert to the fraudulent and mechanical rhetoric of commercial performance. Or, even more darkly, he views it as a kind of *danse macabre* on the charnelhouse floor—a performance of which Rosanette's all-night costume party is, in this case, the appropriate model. At the height of the revels, Frédéric notices one figure (dressed as "the Sphinx"—here with a clear message) coughing blood into a napkin and suggests that she go home and take care of herself. She refuses ("Oh, what's the use? If it wasn't this, it would be something else. Life isn't much fun."), and Frédéric has a moment of terrible insight: "He shivered, seized with an icy melancholy, as if he had caught a glimpse of whole worlds of misery and despair, a charcoal stove beside a trestle bed, and the corpses at the mortuary in their leather aprons, with the cold tap-water running over their hair" (SE, 130–31). If, for Flaubert, the ideal is impossibly remote and immaculate, reality shades off from banality into enveloping horror. In sensibility he is closer to Poe and Baudelaire than to Cervantes, Stendhal, and Byron.

Although Frédéric's honest insights as observer and his sincere but inactive passion are relatively more attractive than the insensate activity of most of the other characters, there is actually no substantial heroic dimension in the novel. The existence of such a dimension is acknowledged only in faint emanations from the past, the most notable of which occurs on the occasion of the visit of Frédéric and Rosanette to Fontainebleau. They visit, among other rooms, the Banqueting Hall of the palace and view the magnificent painted ceiling. It is a beautiful day, the windows are open, and

> from the depths of the forest, whose misty tree-tops filled the horizon, there seemed to come an echo of the morts sounded on ivory hunting-horns,an echo of the mythological ballets which had brought together under the trees prin-

cesses and noblemen disguised as nymphs and satyrs, an echo of an age of primitive science, violent passions, and sumptuous art, when mankind sought to transform the world into a dream of the Hesperides, and when the mistress of kings vied with the constellations. The most beautiful of these legendary creatures was shown in a painting on the right, in the character of Diana the huntress, and indeed of Diana of the Underworld, no doubt to indicate the power she wielded even beyond the grave. All these symbols confirmed her fame; and something of her still remained here, a faint voice, a lingering splendour. [*SE*, 319–20]

Flaubert defines authentic heroism as passionate energy linked to ideal ends in a world somehow responsive to heroic aspirations and transformed by them, with art mirroring the entire process. The goddess-woman is at the center of aspirations and energy, both source and focus. In the mock-heroic mode something of the energy, the dream, and the actual quest or adventure remains (and often some form of the goddess), but it is countered sharply by a sense of the world's invincible banality. The hero is reduced from a triumphant or tragic figure to tragicomic madness or absurdity. In *The Sentimental Education*, however, energy and the goddess have failed almost completely; banality is within as well as without. Frédéric in the Banqueting Hall responds momentarily to the lingering echo of Diana and asks Rosanette if she would like to have been the woman in the painting. She is uncomprehending, and he explains that he means Diane de Poitiers, mistress of Henri II. To this she can still only murmur, "Ah!" Flaubert goes on to make the point explicit: "Her silence clearly proved that she knew nothing and did not understand" (*SE*, 320). Rosanette is, of course, already in spirit the *petite bourgeoise* that she pathetically tries to become later in the novel.

It is perhaps significant that even in Henri II's time Flaubert makes great art the central and most effective expression of heroic energy. Certainly, in its own fashion, aesthetic expression was to become his personal solution to the problem of heroism. This option he, nevertheless, denies to his protagonists along with all other possibilities. It is, however, the categorical quality of these denials that takes his work finally beyond the limits of the more tentative and ambivalent mock-heroic vision. In Madame Bovary's corruption and Frédéric's flaccidity we move on to darker forms of modern narrative.

The "limits" of the mock-heroic are reached at the aesthetic point at which the mode's inherent delicacy of balance is destroyed by a preponderance of one of its components. We reach these limits again with the metafictionists, among whom John Barth may be taken as contemporary representative, especially because he is so obviously identified with mock-heroic devices. Like Flaubert, Barth is a dedicated student of Cervantes, but he is also well aware of the special significance of Flaubert, aware too of his own relationship with the French writer. Using Barth, then, as a second exemplary figure, I want briefly to explore further the limits of mock-heroic narrative so as to put the mode into a secure final perspective, all the more necessary in this case given the present ubiquity of metafictional criticism. I cannot stress enough that the fundamental concerns of mock-heroic are different from those of metafiction—regardless of common ancestry, regardless of qualities it may share with metafiction, regardless even of its influence on metafictionists.

In Barth's story "Echo" (and generally throughout his other work), the prophet Tiresias and the seeker Narcissus are both subsumed in the figure of Echo. Her credo, which I include as epigraph to this chapter, locates the crucial shift in John Barth's work from commitment to heroic illusions for moral and spiritual purposes—indexes of extraordinary desire and effort toward finally impossible ends—to an overriding interest in fictions per se as beautiful and entertaining, perhaps adequate ends in themselves. Echo, moreover, does not so much generate fictions as edit those that have already been told. "We linger forever on the autognostic verge," she notes but then adds that, in fact, "our story's finished before it starts." In her editing function, nevertheless, remains the possibility of some variation; she "never . . . repeats all, like gossip or mirror . . .[rather] heightens, mutes, turns others' words to her end."[9] The linkage here goes back to Flaubert's sense of universal banality, boredom, and satiety and Joyce's role as plagiarist. In another story, Barth explicitly associates his own work with that of Flaubert: "Pathological boredom leads to a final desire for death and nothingness. . . . If . . . we . . . understand satiety to include a large measure of vicariousness, this description [Barth is apparently referring to an essay on Flaubert by V. S. Pritchett] undeniably applies to one aspect of yourself and your work" (LF, 123–24). In Echo's world, of course, all experience is vicarious. One direction of Barth's work has been to express a sense of "death and nothingness"; another celebrates the pleasure of aesthetic games as a response to death, games that express not value systems but only their internal complexity and inclusiveness as aesthetic demonstrations. Barth signals sharply new directions in his early work, which, as he has explained, "carr[ies] all non-mystical value-thinking to the end of the road."[10] This point is made even more bluntly in one of his short stories: "In this dehuman, exhausted, ultimate adjective hour . . . every humane value has become untenable" (LF, 107).

Flaubert collapsed the crucial mock-heroic tension between opaque reality and still vital illusion in the name of a hateful reality so overwhelming as to destroy all value except that found in the autonomy of style and the integrity of the artist. Approaching the same issues less from a moral basis than from the epistemological concerns of contemporary philosophy, Barth collapses the same tensions in the name of a ubiquitous fictionality. For Barth, this world of fictions, having swallowed reality, now threatens to share the same enervation, ennui, and sterility identified earlier by Flaubert with reality. Barth's comments on the "literature of exhaustion" are well known, but we must keep in mind that they are based on premises that go far beyond the technical discussion of literature. What if the artist as Joycean "chronic forger" has nothing worth even forging, the writer thus "committed to the pen for life. Which is to say, death"? (*LF*, 107). The Beckett-like voice in Barth's story "Title" is categorical in its nihilism: "Everything's finished. Name eight. Story, novel, literature, art, humanism, humanity, the self itself. Wait: the story's not finished" (*LF*, 107–8). The voice—just barely—refuses to stop, but it certainly includes silence as one of its options: "Silence. There's a fourth possibility, I suppose. Silence. General anesthesia. Self-extinction. Silence" (*LF*, 110).

Obviously Beckett's option does not represent the direction taken by Barth's work. Another "possibility" mentioned in the same story gives us a better clue: "To turn ultimacy against itself to make something new and valid, the essence whereof would be the impossibility of making something new" (*LF*, 109). On this theme Barth has played many brilliant variations, but for our present purposes it is more important to remember what is no longer possible. In particular, a monistic "ultimacy" destroys the vital dualism on which the mock-heroic mode is based. Gone, in the first place, is any significant distinction between reality and dreams and thus the possibility of ambivalent commitment to both. Lost also in the "raveled fabrication" (*LF*, 150) that constitutes time, myth, and history is any sense of the past as sharply isolate, uniquely valuable, worthy of poignant memory—whether Golden Age or childhood or some heroic culture; lost, at the same time, is all possibility of an anachronistic identity built on some ideal structure from the past. Gone, finally, is the chance of meaningful identity in a world of shifting masks and roles whose only "real" inhabitant is Proteus. Jerome Bray, a recent Barthian version of Proteus, leaves us with no doubt as to what he represents: *"Art is as natural an artifice as nature; the truth of fiction is that fact is fantasy; the made-up story is a model of the world."*[11]

The mock-heroic writer mocks the inefficacy of personality, the unbridgeable gap between desire and consummation, not its values, efforts, or very existence. Barth's protagonists, however, do not passionately and willfully model previous roles. Either they arbitrarily invent and multiply alternatives or they are already the incarnation of a prototype and self-consciously seek to realize its implications. Ebenezer Cooke, for example, in *The Sot-Weed Factor* is (in Manfred Puetz's excellent phrase) "born out of the innocence of new beginnings."[12] Giles Goat-Boy, however, is born to live out the Ur-myth. From arbitrary invention or the mechanical enactment of prototype comes lack of

serious commitments, what Tony Tanner calls the lack of a "committing enthusiasm" to any one cause, direction, or vision.[13] Although Barth by no
means totally ignores the possibility of humanistic "as if" affirmations (particularly dedication to love—"as if" it worked, lasted, had meaning), these affirmations when present lack any context of passionate pursuit because nothing
has "really" been lost whose recovery becomes the focus of singular and obsessive questing. In general, Burlingame's advice to Ebenezer looms large in
Barth's work: "One must choose his gods and devils on the run, quill his own
name upon the universe, and declare, ''Tis I, and the world stands such-a-
way!' One must *assert, assert, assert,* or go screaming mad. What other course
remains?"[14]

If assertion is the goal of the artist and his protagonists, then parody is its
central mechanism. Barth's parody reflects and fulfills the expectations of recent metafictionist criticism, namely that parody is a "reflexive form of metafiction which 'lays bare' the devices of fiction to refunction them for new
purposes." Such criticism emphasizes the role of parody "as the carrier of the
'discontinuous' in epistemological history,"[15] and it is this dimension that
clearly appeals to Barth—the opportunity, that is, for fiction to free itself for
"new purposes" within the context of its fictionality. Parody from this perspective reminds us not so much of the authenticity of the original (or, if a
literary convention, of the authentic relation of the convention to its culture)
as of its falsity or artificiality or both. Whereas the mock-heroic mode still
somehow involves serious imitation and still seeks in parody a method for
sustaining heroic continuity (granted the simultaneous mockery of such
aims), Barth celebrates rather the sheer liberating quality of parody, the "devices of fiction" revitalized for the perpetuation of fiction—for what Barth
calls "the aesthetic pleasure of complexity." As he has explained to an interviewer: "If you are working the comic mode, you may be free *ipso facto* to
make use of all sorts of conventions because you're parodying them."[16]

The continued discovery and exploitation of such freedom increasingly
mark the direction of Barth's work, moving, as he does, beyond the prison of
valueless, repetitive, and exhausted forms—"petrification," the glance of
Medusa, he calls it in the "Perseid"—to the treasure house of metafiction,
where, he points out correctly, "the key to the treasure is the treasure."[17]
And, we might add, the key to the key is Barth's parody, which reminds us
both of the reflexivity and circularity of art within a closed system and its
limitless possibilities within that same system. In his commitment to these
possibilities and his simultaneous expression of their full ironic context, Barth
moves closest to certain aspects of the mock-heroic sensibility—in particular,
its manic quest to escape the prison house of circumstances and its tendency

to find escape in aesthetic experience and in identification with the artist. For the mock-heroic writer and his protagonists, fictions are the instrument of liberation, mocked everywhere by opaque reality and, additionally, by the inherent limits even of the instrument. For Barth, fictions retain such instrumentality, while becoming, at the same time, both their own end and their own most devastating mocker.[18] In other words, the mock-heroic writer uses artifice to sustain the heroic quest; with Barth, artifice sustains only itself, still mocked, however, by the chaotic nonsense that constitutes its particular dimension of nothingness. Writing of this sort, nevertheless, continues to generate significant tensions. To the extent that Barth's later work reaches toward a fully articulated double vision of affirmation and denial, it represents a final tenuous echo within the literature of echo that I have been describing.

The Continuing Quest for Heaven

The mock-heroic writer deals in mirrors, echoes, and "shades" but finds (or tries to find) in them the traditional epic values. Even in exile, he strives valiantly to be "pater-son," the worthy heir of Western humanism. For the mock-heroic writer, art remains the epic and romantic vehicle for spiritual transcendence, albeit mock-transcendence, the experience of supreme fictions. Joyce is the parodist of Dante, Blake, and Homer and himself the creator of a universe exquisitely complete—heaven and earth in their own perfect relation. These writers and their parodists are builders of ideal moral and spiritual systems, yet centrally concerned with the relation of system to daily human experience. Barth, on the other hand, is the parodist of the compilers, those like his mad editor Jerome Bray (Kinbote without tragic sense or moral passion) who encyclopedically collect and collate formal patterns complete from some remote beginning and already detached from moral contexts, patterns approaching both a "perfect model" and "pure nothingness" (C, 256–57). To be more precise, Barth's parody illuminates the very act of compiling: its celebration of imaginative energy, its nonsensicality. His parody deliberately creates a context of fabrication so hermetic and so complete that anything he calls "unrefracted fact" (LF, 149) has almost disappeared from view. Certainly any concern for human nobility and the traditional moral and spiritual concerns of the hero has been lost. Tony Tanner (also relating Barth to Joyce) is essentially correct in observing that "what Barth seems to have lost is a sense of the value of fictions and any conviction that they may be significantly related to our experience of reality."[19] Barth's commitment, such as it is, is not to the continuance of spiritual and moral questing by means of fictions but to the very continuance of fictions themselves, at a time when their fresh imaginative possibilities have been called into question, let alone any relationship they might have to humanistic values.

Even in relation to that of his chief literary mentor, Jorge Luis Borges, Barth's work represents an attenuation of the mock-heroic impulse, a further turning away from commitment to the nobility of the mad system builders to mere affirmation of the impulse to identify and catalog systems. Such a turning away is apparent in the emphases of Barth's famous essay in praise of Borges, "The Literature of Exhaustion." Though pointing out that Borges is essentially in pursuit of a "passionately relevant metaphysical position" and that his work illustrates "how an artist may paradoxically turn the felt ultimacies of our time into material and means for his work"—both statements descriptive of the context of mock-heroic narrative—Barth, nevertheless, concerns himself largely with Borges's technical triumph as a writer of "footnotes" to other people's books (in effect, an editor). Borges does this, according to Barth, to remind us of "the fictitious aspect of our own existence" and the endless repetition and "dizzying multiples" of the world.[20]

In emphasizing such issues, Barth plays down the religious parody of much of Borges's work, the degree to which his protagonists are spiritual questers. Seeking the Word under the usual sentence of death, they involve themselves with the much more ambiguous "word"; seeking to destroy time and "inhuman" reality, they weave "lofty invisible" human labyrinths.[21] These protagonists—the philosophers, writers, detectives, raisonneurs, hasidic searchers—all possess a "singular intellectual passion" and their projects (as Borges describes those of Fumes, the Memorius) "are lacking in sense but they reveal a certain stammering greatness."[22]

Borges's humanistic concern is precisely that of mock-heroic narrative: heroism redeemed in the context of mockery, the ideal affirmed in the symbiosis of its degraded and absurd context. He emphasizes this point in "Three Versions of Judas," a story in which his "deeply religious" metaphysician protagonist, Nils Runeberg, is another anachronistic hero: "His name might have augmented the catalogues of heresiarchs . . . instead God assigned him to the twentieth century." Runeberg argues that God to redeem us becomes Judas and that Judas's specific role (in his own degradation and Christ's suffering) is to prophesy "all the atrocious future, in time and eternity, of the word made flesh." As Borges summarizes his protagonist's position and significance, "he added to the concept of the Son, which seemed exhausted, the complexities of calamity and evil." The "informer," in short, is somehow double to the word carrier, "the lower order is a mirror of the superior order . . . the stains on the skin are a map of the incorruptible heavens."[23] Borges's mock-heroic acknowledges exhaustion yet finds in a parodic "lower order"—that "mirror" world that constitutes the essential environment of all

the works I have examined—continuing opportunities for redemptive questing that are humanistically more inclusive, more squarely assertive of spiritual claims than Barth's narrower aesthetic version.

Borges's work, in short, reminds us again of the sustained and categorical
dualism on which the mock-heroic mode depends, its delicate, resilient antiphony of skepticism and commitment to heroic ends in the continuing (albeit
nightmarish and absurd) context of historical time. At its best, the mock-
heroic mode is a triumph of ironic balance, the aesthetic manifestation and
equivalent of Herzog's claim that his "balance comes from instability" (*H*,
330). Or perhaps rather a triumph of effort. Effort is its theme: at least Virginia
Woolf thought so in commenting upon her plan to give Bernard, her own
mock-hero, the long final monologue in *The Waves:* "This is . . . to show that
the theme effort, effort, dominates: not the waves: and personality: and defiance." Yet she remains aware of how all such efforts must end: "I am not
sure of the effect artistically; because the proportions may need the intervention of the waves finally so as to make a conclusion."[24] Balance reasserts itself
after all; less brutally than Stevens, Woolf, nevertheless, reminds herself
and her potential readers that relations will be clipped, that "be" is inevitably
the "finale of seem."

Notes

Introduction

1   Vladimir Nabokov, *Lectures on Don Quixote*, ed. Fredson Bowers (New York: Harcourt Brace Jovanovich, 1983), p. 1n.

2   Herman Melville, *The Confidence Man: His Masquerade* (New York: Grove Press, 1949), p. 278.

3   For Cook's theory of tragedy and comedy see *The Dark Voyage and the Golden Mean: A Philosophy of Comedy* (Cambridge, Mass.: Harvard University Press, 1969). My concept of the "power of abstraction" as the blocking force removed by an appeal to reason and social norms in comic resolutions is indebted to A. N. Kaul, *The Action of English Comedy: Studies in the Encounter of Abstraction and Experience from Shakespeare to Shaw* (New Haven: Yale University Press, 1970), esp. pp. 45–48.

4   George Gordon, Lord Byron, *Don Juan*, ed. Leslie A. Marchand (Boston: Houghton Mifflin, 1958), 11.82 (hereafter cited in the text by canto and stanza).

5   Robert Kiely, *Robert Louis Stevenson and the Fiction of Adventure* (Cambridge, Mass.: Harvard University Press, 1964), p. 247. For Kiely's excellent treatment of Stevenson's early novels see pp. 50–105. I deal briefly with other significant evasions of the full, delicate balance of mock-heroic in Chapter 10.

6   Walter Kaiser, *Praisers of Folly* (Cambridge, Mass.: Harvard University Press, 1963), pp. 278–91. Other versions of mock-heroic that, though fundamentally non-satiric, are still not Cervantine have been carefully discussed by George Lord, *Heroic Mockery: Variations on Epic Themes from Homer to Joyce* (Newark: University of Delaware Press, 1977).

7   For Muecke's thoughtful yet traditional treatment of mock-heroic see *The Compass of Irony* (London: Methuen, 1969), pp. 78–79.

8   Miguel de Cervantes Saavedra, *The Adventures of Don Quixote*, trans. J. M. Cohen (London: Penguin, 1950), p. 29 (hereafter cited in the text by title [*DQ*] and page). Since my study, on the whole, concerns itself with larger questions of form rather than fine nuances of style and since my examples are chosen primarily from literature in English, I have not scrupled when necessary to use good English translations of works in other languages.

9   Robert Alter, *Partial Magic: The Novel as Self-Conscious Genre* (1975; Berkeley and Los Angeles: University of California paperback, 1978), pp. x–xiii. Since Alter argues that fictionality is the central concern of *Don Quixote*, he would not, obviously, agree that *Tristram Shandy* reduces the complex dialectic of the earlier book. Other influential critics, in particular Michel Foucault (*The Order of Things: An Archaeology of the Human Sciences* [New York: Vintage–Random House, 1973, pp. 46–50]), have advanced a meta-fictional interpretation of *Don Quixote*, a critical point of view which, of course, enjoys strong popularity at the moment. In my discussions of many of the writers to follow, I

shall return often to the distinction between the metafictional and the mock-heroic mode. They share much in common but remain different in crucial ways.

10   Marthe Robert, *The Old and the New: From "Don Quixote" to Kafka*, trans. Carol Cosman (Berkeley and Los Angeles: University of California Press, 1977), p. 27.

11   For Levin's comments on heroic models in nineteenth-century fiction see "The Quixotic Principle: Cervantes and Other Novelists," in Morton W. Bloomfield, ed., *The Interpretation of Narrative: Theory and Practice* (Cambridge, Mass.: Harvard University Press, 1970), pp. 61–64. Levin makes the same essential point in his two other important works on the Cervantes tradition, *Contexts of Criticism* (New York: Atheneum, 1957), pp. 79–109, and *The Gates of Horn: A Study of Five French Novelists* (New York: Oxford University Press, 1963).

12   Robert, *The Old and the New*, p. 27.

13   The naturalistic and mundane environment of the book remains strongly felt as the essential "setting" of events, regardless of whether or not we finally think of these events as filtered through complex fictional frames. Even Robert Alter notes that the "juxtaposition of high-blown literary fantasies with grubby actuality point[s] the way to the realists" (*Partial Magic*, p. 3). Yet he quickly drops the issue because he is tracing the presumably alternate tradition of the self-conscious or metafictional novel.

14   Ronald Paulson, *The Fictions of Satire* (Baltimore: Johns Hopkins Press, 1967), pp. 100–105. In her other major book based on a reading of *Don Quixote*, Marthe Robert argues that "the birth of the novel coincides with that moment of suspense and conflict when, without entirely giving up his visions of paradise, he [the protagonist, specifically Don Quixote] can no longer ignore his newly acquired experience nor by-pass necessity. . . . And although he is still, perhaps more than ever, the incorrigible wanderer dominated by the creations of his unbridled imagination, he is no longer surrounded by things that correspond to his desires but by a real world and a society which derides him." (*Origins of the Novel*, trans. Sacha Rabinovitch [Bloomington: Indiana University Press, 1980], p. 81). The mock-heroic mode exploits this disjunction and steadily denies the possibility of resolution.

15   James Joyce, *Scribbledehobble, the Ur-Workbook for Finnegans Wake*, ed. T. E. Connolly (Evanston: Northwestern University Press, 1961), p. 25. Joyce's phrase in its larger context is used as epigraph to this Introduction.

16   Nabokov, *Lectures on Don Quixote*, p. 16. Feeling likewise that this point should be steadily "kept in mind," I use it as an epigraph to the chapter—and really the entire book.

17   Alistair Fowler, *Kinds of Literature: An Introduction to the Theory of Genres and Modes* (Cambridge, Mass.: Harvard University Press, 1982), p. 107. The theory of genres as "more like families than classes" is also from Fowler (p. 41), though he acknowledges that it did not originate with him.

18   Anne Mellor, *English Romantic Irony* (Cambridge, Mass.: Harvard University Press, 1980), p. 195, n. 47. Frederic Jameson, "Magical Narratives: Romance as Genre," *New Literary History* 7 (1975): 136–37, has noted that contemporary approaches to genre are either semantic (genre as meaning or mode) or syntactic (genre as model or fixed form). His own definition insists on both dimensions: "that literary phenomenon which may be articulated *either* in terms of a fixed form *or* in terms of a mode, and

which *must* be susceptible of expression in *either* of these critical codes optionally." I have simply incorporated both dimensions within an enlarged concept of mode.

19 Mark Rose, *Alien Encounters: Anatomy of Science Fiction* (Cambridge, Mass.: Harvard University Press, 1981), p. 23.

20 Margaret Rose, in discussing the role of parody in transforming literary history, describes how "the structure of the parody . . . creates a dialectic of imitation and transformation, superseding the act of imitation itself, and uniting the parody work within another text and literary tradition, while at the same time changing the direction of this tradition through its refunctioning of its model. Hence parody has been able to transform the limits of other genres in the act of defining them" (*Parody/Meta-Fiction: An Analysis of Parody as a Critical Mirror to the Writing and Reception of Fiction* [London: Croom Helm, 1979], p. 158).

21 Rose, *Alien Encounters*, p. 4. Claudio Guillén, in perhaps the most influential contemporary essay on genre, stresses its instrumentality as a critical tool. See "On the Uses of Literary Genre," in *Literature as System: Essays toward a Theory of Literary History* (Princeton: Princeton University Press, 1971), esp. p. 122: "The process of classification that genre theory implies is but one part of a broader process of definition and interpretation."

Chapter 1

1 Leon Gottfried, "The Odysseyan Form: An Exploratory Essay," in Egon Schwartz and Peter Hohendahl, eds., *Festschrifte for Liselotte Dieckmann* (Seattle: University of Washington Press, 1972), pp. 20–24.

2 Alexander Welsh, *Reflections on the Hero as Quixote* (Princeton: Princeton University Press, 1981), p. 21.

3 Marthe Robert, *Origins of the Novel*, trans. Sacha Rabinovitch (Bloomington: Indiana University Press, 1980), p. 129. See also her comment that the novel "consists not in a series of progressive episodes, but in a system of duplicates having identical meanings [and] incessantly turns in its inexorable circle of repetitions" (p. 128).

4 I echo and paraphrase Nabokov here; see *Lectures on Don Quixote,* ed. Fredson Bowers (New York: Harcourt Brace Jovanovich, 1983), pp. 1, 134–35, 182–83. I shall demonstrate in a later chapter the crucial relevance of acts of transformation to Nabokov's own art. Everywhere in his work are "magical" experiences similar to those he notes in Cervantes.

5 Nabokov, *Lectures on Don Quixote,* p. 70.

6 Robert Alter has demonstrated at length how the parodic Journey is itself parodied. He concludes: "The novel creates a world at once marvelous and credible, but the most splendid evocations of character or action bear within them the visible explosive freight of their own parodistic negation" (*Partial Magic: The Novel as Self-Conscious Genre* [1975; Berkeley and Los Angeles: University of California paperback, 1978], pp. 23–25). See also my discussion of parody in this chapter.

7 From her psychological perspective, Robert makes the same point: "Don Quixote's advent reveals the omnipotence of desire—and the desire of omnipotence—peculiar to childish imagination" (*Origins of the Novel,* p. 119). René Girard also associ-

276 Notes to Chapter 1

ates what he calls "triangular" desire (desire defined externally by an imitated model) with Don Quixote and childhood. See *Deceit, Desire, and the Novel*, trans. Yvonne Freccero (Baltimore: Johns Hopkins Press, 1966), pp. 32–37 and passim. Both critics treat this issue more negatively than I do.

8 Robert, *Origins of the Novel*, p. 109. Howard Mancing has exhaustively analyzed both the Knight's imitation of chivalric models (themselves timeless models of ideal behavior) and his deliberate and persistent speech archaisms. See *The Chivalric World of Don Quijote: Style, Structure, and Narrative Technique* (Columbia: University of Missouri Press, 1982), esp. pp. 9–48.

9 "Don Quixote, Cervantes," in *The Literary Remains of Samuel Taylor Coleridge*, 4 vols. (London: W. Pickering, 1836), 1: 113–31, rpt. Raymond E. Barbera, ed., *Cervantes: A Critical Trajectory* (Boston: Mirage Press, 1971), p. 34.

10 The concept of the enchanters as rationalizing devices is borrowed from Richard Predmore, *The World of Don Quixote* (Cambridge, Mass.: Harvard University Press, 1967), p. 52.

11 N. N. Evreinoff, *The Theater in Life*, ed. and trans. A. I. Nazaroff (New York, 1927), pp. 86–89, quoted in Ludmilla B. Turkevich, *Cervantes in Russia* (Princeton: Princeton University Press, 1950), p. 175. Alter changes the literary metaphor only slightly when he writes that "Don Quixote, a bookish man, actually wants to become a book" (*Partial Magic*, pp. 8–9).

12 Jorge Luis Borges, "Pierre Menard, Author of Don Quixote," trans. Anthony Bonner, in Anthony Kerrigan, ed., *Fictions* (London: John Calder, 1965), pp. 42–51. Howard Mancing has observed that the gratuitousness of Don Quixote's feats constitutes both the essence of his life lived according to heroic models and paradoxically "reduces in great measure the authenticity of the art-inspired existence that is the hallmark of Don Quijote's chivalric world" (*Chivalric World of Don Quijote*, p. 83). The relation of games and play to human creativity and what Freud calls the general "urge to mastery" has been widely explored in contemporary thought, not only by Freud himself but by Johan Huizinga, Erik Erikson, Jean Piaget, and others.

13 Predmore, *World of Don Quixote*, p. 82.

14 Leo Spitzer, "Perspectivism in 'Don Quijote,'" in *Linguistics and Literary History: Essays in Stylistics* (Princeton: Princeton University Press, 1948), p. 62.

15 Mancing, *Chivalric World of Don Quijote*, p. 215. Mancing is here following the lead of the Cervantes scholar Juan Bautista Avalle-Arce, *Don Quijote como forma de vida* (Madrid: Fundación Juan March/Editorial Castalia, 1976).

16 Nabokov, *Lectures on Don Quixote*, p. 63. Alternatively he refers to "the Diabolical Diana and her Duke." Nabokov clearly recognizes and emphasizes the moral dimension of the book, indeed, puts the issue here in extreme terms—"devils" versus a Christ-figure.

17 Robert Scholes and Robert Kellogg, *The Nature of Narrative* (New York: Oxford University Press, 1966), p. 15; Leo Spitzer, "On the Significance of Don Quijote," *Modern Language Notes* 77 (1962): 113–29, rpt. in Lowry Nelson, Jr., ed., *Cervantes: A Collection of Critical Essays* (Englewood Cliffs, N.J.: Prentice-Hall, 1969), p. 88; Gary Morson, *The Boundaries of Genre: Dostoevsky's Diary of a Writer and the Traditions of Literary Utopia* (Austin: University of Texas Press, 1981), pp. 48–52.

18   Morson, *Boundaries of Genre*, p. 108. Morson is referring to the recently influential theories of Mikhail Bakhtin as found in *Problems of Dostoevsky's Poetics*, trans. R. W. Rotsel (Ann Arbor: Ardis Press, 1973). I have already noted (Introduction, n. 20) this tendency of contemporary critics to stress the transformational and reconstructive as much as the deconstructive dimensions of parody. Such "refunctioning" indeed is part of Margaret Rose's definition: Parody, she writes, is "the critical refunctioning of pre-formed literary material with comic effect" (*Parody/Meta-Fiction: An Analysis of Parody as a Critical Mirror to the Writing and Reception of Fiction* [London: Croom Helm, 1979], p. 35). Morson feels that parody need not always even be comic (p. 111).

19   My terms are from Rose (*Parody/Meta-Fiction*, p. 107), who speaks of the "two fictional worlds" of parody—"the one 'preformed' and the other, the parody itself, a new world which offers a critical context for the re-coding and re-reception of the for-mer." She also (following Foucault) notes the archaeological function of parody.

20   Spitzer, "Perspectivism in 'Don Quijote,'" p. 52. Spitzer's comments everywhere anticipate the dimension of the novel most attractive to contemporary criticism. For a more recent version see Alter, *Partial Magic*, p. 11: "For Cervantes, the word simul-taneously resonates with its old magic quality and turns back on itself, exposing its own emptiness as an arbitrary or conventional construct."

21   Nabokov, *Lectures on Don Quixote*, p. 39. Elsewhere he notes that "both parts of *Don Quixote* form a veritable encyclopedia of cruelty. From that viewpoint it is one of the most bitter and barbarous books ever penned" (p. 52).

22   The elements of chance and surprise, wonder and astonishment have been noted by Predmore in *The World of Don Quixote*, and Cervantes's linguistic formulas for expressing these elements carefully documented. See especially pp. 22–23, 84–87. As Predmore observes categorically: "What is it that so frequently surprises the inhabi-tants of the world of *Don Quixote*? Simply everything: the appearances of their world, the situations they fall into, and above all, the conduct of the people they encounter" (p. 87). More recently, Alexander Welsh has demonstrated brilliantly the relation of "practical jokes, which confound desire, belief, trustfulness with materiality" to the quixotic tradition in literature and the larger movement of nineteenth-century realism. See his entire discussion in *Reflections on the Hero as Quixote*, p. 81–123. Marthe Robert has also noted how Don Quixote is endlessly "corrected" by the "unperturbable course of established events." She argues that "such automatic corrections of uncorrigibility dominate the structure of the story from start to finish" (*Origins of the Novel*, p. 128).

23   See especially the narrator's savage attack on the "grave ecclesiastic" in the Duke and Duchess's household, "one of those . . . who, not being born princes themselves, do not succeed in teaching those who are how to behave as such; who would have the greatness of the great measured by the narrowness of their own souls; who, wanting to show those they rule how to be frugal, make them miserly" (*DQ*, 670). This ecclesiastic, significantly, is the figure in the book most violently hostile to Don Quixote, and, at one point (*DQ*, 674), receives a telling rebuke from the Knight.

24   Robert Adams, *Strains of Discord: Studies in Literary Openness* (Ithaca: Cornell University Press, 1958), argues persuasively against the authority in the novel of Aris-totelian moderates such as the Gentleman in Green. Adams defines the Cervantes tra-dition as follows: "openness of form, ambivalence of judgement, and indefinite equivo-

cation" (p. 84). The concept of the ambivalence (variously defined) of *Don Quixote* is one widely shared by modern critics of Cervantes, for example, Scholes and Kellogg, Erich Auerbach, Leo Spitzer, Thomas Mann, Américo Castro, Marthe Robert, and others.

25   Anne Mellor, *English Romantic Irony* (Cambridge, Mass.: Harvard University Press, 1980), p. 17. The persona of the theatrical clown will figure prominently in later mock-heroic narrative. For the precise relation between the two modes see my discussion of Byron's *Don Juan*. D. C. Muecke, *The Compass of Irony* (London: Methuen, 1969), p. 143.

26   Nabokov, *Lectures on Don Quixote*, p. 160.

27   Schlegel's phrase is from *Lyceum* fragment 108, in Friedrich Schlegel's *Lucinde and the Fragments*, trans. Peter Firchow (Minneapolis: University of Minnesota Press, 1971), quoted in Mellor, *English Romantic Irony*, p. 12.

Chapter 2

1   Stendhal, *The Life of Henry Brulard*, trans. Jean Steward and B.C.J.G. Knight (1958; rpt. New York: Minerva Press, 1968), p. 8 (hereafter cited in the text by title[*HB*] and page). See also Harry Levin's apt description of the early nineteenth century as "an age of disappointed hero-worship" in *The Gates of Horn: A Study of Five French Novelists* (New York: Oxford University Press, 1963), p. 58.

2   Raymond Giraud, *The Unheroic Hero in the Novels of Stendhal, Balzac, and Flaubert* (Rutgers: Rutgers University Press, 1957), pp. 10, 47. Giraud has some useful insights into this divided sensibility but unfortunately limits his discussion unduly by taking a very narrow view of *Don Quixote* and virtually denying the book's relevance. Eric Auerbach has commented thoughtfully on Stendhal's split life in *Mimesis*, trans. Willard Trask (Princeton: Princeton University Press, 1953), pp. 458–63.

3   Victor Brombert, *Stendhal: Fiction and the Themes of Freedom* (New York: Random House, 1968), pp. 4–5. In dealing with documents in the mock-heroic mode, the term *Bildungsroman* can be misleading, even if we define the developmental process as one of disillusionment. See Harry Levin's sweeping use of the term in *Gates of Horn*, p. 52. M. K. Joseph carefully makes a point of dissociating Byron's method from *Bildungsroman* in *Byron the Poet* (London: Gollanz, 1966), p. 197.

4   The Gagnons (originally, says Stendhal, Guadagni or Guadaniamo) are his mother's family, Beyle, his father's: "I considered myself a Gagnon and I never thought of the Beyles except with a distaste which I still feel in 1835" (*HB*, 58). Often the displacement felt by the mock-hero is expressed as loss of class—usually from aristocratic to bourgeois.

5   Stendhal even directs the *Life of Brulard* to the young reader: "If you are over thirty or if, being under thirty, you belong to the prosaic order, close this book!" (*HB*, 345). Stendhal's preservation of youthfulness into maturity is noted by Levin in *Gates of Horn*, p. 149. He points out how Stendhal defined the modern ideal in his *Histoire de la peinture en Italie* (Paris: Le Divan), 2:156, as "above all, the agile air of youth."

6   We must, it is true, be careful in drawing conclusions about style from a work that exists only in draft form. Nevertheless, much of its roughness and disorganization

seems intentional. One of his notes to himself, for example, reads: "Idea: Perhaps if I do not correct this first draft I shall manage to escape lying through vanity" (*HB*, 55). At another point he suggests that chronology is unimportant, that he is concerned only with writing down his impressions of the past as they occur to him (*HB*, 160).

7 Stendhal, *Red and Black*, trans. and ed. Robert M. Adams (New York: Norton, 1969), p. 251 (hereafter cited in the text by title [*RB*] and page).

8 I have noted already that Marthe Robert in *Origins of the Novel* relates Don Quixote's experience to that of childhood. Her psychoanalytic study of the novel traces the writer's need to express one of two primary attitudes toward human development, and she uses *Robinson Crusoe* and *Don Quixote* as prototypal revelations of these attitudes as they are exemplified in the lives of the protagonists: the hero as Bastard (the outcast who matures, innovates, and finally returns to society) and as Foundling. The author sees Don Quixote as a lifelong "foundling" stuck at an early stage of psychic growth, which keeps him hopelessly socially maladjusted through life. Of course, with Stendhal, Cervantes, and others this "maladjustment" reflects a crucial psychological problem (the "madness" in various forms of the mock-hero), but at the same time it is a measure of relative spiritual strength and distinction. The ambiguities of literature begin where traditional psychoanalysis leaves off. Victor Brombert (*Stendhal*, p. 98) has noted that in Stendhal's novels the pursuit of the father figure is essentially pursuit of authentic heroism.

9 Robert Adams, in a footnote to this line in the Norton Edition, points out its relation to romanticism as a register of the gap between desire and reality and cross references it with *Life of Brulard* and *The Charterhouse*, chap. 5 (Fabrizio's response to Waterloo).

10 Stendhal, *The Charterhouse of Parma*, trans. Lowell Bair (New York: Bantam, 1960), p. 164 (hereafter cited in the text by title [*CP*] and page).

11 Romantic orthodoxy or, perhaps better, orthodox criticism about romanticism is itself fast fading in the light of deconstructionist perspectives. In *The Subterfuge of Art: Language and the Romantic Tradition* (Baltimore: Johns Hopkins University Press, 1978), Michael Ragussis treats romantic writing as a series of language acts seeking to interpret or otherwise recover a transcendent text (including memories of childhood and heroic myth), which resists complete decipherment. He argues that the most important romantic writers are skeptical about the final truth of language and incorporate this skepticism into their art. I relate the mock-heroic mode below to tensions inherent in literary realism, but, in an explicit, dramatic, categorical fashion, it equally reveals those of romanticism. Stendhal, in effect, explores every tendency of desire and its mockery during this period.

12 See Levin, *Gates of Horn*, p. 289. Flaubert's description of the stages of human history—"Paganisme, christianisme, muflisme"—is from *Correspondance entre George Sand et Gustave Flaubert* (Paris: Conard, n.d.), 6: 201.

13 Brombert (*Stendhal*, pp. 82–83) has noted the mocking echo of heroic activity in the amorous combat of Julien and Mathilde.

14 I am omitting any detailed discussion of these intrusions because they have been mentioned and often carefully analyzed by Victor Brombert, Robert Adams, Raymond

Giraud, Jean Prévost, Paul Valéry, and others. The idea of multiple perspectives or judgments is borrowed specifically from Jean Prévost, *La Création chez Stendhal* (Paris, 1951), rpt. *RB*, 463.

15   The relation of the different kinds of games to each other in *The Charterhouse* has been noted by Judd D. Hubert, "The Devaluation of Reality in the *Chartreuse de Parme*," *Stendhal Club*, October 15, 1959, rpt. Victor Brombert, ed., *Stendhal: A Collection of Critical Essays* (Englewood Cliffs, N.J.: Prentice-Hall, 1962), pp. 96–97. All the games, he points out, serve to "devaluate the present, to destroy the material world, thereby setting up an ideal form of happiness, timeless and yet perfectly human." Judd is particularly good on Fabrizio's games with Clelia, though he stresses the "mock" elements far less than I do.

16   Hubert, "Devaluation of Reality," pp. 98–99.

17   Georges Poulet, "Stendhal and Time," *Revue Internationale de Philosophie* 16 (1962): 395–412, rpt. *RB*, 477–78.

18   Stephen Spender, "Inside the Cage: Reflections on Conditioned and Unconditioned Imagination," in Derek Hudson, ed., *English Critical Essays: Twentieth Century*, 2d ser. (London: Oxford University Press, 1958), pp. 272–73.

Chapter 3

1   Karl Kroeber, *Romantic Narrative Art* (Madison: University of Wisconsin Press, 1960), p. 146. *Don Juan* slightly antedates Stendhal's major fiction, but I have delayed my comments on the poem so as to approach it from the firm context of a sympathetic contemporary working in the same mode.

2   Edward Bosteller, in his Introduction to a collection of essays on *Don Juan*, has noted the problem of giving the poem "a name and habitation among the genres" and, in what may be either the rhetoric of anticipation or despair, reviews some contemporary efforts: "What is it to be called? Epic? Epic of negation? Anti-epic? Epic Satire?" (*Twentieth Century Interpretations of Don Juan* [Englewood Cliffs, N.J.: Prentice-Hall, 1969], p. 11). He might equally well have mentioned frequent attempts to link the poem with the larger genres of satire, tragedy, and comedy or with historical groupings such as romantic narrative. In my opinion, the most interesting generic suggestions have been those, like Kroeber's comment, relating *Don Juan* to Bryon's acknowledged models in earlier mock-epic and those that have seen in the poem's narrative method a proto-novel of the nineteenth century. But one approach has tended to be too limited in its exploration of the nature of mock-epic and sometimes too literal (too involved in questions of explicit influence), the other too vague in its genre identification. In *English Romantic Irony* (Cambridge, Mass.: Harvard University Press, 1980), Anne Mellor usefully approaches many of the same issues I develop from within the tensions of romanticism. At the same time, she disavows any substantial genre link with *Don Quixote*, even though acknowledging (following Byron) that the book is somehow a "model" (see pp. 58–59). At issue between the two modes of romantic irony and mock-heroic are nuances of ontology: romantic irony involves an "ontology of becoming" based on a "sense of exuberant freedom in an infinitely various and infinitely possible world" (pp. 186–87); mock-heroic, however, mirrors an ontology of effort based on a sharp

sense of loss and a concept of reality far more opaque, far less consonant with the dreams of the creative self, albeit still providing the chance for some sort of "adventure."

3   George Gordon, Lord Byron, *Letters and Journals*, ed. R. E. Prothero, 6 vols. (London, 1898–1905), 5:426, quoted in E. D. Hirsch, Jr., "Byron and the Terrestrial Paradise," in Frederick H. Hilles and Harold Bloom, eds., *From Sensibility to Romanticism: Essays Presented to Frederick H. Pottle* (New York: Oxford University Press, 1965), p. 474. Hirsch argues that the most important Edenic vision in Byron is that of "a totally selfless and totally fulfilling love relationship" (p. 474).

4   See M. K. Joseph, *Byron the Poet* (London: Gollancz, 1966), pp. 163–64. More recently, Anne Mellor makes the same point: "Passionate love, and the acts of sexual reproduction that naturally grow from that emotion . . . are presented as the ultimate human consciousness" (*English Romantic Irony*, pp. 39–40).

5   See Byron's comparison of a beautiful woman with a statue:

> . . . she was one
> Fit for the model of a statuary
> (A race of mere impostors, when all's done—
> I've seen much finer women, ripe and real,
> Than all the nonsense of their stone ideal).   [2.118]

6   Epic parallels in *Don Juan* are traced by, among others, Brian Wilkie, *Romantic Poets and Epic Tradition* (Madison: University of Wisconsin Press, 1965), esp. pp. 198–215.

7   Alvin Kernan, *The Plot of Satire* (New Haven: Yale University Press, 1965), pp. 187–93. Kernan has noted about *Don Juan* that "what we are faced with is not a simple irony, which involves only two points, what seems and what is, but an endlessly complicating ambiguity, a series of perspectives, each one of which is as true as any other" (p. 183). Kernan labels these perspectives as comic, satiric, and tragic and discusses each separately.

Chapter 4

1   *The Works of Mark Twain*, 37 vols. (New York: Gabriel Wells, 1922–25), 5:176–77 (hereafter cited in the text by volume and page); Henry James, *The Art of Travel*, ed. Morton Dauwen Zabel (New York: Doubleday, 1958), p. 518; John Ruskin, *Fors Clavigera*, quoted in John D. Rosenberg, *The Darkening Glass: A Portrait of Ruskin's Genius* (New York: Columbia University Press, 1961), pp. 190–91; Tennyson to Emily Sellwood in Hallam Lord Tennyson, *Alfred Lord Tennyson: A Memoir* (New York, 1897), pp. 171–72, in James Kissane, "Tennyson: The Passion of the Past and the Curse of Time," *English Literary History* 32 (1965): 87. Using Tennyson as an example, Kissane exhaustively explores Victorian dislocation and nostalgia.

2   The literary and cultural image of childhood in the nineteenth century has been a good deal studied in recent years. I am particularly indebted to the following: Peter Coveney, *The Image of Childhood: The Individual and Society: A Study of the Theme in English Literature*, rev. ed. (London: Barrie & Jenkins, 1967); Albert E. Stone, Jr., *The Innocent Eye: Childhood in Mark Twain's Imagination* (New Haven: Yale University Press, 1961); Jan

B. Gordon, "The *Alice* Books and the Metaphors of Victorian Childhood," in Robert Phillips, ed., *Aspects of Alice: Lewis Carroll's Dreamchild as Seen through the Critics' Looking-Glasses, 1865–1971* (London: Gollancz, 1972); Elsie Leach, "*Alice in Wonderland* in Perspective," *Victorian Newsletter* 25 (1964), rpt. in Phillips, ed., *Aspects of Alice*, and Gilliam Avery, *Nineteenth Century Children: Heroes and Heroines in English Children's Stories, 1780–1900* (London: Hodder and Stoughton, 1965). Everyone, of course, is indebted to William Empson's classic "The Child as Swain," in *Some Versions of Pastoral* (London: Chatto & Windus, 1935).

3 Twain to Aldrich, December 6, 1893, Clemens Collection, Houghton Library, Harvard University, quoted in Stone, *Innocent Eye*, p. 31; Kenneth Grahame, *The Golden Age* and *Dream Days* (New York: Signet, 1964), p. 106 (hereafter cited in the text by titles [*GA* and *DD*] and page). It is always a temptation to oversimplify literary history. Obviously, alternatives to the mock-heroic mode were pursued by other writers: straight nostalgia, of course, or works of categorical disillusionment such as I ascribe in a later chapter to Flaubert, or those more positive narratives of change and maturation (e.g., *David Copperfield*) particularly characteristic of the English novel. Alexander Welsh describes the alternatives succinctly: "When the cure for quixotism consists simply in growing up, the nineteenth-century novel of disillusionment has been founded" (*Reflections on the Hero as Quixote* [Princeton: Princeton University Press, 1981], p. 150).

4 Lewis Carroll, *Alice in Wonderland, Through the Looking-Glass, The Hunting of the Snark*, ed. Donald J. Grey (New York: Norton, 1971), pp. 7, 15–16 (hereafter cited in the text by titles [*AW* and *LG*] and page).

5 See especially George Pitcher, "Wittgenstein, Nonsense, and Lewis Carroll," *Massachusetts Review* 6 (1965): 591–611, rpt. in *AW, LG*, pp. 387–402; and Donald Racklin, "Alice's Journey to the End of Night," *PMLA* 71 (1966): 313–26, rpt. in Phillips, ed., *Aspects of Alice*, pp. 391–416. Pitcher carefully compares aspects of Carroll's nonsense with points raised by Wittgenstein in his attacks on the semantic basis of traditional philosophy; Racklin reads Alice's experience in Gothic terms as "an almost total destruction of the fabric of our so-called logical, orderly, and coherent approach to the world. Practically all pattern, save the consistency of chaos, is annihilated" (p. 393). Racklin emphasizes qualities of fright and horror; I am stressing more the sense of liberation and escape from dull and banal "sanity."

6 John Hinz, "Alice Meets the Don," *South Atlantic Quarterly* 52 (1953): 253–66, rpt. in Phillips, ed., *Aspects of Alice*, pp. 143–55, esp. p. 149; *The Diaries of Lewis Carroll*, ed. Roger Lancelyn Green, 2 vols. (New York: Oxford University Press, 1954), 1:76, rpt. in *AW, LG*, p. 245.

7 See Anne Mellor's treatment of Carroll in *English Romantic Irony* (Cambridge, Mass.: Harvard University Press, 1980). She compares him with his persona Humpty Dumpty: "As an author and game-creator, Humpty Dumpty shows us one way to deal with a frightening Chaos . . . to force signs to mean what you stipulate they mean, to impose a self-referential linguistic system upon a resisting chaos" (p. 176). But (she notes) Humpty Dumpty falls down. Mellor stresses the anxious and fearful side of Carroll's gamesmanship, a mood she places closer to that of Kierkegaard than Cervantes.

8 Elizabeth Sewell, *The Field of Nonsense* (London: Chatto & Windus, 1952), rpt. in

AW, LG, p. 382. Beyond the limits of Victorian nonsense lurks a darker mockery: the potential of nonsense to deconstruct all systems as arbitrary and self-referential. Mellor emphasizes this point. I discuss nonsense further in Chapter 8. For an exhaustive study of the relation of Carroll's work to Victorian play and game see Kathleen Blake, *Play, Games, and Sport: The Literary Works of Lewis Carroll* (Ithaca: Cornell University Press, 1974).

9 Quoted in Harry Levin, "Wonderland Revisited," *Kenyon Review* 27 (1965): 594, rpt. in Phillips, ed., *Aspects of Alice*, p. 178.

10 See Thomas Fensch, "Lewis Carroll: The First Acidhead," *Story: The Yearbook of Discovery* (New York, 1969), pp. 153–56, rpt. in Phillips, ed., *Aspects of Alice*, pp. 421–24.

11 Hjalmar Boyesen, *Gunnar: A Tale of Norse Life* (Boston: James R. Osgood, 1874), p. 33.

12 Alphonse Daudet, *Tartarin of Tarascon, Tartarin on the Alps* (London: Dent, 1910, p. 156 (hereafter cited in the text by titles [*TT* or *TA*] and page).

13 James Joyce, *Ulysses*, 2d ed. (New York: Random House, 1961), p. 377.

14 Murray Sachs, *The Career of Alphonse Daudet* (Cambridge, Mass.: Harvard University Press, 1965), pp. 138–39, has noted that the book was affected by the pessimism and dark mood of this time in Daudet's life. He also points out that its immediate occasion was as a satire on the mountain-climbing craze promoted in the 1880s by the Swiss Tourist Office. In addition, Franklin Rogers, "Mark Twain and Alphonse Daudet: *A Tramp Abroad* and *Tartarin sur les Alpes*," *Comparative Literature* 16 (1964): 254–63, has demonstrated Daudet's strong borrowings from Twain, though Rogers argues correctly that Daudet's protagonist is a more complex figure than Twain's persona, a simple satiric butt for tourist vanity and pretensions.

15 Alphonse Daudet, *Notes sur la vie*, in *Oeuvres complètes illustrées* (Paris, 1929–31), 16:1, quoted in Sachs, *Career of Alphonse Daudet*, p. 15.

16 Rpt. in Clara Kirk and Rudolph Kirk, eds., *European and American Masters* (New York: Collier Books, 1963), p. 151.

17 Notebook 35 (1902), Mark Twain Papers, University of California Library, p. 20, quoted in Roger B. Salomon, *Twain and the Image of History* (New Haven: Yale University Press, 1961), p. 156.

18 *Mark Twain-Howells Letters*, ed. Henry Nash Smith and William M. Gibson, 2 vols. (Cambridge, Mass.: Harvard University Press, 1960), 1:47.

19 Mary N. Murfree, *In the Tennessee Mountains* (Boston: Houghton, Mifflin, 1884), pp. 134–35; *Mark Twain-Howells Letters*, 1:46.

20 Kirk and Kirk, eds., *European and American Masters*, p. 35.

21 Alice Brown, *Meadow-Grass: Tales of New England Life* (Boston: Copland and Day, 1895), p. 1.

22 Leo Marx, *The Machine in the Garden: Technology and the Pastoral Ideal in America* (New York: Oxford University Press, 1964), p. 22.

23 Brown, *Meadow-Grass*, pp. 6, 11.

24 See Alexander Welsh's excellent discussion of Huck and Tom's mock rescue of Jim in *Reflections on the Hero as Quixote*, pp. 94–97. For Welsh, Tom's "practical joke" of withholding the information that Jim had been freed "functions both as realism and as . . . a critique of the entire novelistic enterprise as inescapable fiction."

25   See Salomon, *Twain and the Image of History*, pp. 176–77.

26   This point has been demonstrated with great brilliance by Walter Blair, *Mark Twain and Huck Finn* (Berkeley and Los Angeles: University of California Press, 1962).

27   Ibid., pp. 117–19. See also Olin H. Moore, "Mark Twain and Don Quixote," *PMLA* 37 (1922): 337–38. Blair says that Twain read Cervantes in 1860.

28   Notebook 15, p. 2, Mark Twain Papers, quoted in Salomon, *Twain and the Image of History*, p. 77. See my entire discussion of the origins of the book, pp. 77–78, 114–17.

Chapter 5

1   James Joyce, *The Critical Writings*, ed. Ellsworth Mason and Richard Ellmann (New York: Viking Press, 1959), pp. 44–45 (hereafter cited in the text by title [*CW*] and page).

2   James Joyce, *Stephen Hero*, 2d ed. (New York: New Directions, 1963), p. 77 (hereafter cited in the text by title [*SH*] and page).

3   Flaubert's complex mediation between romanticism and realism was another important model for the young Joyce. See Richard K. Cross, *Flaubert and Joyce: The Rite of Fiction* (Princeton: Princeton University Press, 1971). I am not attempting to give a survey of Joyce's intellectual backgrounds, a topic exhaustively explored elsewhere. Rather, my sole concern is to isolate briefly and sharply those assumptions which lead to his use of the mock-heroic mode and locate them in the contexts most immediately germane to their expression.

4   James Joyce, *Finnegans Wake* (London: Faber & Faber, 1939), p. 134 (hereafter cited in the text by title [*FW*] and page). Hugh Kenner, *Dublin's Joyce* (Bloomington: Indiana University Press, 1955), has related Joyce's parodic sense to his awareness of Ireland's decline from an eighteenth-century culture that fused form and rhetoric with social reality. I do not, obviously, share the reductive and negative interpretation of Joycean parody developed in this book.

5   Stephen Heath, "Ambiviolences: Notes pour la Lecture de Joyce," *Tel Quel* 50 (1972): 37. An English version of this seminal poststructuralist essay can be found in Derek Attridge and Daniel Ferrer, eds., *Post-Structuralist Joyce: Essays from the French* (Cambridge: Cambridge University Press, 1984).

6   John Paul Riquelme, *Teller and Tale in Joyce's Fiction: Oscillating Perspectives* (Baltimore: Johns Hopkins University Press, 1983), p. 62.

7   L. A. Murillo, *The Cyclical Night: Irony in James Joyce and Jorge Luis Borges* (Cambridge, Mass.: Harvard University Press, 1968), p. 32.

8   James Joyce, *A Portrait of the Artist as a Young Man* (New York: Viking Press, 1964), p. 7 (hereafter cited in the text by title [*PA*] and page).

9   See Chapter 2, note 8. I borrow the phrase "desire of omnipotence" from Robert (see also Chapter 1, note 7).

10   See, for example, Marilyn French, *The Book as World: James Joyce's Ulysses* (Cambridge, Mass.: Harvard University Press, 1976). French is correct in pointing out that very quickly in the book we become aware that "the point of view resides not just with Stephen, nor with Stephen and Bloom, but somewhere else" (p. 14), and she sees the "Aeolus" chapter as specifically announcing the universal mockery that underlies

the book. But she conceives of mockery as the expression of a "contemptuous intellect" which "batters" the human reality of the book (pp. 12–13). My own view, of course, is that Joyce's mockery is essentially defensive and instrumental, systematically reducing the fictions of reality to their human dimensions so as to be able to celebrate them imaginatively (and the humanistic values they represent) as fictions. Irony alone permits Joyce to be the new Homer or Dante, but that remains his firm intention. Lately, the attack against what Riquelme calls "the myth of Joyce's impersonal narration" (*Teller and Tale in Joyce's Fiction,* p. 131) has intensified. See also Karen Lawrence, *The Odyssey of Style in Ulysses* (Princeton: Princeton University Press, 1982). This is not to mention poststructuralist criticism of Joyce, some of the best of which has recently been collected in Attridge and Ferrer, eds., *Post-Structuralist Joyce.*

11   Frank Budgen, *James Joyce and the Making of "Ulysses"* (Bloomington: Indiana University Press, 1960), p. 17.

12   French, *The Book as World,* p. 110.

13   James Joyce, *Ulysses,* 2d ed. (New York: Random House, 1961), pp. 184, 187 (hereafter cited in the text by title [*U*] and page).

14   Don Gifford, with Robert J. Seidman, *Notes for Joyce: An Annotation of James Joyce's Ulysses* (New York: E. P. Dutton, 1974), p. 159. Gifford and Seidman are, in turn, quoting Annie Besant, *Esoteric Christianity* (1901). I am generally in debt to Gifford and Seidman for certain technical details in this and other chapters of *Ulysses.*

15   Michael Seidel, *Epic Geography: James Joyce's Ulysses* (Princeton: Princeton University Press, 1976), p. 174.

16   Bernard Benstock's valuable book *Joyce-Again's Wake: An Analysis of Finnegans Wake* (Seattle: University of Washington Press, 1965), first brought the "biblical" dimension of the *Wake* to my attention and Joyce's role as forger. Benstock notes the pun on "forgery" (creativity/fakery), but his discussion ultimately suffers, in my opinion, from an inadequate concept of mock-heroic and, generally, from a tendency to play down the implications of Joycean irony. See pp. 179, 214, 222–23. Riquelme, in his important chapter on the *Wake,* notes that "Shem's aesthetic creations, like Joyce's books, emerge from detritus, from the waste of earlier creative acts" (*Teller and Tale in Joyce's Fiction,* p. 5). Elsewhere he compares the *Wake* to Poe's "Purloined Letter": in both, "the undecipherable, perhaps unknowable, always false or stolen document within the tale represents the tale itself" (p. 29). Section V of Stephen Heath's essay "Ambiviolences" also deals well with plagiarism and forgery.

17   Heath, "Ambiviolences," p. 24.

18   Jorge Luis Borges, *Other Inquisitions, 1937–1952,* trans. Ruth L. C. Simms (Austin: University of Texas Press, 1964), pp. 102, 104.

19   Richard Ellmann, *James Joyce* (London: Oxford University Press, 1959), p. 28. Michael Seidel in *Epic Geography* uses John Joyce's statement as epigraph and then goes on to document in extraordinary detail Joyce's topological and geodetic imagination.

20   Marthe Robert, *The Old and the New: From "Don Quixote" To Kafka,* trans. Carol Casman (Berkeley and Los Angeles: University of California Press, 1977), pp. 99–100.

21   Margot Norris, *The Decentered Universe of Finnegans Wake: A Structuralist Analysis* (Baltimore: John Hopkins University Press, 1976), p. 61. Norris carelessly describes Joyce's notion of fatherhood as "cynical," a term that scarcely does justice to the deli-

cate ironic balance of his work. Perhaps for this reason, she has trouble reconciling what amounts to her elaborate identification of a monomyth with her equally pointed comments on the *Wake*'s "decentered" qualities.

22   Among these connotations is an important echo from *Coriolanus* (5.4.51). Announcing that Coriolanus has abandoned his revenge, the messenger says that "the trumpets, sackbuts, psalteries and fifes, / Tabors and cymbals and the shouting Romans / make the sun dance."

23   James Joyce, *Letters*, 3 vols.; vol. 1 ed. Stuart Gilbert, vols. 2 and 3 ed. Richard Ellmann (London: Faber & Faber, 1957–66), 1:159–60.

24   F. R. Jameson, "Seriality in Modern Literature," *Bucknell Review* 18 (1970): 69.

25   With regard to Wakean borrowing, see Margot Norris's excellent discussion of bricolage, *Decentered Universe of Finnegans Wake*, pp. 130–40.

26   Joyce, *Letters*, 1:139.

27   See Joyce's question to Harriet Weaver in a letter of 16 August 1920, *Letters* 3:16: "Do you mean that the *Oxen of the Sun* episode resembles *Hades* because the nine circles of development (enclosed between a headpiece and tailpiece of opposite chaos) seem to you to be peopled by extinct beings?" According to Ellmann, Weaver had written him that reading it was "like being taken the rounds of hell." In *Ulysses on the Liffey* (London: Faber & Faber, 1972), p. 136, Ellmann identifies these head and tailpieces as the "excessive order" of the beginning translation of medieval Latin and the final burst of contemporary slang. Possibly Joyce refers, however, to the mock-religious invocations with which the chapter begins and ends. Ellmann's comment (pp. 135–36) seems to me a non sequitur: "The styles cannot be futile any more than ontogeny is futile. They represent orderly stages of literary genesis." He bases his interpretation, to be sure, on a Viconian sense of historical rhythms and continuity, but clearly Joyce's awareness of chaos mocks systems of temporal order as much as any others.

28   Norris, *Decentered Universe of Finnegans Wake*, p. 110. Norris also uses the term "double talk" (though discussing primarily its psychological significance as a censoring device in dream language), which again I have borrowed. See pp. 101–3.

29   Benstock, *Joyce-Again's Wake*, p. 124. See also Riquelme's suggestive description of Joyce's punning in the *Wake*: "Each pun enacts the title as a linguistic phoenix whose meaning arises from the capsizing in its wake of the word that it at once suggests and partially drowns" (*Teller and Tale in Joyce's Fiction*, p. 33).

Chapter 6

1   William Carlos Williams, *Imaginations*, ed. Webster Schott (New York: New Directions, 1970), p. 27 (hereafter cited in the text by title [*I*] and page).

2   Joseph Riddel, *The Inverted Bell: Modernism and the Counterpoetics of William Carlos Williams* (Baton Rouge: Lousiana State University Press, 1974), p. 46.

3   This latter point is made by Riddel in *Inverted Bell*, pp. 72–73, who refers, in turn, to Geoffrey Hartman, *Beyond Formalism: Literary Essays, 1958–1970* (New Haven: Yale University Press, 1970), pp. 3–23, 287–310, 311–36. I noted in Chapter 2, note 11 Michael Ragussis's important treatment of these issues in *The Subterfuge of Art: Language and the Romantic Tradition* (Baltimore: Johns Hopkins University Press, 1978).

4 William Carlos Williams, *Paterson* (New York: New Directions, 1963), p. 140 (hereafter cited in the text by title [*P*] and page).

5 Wallace Stevens, "Reply to Papini," in *Collected Poems* (New York: Alfred Knopf, 1964), p. 446 (hereafter cited in the text by title [*CP*] and page).

6 Américo Castro, "The Structure of the *Quixote*," in Raymond E. Barbera, ed., *Cervantes, A Critical Trajectory* (Boston: Mirage Press, 1971), p. 193, translated by the editor.

7 Ibid., p. 183.

8 See ibid., p. 198: "The epic-chivalric hero could not allow the meaning of his heroic life to be doubted."

9 Wallace Stevens, *The Necessary Angel: Essays in Reality and the Imagination* (New York: Vintage–Random House, 1951), pp. 9–10.

10 William Carlos Williams, *In the American Grain* (New York: New Directions, 1956), p. 136 (hereafter cited in the text by title [*IAG*] and page).

11 Fritz Mauthner, *Beiträge zu einer Kritik der Sprache*, 3 vols. (Stuttgart: J. G. Cotta, 1901–3), 1:25, quoted in Allan Janik and Stephen Toulmin, *Wittgenstein's Vienna* (New York: Simon and Schuster, 1973), p. 126, translation by the authors. Contemporary criticism has strongly returned to this issue. For Michel Foucault it constitutes the central significance of *Don Quixote*, which is "the first modern work of literature, because in it we see the cruel reason of identities and differences make endless sport of signs and similitudes; because in it language breaks off its old kinship with things and enters into that lonely sovereignty from which it will reappear, in its separated state, only as literature; because it marks the point where resemblance enters an age which is, from the point of view of resemblance, one of madness and imagination" (*The Order of Things: An Archaeology of the Human Sciences* [New York: Vintage–Random House, 1973], pp. 48–49).

12 Wallace Stevens, *Selected Poems* (New York: New Directions, 1963), p. 3 (hereafter cited in the text by title [*SP*] and page).

13 William Carlos Williams, *Pictures from Brueghel and Other Poems* (New York: New Directions, 1962), pp. 110–20 (hereafter cited in the text by title [*PB*] and page).

14 William Carlos Williams, *Collected Later Poems* (New York: New Directions, 1967), p. 75 (hereafter cited in the text by title [*CLP*] and page).

15 Riddel, *Inverted Bell*, p. 93. Riddel has many brilliant things to say about Williams's aesthetic theory. In bringing him under the aegis of structuralist poetics, however, he makes a positive program out of Williams's commitment to the new without being enough aware, as I think Williams was, of the degree to which this commitment was the quixotic strategy of one who, like Joyce, lives in the intractable environment of diminished times (more "realistic" than "romantic") and whose doubts are in constant dialogue with his vision. Riddel's strong focus on aesthetic theory tends to neglect the actual nature of Williams's personae. The pain, the struggle, the approaches to despair, the frequent mockery, the incessant anticlimax, and the counterrhythms of much of Williams's work, including at least the first four books of *Paterson*, are, by and large, ignored by Riddel. Ironically, he makes Williams into the authentic hero of the new world that Paterson and the other personae are always trying to be. Paterson is, in effect, a parody of Riddel's own critical dream.

16   Ralph Waldo Emerson, "Nature," in *The Complete Essays and Other Writings*, ed. Brooks Atkinson (New York: Modern Library, 1940), p. 20.

Chapter 7

1   Harold Bloom, *Wallace Stevens: The Poems of Our Climate* (Ithaca: Cornell University Press, 1977), p. 170. As Bloom puts it, Stevens's "whole art is an aftering that battles belatedness." In spite of his many acute statements about Stevens's disjunctiveness, his "intricate evasions," his equivocations, irresolutions, deconstructions, and willed self-deception, Bloom, nevertheless, remains unhappy with an ambivalent Stevens and attempts to salvage him for the Emersonian tradition of "sage and seer" (p. 156). He tries to make of belatedness not a fundamental ironic duality but a step in a dialectical process of revision "into a new meaning of augmented psychical effectiveness" (p. 170). Bloom is himself (quixotically?) battling to salvage romanticism and secure the triumph of the Freudian "son" against the ironists, the philosophical deconstructionists, and the minimalist readers of Stevens, among whom Helen Vendler is the most notable and persuasive.

2   Wallace Stevens, *Opus Posthumous* (New York: Alfred Knopf, 1957), p. 166 (hereafter cited in the text by title [*OP*] and page).

3   Wallace Stevens, *The Necessary Angel: Essays in Reality and the Imagination* (New York: Vintage–Random House, 1951), pp. 9, 24.

4   In his prefaces dealing with Valéry, Stevens notes from Valéry's *Eupalinos* Socrates' description of himself to Phaedrus as "an imaginary hero." Another passage quoted from Valéry has Socrates saying that "by dint of constructing . . . I truly believe I have constructed myself" (*OP*, 269–72).

5   Michel Foucault, *The Order of Things: An Archaeology of the Human Sciences* (New York: Vintage–Random House, 1973), pp. 49–50.

6   See especially Robert Buttel, *The Making of Harmonium* (Princeton: Princeton University Press, 1967); Daniel Fuchs, *The Comic Spirit of Wallace Stevens* (Durham: Duke University Press, 1963); and A. Walton Litz, *Introspective Voyager: The Poetic Development of Wallace Stevens* (New York: Oxford University Press, 1972). Fuchs's book remains the most useful study of Stevens's comic irony, although it tends to emphasize deconstructive elements rather than the full unresolved and unresolvable tensions of mock-heroic.

7   Harold Bloom, for example, very usefully calls "The Comedian" "the satyr-poem or parody that culminates and almost undoes the tradition of the High Romantic quest poem," but then goes on to remark that "it shares fully in the obsessive quest that it only ostensibly mocks" and finally quotes Helen Vendler's formula with approval: "In spite of its mock-heroic mode the poem conveys some sort of heroism." See *Wallace Stevens*, pp. 70–71, and Helen Vendler, *On Extended Wings: Wallace Stevens' Longer Poems* (Cambridge, Mass.: Harvard University Press, 1969), p. 38. These and similar comments from others show little insight into the complex commitments of mockery and parody and perpetuate a very narrow view of mock-heroic.

8   See Introduction, note 12.

9   Stevens's description of "The Comedian" as "rudimentary" can be found in *Letters of Wallace Stevens*, ed. Holly Stevens (London: Faber & Faber, 1967), p. 230.

10   Ibid., p. 778.

11   Howard Mancing, *The Chivalric World of Don Quixote: Style, Structure, and Narrative Technique* (Columbia: University of Missouri Press, 1982), p. 49.

12   Litz, *Introspective Voyager*, p. 121. Revision of the poem is mentioned in *Letters*, ed. Stevens, p. 229.

13   *Letters*, ed. Stevens, p. 294.

14   Ibid., p. 293.

15   Bloom, *Wallace Stevens*, p. 94. Bloom has Stevens, after "The Comedian," recovering his strength as a poet only "when he ceased to fear his own solipsism," a phrase that, in my opinion, does not suggest enough Stevens's consistent development toward a solipsism within a secure ironic context but, rather, sees ironic tendencies as essentially negative in effect, something to overcome.

16   Since we are dealing here only in mock-heroes, it might be useful, by way of comparison, to invoke briefly the authentic prototype which Stevens parodies. According to Emerson, "The office of the scholar is to cheer, to raise, and to guide men by showing them facts amidst appearances. He plies the slow, unhonored, and unpaid task of observation." Elsewhere he describes him even more grandiosely as "one who raises himself from private considerations and breathes and lives on public and illustrious thoughts. He is the world's eyes. He is the world's heart" (*Complete Works*, 14 vols. [Boston: Houghton Mifflin, 1894], 1:101–2). In "The American Scholar" Emerson also speaks at some length of "the great principle of Undulation in Nature . . . deeply ingrained in every atom and every fluid" (p. 99).

17   Vendler, *On Extended Wings*, pp. 14–35, 196. In spite of the brilliance of much of her analysis of Steven's equivocations, Vendler, in my opinion, tends to dismiss too quickly as soft or dubious Stevens's willed strategies of desire, his heroic expansions, in favor of certain "severely refined" poems that make minimal claims. She thus reduces or ignores the full mock-heroic dialectic or tension, its continuing, distinctive, and central role.

18   Stevens, *Necessary Angel*, p. 35.

19   Such self-composition, as Stevens develops the concept, is also a parody of the formal meditations of heroic Church Fathers such as Saint Ignatius. Without, I believe, stressing the ironic contexts sufficiently, Louis Martz, nevertheless, defines meditation in terms relevant to the point I am making. He writes that "meditation is the essential exercise which, constantly practiced, brings the imagination into play, releases creative power, enables the human being to compose a sensitive, intelligent, and generous self." See "Wallace Stevens: The World as Meditation," in Ashley Brown and Robert S. Haller, eds., *The Achievement of Wallace Stevens* (Philadelphia: Lippincott, 1962), p. 213. Stephen Dedalus's "performance" in the National Library is, as I noted earlier, another such parody of religious meditation.

Chapter 8

1   Vladimir Nabokov, *The Annotated Lolita*, ed. Alfred Appel, Jr. (New York: McGraw-Hill, 1970), p. 15 (hereafter cited in the text by title [L] and page). I am, in general, much indebted to the scholarship of Appel's edition.

2   Vladimir Nabokov, *Ada or Ardor: A Family Chronicle* (New York: McGraw-Hill, 1969), p. 414 (hereafter cited in the text by title [*A*] and page).

3   Vladimir Nabokov, *Pnin,* in *The Portable Nabokov,* ed. Page Stegner (New York: Penguin, 1971), p. 423 (hereafter cited in the text by title [*PN*] and page).

4   Vladimir Nabokov, *The Defense,* trans. Michael Scammell (New York: Putnam, 1964), p. 25.

5   Vladimir Nabokov, *Speak, Memory* (New York: Putnam, 1966), p. 73 (hereafter cited in the text by title [*SM*] and page).

6   I obviously disagree with the still popular view of Nabokov as an aesthete whose art is principally concerned with exploring the nature of its own fictionality. Concerned with its refutation, Robert Merrill admirably sums up the dominant thesis of Nabokov studies: "He has been labeled a metafictionist, a parafictionist, a fabulator, a pattern maker, and an artificer. . . . The writers with whom he is most often associated are Beckett, Borges, and John Barth; repeatedly we are assured that Nabokov, like his fellow illusionists, 'dismisses mimesis and identification with the hero distainfully as mythology,' and that his subject is either the conflict 'between different concepts of art' or nothing less than 'form itself'" ("Nabokov and Fictional Artifice," *Modern Fiction Studies* 25 [Autumn 1979]: 439–40). Merrill quotes representative views from various books and articles on Nabokov. I will argue that, as with other writers using the mock-heroic mode, it is less accurate to say that Nabokov's work is metafictional, reflexively "about" art and the artist, than that in his work the role of art and the nature of the artist's qualities are functional to a value system that continues to embrace most of the traditional concerns of the hero and whose delineation constitutes its major theme.

7   Vladimir Nabokov, *The Gift,* trans. Michael Scammell (New York: Putnam, 1963), p. 73 (hereafter cited in the text by title [*G*] and page).

8   Vladimir Nabokov, *Invitation to a Beheading* (New York: Putnam, 1959), p. 37 (hereafter cited in the text by title [*IB*] and page).

9   Vladimir Nabokov, *The Real Life of Sebastian Knight* (New York: New Directions, 1959), p. 27 (hereafter cited in the text by title [*SK*] and page).

10   From a poem in his collection *Drops of Paint,* quoted in Andrew Field, *Nabokov: His Life in Art* (Boston: Little, Brown, 1967), p. 71. Field traces Nabokov's own "Georgian" phrase at some length. Nabokov has argued that Fyodor's experience should not be construed as his, and this is true enough on the literal level. As my comments everywhere suggest, however, I view Fyodor's quest for an adequate form, both its dynamics and its outcome, as essentially Nabokov's own. In my discussion of *Invitation to a Beheading,* I have already argued that Nabokov's "prison" is only a more expansive version of the cell that confines Cincinnatus. For Nabokov's disclaimer concerning *The Gift,* see the Foreword, p. 9.

11   Margaret Rose, *Parody/Meta-Fiction: An Analysis of Parody as a Critical Mirror to the Writing and Reception of Fiction* (London: Croom Helm, 1979), p. 132. See also Michel Foucault, *The Order of Things: An Archaeology of the Human Sciences* (New York: Vintage–Random House, 1973), p. 48. To the extent that the protagonist/persona learns how to become a mock-hero the term *Bildungsroman,* used in connection with mock-heroic narrative, may perhaps have some relevance. See Rose's description (p. 130) of Don Quixote as "a 'Bildungsroman' in the art of learning how to live the fictional life, and

the art of masking." Cf. my earlier comment on references to *Bildungsroman* (Chapter 2, note 3).

12   "A University Poem," quoted in Field, *Nabokov*, p. 84.

13   I am not arguing that Nabokov, like Fyodor, discovers this formula in *The Gift*. He had, of course, used it already in such novels as *The Defense* (1930). My point, rather, is that Fyodor's analytic quest for this formula, his growing awareness of its significance, its certain equivalence to the earlier straight heroics and nostalgia—all are the concern of *The Gift*; Fyodor's own quest, in other words, becomes Nabokov's self-conscious subject. As Nabokov's first major book, the culmination of his writing in Russian, *The Gift* is his most complete and explicit description of the development of his mock-heroic art. Like most major work, it both summarizes past achievement and marks out new directions, thus a beginning as much as an end.

14   Vladimir Nabokov, *Pale Fire* (New York: Putnam, 1962), pp. 62–63 (hereafter cited in the text by title [*PF*] and page).

15   Paranoia—the persistent will to believe, read signs, create "plots" and patterns from apparently disparate events—in Nabokov and certain other contemporary writers not necessarily identified with the mock-heroic mode was first pointed out to me by one of my graduate students in an excellent dissertation. See Mary Gourevitch, "The Writer as Double Agent: Essays on the Conspiratorial Mode in Contemporary Fiction" (Ph.D. dissertation, Case Western Reserve University, 1970). Paranoia (at least in its literary treatment) is essentially parody religion, whether we think of "sign-reading" in essentially Christian or romantic terms. Kinbote, significantly, is an orthodox believer, whose credo affirms that God's sign is "at every turn of the trail, painted on the boulder and notched on the fir trunk . . . [that] every page in the book of one's personal fate bears His watermark" (*PF*, 221–22). Kinbote, of course, brings to "every page" of Shade's manuscript this same zealous commitment to signs.

16   *Vladimir Nabokov: Lectures on Literature*, ed. Fredson Bowers (New York: Harcourt Brace Jovanovich & Bruccoli Clark, 1980), p. 377.

17   *New York Times*, 1 March 1981, Sec. 2, p. 4, Col. 1.

18   Alfred Appel, Jr., "*Lolita*: The Springboard of Parody," in L. S. Dembo, ed., *Nabokov: The Man and His Work* (Madison: University of Wisconsin Press, 1967), p. 109. Appel's treatment of Nabokov's parody, here and in his Preface to *The Annotated Lolita*, stresses its negative implications at the cost of fully exploring the total perspective involved in the mechanics of ironic affirmation. His comments can be taken as representative of current critical discussion. See also Dabney Stuart, *Nabokov: The Dimensions of Parody* (Baton Rouge: Louisiana State University Press, 1978).

19   Quoted by Appel in n. 5/3, *L*, 321–22. I am indebted to Appel's entire gloss of the name Humbert Humbert.

20   In 1923 Nabokov translated *Alice in Wonderland* into Russian. Nabokov remarked to Appel during an interview that Lewis Carroll "has a pathetic affinity with Humbert Humbert but some odd scruple prevented me from alluding in *Lolita* to his wretched perversion and to those ambiguous photographs he took in dim rooms. He got away with it, as so many other Victorians got away with pederasty and nympholepsy." Nabokov added that he was fond of Carroll and that Carroll was a part of his "English" childhood (Alfred Appel, Jr., "An Interview with Vladimir Nabokov," in Dembo, ed.,

Nabokov, p. 35. Remote as it seems at first glance, *Lolita*, along with *The Gift* and *Ada*, is among the most obvious examples of Nabokov's transformation of nostalgia into mock-heroic.

21   Alexander Welsh, *Reflections on the Hero as Quixote* (Princeton: Princeton University Press, 1981), p. 217.

22   Susan Stewart, *Nonsense: Aspects of Intertextuality in Folklore and Literature* (Baltimore: Johns Hopkins University Press, 1979), p. 155. Appel relates "quilted Quilty" to what he calls Humbert's "patchwork self" and to the crazy-quilt of forty-eight states through which Humbert and Lolita aimlessly wander (*L*, lxiii–lxvii, 382, n. 154/1).

23   The quotation is from Appel (*L*, 360, n. 53/2), who exhaustively lists the doubles and twins of the book.

24   Ellen Pifer, "Dark Paradise: Shades of Heaven and Hell in *Ada*," *Modern Fiction Studies* 25 (Autumn 1979): 482.

25   See Nabokov's specific reference to the fairy-tale formula in describing the young lovers together: "For yet another immortal moment they stood embraced in the hushed avenue, enjoying, as they had never enjoyed before, the 'happy-forever' feeling at the end of never-ending fairy tales." Ada interpolates—"That's a beautiful passage, Van. I shall cry all night"—and the passage goes on: "As the last moonbeam struck Ada, her mouth and chin shone drenched with his poor futile kisses" (*A*, 304). This scene is just before Van learns of Ada's betrayal of him. For Nabokov, "forever" is only a moment of aesthetic and emotional consummation experienced, remembered, recorded—but always in a context of loss and futility.

26   Stewart, *Nonsense*, pp. 118–19, 186.

27   Van Veen's speculations are part of Nabokov's comprehensive parody of the nineteenth-century novel in *Ada*. At one point he describes fictional "explanations" as "empty formulas befitting the solemn novelists of former days who thought they could explain everything" (*A*, 505). The immediate reference here is to psychological explanation, but the comment cuts deeply into the total didactic possibility of fiction. See Alfred Appel, Jr.'s, comment on *Ada* in *"Ada* Described," *TriQuarterly* 17 (Winter, 1970): 161: "As the family chronicle to end all such chronicles, it is also a museum of the novel, and it employs parody to rehearse its own history." Appel's further suggestion (p. 168) that the novel is a particular tribute to Tolstoy throws light on Van Veen's role as "philosopher."

28   Both Ellen Pifer, "Dark Paradise," and Alfred Appel, Jr., *"Ada* Described," have explored these etymologies, and I have relied on their knowledge.

Chapter 9

1   Occasionally, earlier criticism can be positively misleading. John Clayton in *Saul Bellow: In Defense of Man* (Bloomington: Indiana University Press, 1968), pp. 6–7, describes the Bellow hero as a redeemer struggling to rescue his own and the common life from the past seen as a burden. This formula is true enough insofar as it refers to a past made up of the hero's personal failures—the incessant mockery of reality impinging on the hero's life. It is not at all true about the past as model and value system to which the

hero remains committed, a past, incidentally, about which Clayton has many illuminating things to say in his book.

2   Saul Bellow, *Herzog* (New York: Viking Press, 1964), p. 286 (hereafter cited in the text by title [*H*] and page).

3   Daniel Hughes, "Reality and the Hero: *Lolita* and *Henderson the Rain King*," in Irving Malin ed., *Saul Bellow and the Critics* (New York: New York University Press, 1967), p. 90. For Heller's comment on higher parody see *The Ironic German: A Study of Thomas Mann* (Boston: Little, Brown, 1958), p. 272.

4   Saul Bellow, *Humboldt's Gift* (New York: Viking Press, 1975), pp. 476–77 (hereafter cited in the text by title [*HG*] and page).

5   Sarah Blacher Cohen, *Saul Bellow's Enigmatic Comedy* (Urbana: University of Illinois Press, 1974), p. 116. Cohen's book is excellent as a discussion of comic devices in Bellow's work, less useful in the conclusions she draws from the evidence because of her mistaken dependence on Bergsonian comic theory, which postulates an "alive" and flexible common humanity against which the rigid and mechanical comic figure can be measured and found wanting. Mock-heroic narrative, however, has no such simple and reductive yardstick. Its complex irony—the encounter of truly contradictory perspectives, the duality generated by affirmation and commitment in an inexorable context of mockery—goes well beyond the more limited (however powerful and effective) Bergsonian comedy of mental or physical rigidity. In mock-heroic narrative, the "rigid" heroic dimension (now the very source in the fiction of that which is "alive" and "human" as opposed to the "dead" mass of humanity) paradoxically survives its traduction in absurdity to remain of continuing value in and for itself. Cohen has no trouble recognizing the model of Don Quixote in Henderson, but she does have great difficulty in relating model to theory. For her entire discussion see pp. 116–42.

6   See Nina Steers, "Successor to Faulkner? An Interview with Saul Bellow," *Show* 4 (September 1964): 38. I have used the question and answer from this interview giving Bellow's description of Henderson as an epigraph to this chapter.

7   Saul Bellow, *Mr. Sammler's Planet* (New York: Viking Press, 1970), p. 30 (hereafter cited in the text by title [*MSP*] and page).

8   Saul Bellow, *Henderson the Rain King* (New York: Viking Press, 1959), p. 266 (hereafter cited in the text by title [*HRK*] and page).

9   Steers, "Successor to Faulkner?" p. 38.

10   Cohen, *Saul Bellow's Enigmatic Comedy*, p. 119. Cohen also identifies Henderson as a "Knight of the Woeful Countenance" (p. 122), an identification I develop further in the next paragraph.

11   Ibid., p. 119.

12   Cohen (p. 178) responds to this position but only by cataloging Sammler's "imperfect fundamentals" and those of the other characters as deviations from a comic norm.

13   Marcus Klein, "A Discipline of Nobility: Saul Bellow's Fiction," in Malin, ed., *Saul Bellow and the Critics*, p. 107.

14   Clayton, *Saul Bellow*, pp. 31–34. The Rosenberg quotation is from *An Age of Enormity* (Cleveland, 1962), p. 150. Clayton (p. 36) also refers to Irving Malin's statement in *Jews and Americans* (Carbondale, 1965), p. 132, that Bellow's heroes "walk the line be-

tween dream and fact, laughing at their precarious position. They are Jewish ironists."

15 I am greatly indebted to Michael J. Hoffman's gloss of the name in "From Cohn to Herzog," *Yale Review* 58 (Spring 1969): 355.

16 *Writers at Work: The Paris Review Interviews*, 3d ser. (New York: Viking Press, 1967), p. 192, interview with Gordon L. Harper.

17 Ibid., pp. 187–89: Of the mock-hero in prison, see Bellow's further comment on the novel: "To me the significant theme of *Herzog* is the imprisonment of the individual in a shameful and impotent privacy" (p. 194).

18 Bellow, in his interview with Gordon Harper in *Writers at Work*, p. 192, has observed that the book "simply points to the comic impossibility of a synthesis that can satisfy modern demands." Herzog's own mockery of his intellectual aims is well known: "*What this country needs is a good five-cent synthesis*" (*H*, 207).

19 Earl Rovit, "Bellow in Occupancy," in Malin, ed., *Saul Bellow and the Critics*, p. 181. Rovit has noted the connection with the Emersonian hero.

20 Hoffman, "From Cohn to Herzog," also argues against even a cyclic reading of the book and notes that the final peace and serenity will be just temporary (pp. 357–58). The familiar charges brought against Bellow that his works lack denouement, resolution, or coherent visions of social possibility seem to me to miss the point completely because of a failure to identify and understand the modal form. Equally wrongheaded is any idea that he simply *indulges* his characters in their romantic selfhood, what Josephine Hendin, for example, calls Bellow's "sentimental infatuation with his characters" in *Vulnerable People: A View of American Fiction since 1945* (New York: Oxford University Press, 1978), p. 103.

21 His commitment may be more Platonic than Wordsworthian. Citrine speaks of Fleisher's ballads as "pure, musical, witty, radiant, humane" and adds: "I think they were Platonic. By Platonic I refer to an original perfection to which all human beings long to return" (*HG*, 11). See also his statement: "Humboldt was forever talking about something he called 'the home-world,' Wordsworthian, Platonic, before the shades of the prison house fell" (*HG*, 443). In Bellow's perpetual "boy" heroes there is also something of the American Adamic tradition, or rather, the American context reinforces the youthfulness always associated with the mock-hero as I have described him.

Chapter 10

1 Victor Brombert, *The Novels of Flaubert: A Study of Themes and Techniques* (Princeton: Princeton University Press, 1966), p. 148.

2 See Jules de Gaultier, *Le Bovarysme* (Paris: Librarie Léopold Cerf, 1892).

3 Eric Gans, *The Discovery of Illusion: Flaubert's Early Works, 1835–1837* (Berkeley and Los Angeles: University of California Press, 1971), pp. 9–10; *The Selected Letters of Gustave Flaubert*, trans. and ed. Francis Steegmuller (London: Hamish Hamilton, 1954), pp. 131, 173.

4 Gans, *Discovery of Illusion*, p. 166.

5 Gustave Flaubert, *Madame Bovary, Nouvelle version precédée de scenarios inédits*, ed. Jean Pommier and Gabrielle Leleu (Paris: Librarie José Corti, 1949), rpt. in *Madame Bovary*, trans. and ed. Paul de Man (New York: Norton, 1965), p. 165 (hereafter cited in the

text by title [*MB*] and page). Flaubert significantly describes Madame Bovary's voluptuous appearance in the first flush of her adultery with Rodolphe as that devised by "some artist skilled in corruption" (*MB,* 140).

6 See Alexander Welsh's comment on the power of reality in Flaubert's major novels: "Circumstances do not merely oppose the individual will but infect it" (*Reflections on the Hero as Quixote* [Princeton: Princeton University Press, 1981], p. 160). Welsh reminds us of Georg Lukács's distinction between modes in which illusion remains vital and sustained and Flaubert's novels of disillusionment. He quotes Lukács on *The Sentimental Education:* "In it an impotent subjectivity faces the meaningless objectivity of the external world" (pp. 161–62). See Lukács, *Studies in European Realism,* no trans. (New York: Grosset and Dunlap, 1964), p. 190.

7 Gustave Flaubert, *The Sentimental Education,* trans. Robert Baldick (Baltimore: Penguin, 1964), p. 79 (hereafter cited in the text by title [*SE*] and page).

8 Brombert, *Novels of Flaubert,* discusses the polarization of the female image at length in his chapter on *The Sentimental Education* (pp. 125–85).

9 John Barth, *Lost in the Funhouse* (New York: Doubleday, 1968), pp. 100–103. The epigraph is found on p. 100 (hereafter cited in the text by title [*LF*] and page). Compare Echo's credo with the comment of "Editor B" in *Giles Goat-Boy* (New York: Doubleday, 1966), p. xii: "Where other writers seek fidelity to the fact of modern experience and expose to us the emptiness of our lives, he declares it his aim purely to *astonish;* where others strive for truth, he admits his affinity for lies, the more enormous the better." Unlike many such "editorial" intrusions in fiction, the irony of this statement lies more in its truth than in any presumption of comic opacity.

10 Quoted in David Morrell, *John Barth: An Introduction* (University Park: Pennsylvania State University Press, 1976), p. 16.

11 John Barth, *Letters* (New York: Putnam, 1979), p. 33 (hereafter cited in the text by title [*L*] and page). The statement is found also in *Chimera.*

12 Manfred Puetz, "John Barth's *The Sot-Weed Factor:* The Pitfalls of Mythopoesis," in Joseph J. Waldmeir, ed., *Critical Essays on John Barth* (Boston: G. K. Hall, 1980), p. 135. Puetz compares the capacity of Barth's characters to invent and reinvent their past as they go along with their author's own willingness to invent history and notes the significance: "Barth's toying with history aims at our vital assumption that there are facts which can be indisputably established" (p. 143). See also Alan Holder's comment in the same volume: "*The Sot-Weed Factor's* own relation to the past would appear to be that of Cosmic Lover as well [he refers to Henry Burlingame's name for himself, Burlingame the supreme "shape-shifter" in the book], in the sense that the book refuses to commit itself to a particular conception of the past, of historical truth, but wants the freedom to embrace simultaneously a variety of possibilities" ("'What Marvelous Plot . . . Was Afoot?': John Barth's *The Sot-Weed Factor,*" ibid., p. 130).

13 Tony Tanner, *City of Words: American Fiction, 1950–70* (New York: Harper & Row, 1971), p. 236.

14 John Barth, *The Sot-Weed Factor* (New York: Grosset & Dunlap), p. 365. Both Holder and Puetz emphasize this issue in their essays. See, for example, pp. 130, 136, in Waldmeir, ed., *Critical Essays.* Morrell develops the same point also in *John Barth,* pp. 102–3.

15   Margaret Rose, *Parody/Meta-Fiction: An Analysis of Parody as a Critical Mirror to the Writing and Reception of Fiction* (London: Croom Helm, 1979), pp. 14, 133. See also her summary of Foucault's position: "Foucault has shown how parody has served to criticize such categories [those which in the past defined parody "according to its relationship to its model in terms of imitation"], and how modern parody has taken on a meta-critical form which raises the specific critical functions of the parody of texts to the role of a critique of its historical epistema" (p. 134).

16   "Having It Both Ways: A Conversation between John Barth and Joe David Bellamy," *New American Review* 15 (April 1972): 148. I am undoubtedly oversimplifying Barth's concept of parody so as to make a sharp distinction between his metafictions and mock-heroic as a formal mode. *Giles Goat-Boy*, for example, may be an exception to what I am saying, depending on one's reading of that complex novel. James Gresham argues that the book is a Menippean satire, a form which, he claims, mediates between romance and reality and whose prototype is *Don Quixote* ("*Giles Goat-Boy:* Satyr, Satire, and Tragedy Twined," in Waldmeir, ed., *Critical Essays*, pp. 157–71). In the interview to which I have just referred, Barth takes a somewhat different approach to parody when discussing *Giles:* "What I did in the case of the *Goat-Boy* novel was to try to abstract the patterns, and then write a novel which would consciously, even self-consciously, follow the patterns, parody the patterns, satirize the patterns, but with good luck transcend the satire a little bit in order to say some of the serious things I had in mind to say. Otherwise it would be a farce, a great trifle—which, of course, some readers found it to be. But the intention was to escalate the farce, to escalate the parody, until the thing took on a genuine dramatic dimension of its own. This may not be making up a new myth, but it's getting to a dimension of response that we can associate with myth, through a comical and farcical mode" (p. 146). Elsewhere in this same interview he argues for the passionate nature of parody in *Don Quixote* in response to Robert Scholes's theory that self-consciousness about myth precludes its serious use (p. 144). Appropriately enough, this issue comes up in the frequent critical comparisons of Barth and Nabokov. Earl Rovit, for example, claims that both men have been engaged in the creation of a new kind of parodic novel based on the concept that nothing has value ("The Novel as Parody: John Barth," in Waldmeir, ed., *Critical Essays*, pp. 116–22). Jerry Powell feels, however, that in playing "as if" games, Nabokov finds "some kind of absolute value, whereas Barth appears to believe he is accepting a relative value for lack of any absolute values in life" ("John Barth's *Chimera:* A Creative Response to the Literature of Exhaustion," in ibid., pp. 238–39).

17   See "Dunyazadiad," in John Barth, *Chimera* (New York: Random House, 1972), pp. 11 or 56 (hereafter cited in the text by title [C] and page).

18   Again I am probably overstating the case for my own purposes. A real sense of death and doom hangs over Barth's fiction, however much it is encapsulated in the Chinese box of fiction. The "Belleroponiad," for example, resounds to the litany of "dead, dead, dead," to the pain of middle-aged failure, to the awareness of youth growing into "commonplace adults, grasping, doomed" (C, 302–3). The horror, catastrophe, and anticlimax endemic to Barth's heavily plotted fiction produces much the same effect.

19   Tanner, *City of Words*, p. 253.

20   John Barth, "The Literature of Exhaustion," *Atlantic Monthly* 220 (August 1967): 32–33. For Barth, Borges is the central figure of the artist as "virtuoso," who, confronted with the modern labyrinth, like Theseus "go[es] straight through the maze to the accomplishment of his work" (p. 34). In this case, Barth shares the general concern of mock-heroic with the virtuoso "performer."

21   Jorge Luis Borges, *Fictions*, ed. Anthony Kerrigan (London: John Calder, 1965), pp. 33, 132–37, trans. Alastair Reed, Anthony Kerrigan.

22   Ibid., pp. 139, 103, trans. Anthony Kerrigan.

23   Ibid., pp. 138–43, trans. Anthony Kerrigan.

24   *The Diary of Virginia Woolf*, ed. Ann Olivier Bell, 5 vols. (New York: Harcourt Brace Jovanovich, 1980), 3:339.

Index